유희태
일반영어 ⑤

기출 VOCA
30days

LSI 영어연구소 유희태 박사 저

Contents

Day
01

유희태 일반영어 ⑤
VOCA
기출 VOCA 30 days

facetious	☐☐☐	wrath	☐☐☐
reincarnation	☐☐☐	catastrophe	☐☐☐
straight-face	☐☐☐	represent	☐☐☐
dodo	☐☐☐	benediction	☐☐☐
kowtow	☐☐☐	disaffect	☐☐☐
looking-glass	☐☐☐	advocate	☐☐☐
makeweight	☐☐☐	classify	☐☐☐
statute	☐☐☐	delegate	☐☐☐
turret	☐☐☐	dissertation	☐☐☐
freckle	☐☐☐	interrogation	☐☐☐
speck	☐☐☐	drawback	☐☐☐
toss	☐☐☐	reflect	☐☐☐
teetotal	☐☐☐	anatomy	☐☐☐
abstain	☐☐☐	dreary	☐☐☐
nudge	☐☐☐	denote	☐☐☐
gossamer	☐☐☐	redundant	☐☐☐
warp	☐☐☐	incantation	☐☐☐
derogatory	☐☐☐	audacity	☐☐☐
compunction	☐☐☐	eminent	☐☐☐
abbreviate	☐☐☐	recoup	☐☐☐
confront	☐☐☐	dawdle	☐☐☐
besiege	☐☐☐	contingent	☐☐☐
conciliate	☐☐☐	empirical	☐☐☐
ameliorate	☐☐☐	catalyst	☐☐☐
collocate	☐☐☐	adversity	☐☐☐
abstinence	☐☐☐	heterogeneous	☐☐☐
breadwinner	☐☐☐	enumerate	☐☐☐
pejorative	☐☐☐	altitude	☐☐☐
dispense	☐☐☐	sabotage	☐☐☐
altruistic	☐☐☐	oblique	☐☐☐

0001 ■■■

facetious
[fəsíːʃəs]

우스운, 익살맞은, 경박한
ⓐ treating serious issues with deliberately inappropriate humor
ⓢⓨⓝ flippant, flip, waggish
ⓞⓟⓟ serious
ⓔ.ⓖ. That is a serious, not a **facetious** point.

0002 ■□□

reincarnation
[rèincarnátion]

환생
ⓝ the rebirth of a soul in a new body
ⓢⓨⓝ metempsychosis, samsara
ⓔ.ⓖ. Of course, we Indians believe in **reincarnation**.
ⓝ reincarnationist 환생론자

0003 ■■□

straight-face
[streit-feis]

무표정
ⓝ a serious facial expression, esp one that conceals the impulse to laugh
ⓔ.ⓖ. He kept a **straight face**.

0004 ■■■

dodo
[dóudou]

얼간이
ⓝ If you refer to someone as a dodo, you think they are foolish or silly.
ⓔ.ⓖ. He's so stupid; he's a **dodo**.

0005 ■■■

kowtow
[káutáu]

~에게 굽실거리다(남한산성의 삼두고구 연상)
ⓥ act in an excessively subservient manner (kneel and touch the ground with the forehead in worship or submission as part of Chinese custom)
ⓢⓨⓝ grovel, crawl, toady
ⓔ.ⓖ. Just look at how they cower and **kowtow** to him now even in public.

0006 ■□□

looking-glass
[lóok·ing-glæs]

거울
ⓝ a mirror
ⓔ.ⓖ. Every man's neighbor is his **looking-glass**.

0007 ■■□

makeweight
[máke·wèight]

(정확한 수 · 양 등을 채우기 위해 포함하는 별로 중요하지 않은) 보충물, 보충인원

ⓝ They are not good or valuable and have been included in an activity in order to fill up a gap.

ⓔ.ⓖ. He has not been signed to the club as a **makeweight** to fill out the numbers.

0008 ■□□

statute
[stǽtʃuːt]

규칙, 정관, 법률

ⓝ a written law passed by a legislative body

ⓢⓨⓝ law, regulation, pronouncement, ratification

ⓔ.ⓖ. Corporal punishment was banned by **statute** in 1987.

ⓐ statutory 법에 명시된

0009 ■■□

turret
[tɜːrət]

포탑

ⓝ gun tower

ⓢⓨⓝ tower

ⓔ.ⓖ. He stood in the middle of the Humvee and manned a machine gun in a **turret** sticking out of the top.

0010 ■□□

freckle
[frekl]

주근깨

ⓝ small light brown spots on someone's skin, especially on their face

ⓔ.ⓖ. He had short ginger-coloured hair and **freckles**.

0011 ■□□

speck
[spek]

작은 얼룩(자국), 반점; 작은 알갱이, 입자

ⓝ a very small stain, mark, or shape

ⓢⓨⓝ mark, dot, spot

ⓔ.ⓖ. The ship was now just a **speck** in the distance.

0012 ■□□

toss
[tɔːs]

(가볍게 · 아무렇게나) 던지다

ⓥ to throw it there lightly, often in a rather careless way

ⓢⓨⓝ throw, flip

ⓔ.ⓖ. I **tossed** the book aside and got up.

0013 ■■■

teetotal
[tiːtoʊtl]

술을 입에도 대지 않는

ⓐ Someone who is teetotal does not drink alcohol.
ⓔ.ⓖ. He's strictly **teetotal**.

0014 ■■☐

abstain
[əbsteɪn]

(특히 자기가 좋아하는 것을 건강·도덕상의 이유로) 자제하다(삼가다)

ⓥ deliberately not to do it
ⓢyn cease, stop
ⓔ.ⓖ. It is a good habit to **abstain** from any kind of abuse.

0015 ■■■

nudge
[nʌdʒ]

(특히 팔꿈치로 살짝) 쿡 찌르다

ⓥ to push someone gently, usually with one's elbow
ⓢyn push, poke, shove
ⓔ.ⓖ. He **nudged** me and whispered, 'Look who's just come in.'

0016 ■■■

gossamer
[gɑːsəmə(r)]

(아주 가볍고) 고운(섬세한)

ⓐ something very light, thin, or delicate
ⓢyn light, delicate, fine
ⓔ.ⓖ. That's not one of my **gossamer** landings.

0017 ■■☐

warp
[wɔ́ːrp]

휘게 하다, 뒤틀다, 구부리다; 왜곡하다

ⓥ to bend or twist out of shape, esp. from a straight or flat form, as timbers or flooring; to distort or cause to distort from the truth, fact, true meaning, etc.
ⓢyn contort, distort, bias, falsify
ⓔ.ⓖ. Fear **warps** the mind.
ⓝ warpage 굽힘, 뒤틀림, 왜곡

0018 ■■☐

derogatory
[dirάgətɔ́ːri]

손상하는, 경멸적인

ⓐ tending to lessen the merit or reputation of a person or thing
ⓢyn disparaging, depreciatory, belittling, uncomplimentary
ⓔ.ⓖ. Their conversation contained a number of **derogatory** racial remarks.
ⓥ derogate (명성, 품위, 가치를) 떨어뜨리다

0019 ■■■

compunction
[kəmpʌ́ŋkʃən]

양심의 가책, 회한, 후회

ⓝ a feeling of uneasiness or anxiety of the conscience caused by regret for doing wrong or causing pain

ⓢⓨⓝ contrition, remorse

ⓔ.ⓖ. He said "sorry" to her without **compunction**.

ⓐ compunctious 양심의 가책이 되는, 후회하는

0020 ■■□

abbreviate
[əbríːvièit]

줄여 쓰다, 생략하다, 단축하다

ⓥ to shorten (a word or phrase) by omitting letters, substituting shorter forms, etc.

ⓢⓨⓝ abridge, foreshorten, shorten, cut

ⓔ.ⓖ. "San Francisco" is commonly **abbreviated** to "SF".

ⓝ abbreviation 생략, 단축

0021 ■■□

confront
[kənfrʌ́nt]

직면하다, 맞서다

ⓥ to come face to face with, especially with defiance or hostility

ⓢⓨⓝ encounter, face, front

ⓔ.ⓖ. It is time to **confront** the President about his poor leadership.

ⓝ confrontation 대면, 직면, 대립

0022 ■■■

besiege
[bisíːdʒ]

포위하다, 공격하다

ⓥ surround so as to force to give up

ⓢⓨⓝ surround, circumvent

ⓔ.ⓖ. The army moved to **besiege** the base.

ⓝ besiegement 공격

0023 ■■□

conciliate
[kənsílièit]

달래다, 회유하다, 조정하다

ⓥ to become agreeable or reconciled

ⓢⓨⓝ reconcile, pacify, appease, placate

ⓔ.ⓖ. The two countries moved to **conciliate** for the sake of peace.

ⓐ conciliatory 달래는 듯한, 회유적인

0024 ■■■

ameliorate
[əmíːljərèit]

좋아지다, 향상하다
ⓥ to make or become better, more bearable, or more satisfactory
ⓢⓨⓝ advance, improve, progress
ⓔ.ⓖ. In every human being there is a wish to **ameliorate** his own situation.
ⓝ ameliorator 개량자

0025 ■■■

collocate
[kάləkèit]

나란히 놓다, 배열하다, 연어(특정 단어가 함께 쓰임)를 이루다
ⓥ to set or place together, esp. side by side
ⓢⓨⓝ arrange, parallel
ⓔ.ⓖ. Rancid often **collocates** with heat.
ⓝ collocation 나란히 놓음, 배치, 배열

0026 ■■□

abstinence
[ǽbstənəns]

절제, 금욕
ⓝ the act or practice of refraining from indulgence in an appetite, as for certain foods, drink, alcoholic beverages, drugs, or sex
ⓢⓨⓝ forbearance, temperance
ⓔ.ⓖ. The CEO set an example of **abstinence** for our company.
ⓐ abstinent 절제하는, 참는

0027 ■□□

breadwinner
[brédwinər]

집안의 벌이를 하는 사람, 가족 부양자
ⓝ a person who earns a livelihood, esp. one who also supports dependents
ⓔ.ⓖ. He is the **breadwinner**, but he has to do his laundry and cook for his children as well.

0028 ■■■

pejorative
[pidʒɔ́ːrətiv]

가치를 떨어뜨리는, 경멸적인
ⓐ having a disparaging, derogatory, or belittling effect or force
ⓢⓨⓝ disparaging, derogatory, belittling
ⓔ.ⓖ. He called me a student as a **pejorative** term, implying I was inexperienced or ignorant.

0029 ■■□

dispense
[dispéns]

분배하다, 베풀다
ⓥ to deal out
ⓢⓨⓝ distribute
ⓔ.ⓖ. We **dispensed** food and clothing to the poor.
ⓝ dispensation 분배, 분배품

0030 ■■□

altruistic
[æ̀ltruːístik]

이타적인
ⓐ unselfishly concerned for or devoted to the welfare of others
ⓢⓨⓝ selfless
ⓔ.ⓖ. **Altruistic** love is associated with greater happiness, in general.
ⓝ altruism 이타주의

0031 ■■□

wrath
[ræθ, rɑ́ːθ]

격노, 분노
ⓝ strong, stern, or fierce anger; deeply resentful indignation
ⓢⓨⓝ anger, rage, resentment, fury
ⓔ.ⓖ. If you don't apologize soon, you will face his **wrath**.
ⓐ wrathful 몹시 노한

0032 ■■□

catastrophe
[kətǽstrəfi]

대참사, 큰 재앙
ⓝ a sudden and widespread disaster
ⓢⓨⓝ disaster
ⓔ.ⓖ. By planning we will avoid **catastrophes** in the future.
ⓐ catastrophic 큰 재앙의, 파멸적인

0033 ■□□

represent
[rèprizént]

나타내다
ⓥ to serve to express, designate, stand for, or denote, as a word or symbol
ⓢⓨⓝ exemplify, illustrate, stand for
ⓔ.ⓖ. The rose **represents** his prized love.
ⓝ representative 대표자, 대리인

0034 ■■■

benediction
[bènədíkʃən]

축복, 감사 기도
ⓝ an utterance of good wishes
ⓢⓨⓝ blessing
ⓔ.ⓖ. The pastor pronounced the **benediction** for his congregation.
ⓐ benedictive 소원의, 소망의

0035 ■■□

disaffect
[dìsəfékt]

~에게 불평(불만)을 품게 하다
ⓥ to alienate the affection, sympathy, or support of; make discontented
    or disloyal
ⓢⓨⓝ alienate, disquiet
ⓔ.ⓖ. The dictator's policies had soon **disaffected** the population.
ⓐ disaffected 불만(반감)을 품은

0036 ■■□

advocate
[ǽdvəkèit]

변호하다, 주장하다
ⓥ to speak or write in favor of; support or urge by argument
ⓢⓨⓝ recommend, urge
ⓔ.ⓖ. He **advocated** higher salaries for the teaching staff.
ⓝ advocator 주창자, 창도자

0037 ■□□

classify
[klǽsəfài]

분류하다, 나누다
ⓥ to arrange or organize by classes; order according to class
ⓢⓨⓝ class, sort, assort, categorize
ⓔ.ⓖ. This company is **classified** as a charity organization.
ⓝ classification 분류

0038 ■■□

delegate
[dél-igət]

대표, 사절, 파견의원
ⓝ a person designated to act for or represent another or others;
    deputy; representative, as in a political convention
ⓢⓨⓝ deputy, emissary, envoy, agent
ⓔ.ⓖ. **Delegates** visited several African nations last month.
ⓝ delegation 대표 임명(파견), 대표단

0039 ■□□

dissertation
[dìsərtéiʃən]

학술논문, 박사논문
ⓝ a written essay, treatise, or thesis, esp. one written by a candidate for the degree of Doctor of Philosophy
ⓢⓨⓝ treatise, disquisition
ⓔ.ⓖ. He had to present his **dissertation** before a panel of examiners.
ⓥ dissert 논하다, 논문을 쓰다

0040 ■■□

interrogation
[intèrəgéiʃən]

질문, 심문, 의문
ⓝ the act of interrogating; questioning
ⓢⓨⓝ inquisition, inquiry, investigation
ⓔ.ⓖ. The thief was taken to the police station for **interrogation**.
ⓥ interrogate 심문하다, 질문하다

0041 ■□□

drawback
[drɔ́ːbæ̀k]

약점, 결점, 장애
ⓝ a hindrance or disadvantage; an undesirable or objectionable feature
ⓢⓨⓝ defect, handicap, disadvantage
ⓔ.ⓖ. Success has its **drawbacks**.

0042 ■□□

reflect
[riflékt]

반사하다, 반영하다
ⓥ to cast back (light, heat, sound, etc.) from a surface
ⓢⓨⓝ reverberate
ⓔ.ⓖ. The mirror **reflected** the family's image perfectly.
ⓝ reflection 반영

0043 ■□□

anatomy
[ənǽtəmi]

해부학, 해부, 분석
ⓝ the science dealing with the structure of animals and plants
ⓔ.ⓖ. **Anatomy** is an important part of biology.
ⓥ anatomize 해부하다, 분석하다

0044 ■□□

dreary
[dríəri]

적적한, 쓸쓸한, 음울한
ⓐ causing sadness or gloom
ⓢⓨⓝ gloomy, doleful, bleak
ⓔ.ⓖ. Despite a **dreary** start to the day, the skies will brighten by midday.

0045 ■■□

denote
[dinóut]

표시하다, 나타내다
ⓥ to be a mark or sign of
ⓢⓨⓝ indicate, mark
ⓔ.ⓖ. This mark in this book **denotes** an overdue account.
ⓝ denotation 표시, 지시

0046 ■□□

redundant
[ridʌ́ndənt]

과다한, 남아도는, 불필요한
ⓐ being in excess; exceeding what is usual or natural; not needed or useful
ⓢⓨⓝ superfluous, excess
ⓔ.ⓖ. The boom of mobile phone has made phone boxes totally **redundant**.
ⓝ redundancy 여분, 과잉

0047 ■■□

incantation
[ìnkæntéiʃən]

주문
ⓝ the chanting or uttering of words purporting to have magical power
ⓔ.ⓖ. The idea that saying some sort of **incantation** or prayer will bring a good luck is quite appealing.
ⓐ incantatory 주문의

0048 ■■■

audacity
[ɔːdǽsəti]

대담, 담대함, 무모함
ⓝ boldness or daring, esp. with confident or arrogant disregard for personal safety, conventional thought, or other restrictions
ⓢⓨⓝ boldness, discourtesy
ⓔ.ⓖ. He had the **audacity** to ask me for money.
ⓐ audacious 담대한, 무모한

0049 ■■□

eminent
[émənənt]

높은, 저명한
ⓐ high in station, rank, or repute
ⓢⓨⓝ prominent, distinguished, lofty, famous
ⓔⓖ He was known for his **eminent** achievements.
ⓝ eminence 고귀, 높음, 저명, 명성

0050 ■■□

recoup
[rikúːp]

되찾다, 벌충하다, 공제하다
ⓥ to get back or regain
ⓢⓨⓝ recover, restore, retrieve, recompense
ⓔⓖ If we sell off some of our kitchen appliances, we can **recoup**
the loss for restaurant.
ⓝ recoupment 공제, 보상

0051 ■■□

dawdle
[dɔ́ːdl]

빈둥거리다, 시간을 낭비하다
ⓥ to waste time
ⓢⓨⓝ idle, trifle, loiter
ⓔⓖ Stop **dawdling** and help me with these chores!
ⓝ dawdler 굼벵이, 게으름뱅이

0052 ■■■

contingent
[kəntíndʒənt]

~에 부수하는, ~을 조건으로 하는
ⓐ dependent for existence, occurrence, character, etc., on something
not yet certain
ⓢⓨⓝ incidental, conditional
ⓔⓖ Our soccer schedule is **contingent** on the weather.
ⓐ contingently 우연히, 의존적으로

0053 ■■□

empirical
[impírikəl]

경험적인, 경험상의
ⓐ derived from or guided by experience or experiment
ⓢⓨⓝ experimental, pragmatic, practical
ⓔⓖ Until recently, very little **empirical** work had been done, a side
from the professor's initial experiment.
ⓝ empiricism 경험주의

0054 ■□□

catalyst
[kǽtəlist]

촉매제, 촉매, 자극
ⓝ a substance that causes or accelerates a chemical reaction without itself being affected
ⓢⓨⓝ impetus, incitation
ⓔⓖ The protests became the **catalyst** for political change.
ⓥ catalyze 촉진시키다

0055 ■■□

adversity
[ædvə́ːrsəti]

불행, 역경, 불운
ⓝ adverse fortune or fate; a condition marked by misfortune, calamity, or distress
ⓢⓨⓝ affliction, distress, misery, disaster
ⓔⓖ A friend will show his or her true colors in times of **adversity**.
ⓐ adverse 거스르는, 반대의

0056 ■■■

heterogeneous
[hètərədʒíːniəs]

이질적인, 이류의, 혼성의
ⓐ different in kind; unlike
ⓢⓨⓝ mixed, incongruous
ⓔⓖ America is a **heterogeneous** nation, they call it "the melting pot", because of this mixture.

0057 ■■□

enumerate
[injúːmərèit]

열거하다, 낱낱이 세다, 계산하다
ⓥ to mention separately as if in counting; name one by one; specify, as in a list
ⓢⓨⓝ count, number, calculate
ⓔⓖ Let me **enumerate** the many flaws in your hypothesis.
ⓝ enumeration 셈, 계산, 열거

0058 ■□□

altitude
[ǽltətjùːd]

고도, 높이
ⓝ the height of anything above a given planetary reference plane, esp. above sea level on earth.
ⓢⓨⓝ height
ⓔⓖ The **altitude** gave him a headache.

0059 ■□□

sabotage
[sǽbətɑ̀:ʒ]

파괴(방해) 행위

ⓝ any underhand interference with production, work, etc., in a plant, factory, etc., as by enemy agents during wartime or by employees during a trade dispute

ⓢⓨⓝ demolition, destruction

ⓔ.ⓖ. The factory will be out of order because of **sabotage**.

0060 ■■□

oblique
[əblíːk]

에두른, 비스듬한, 기울어진

ⓐ indirect; neither perpendicular nor parallel to a given line or surface

ⓢⓨⓝ slanting, sloping

ⓔ.ⓖ. 1. The criminals' answers to the police were **oblique**.
      2. The line on the road is **oblique**.

ⓝ obliquity 경사진 것, 기울어진 상태

Day

02

gnash	□□□	**attach**	□□□
recount	□□□	**literary**	□□□
transition	□□□	**compatible**	□□□
synthesize	□□□	**flippant**	□□□
chasm	□□□	**arena**	□□□
affect	□□□	**pliable**	□□□
insulate	□□□	**acute**	□□□
contrived	□□□	**obstinate**	□□□
strand	□□□	**allot**	□□□
hummable	□□□	**accordance**	□□□
jockey	□□□	**conscience**	□□□
mince	□□□	**hibernate**	□□□
imbibe	□□□	**consolidate**	□□□
whirl	□□□	**crumble**	□□□
unbearable	□□□	**lag**	□□□
perpendicular	□□□	**humiliate**	□□□
hawk	□□□	**backlash**	□□□
intensity	□□□	**impediment**	□□□
exasperate	□□□	**abstract**	□□□
arbitrary	□□□	**plead**	□□□
categorize	□□□	**antagonism**	□□□
compel	□□□	**authenticate**	□□□
merchandise	□□□	**decipher**	□□□
excursion	□□□	**consume**	□□□
actualize	□□□	**infatuate**	□□□
exhort	□□□	**convince**	□□□
deviant	□□□	**celibacy**	□□□
norm	□□□	**intricate**	□□□
fetter	□□□	**shed**	□□□
blatant	□□□	**lavish**	□□□

0061 ■□□

gnash
[næʃ]

(분노로) 이를 갈다
ⓥ grind (one's teeth) together, typically as a sign of anger
ⓢⓨⓝ grind, rasp
ⓔ.ⓖ. He is **gnashing** his teeth because he is so angry.

0062 ■□□

recount
[rikáunt]

~을 이야기하다
ⓥ to tell one by one
ⓢⓨⓝ narrate, delineate, rehearse
ⓔ.ⓖ. This book has the author **recount** the story as an omniscient narrator.

0063 ■□□

transition
[trænzíʃən]

이행
ⓝ the process or a period of changing from one state or condition to another
ⓢⓨⓝ move, adaptation
ⓔ.ⓖ. His life was a **transition** from poverty to power.

0064 ■□□

synthesize
[sínθəsàiz]

(화학 물질 따위를) 합성하다, (사상·스타일 등을) 종합(통합)하다
ⓥ to combine (constituent elements) into a single or unified entity
ⓔ.ⓖ. They **synthesized** a new chemical product.

0065 ■□□

chasm
[kǽzəm]

(땅·바위·얼음 속 등에 난) 아주 깊은 틈(구멍), (사람·집단 사이의) 큰 차이(골)
ⓝ a yawning fissure or deep cleft in the earth's surface
ⓢⓨⓝ gorge, cavity, breach, gulf
ⓔ.ⓖ. There is now a major gap and **chasm** in the process.

0066 ■□□

affect
[əfékt]

~에 영향을 끼치다; ~인 척하다
ⓥ influences something or causes something to change in some way
ⓢⓨⓝ influence, touch, bias, sham, feign
ⓔ.ⓖ. Space fever does not significantly **affect** an astronaut's health.

0067 ■□□

insulate
[ínsəlèit]

절연(단열)시키다, 보호(격리)시키다

ⓥ to cover, line, or separate with a material that prevents or reduces the passage, transfer, or leakage of heat, electricity, or sound

ⓢⓨⓝ wrap, soundproof, cocoon

ⓔ.ⓖ. **Insulating** your hot water cylinder is one of the simplest ways to save energy and money.

0068 ■□□

contrived
[kənˈtraɪvd]

억지로 꾸민 듯한, 부자연스러운

ⓐ deliberately created rather than arising naturally or spontaneously

ⓢⓨⓝ pretended, feigned

ⓞⓟⓟ spontaneous

ⓔ.ⓖ. The humour of the play is self-conscious and **contrived**.

0069 ■■□

strand
[strænd]

좌초시키다, 오도 가도 못하게 하다

ⓥ to drive or leave (a ship, fish, etc.) aground or ashore

ⓢⓨⓝ desert, shipwreck, abandon

ⓔ.ⓖ. Ten miles beyond the islands was **stranded** a sailboat, with its sail lowered in a distress signal.

0070 ■□□

hummable
[hʌ́məbl]

(곡이) 쉽게 흥얼거릴 수 있는; (가락이) 아름다운

ⓔ.ⓖ. Yet it's also roaringly mawkish, which might barely matter if it were packed full of **hummable** song.

0071 ■■■

jockey
[|dʒɑːki]

(남을 앞서기 위해) 다투다

ⓥ to use whatever methods someone can in order to get it or do it before their competitors can get it or do it

ⓔ.ⓖ. The runners **jockeyed** for position at the start.

0072 ■■□

mince
[mɪns]

(특히 고기를) 갈다, 다지다

ⓥ to put food such as meat into a machine which cuts it into very small pieces

ⓢⓨⓝ chip, cut, divide

ⓔ.ⓖ. **Mince** two pounds of chicken finely.

0073 ■■■

imbibe
[ɪm|baɪb]

(특히 술을) 마시다
ⓥ to drink, especially alcohol
ⓢⓨⓝ absorb, consume
ⓔ.ⓖ. If you **imbibe** too much alcohol, you will get drunk.

0074 ■□□

whirl
[wɜːrl]

빙그르르 돌다
ⓥ turn around in circles
ⓢⓨⓝ round, turn
ⓔ.ⓖ. He stepped out into the night and the **whirling** snow.

0075 ■■□

unbearable
[ʌn|berəbl]

참을 수 없는
ⓐ too painful or unpleasant for you to continue to experience
ⓢⓨⓝ insufferable, intolerable, unendurable
ⓔ.ⓖ. **unbearable** pain

0076 ■■□

perpendicular
[pɜːrpən|dɪkjələ(r)]

수직의
ⓐ at an angle of 90° to a horizontal line or surface
ⓢⓨⓝ vertical
ⓔ.ⓖ. The staircase was almost **perpendicular**.

0077 ■□□

hawk
[hɑːk]

매
ⓝ a type of large bird that catches small birds and animals for food
ⓔ.ⓖ. A **hawk** flew with flaps of the wings in the sky.

0078 ■□□

intensity
[inténsəti]

강렬, 맹렬
ⓝ great energy, strength, concentration, vehemence, etc., as of activity, thought, or feeling
ⓢⓨⓝ ferociousness, ferocity, fury
ⓔ.ⓖ. The **intensity** of his stare made it difficult to look him in the eye.
ⓐ intensive 강렬한

0079 ■■■

exasperate
[igzǽspərèit]

성나게 하다, 격분시키다

ⓥ to irritate or provoke to a high degree; annoy extremely
㊂ aggravate, enrage
ⓔ.ɡ. He was **exasperated** by the traffic.
ⓝ exasperation 격노, 분노, 격화

0080 ■■□

arbitrary
[ɑ́ːrbətrèri]

제멋대로인, 독단적인, 변덕스러운

ⓐ subject to individual will or judgment without restriction
㊂ capricious, impulsive, autocratic
ⓔ.ɡ. He made an **arbitrary** choice of the red shirt instead of the
    white.
ⓐⓓ arbitrarily 독단적으로, 제멋대로

0081 ■□□

categorize
[kǽtəgəràiz]

~의 범주에 넣다, 분류하다

ⓥ to arrange in categories or classes
㊂ classify, class, sort, assort, sort out
ⓔ.ɡ. Scientists have been **categorizing** new minerals.
ⓝ categorization(category) 분류

0082 ■■□

compel
[kəmpél]

억지로 시키다, 강요하다

ⓥ to force or drive, esp. to a course of action
㊂ force, enforce, drive, constrain
ⓔ.ɡ. His disregard of the rules **compels** us to fire him.
ⓝ compulsion 강제, 강박

0083 ■□□

merchandise
[mə́ːrtʃəndàiz]

상품, 물품

ⓝ the manufactured goods bought and sold in any business
㊂ goods
ⓔ.ɡ. The man is examining the **merchandise**.
ⓝ merchandiser 판매인

0084 ■□□

excursion
[ikskə́ːrʒən]

소풍, 짧은 여행
ⓝ a short trip or outing to some place, usually for a special purpose and with the intention of a prompt return
ⓢⓨⓝ jaunt, journey, outing, travel
ⓔ.ⓖ. If you want to make reservations for the **excursion** tomorrow, let me know some time this afternoon.
ⓥ excurse 잠깐 여행하다, 소풍 가다

0085 ■□□

actualize
[ǽktʃuəlàiz]

실현시키다
ⓥ to make actual or real; turn into action or fact
ⓢⓨⓝ realize, substantiate
ⓔ.ⓖ. To **actualize** one's master piece, many sketches must be made and thrown away first.
ⓝ actualization 실현

0086 ■■■

exhort
[igzɔ́ːrt]

간곡히 타이르다, 권하다, 훈계하다
ⓥ to urge, advise, or caution earnestly; admonish urgently
ⓢⓨⓝ urge, admonish
ⓔ.ⓖ. The teacher **exhorted** students to do good work.
ⓝ exhortation 권고, 장려, 훈계

0087 ■■□

deviant
[díːviənt]

정상이 아닌, (표준에서) 벗어난
ⓐ deviating or departing from the norm
ⓢⓨⓝ abnormal, atypical, freaky
ⓔ.ⓖ. They found that the rate of **deviant** behavior increased with the rate of popularity.
ⓝ deviance 이상, 일탈

0088 ■■□

norm
[nɔ́ːrm]

표준, 규범, 일반
ⓝ a standard, model, or pattern
ⓢⓨⓝ commonplace, ordinary, rule
ⓔ.ⓖ. After the fight, things returned to the **norm**.
ⓐ normal 전형적인

0089 ■□□

fetter
[fétər]

족쇄
ⓝ a chain or shackle placed on the feet
ⓢⓨⓝ manacle, shackle
ⓔⓖ We must free ourselves from the **fetters** of censorship.
ⓐ fetterless 족쇄(속박)이 없는

0090 ■■□

blatant
[bléitənt]

노골적인, 뻔한
ⓐ brazenly obvious
ⓢⓨⓝ flagrant, obvious, evident, noticeable
ⓔⓖ His **blatant** disregard for the rules up set the police officer from the start.
ⓝ blatancy 노골적임

0091 ■□□

attach
[ətǽtʃ]

붙이다
ⓥ to fasten or affix; join; connect
ⓢⓨⓝ link, tie, link up
ⓔⓖ I **attach** no importance to what he said.
ⓝ attachment 첨부, 붙임

0092 ■□□

literary
[lítərèri]

문학의
ⓐ pertaining to or of the nature of books and writings, esp. those classed as literature
ⓢⓨⓝ academic, bookish
ⓔⓖ He was somewhat **literary** in his speaking.
ⓝ literacy 읽고 쓸 줄 앎   ⓐ literate 읽고 쓸 줄 아는
ⓐ literal 글자 그대로의   ⓝ literature 문학

0093 ■■□

compatible
[kəmpǽtəbl]

양립할 수 있는, 호환되는
ⓐ capable of existing or living together in harmony
ⓢⓨⓝ consistent, harmonious
ⓔⓖ The following items are not **compatible** with Apple computers.
ⓝ compatibility 호환성, 양립성

0094 ■□□

flippant
[flípənt]

경박한, 경솔한, 무례한

ⓐ frivolously disrespectful, shallow, or lacking in seriousness; characterized by levity

ⓢⓨⓝ disrespectful, bold

ⓔ.ⓖ. The audience was shocked by his **flippant** remarks about celebrities.

ⓝ flippancy 경솔, 경박

0095 ■□□

arena
[ərí:nə]

투기장, 경기장

ⓝ a central stage, ring, area, or the like, used for sports or other forms of entertainment

ⓢⓨⓝ field

ⓔ.ⓖ. His pop concert was held in a sports **arena**.

0096 ■■□

pliable
[pláiəbl]

휘기 쉬운, 융통성 있는, 유순한

ⓐ easily bent; easily influenced or persuaded

ⓢⓨⓝ supple, docile, flexible

ⓔ.ⓖ. Work to form a soft **pliable** dough.

ⓝ pliability 유연성, 유순

0097 ■■□

acute
[əkjú:t]

날카로운, 예리한, 격렬한

ⓐ sharp or severe in effect

ⓢⓨⓝ intensive, keen, sharp, sensitive

ⓔ.ⓖ. He is afraid of an **acute** pain in his back.

ⓝ acuteness 날카로움, 격렬함

0098 ■■■

obstinate
[ábstənət]

완고한, 고집 센

ⓐ firmly or stubbornly adhering to one's purpose, opinion, etc.; not yielding to argument, persuasion, or entreaty

ⓢⓨⓝ stubborn, headstrong, incompliant

ⓔ.ⓖ. He is the most **obstinate** fellow I have ever met.

ⓝ obstinacy 완고함, 고집, 집요함; (병의) 난치

0099 ■■□

allot
[əlát]

할당하다, 분배하다
ⓥ to divide or distribute by share or portion
ⓢⓨⓝ assign, distribute
ⓔ.ⓖ. We were **allotted** new uniforms by our coach.
ⓝ allotment 할당, 배분

0100 ■□□

accordance
[əkɔ́ːrdəns]

일치, 조화
ⓝ agreement; conformity
ⓢⓨⓝ harmony, unison, coincidence
ⓔ.ⓖ. We are in total **accordance** with your proposal.
ⓥ accord 일치하다, 조화하다

0101 ■□□

conscience
[kánʃəns]

양심, 도의심
ⓝ the inner sense of what is right or wrong in one's conduct or motives, impelling one toward right action
ⓢⓨⓝ virtue
ⓔ.ⓖ. You should not do what clearly troubles your **conscience**.
ⓐ conscientious 양심적인, 성실한, 진실한

0102 ■□□

hibernate
[háibərnèit]

동면하다, 겨울잠 자다
ⓥ to spend the winter in close quarters in a dormant condition, as bears and certain other animals
ⓔ.ⓖ. Bears **hibernate** during the winter.
ⓝ hibernation 동면, 겨울잠

0103 ■■□

consolidate
[kənsálədèit]

합병하다, 통합하다
ⓥ to bring together (separate parts) into a single or unified whole
ⓢⓨⓝ unite, combine
ⓔ.ⓖ. We decided to **consolidate** our company holdings because of financial difficulty.
ⓝ consolidation 합병, 통합

0104 ■■□

crumble
[krÁkrmb]

부스러지다, 산산이 무너지다

ⓥ to break into small fragments or crumbs
ⓢⓨⓝ crush, break
ⓔ.ⓖ. The cake is so dry, it **crumbles** when you touch it.
ⓐ crumbly 부서지기 쉬운, 푸석푸석한

0105 ■■□

lag
[lǽg]

뒤처지다, 뒤떨어지다

ⓥ to fail to maintain a desired pace or to keep up; fall or stay behind
ⓢⓨⓝ delay, linger, loiter
ⓔ.ⓖ. My partner is **lagging** in our project, I can't stand it.
ⓝ laggard 느린 사람, 꾸물거리는 사람

0106 ■■□

humiliate
[hju:mílièit]

굴욕감을 느끼게 하다, 창피를 주다

ⓥ to cause (a person) a painful loss of pride, self-respect, or dignity; mortify
ⓢⓨⓝ degrade, derogate, disgrace
ⓔ.ⓖ. He was **humiliated** by the rude behavior of his family.
ⓝ humiliation 창피 줌, 굴욕

0107 ■■□

backlash
[bǽklæ̀ʃ]

(사회 변화 등에 대한 대중의) 반발

ⓝ a sudden, forceful backward movement; a strong or violent reaction, as to some social or political change
ⓢⓨⓝ resistance, retaliation, counteraction
ⓔ.ⓖ. The **backlash** of the new tax raise was a great deal of rioting.

0108 ■■□

impediment
[impédəmənt]

방해, 지장, 장애

ⓝ obstruction; hindrance; obstacle
ⓢⓨⓝ encumbrance, obstruction, hindrance, obstacle
ⓔ.ⓖ. There are a lot of **impediments** to building my new house.
ⓥ impede 방해하다, 지연시키다

0109 ■■□

abstract
[ǽbstrǽkt]

추상적, 관념적

ⓐ thought of apart from concrete realities, specific objects, or actual instances

ⓢⓨⓝ conceptional, ideational, notional

ⓔ.ⓖ. While most people clearly understand this work, it all seemed rather **abstract**.

ⓝ abstraction 추상, 추상적 개념

0110 ■■■

plead
[plíːd]

변호하다, 변론하다, 항변하다

ⓥ to appeal or entreat earnestly

ⓢⓨⓝ advocate, implore, entreat

ⓔ.ⓖ. She **pleaded** that he was to blame for the car accident.

ⓝ pleader 변호사, 항변하는 사람

0111 ■□□

antagonism
[æntǽgənìzm]

적개, 반목, 대립

ⓝ an active hostility or opposition, as between unfriendly or conflicting groups

ⓢⓨⓝ opposition, hostility

ⓔ.ⓖ. The demonstration began of **antagonism** to the President.

ⓝ antagonist 적대자, 경쟁자, 적

0112 ■■□

authenticate
[ɔːθéntikèit]

입증하다, 증명하다

ⓥ to establish as genuine; to make authoritative or valid

ⓢⓨⓝ confirm, validate, prove

ⓔ.ⓖ. It was not possible to **authenticate** the claim.

ⓝ authentication 입증, 인증

0113 ■■■

decipher
[disáifər]

해독하다, 암호를 풀다

ⓥ to make out the meaning of (poor or foreign writing, etc.)

ⓢⓨⓝ decode, analyze, translate

ⓔ.ⓖ. The professor **deciphered** the writing on the door.

0114 ■□□

consume
[kənsúːm]

소비하다, 소모하다

ⓥ to destroy or expend by use; use up
ⓢⓨⓝ spend, expend, use
ⓔⓖ How much salt do you **consume** in a meal?
ⓝ consumption 소비, 소모

0115 ■■■

infatuate
[infǽtʃuèit]

얼빠지게 하다, 홀리다, 열중하게 하다

ⓥ to inspire or possess with a foolish or unreasoning passion, as of love
ⓢⓨⓝ seduce, allure, tempt
ⓔⓖ After the ballet, he was completely **infatuated** with the lead ballerina.
ⓝ infatuation 정신을 잃게 함, 홀림, 심취

0116 ■■□

convince
[kənvíns]

확신시키다, 납득시키다

ⓥ to move by argument or evidence to belief, agreement, consent, or a course of action
ⓢⓨⓝ assure, persuade
ⓔⓖ The teacher tried patiently to **convince** hers on of his mistake.
ⓝ conviction 확신, 납득

0117 ■■■

celibacy
[séləbəsi]

독신주의(생활), 금욕적 순결

ⓝ abstention from sexual relations or by vow from marriage
ⓢⓨⓝ abstinence, chastity, purity
ⓔⓖ Clerical **celibacy** is the practice in most religious traditions.
ⓝ celibatarian 독신주의자

0118 ■■■

intricate
[íntrikət]

얽힌, 복잡한, 난해한

ⓐ having many interrelated parts or facets; entangled or involved
ⓢⓨⓝ complicated, abstruse
ⓔⓖ The plot of this television series is very **intricate**.
ⓝ intricacy 얽힘, 복잡함

0119 ■■□

shed
[ʃéd]

껍질을 벗다; (눈물 따위를) 흘리다, 떨어뜨리다, 치료하다(=cure)

ⓥ of a reptile, insect, etc. allow its skin or shell to come off, to be replaced by another one that has grown underneath; to pour forth (water or other liquid), as a fountain

ⓢⓨⓝ exuviate; emit, pour, sprinkle

ⓔ.ⓖ. 1. Who can tell me why snakes **shed** their skins in the summer?
   2. According to research, **shedding** tears lowers blood pressure and eases us of stress through relaxation.

ⓝ shedding 흘리기, 발산

0120 ■■□

lavish
[lǽviʃ]

아끼지 않는, 후한, 사치스러운

ⓐ expended, bestowed, or occurring in profusion

ⓢⓨⓝ luxurious, abundant, affluent

ⓔ.ⓖ. She is known for her **lavish** spending habits, and her taste for things expensive and exotic.

ⓝ lavisher 낭비자

Day

03

intrusive	☐☐☐	discipline	☐☐☐
jaunt	☐☐☐	prerogative	☐☐☐
beastie	☐☐☐	converge	☐☐☐
illuminated	☐☐☐	afterward	☐☐☐
tapestry	☐☐☐	integrate	☐☐☐
antelope	☐☐☐	propulsion	☐☐☐
power broker	☐☐☐	amendment	☐☐☐
afield	☐☐☐	puberty	☐☐☐
transform	☐☐☐	calumny	☐☐☐
authority	☐☐☐	adjust	☐☐☐
radiation	☐☐☐	compound	☐☐☐
preliminary	☐☐☐	quaint	☐☐☐
ascertain	☐☐☐	constraint	☐☐☐
gyre	☐☐☐	mere	☐☐☐
fraudulent	☐☐☐	refrain	☐☐☐
decimeter	☐☐☐	antiseptic	☐☐☐
underrepresented	☐☐☐	blast	☐☐☐
agitation	☐☐☐	constitute	☐☐☐
dedicate	☐☐☐	abide	☐☐☐
applaud	☐☐☐	passion	☐☐☐
benighted	☐☐☐	relish	☐☐☐
ensure	☐☐☐	burst	☐☐☐
bias	☐☐☐	deviate	☐☐☐
lukewarm	☐☐☐	state	☐☐☐
multiply	☐☐☐	alter	☐☐☐
sway	☐☐☐	alliteration	☐☐☐
proficient	☐☐☐	reminiscence	☐☐☐
creep	☐☐☐	bide	☐☐☐
meticulous	☐☐☐	trait	☐☐☐
circulate	☐☐☐	render	☐☐☐

0121 ■□□

intrusive
[intrúːsiv]

침입하는, 거슬리는
ⓐ disturbs your mood or your life in a way you do not like
ⓢⓨⓝ meddling
ⓞⓟⓟ low-key
ⓔ.ⓖ. Overflying helicopters represent a noisy, **intrusive** assault on quality of life.

0122 ■□□

jaunt
[dʒɔːnt]

(짧은) 여행
ⓝ a short excursion or journey for pleasure
ⓢⓨⓝ drive, junket
ⓔ.ⓖ. With Mother's Day approaching, I decide it's time for our annual **jaunt**.

0123 ■□□

beastie
[bíːsti]

짐승
ⓝ a small animal, especially one toward which affection is felt
ⓔ.ⓖ. "I'm not SO hungry any more," says the **Beastie**.

0124 ■□□

illuminated
[iˈluːmə.nātid]

(불빛이) 환한, (손으로 금, 은, 물감을) 채색한
ⓐ shine light on it and to make it brighter and more visible
ⓔ.ⓖ. The remains of the star were found as they were **illuminated** by the light from a nearby black hole.

0125 ■■□

tapestry
[tǽpistri]

태피스트리(색색의 실로 수놓은 벽걸이나 실내 장식용 비단), 그런 직물의 무늬
ⓝ cloth with a picture sewn on it using coloured threads
ⓔ.ⓖ. crafts such as embroidery and **tapestry**

0126 ■■□

antelope
[ǽntəlòup]

(동물) 영양
ⓝ an animal like a deer, with long legs and horns, that lives in Africa or Asia.
ⓔ.ⓖ. Bears, elk, deer, **antelope** and bison live in the park.

0127 ■□□

power broker
['pou(ə)r,brōkər]
정계 실력자, 막후실세

ⓝ someone who has a lot of influence, especially in politics, and uses it to help other people gain power

e.g. Ken Clarke is the real **power broker** in the Tory party.

0128 ■□□

afield
[əfiːld]
~에서 멀리 떨어져

ⓐ to or at a distance

e.g. The company is working as far **afield** as Indonesia and Kazakhstan.

0129 ■□□

transform
[trænsfɔ́ːrm]
변형시키다, 바꾸다, 전환하다

ⓥ to change in form, appearance, or structure

syn metamorphose, transfigure, renovate

e.g. His imagination **transformed** windmills into giants.

ⓝ transformation 변형, 변모, 변질

0130 ■■□

authority
[əθɔ́ːrəti]
권위, 권력, 권한

ⓝ the power to determine; the right to control, command, or determine

syn right, power, jurisdiction

e.g. He has no **authority** to make that decision.

ⓐ authoritarian 권위주의의, 독재주의의

0131 ■■□

radiation
[reɪd|eɪʃn]
(열·에너지 등의) 복사

ⓝ energy from heat or light that you cannot see

e.g. ultraviolet **radiation**

0132 ■■□

preliminary
[prɪlɪmɪneri]
예비의; 예선전

ⓐ coming before a more important action or event, especially introducing or preparing for it

syn introductory, initial

e.g. **preliminary** results

0133 ■■■

ascertain
[æsərteɪn]

확인하다, 발견하다

ⓥ If you ascertain the truth about something, you find out what it is, especially by making a deliberate effort to do so.
ⓢⓨⓝ confirm, discover
ⓔ.ⓖ. It can be difficult to **ascertain** the facts.

0134 ■■■

gyre
[dʒáiər]

나선형

ⓝ a circular or spiral movement or path

0135 ■■■

fraudulent
[|frɔ:dʒələnt]

사기 치기 위한

ⓐ dishonest and illegal
ⓢⓨⓝ fake, deceitful
ⓔ.ⓖ. **fraudulent** advertising

0136 ■■■

decimeter
[désəmì:tər]

10분의 1미터

ⓝ one tenth of a metre

0137 ■■□

underrepresented
[ʌndərɛprɪˈzɛntɪd]

대표가 제대로 안 된, 충분한 숫자가 드러나지 않은

ⓐ not present or shown in sufficient numbers
ⓢⓨⓝ The indigenous group is **underreperesented** in Australia.

0138 ■■□

agitation
[ædʒɪteɪʃn]

불안, 동요

ⓝ If someone is in a state of agitation, they are very worried or upset, and show this in their behaviour, movements, or voice.
ⓢⓨⓝ commotion, tumult, turmoil, upheaval, disquiet
ⓔ.ⓖ. The police have just damped down an **agitation**.
ⓐ agitational, agitative

0139 ■■□

dedicate
[dédikèit]

봉헌하다, 헌납하다, 바치다

ⓥ to set apart and consecrate to a deity or to a sacred purpose
ⓢⓨⓝ devote, donate
ⓔⓖ I would like to **dedicate** this championship award to my mother.
ⓝ dedication 봉헌, 헌납, 헌신

0140 ■■□

applaud
[əplɔ́ːd]

박수를 보내다, 칭찬하다

ⓥ to clap the hands as an expression of approval, appreciation, acclamation, etc
ⓢⓨⓝ cheer, clap, acclaim
ⓔⓖ They **applauded** wildly at the end of the film.
ⓝ applause 박수, 칭찬

0141 ■■■

benighted
[bináitid]

무지몽매한, 미개한, 문화가 뒤떨어진

ⓐ intellectually or morally ignorant; unenlightened
ⓔⓖ Some of the early colonists thought of the native people as **benighted** savages who could be exploited.

0142 ■■□

ensure
[inʃúər]

안전하게 하다, 지키다, 보증하다

ⓥ to secure or guarantee
ⓢⓨⓝ guard, secure, guarantee
ⓔⓖ New drugs are inspected closely to **ensure** their safety.
ⓐ sure 확실한, 틀림없는

0143 ■□□

bias
[báiəs]

선입견, 편견

ⓝ a particular tendency or inclination, esp. one that prevents unprejudiced consideration of a question
ⓢⓨⓝ prejudice, prepossession
ⓔⓖ The legal case should proceed without **bias** and without favor.
ⓐ biased 편향된, 선입견이 있는

0144 ■■□

lukewarm
[lúːkwɔ́ːrm]

미지근한, 미온적인, 내키지 않은, 냉담한

ⓐ moderately warm; having or showing little ardor, zeal, or enthusiasm
ⓢⓨⓝ tepid, indifferent, halfhearted, apathetic
ⓔ.ⓖ. Most children watched the show with **lukewarm** enthusiasm.

0145 ■□□

multiply
[mʌ́ltəplài]

증가시키다, 다양화시키다

ⓥ to make many or manifold; increase the number or quantity
ⓢⓨⓝ increase, propagate, reproduce, augment
ⓔ.ⓖ. Those cells can **multiply** many times, replenishing other cells in different parts of the body.
ⓝ multiplication 증가, 증식, 번식

0146 ■■□

sway
[swéi]

뒤흔들다, 동요시키다

ⓥ to move or swing to and fro, as something fixed at one end or resting on a support
ⓢⓨⓝ swing
ⓔ.ⓖ. The trees are **swaying** in the breeze.
ⓐ swayable 흔들릴 수 있는, 동요할 수 있는

0147 ■□□

proficient
[prəfíʃənt]

익숙한, 숙달된, 능숙한

ⓐ well-advanced or competent in any art, science, or subject
ⓢⓨⓝ skilled, skillful, trained
ⓔ.ⓖ. We can't become language-**proficient** by studying for one year in high school.
ⓝ proficiency 숙달, 능숙, 익숙

0148 ■■□

creep
[kríːp]

기다, 포복하다, 살금살금 걷다

ⓥ to move slowly with the body close to the ground, as a reptile or an insect, or a person on hands and knees
ⓢⓨⓝ crawl, slink, prowl
ⓔ.ⓖ. They **crept** silently through the school.
ⓐ creepy 기어 돌아다니는, 꾸물꾸물 움직이는

0149 ■■■

meticulous
[mətíkjuləs]

꼼꼼한, 세심한
ⓐ taking or showing extreme care about minute details
ⓢⓨⓝ careful, detailed, precise, thorough
ⓔⓖ My father is **meticulous** in all things.
ⓐⓓ meticulously 꼼꼼하게, 세심하게

0150 ■□□

circulate
[sə́ːrkjulèit]

순환하다, 돌다
ⓥ to move in a circle or circuit
ⓔⓖ Without proper hydration, the blood volume decreases, forcing the body to work harder to **circulate** nutrition.
ⓝ circuit 순회, 순환

0151 ■□□

discipline
[dísəplin]

훈련, 단련, 수양
ⓝ training to act in accordance with rule
ⓢⓨⓝ drill, training, conduct
ⓔⓖ The school has a reputation for high standards of **discipline**.
ⓐ disciplined 잘 통솔된, 훈련받은

0152 ■■■

prerogative
[prirágətiv]

특권, 특전
ⓝ an exclusive right, privilege, etc., exercised by virtue of rank or office
ⓢⓨⓝ privilege, right, liberty
ⓔⓖ They needed the strong powers and **prerogatives** of the CEO.

0153 ■■□

converge
[kənvə́ːrdʒ]

모이다, 집중하다
ⓥ to tend to meet in a point or line; incline toward each other, as lines that are not parallel
ⓢⓨⓝ concentrate, gather, focus
ⓔⓖ The two creeks **converged** in the canyon, forming a small river.
ⓝ convergence 수렴, 집합

0154 ■□□

afterward
[ǽftərwərd]

뒤에, 그 뒤
(ad) at a later or subsequent time
(syn) subsequently, later
(e.g.) He's going to the store but he'll come back here **afterward**.
(ad) forward 앞으로

0155 ■■□

integrate
[íntəgrèit]

통합하다, 합치다, 완전하게 하다
(v) to bring together or incorporate (parts) into a whole
(syn) unite, combine, merge
(e.g.) He's a computer scientist working on how to **integrate** technology into education.
(n) integration 통합, 완성, 완전

0156 ■■□

propulsion
[prəpʌ́lʃən]

추진, 추진된 상태
(n) the act or process of propelling
(syn) drive, promotion
(e.g.) When the sail broke, the ship lost all **propulsion**, and laid still in the water.
(v) propel 추진하다, 나아가게 하다

0157 ■■□

amendment
[əméndmənt]

변경, 수정, 개정
(n) the act of amending or the state of being amended
(syn) alteration, change, correction
(e.g.) The government may sometimes show signs of improvement and **amendment**.
(v) amend 수정하다, 변경하다

0158 ■■□

puberty
[pjúːbərti]

사춘기, 성숙기
(n) the period or age at which a person is first capable of sexual reproduction of offspring: in common law, presumed to be 14 years in the male and 12 years in the female
(syn) adolescence, juvenility, youthfulness
(e.g.) Everybody's voice changes and becomes deeper at **puberty**.

0159 ■■□

calumny
[kǽləmni]

중상, 비방, 악담
ⓝ a false and malicious statement designed to injure the reputation of someone or something
ⓢⓨⓝ aspersion, defamation
ⓔⓖ The letter was considered a **calumny** of the administration.
ⓐ calumnious 중상의, 비방하는

0160 ■□□

adjust
[ədʒʌ́st]

적합시키다, 맞추다, 순응하다
ⓥ to change (something) so that it fits, corresponds, or conforms
ⓢⓨⓝ set, correct, adapt, accommodate
ⓔⓖ They had no problems in **adjusting** to the new school.
ⓝ adjustment 조정, 적응, 순응

0161 ■■□

compound
[kámpaund]

합성의, 복합의
ⓐ composed of two or more parts, elements, or ingredients
ⓢⓨⓝ composite, commixture, blend
ⓔⓖ Plastic is a **compound** substance.
ⓐ compoundable 혼합할 수 있는, 타협할 수 있는

0162 ■■■

quaint
[kwéint]

기묘한, 기이한, 별스러워 흥미를 끄는
ⓐ having an old-fashioned attractiveness or charm; oddly picturesque; strange, peculiar, or unusual in an interesting, pleasing, or amusing way
ⓢⓨⓝ grotesque, odd, strange, peculiar
ⓔⓖ The **quaint** art of letter writing won't any longer be practiced soon.
ⓝ quaintness 기묘함, 기이함

0163 ■■□

constraint
[kənstréint]

강제, 압박, 속박
ⓝ limitation or restriction
ⓢⓨⓝ compulsion, obligation
ⓔⓖ Under the **constraint** of his chains, the prisoner couldn't reach his own feet.
ⓥ constrain 억지로 시키다, 강요하다

0164 ■□□

mere
[míər]

단순한, 순전한, 단지, ~에 불과한
ⓐ being nothing more nor better than
ⓢⓨⓝ pure, scant, sheer
ⓔⓖ You should not make light of him being a **mere** boy.
ⓐⓓ merely 단지, 다만

0165 ■■□

refrain
[rifréin]

그만두다, 참다, 삼가다
ⓥ to abstain from an impulse to say or do something (often fol. by from)
ⓢⓨⓝ abstain, inhibit, cease, desist
ⓔⓖ I **refrained** from writing to him what I thought.

0166 ■□□

antiseptic
[æntiséptik]

살균된, 소독된
ⓐ free from or cleaned of germs and other microorganisms
ⓢⓨⓝ sterile, aseptic, germ-free
ⓔⓖ I just take an **antiseptic** cream with me to hot places to put on bites and scratches to prevent infection.
ⓥ antisepticise 소독하다, 멸균하다

0167 ■□□

blast
[blǽst, blάːst]

돌풍, 센 바람
ⓝ a sudden and violent gust of wind
ⓢⓨⓝ gust, storm, gale
ⓔⓖ The **blasts** of cannons chilled us to the marrow.

0168 ■■□

constitute
[kánstətjùːt]

구성하다, ~의 구성 요소가 되다, (상태를) 성립시키다, 만들어내다
ⓥ be a part of a whole; to compose
ⓢⓨⓝ compound, compose, form, add up to
ⓔⓖ These elements combine to **constitute** a compound.
ⓝ constitution 구성, 구조, 조직
ⓐ constitutive

0169 ■■■

abide
[əbáid]

머무르다, 체류하다, 살다
ⓥ to remain; continue
ⓢⓎⓝ stay, continue, remain
ⓔ.ⓖ. Let her **abide** by the rules a few days longer.
ⓝ abider (관례, 명령 등을) 따르는 사람

0170 ■□□

passion
[pǽʃən]

열정, 정열, 격정
ⓝ any powerful or compelling emotion or feeling, as love or hate
ⓢⓎⓝ dedication, desire, devotion
ⓔ.ⓖ. Having a **passion** for one's career contributes significantly to
overall good health.
ⓐ passionate 열렬한, 열정적인

0171 ■□□

relish
[réliʃ]

맛, 풍미, 향기
ⓝ liking or enjoyment of the taste of something
ⓢⓎⓝ taste, flavor, savor
ⓔ.ⓖ. The hungry gives **relish** to any food.
ⓝ disrelish 싫음, 혐오

0172 ■□□

burst
[bə́ːrst]

폭발하다, 파열하다, 갑자기 튀다
ⓥ to break, break open, or fly apart with sudden violence
ⓢⓎⓝ explode, pop, blast
ⓔ.ⓖ. The bitter cold caused the pipes to **burst**.
ⓝ burster 파열시키는 것, 작약

0173 ■■□

deviate
[díːvièit]

빗나가게 하다, 일탈시키다
ⓥ to turn aside, as from a route, way, course, etc.
ⓢⓎⓝ divert, depart, digress
ⓔ.ⓖ. If you walk straight in that direction, without **deviating**, you will
come to the station.
ⓝ deviation 탈선, 일탈

0174 ■□□

state
[stéit]

상태, 형편, 사정
ⓝ the condition of a person or thing, as with respect to circumstances or attributes
ⓢⓨⓝ condition, circumstance, situation
ⓔ.ⓖ. The city was in a chaotic **state** because of a serious fire.

0175 ■■□

alter
[ɔ́:ltər]

변경하다, 바꾸다
ⓥ to make different in some particular, as size, style, course
ⓢⓨⓝ change, convert, modify
ⓔ.ⓖ. He **altered** his house a little to better suit the weather.
ⓐ alterable 변경할 수 있는

0176 ■■■

alliteration
[əlìtərèiʃən]

두운법, 두운체
ⓝ the commencement of two or more stressed syllables of a word group either with the same consonant sound or sound group (consonantal alliteration), as in from stem to stem, or with a vowel sound that may differ from syllable to syllable (vocalic alliteration), as in each to all
ⓔ.ⓖ. "Go get gold" is an example of **alliteration**.
ⓐ alliterative 두운법의, 두운체의

0177 ■■□

reminiscence
[rèmənísns]

회상, 추억, 기억
ⓝ the act or process of recalling past experiences, events, etc.
ⓢⓨⓝ memory, recollection, remembrance
ⓔ.ⓖ. We often live in **reminiscence** of our beloved childhoods.
ⓐ reminiscent 상기시키는, 연상시키는, 회상하게 하는

0178 ■■□

bide
[báid]

기다리다, 견디다
ⓥ to endure, bear
ⓢⓨⓝ wait, endure, bear
ⓔ.ⓖ. He's **biding** his time for the market to shift in his favor.

0179 ■□□

trait
[tréit]

특성, 특색, 특징

ⓝ a distinguishing characteristic or quality, esp. of one's personal nature

ⓢⓨⓝ characteristic, feature, particularity

ⓔ.ⓖ. The most important **trait** in business is not giving up.

0180 ■■■

render
[réndər]

~을 하게 하다, 되게 하다

ⓥ to cause to be or become

ⓢⓨⓝ make

ⓔ.ⓖ. His research **rendered** great service to the journalist profession.

DAY
03

Day

04

last-minute	☐☐☐	valid	☐☐☐
plot	☐☐☐	beacon	☐☐☐
dispatch	☐☐☐	provenance	☐☐☐
heraldry	☐☐☐	dictator	☐☐☐
feature	☐☐☐	condescending	☐☐☐
ring	☐☐☐	deploy	☐☐☐
recurrence	☐☐☐	salient	☐☐☐
entity	☐☐☐	contagious	☐☐☐
remorse	☐☐☐	clumsy	☐☐☐
overcome	☐☐☐	scorn	☐☐☐
attire	☐☐☐	dogma	☐☐☐
altar	☐☐☐	articulate	☐☐☐
august	☐☐☐	constrained	☐☐☐
austere	☐☐☐	scrutiny	☐☐☐
blaze	☐☐☐	comply	☐☐☐
blindly	☐☐☐	shatter	☐☐☐
bliss	☐☐☐	envoy	☐☐☐
bustle	☐☐☐	prolific	☐☐☐
choral	☐☐☐	amiable	☐☐☐
repent	☐☐☐	bizarre	☐☐☐
daunt	☐☐☐	thrive	☐☐☐
trivial	☐☐☐	explicit	☐☐☐
decompress	☐☐☐	shrill	☐☐☐
thorough	☐☐☐	conform	☐☐☐
converse	☐☐☐	shuffle	☐☐☐
forensic	☐☐☐	arid	☐☐☐
entice	☐☐☐	bitterness	☐☐☐
consent	☐☐☐	sluggish	☐☐☐
tremendous	☐☐☐	hazard	☐☐☐
tranquil	☐☐☐	armistice	☐☐☐

0181 ■□□

last-minute
[lást-mínute]

최후 순간의, 마지막 순간의, 급조한
ⓐ the latest possible time before an event
(e.g.) With the Olympics only a month away, the athletes are sweating it out in **last-minute** training.

0182 ■□□

plot
[plɑt]

땅, 도면
ⓝ a small piece of ground marked out for a purpose such as building or gardening
(syn) acreage, area
(e.g.) a vegetable **plot**

0183 ■■□

dispatch
[dispǽtʃ]

급송하다, 급히 해치우다
ⓥ to send off or away with speed
(syn) send, freight
(e.g.) Many armored vehicles are ready for immediate **dispatch**.

0184 ■■■

heraldry
[hérəldri]

(가문의) 문장
ⓝ symbol of families of medieval Europe
(e.g.) **Heraldry** developed as a means of identifying knights on the battlefield.

0185 ■□□

feature
[fíːtʃər]

~을 특징으로 삼다
ⓥ be a significant characteristic of or take an important part in
(syn) appear
(e.g.) Problems of family relationships **feature** prominently in her novels.

0186 ■■□

ring
[riŋ]

둘러싸다
ⓥ surround (someone or something), especially for protection or containment
(syn) surround, circle, embrace
(e.g.) You have to **ring** yourself with people you can trust.

0187 ■□□

recurrence
[rikə́:rəns]

되풀이 발생, 반복

ⓝ an act or instance of recurring
(e.g.) This should obviate a **recurrence** of the same problem!

0188 ■□□

entity
[éntəti]

실재(물); 존재; 실체

ⓝ something that has a real existence
(syn) thing, being, individual
(e.g.) Time is not an abstract **entity**.

0189 ■■□

remorse
[rimɔ́:rs]

후회, 양심의 가책, 자책

ⓝ deep and painful regret for wrongdoing
(syn) compunction, repentance, contrition
(e.g.) She hasn't shown a bit of **remorse**.
ⓐ remorseful 후회하는, 자책하는

DAY
04

0190 ■□□

overcome
[òuvərkʌ́m]

이기다, 압도하다

ⓥ to get the better of in a struggle or conflict
(syn) conquer, defeat
(e.g.) Napoleon **overcame** his slight height and ended up conquering most of Europe.

0191 ■□□

attire
[ətáiər]

차려입다

ⓥ to dress, array, or adorn, esp. for special occasions, ceremonials, etc.
(syn) overdress, dress up, fig out
(e.g.) My boyfriend looked so handsome neatly **attired**.
ⓐ attired 복장의, 복장을 한

0192 ■□□

altar
[ɔ́:ltə(r)]

제단

ⓝ An altar is a holy table in a church or temple.
(e.g.) The priest said a prayer at the **altar**.

0193 ■■■

august
[ɔːgʌst]

위엄 있는

ⓐ Someone or something that is august is dignified and impressive.
ⓢ dignified, illustrious, lofty
ⓔ The **august** surroundings of the Liberal Club made me exciting.
ⓝ augustness

0194 ■■■

austere
[ɔːstɪr]

소박한; 엄격한; 금욕적인

ⓐ If you describe something as austere, you approve of its plain and simple appearance.
ⓢ harsh, severe, stern, strict
ⓔ The monks' **austere** way of life was amazing.
ⓐⓓ austerely

0195 ■■□

blaze
[bleɪz]

활활 타다

ⓥ When a fire blazes, it burns strongly and brightly.
ⓢ burn, glow, flare
ⓔ A huge fire was **blazing** in the fireplace.
ⓐ ablaze

0196 ■□□

blindly
[|blaɪndli]

맹목적으로

ⓐⓓ If you say that someone does something blindly, you mean that they do it without having enough information, or without thinking about it.
ⓢ thoughtlessly, carelessly, recklessly
ⓔ He wanted to decide for himself instead of **blindly** following his parents' advice.

0197 ■■□

bliss
[blɪs]

더없는 행복

ⓝ Bliss is a state of complete happiness.
ⓢ ecstasy
ⓔ She could read the connubial **bliss** on his face.
ⓐ blissful
ⓐ blissless

0198 ■■□

bustle
[bʌsl]

바삐 움직이다, 서두르다
ⓥ If someone bustles somewhere, they move there in a hurried way, often because they are very busy.
ⓢⓨⓝ hurry, rush, fuss
ⓔ.ⓖ. Let's **bustle** up to finish our work.

0199 ■■□

choral
[kɔ́:rəl]

합창의
ⓐ Choral music is sung by a choir.
ⓔ.ⓖ. He bought a piano to use for **choral** practice.
ⓐⓓ chorally

0200 ■■□

repent
[ripént]

후회하다, 뉘우치다, 회개하다
ⓥ to feel sorry, self-reproachful, or contrite for past conduct; regret or be conscience-stricken about a past action, attitude, etc.
ⓢⓨⓝ regret, grieve, lament
ⓔ.ⓖ. She **repented** after her hurtful remark.
ⓝ repentance 후회, 회한, 회개

0201 ■■■

daunt
[dɔ́:nt]

위압하다, 기세를 꺾다
ⓥ to overcome with fear
ⓢⓨⓝ intimidate
ⓔ.ⓖ. The initial rejection **daunted** his ardor.
ⓐ dauntless 겁 없는, 불굴의

0202 ■□□

trivial
[tríviəl]

하찮은, 별것 아닌, 사소한
ⓐ of very little importance or value
ⓢⓨⓝ insignificant, frivolous, inconsiderable
ⓔ.ⓖ. Stop fighting over such **trivial** things.
ⓝ triviality 하찮음, 평범, 진부함

0203 ■■□

decompress
[diːkəmprés]

압력을 감소시키다, 압박을 완화하다
ⓥ to relieve of pressure or compression
ⓢⓨⓝ uncompress
ⓔ.ⓖ. The files are **decompressed** after being removed from storage.
ⓝ decompression 감압

0204 ■□□

thorough
[θɔ́ːrou]

철저한, 완전한, 절대적인
ⓐ executed without negligence or omissions
ⓢⓨⓝ absolute, accurate, complete
ⓔ.ⓖ. Doctors recommend a **thorough** physical exam every six months.
ⓐⓓ thoroughly 철저히, 완전히

0205 ■□□

converse
[kənvə́ːrs]

이야기하다, 담화를 나누다
ⓥ to talk informally with another or others; exchange views, opinions, etc., by talking
ⓢⓨⓝ chat, dialogue, talk, commune
ⓔ.ⓖ. This allows you to **converse** with other participants in our survey.
ⓝ conversation 담화, 회화, 대화

0206 ■■□

forensic
[fərénsik]

법정의, 변론의, 토론의
ⓐ connected with, or used in courts of law or public discussion and debate
ⓢⓨⓝ debatable
ⓔ.ⓖ. **Forensic** investigation revealed much about what happened the night of the murder.
ⓝ forensics 웅변술, 토론학

0207 ■■□

entice
[intáis]

꾀다, 유혹하다
ⓥ to lead on by exciting hope or desire
ⓢⓨⓝ allure, inveigle, induce
ⓔ.ⓖ. They were **enticed** westward by dreams of freedom.
ⓝ enticement 유혹, 꾐

0208 ■■□

consent
[kənsént]

동의하다, 승낙하다, 찬성하다
ⓥ to permit, approve, or agree; comply or yield (often fol. by to or an infinitive)
⑤ⓨⓝ accord, assent, agree, approve
ⓔ.ⓖ. We asked their permission, and they **consented**.
ⓝ consensus 의견의 일치, 합의, 여론

0209 ■□□

tremendous
[triméndəs]

거대한, 대단한
ⓐ extraordinarily great in size, amount, or intensity
⑤ⓨⓝ huge, enormous, gigantic
ⓔ.ⓖ. Breakthroughs in the health sciences sector can present **tremendous** opportunities for growth.

0210 ■■□

tranquil
[trǽŋkwil]

조용한, 고요한, 잔잔한
ⓐ free from commotion or tumult
⑤ⓨⓝ peaceful, quiet, calm
ⓔ.ⓖ. **Tranquil** meadows offer solitude amid the swirl of urban life.
ⓝ tranquility 고요, 평온

0211 ■□□

valid
[vǽlid]

근거가 확실한, 정확한, 타당한
ⓐ sound; just; well-founded
⑤ⓨⓝ authentic, credible, confirmed
ⓔ.ⓖ. When you miss work you must provide a **valid** reason.
ⓥ validate 정당성을 입증하다, 실증하다, 확인하다

0212 ■□□

beacon
[bíːkən]

횃불, 등대, 봉화
ⓝ a guiding or warning signal, as a light or fire, esp. one in an elevated position
⑤ⓨⓝ signal fire, warning light
ⓔ.ⓖ. The fire on the hill was a **beacon** signaling that advance of the enemy.

0213 ■■□

provenance
[právənəns]

기원, 유래

ⓝ place or source of origin
ⓢⓨⓝ derivation, origin
ⓔ.ⓖ. The **provenance** of the bible has been argued for hundreds of years.

0214 ■□□

dictator
[díkteitər]

독재자, 절대 권력자

ⓝ a person exercising absolute power, esp. a ruler who has absolute, unrestricted control in a government without hereditary succession
ⓢⓨⓝ authoritarian, autocrat, totalitarian, tyrant
ⓔ.ⓖ. The **dictator** still held power after the vote against him.
ⓝ dictatorship 절대권, 독재권

0215 ■■■

condescending
[kàndəséndiŋ]

잘난 체하는, 생색내는 듯한

ⓐ showing or implying a usually patronizing descent from dignity or superiority
ⓢⓨⓝ patronizing, disdainful, supercilious
ⓔ.ⓖ. They resented the older neighbors' **condescending** attitude.
ⓥ condescend 잘난 체하다, 거들먹거리다

0216 ■■□

deploy
[diplói]

전개하다, 배치하다

ⓥ to spread out (troops) so as to form an extended front or line
ⓢⓨⓝ arrange, dispose, position
ⓔ.ⓖ. You can choose which air squadron you wish to **deploy**.
ⓝ deployment 전개, 배치

0217 ■■□

salient
[séiliənt]

현저한, 두드러진

ⓐ prominent or conspicuous
ⓢⓨⓝ noticeable, obvious, prominent, conspicuous
ⓔ.ⓖ. The tension between them has become **salient**.
ⓐⓓ saliently 현저하게, 두드러지게

0218 ■□□

contagious
[kəntéidʒəs]

전염성의, 옮기 쉬운

ⓐ capable of being transmitted by bodily contact with an infected person or object
ⓢⓨⓝ epidemic, infectious, pestiferous
ⓔ.ⓖ. An outbreak of the very **contagious** bird flu spread through Asia.
ⓝ contagion 전염, 감염

0219 ■□□

clumsy
[klʌ́mzi]

서투른, 어색한

ⓐ awkward in movement or action; without skill or grace
ⓢⓨⓝ awkward, bungling
ⓔ.ⓖ. He is very **clumsy** and is always falling down.
ⓝ clumsiness 서투름, 어색함

0220 ■□□

scorn
[skɔ́ːrn]

경멸하다, 멸시하다

ⓥ to treat or regard with contempt or disdain
ⓢⓨⓝ disdain, condemn, contemn
ⓔ.ⓖ. Lots of aristocrats used to **scorn** with laughter in the old days.
ⓐ scornful 경멸하는, 멸시하는

0221 ■□□

dogma
[dɔ́ːgmə]

교리, 교의, 신조

ⓝ a system of principles or tenets
ⓢⓨⓝ doctrine, tenet, creed
ⓔ.ⓖ. He sought to separate the philosophy lesson from the religious **dogma**.
ⓐ dogmatic 교리상의, 교리에 관한

0222 ■□□

articulate
[ɑːrtíkjulət]

또렷하게 발음하다

ⓥ to utter clearly and distinctly; pronounce with clarity
ⓢⓨⓝ pronounce, enunciate
ⓔ.ⓖ. You have to **articulate** distinctly so that a foreigner may understand what you are saying clearly.
ⓝ articulation 또렷한 발음, 명확한 표현

DAY
04

0223 ■■□

constrained
[kənstréind]

강제적인, 압박당한

ⓐ forced, compelled, or obliged
ⓔ.ⓖ. We were **constrained** to move out of the town.
ⓐ unconstrained 구속받지 않는

0224 ■■□

scrutiny
[skrúːtəni]

정밀한 조사, 검사

ⓝ a searching examination or investigation; minute inquiry
ⓢⓨⓝ examination, inspection, observation
ⓔ.ⓖ. He was a man under **scrutiny** by the police, so he couldn't do anything freely.
ⓥ scrutinize 세밀히 조사하다, 철저히 검사하다

0225 ■■□

comply
[kəmplái]

응하다, 따르다, 좇다

ⓥ to act or be in accordance with wishes, requests, demands, requirements, conditions, etc.
ⓢⓨⓝ agree, follow, conform, accede
ⓔ.ⓖ. They asked him to leave and he **complied**, after gathering his things.
ⓝ compliance 응함, 순종, 응낙

0226 ■■□

shatter
[ʃǽtər]

산산이 부수다, 분쇄하다

ⓥ to break (something) into pieces, as by a blow
ⓢⓨⓝ break, crash, demolish
ⓔ.ⓖ. The roar of the gunfire **shattered** the morning calm.
ⓐ shattered 엄청난 충격을 받은, 완전히 지친

0227 ■□□

envoy
[énvɔi]

사절, 사신, 대사

ⓝ a diplomatic agent
ⓢⓨⓝ ambassador, deputy, diplomat
ⓔ.ⓖ. Canada hastily sent a senior **envoy** for two days of talks.

0228 ■■□

prolific
[prəlífik]

다산의, 비옥한, 다작의
ⓐ producing offspring, young, fruit, etc., abundantly; highly productive
ⓢⓨⓝ fruitful, fertile, profuse
ⓔ.ⓖ. He was probably th most **prolific** song-writer of his generation.
ⓝ prolificity 다산성, 생산성

0229 ■■□

amiable
[éimiəbl]

호감을 주는, 상냥한, 우호적인
ⓐ having or showing pleasant, good-natured personal qualities
ⓢⓨⓝ affable, agreeable, congenial
ⓔ.ⓖ. He is an **amiable** man and always maintains a smile.
ⓐ unamiable 붙임성 없는, 무뚝뚝한

0230 ■□□

bizarre
[bizáːr]

별난, 기괴한, 이상한
ⓐ markedly unusual in appearance, style, or general character and often involving incongruous or unexpected elements
ⓢⓨⓝ odd, peculiar, cranky
ⓔ.ⓖ. Paleontologists report that the newly discovered species had a **bizarre** lack of recognizable features.
ⓝ bizarreness 괴상함, 이상함

0231 ■□□

thrive
[θráiv]

번영하다, 번성하다, 성공하다
ⓥ to prosper; be fortunate or successful
ⓢⓨⓝ prosper, flourish, boom
ⓔ.ⓖ. While many of our competitors are failing, we continue to **thrive**.
ⓐ thriving 번성하는, 번영하는

0232 ■■□

explicit
[iksplísit]

명백한, 뚜렷한, 명시적인
ⓐ fully and clearly expressed or demonstrated; leaving nothing merely implied
ⓢⓨⓝ clear, unequivocal, absolute, accurate
ⓔ.ⓖ. He was quite **explicit** in his telling of the story.
ⓝ explicitness 명백, 명시

DAY
04

0233 ■□□

shrill
[ʃríl]

(목소리 등이) 날카로운, 높은, 새된

ⓐ high-pitched and piercing in sound quality

ⓢⓨⓝ high-pitched, piercing

ⓔ.ⓖ. A **shrill** cry rang out in the night.

0234 ■■□

conform
[kənfɔ́ːrm]

(행위, 습관을 모범, 범례에) 따르게 하다, 맞게 하다

ⓥ to act in accordance or harmony; to act in accord with the prevailing standards, attitudes, practices, etc., of society or a group

ⓢⓨⓝ comply

ⓔ.ⓖ. The building did not **conform** to safety regulations.

ⓝ conformity 유사, 적합, 일치

0235 ■□□

shuffle
[ʃʌ́fl]

(발을) 질질 끌다, 발을 끌며 걷다

ⓥ to walk without lifting the feet or with clumsy steps and a shambling gait

ⓔ.ⓖ. We watched the princess do the inaugural **shuffle** through the room.

ⓝ shuffler 발을 끌며 걷는 사람, 속이는 사람

0236 ■■□

arid
[ǽrid]

마른, 건조한, 습기가 없는

ⓐ being without moisture; extremely dry

ⓢⓨⓝ dry, waterless

ⓔ.ⓖ. Being **arid**, it is difficult to grow food in deserts.

ⓝ aridness 건조함

0237 ■□□

bitterness
[bítərnis]

고통, 신랄, 비통

ⓝ a feeling of deep and bitter anger and ill-will

ⓢⓨⓝ resentment, agony, acerbity

ⓔ.ⓖ. The president held **bitterness** to ward the other ambassador.

ⓐ bitter 쓴, 쓰라린, 고통스러운

0238 ■■□

sluggish
[slʌ́giʃ]

기능이 둔한, 활발하지 못한, 부진한

ⓐ indisposed to action or exertion; lacking in energy
ⓢⓨⓝ lazy, indolent, inactive
ⓔ.ⓖ. All this weight I put on has made me a bit **sluggish**.

0239 ■□□

hazard
[hǽzərd]

위험, 재난, 해악

ⓝ an unavoidable danger or risk, even though often foreseeable
ⓢⓨⓝ danger, risk, jeopardy
ⓔ.ⓖ. Some sharp toys are a **hazard** for babies.
ⓐ hazardous 위험한, 모험적인

0240 ■■■

armistice
[áːrməstis]

휴전, 정전

ⓝ a temporary cessation of fighting by mutual consent
ⓢⓨⓝ cessation, truce
ⓔ.ⓖ. World War I ended with the **armistice** of 1918.

DAY

04

Day

05

categorical	□□□	bereave	□□□
cavalier	□□□	cease	□□□
haggle	□□□	convey	□□□
gaping	□□□	deliberate	□□□
maw	□□□	audit	□□□
absolution	□□□	aviator	□□□
antibiotic	□□□	collaborate	□□□
ammunition	□□□	discourse	□□□
tempest	□□□	strain	□□□
inherit	□□□	chivalrous	□□□
murky	□□□	crucial	□□□
snatch	□□□	aggression	□□□
consensus	□□□	surge	□□□
contend	□□□	belch	□□□
deceptive	□□□	contemplate	□□□
defer	□□□	stout	□□□
deputation	□□□	beguile	□□□
engaging	□□□	sustain	□□□
ere	□□□	exploit	□□□
eschew	□□□	ritual	□□□
avid	□□□	prodigal	□□□
amenable	□□□	belittle	□□□
demonic	□□□	complexity	□□□
contradict	□□□	rigid	□□□
splendid	□□□	segment	□□□
disengage	□□□	molecule	□□□
versatile	□□□	transact	□□□
ally	□□□	creed	□□□
arbitration	□□□	speculation	□□□
burglary	□□□	enhance	□□□

0241 ■■□

categorical
[kætəgɔ́ːrikəl]

단정적인, 절대적인
ⓐ without exceptions or conditions
ⓢⓨⓝ absolute, unqualified, unconditional, flat, downright
ⓔ.ⓖ. a **categorical** assurance that the government will not raise VAT.
ⓐⓓ categorically
ⓝ categoricalness

0242 ■■□

cavalier
[kæ̀vəlíər]

무관심한, 무신경의
ⓐ haughty, disdainful, or supercilious
ⓢⓨⓝ offhand, uninterested, unconcerned
ⓞⓟⓟ thoughtful
ⓔ.ⓖ. Victoria treated the man with a **cavalier** attitude.

0243 ■■□

haggle
[hǽgəl]

~와 흥정하다, ~와 실랑이하다
ⓥ to bargain in a petty, quibbling, and often contentious manner
ⓢⓨⓝ barter, deal, drive a hard bargain, quibble, wrangle
ⓔ.ⓖ. Always shop around and don't be afraid to **haggle** on price.

0244 ■□□

gaping
[gǽpiŋ]

입을 크게 벌린; 크게 갈라진
ⓐ (mouth) wide open
ⓔ.ⓖ. Their mouths are **gaping** open, they look just ravenous as if they're ready to eat those souls.
ⓐⓓ gapingly

0245 ■■□

maw
[mɔː]

(목)구멍(hole)
ⓝ the mouth, throat, or gullet of an animal, especially a carnivorous mammal
ⓔ.ⓖ. No prayers dare enter this frightful **maw**.

0246 ■□□

absolution
[æbsəlú:ʃən]

면죄, 용서
ⓝ a freeing from blame or guilt
ⓢⓨⓝ clemency, remission, exonerate
ⓞⓟⓟ punishment
ⓔ.ⓖ. The priest gave the woman **absolution**.
ⓥ absolve

0247 ■□□

antibiotic
[antibahyotik]

항생제
ⓝ a medicine that inhibits the growth of or destroys microorganisms
ⓔ.ⓖ. The doctor put him on **antibiotics**.

0248 ■□□

ammunition
[æmjuníʃən]

탄약, 보급
ⓝ any material, means, weapons, etc. used in any conflict
ⓢⓨⓝ bullets, munitions
ⓔ.ⓖ. It'd be a waste of **ammunition**.

0249 ■□□

tempest
[témpist]

폭풍우, 폭설
ⓝ a violent windstorm, esp. one with rain, hail, or snow
ⓢⓨⓝ blizzard, gale, storm, tumult, turmoil
ⓔ.ⓖ. The **tempest** raged unceasingly for ten days.
ⓐ tempestuous 폭풍우의, 폭설의

0250 ■□□

inherit
[inhérit]

상속하다, 물려받다
ⓥ to take or receive (property, a right, a title, etc.) by succession or
   will, as an heir
ⓢⓨⓝ accede
ⓔ.ⓖ. Upon your decease, your family will **inherit** the house.
ⓝ inheritance 상속, 재산, 유산

0251 ■■□

murky
[mə́:rki]

어두운, 음침한, 애매한, 확실치 않은
ⓐ dark, gloomy, vague
ⓢⓨⓝ cheerless, unclear, confused
ⓔ.ⓖ. I looked into the **murky** water of the river.
ⓝ murk 암흑, 우울함

0252 ■■■

snatch
[snætʃ]

와락 붙잡다, 잡아채다, 강탈하다
Ⓥ to make a sudden effort to seize something, as with the hand
ⓢⓨⓝ grab, catch, nab, kidnap, abduct
ⓔⓖ The man **snatched** the purse from that nice old lady.
ⓝ snatcher 날치기, 유괴범인

0253 ■□□

consensus
[kənsensəs]

의견 일치, 합의
ⓝ A consensus is general agreement among a group of people.
ⓢⓨⓝ general agreement, unanimity
ⓔⓖ The **consensus** is against the bill.

0254 ■■□

contend
[kəntend]

~와 다투다, 주장하다, 겨루다
ⓢⓨⓝ argue, compete, contest, jostle
ⓔⓖ Never **contend** with a man who has nothing to lose.
ⓝ contention 논쟁, 언쟁

0255 ■■□

deceptive
[dɪseptɪv]

기만적인, 현혹하는
ⓐ If something is deceptive, it encourages you to believe something which is not true.
ⓢⓨⓝ fraudulent, illusive, misleading
ⓔⓖ The opposition argument is shamefully **deceptive**.
ⓐⓓ deceptively

0256 ■■□

defer
[dɪ|fɜ:(r)]

연기하다
Ⓥ If you defer an event or action, you arrange for it to happen at a later date, rather than immediately or at the previously planned time.
ⓢⓨⓝ postpone, delay, put off
ⓔⓖ The department **deferred** the decision for six months.
ⓐ deferrable

0257 ■■■

deputation
[|depju|teɪʃn]

사절단

ⓝ A deputation is a small group of people who have been asked to speak to someone on behalf of a larger group of people, especially in order to make a complaint.

ⓔ.ⓖ. A **deputation** of elders from the village arrived headed by its chief.

0258 ■■□

engaging
[ɪngeɪdʒɪŋ]

매력적인

ⓐ An engaging person or thing is pleasant, interesting, and entertaining.

ⓢⓨⓝ charming, interesting, pleasing

ⓔ.ⓖ. One of her most **engaging** and least known novels is Justice.

0259 ■■■

ere
[er]

(문예체) ~의 전에

ⓟ Ere means the same as 'before'.

ⓢⓨⓝ before

ⓔ.ⓖ. Take the water **ere** the clock strikes twelve.

0260 ■■■

eschew
[ɪstʃuː]

피하다

ⓥ If you eschew something, you deliberately avoid doing it or becoming involved in it.

ⓢⓨⓝ avoid, forbear, refrain, shun

ⓔ.ⓖ. Although he appeared to enjoy a jet-setting life, he **eschewed** publicity and avoided nightclubs.

ⓝ eschewal

0261 ■■□

avid
[ǽvid]

열망하는, 열심인, 탐하는

ⓐ having an ardent desire or unbounded craving

ⓢⓨⓝ wishful, greedy

ⓔ.ⓖ. My boss had an **avid** desire for making a sustainable, environmental construction company.

ⓝ avidness 열심, 욕심

0262 ■■□

amenable
[əmíːnəbl]

유순한, 다루기 쉬운, 기꺼이 따르는
ⓐ ready or willing to answer, act, agree, or yield
ⓢⓨⓝ compliant, conformable, docile, submissive
ⓔ.ⓖ. The children are generally **amenable** to their English teacher.
ⓝ amenability 복종, 순종

0263 ■□□

demonic
[dimánik]

악마의, 귀신 들린
ⓐ inspired as if by a demon, indwelling spirit, or genius
ⓢⓨⓝ satanic
ⓔ.ⓖ. She accepts the **demonic** staff from the antagonist; and disappears.
ⓝ demon 악마, 정령

0264 ■■□

contradict
[kàntrədíkt]

부정하다, 부인하다, 반박하다
ⓥ to assert the contrary or opposite of; deny directly and categorically
ⓢⓨⓝ deny, disaffirm, controvert
ⓔ.ⓖ. I would argue that this statement is **contradicting** itself.
ⓝ contradiction 부정, 부인

0265 ■□□

splendid
[spléndid]

화려한, 훌륭한, 멋진, 뛰어난
ⓐ gorgeous; magnificent; sumptuous; grand; superb, as beauty
ⓢⓨⓝ gorgeous, magnificent, sumptuous, grand, superb, excellent
ⓔ.ⓖ. The ballet gave us a **splendid** performance.
ⓝ splendor 훌륭함, 장려, 탁월, 빛남

0266 ■■□

disengage
[dìsengéidʒ]

(연결, 접속을) 풀다, 떼다
ⓥ to release from attachment or connection
ⓢⓨⓝ loosen, unfasten
ⓔ.ⓖ. How do I silence or **disengage** the alarm?
ⓝ disengagement 해방, 자유

0267 ■■■

versatile
[vɔ́ːrsətl]

다재다능한, (능력, 재능 등이) 다방면의, 융통성이 있는
ⓐ capable of or adapted for turning easily from one to another of various tasks, fields of endeavor, etc
ⓢⓨⓝ talented, gifted
ⓔ.ⓖ. These offer less memory but make up for that in terms of compact size and **versatile** design.
ⓝ versatility 다재다능, 다예

0268 ■□□

ally
[əlái]

동맹하다, 연합하다
ⓥ to unite formally, as by treaty, league, marriage, or the like
ⓢⓨⓝ consort, associate, affiliate
ⓔ.ⓖ. Russia **allied** itself with France.
ⓝ alliance 동맹, 연합, 결연

0269 ■■□

arbitration
[àːrbətréiʃən]

조정, 중재
ⓝ the hearing and determining of a dispute or the settling of differences between parties by a person or persons chosen or agreed to by them
ⓢⓨⓝ adjustment, agreement, compromise
ⓔ.ⓖ. To make the divorce peaceful, the couple agreed to **arbitration**.
ⓥ arbitrate 중재하다, 조정하다

0270 ■□□

burglary
[bɔ́ːrgləri]

강도, 밤 도둑질, 주거침입
ⓝ the felony of breaking into and entering the house of another at night with intent to steal
ⓢⓨⓝ felony, crime, robbery
ⓔ.ⓖ. There were several **burglaries** in this neighborhood last week.
ⓝ burglar 강도

0271 ■■■

bereave
[biríːv]

앗아가다
ⓥ to deprive and make desolate, esp. by death
ⓢⓨⓝ deprive, rob, bereft
ⓔ.ⓖ. Cancer **bereaved** them of their uncle.
ⓝ bereavement 여읨, 사별

DAY
05

0272 ■■□

cease
[síːs]

그치다, 끝나다, 그만두다
ⓥ to stop
syn discontinue, desist, stop
e.g. Not all medieval beliefs have **ceased** practice.
ⓝ cessation 중지

0273 ■□□

convey
[kənvéi]

나르다, 운반하다
ⓥ to carry, bring, or take from one place to another
syn transport, bear
e.g. The workers are **conveying** the building materials in handcarts.
ⓝ conveyance 운반, 수송

0274 ■■□

deliberate
[dilíbərət]

신중한, 생각이 깊은, 사려 깊은, 계획적인
ⓐ carefully weighed or considered; studied; intentional
syn considered, intentional, planned, premeditated, studied
e.g. The CEO fired them for **deliberate** misrepresentation.
ⓝ deliberation 숙고, 곰곰이 생각함, 신중함

0275 ■□□

audit
[ɔ́ːdit]

회계 감사, 심사, 결산; (회계를) 감사하다
ⓝ an official examination and verification of accounts and records, esp. of financial accounts
syn scrutinize, inspect
e.g. Accountants from outside **audit** the company annually.
ⓝ auditee 회계 감사를 받는 사람

0276 ■□□

aviator
[éivièitər]

비행사, 조종사
ⓝ a pilot of an airplane or other heavier-than-air aircraft
syn pilot
e.g. She has a dream to be the best woman **aviator**.
ⓥ aviate 비행하다, 조종하다

0277 ■■□

collaborate
[kəlǽbərèit]

공동으로 일하다, 합작하다, 협동하다
ⓥ to work, one with another; cooperate, as on a literary work
ⓢⓨⓝ cooperate, participate
ⓔ.ⓖ. We **collaborated** with the best of our skills in our project.
ⓝ collaboration 협동, 합작, 공동연구

0278 ■■□

discourse
[dískɔ:rs]

강연, 설교, 담론, 토론
ⓝ communication of thought by words
ⓢⓨⓝ talk, conversation
ⓔ.ⓖ. The **discourse** of the academy is hostile towards grant funding.

0279 ■■□

strain
[stréin]

잡아당기다, 팽팽하게 하다, 긴장시키다
ⓥ to draw tight or taut, esp. to the utmost tension
ⓢⓨⓝ tighten, overwork
ⓔ.ⓖ. I **strained** my eyes by reading in the dark.
ⓐ strained 팽팽한, 긴장한

0280 ■■■

chivalrous
[ʃívəlrəs]

기사도의, 기사다운, 용기 있는
ⓐ having the qualities of chivalry, as courage, courtesy, and loyalty
ⓢⓨⓝ gallant, knightly
ⓔ.ⓖ. Paul is a man of **chivalrous** spirit.
ⓝ chivalry 기사도(정신)

0281 ■□□

crucial
[krú:ʃəl]

결정적인, 중대한
ⓐ involving an extremely important decision or result
ⓢⓨⓝ decisive, critical
ⓔ.ⓖ. Some investment is a **crucial** resource for any start-up venture.

DAY
05

0282 ■■□

aggression
[əgréʃən]

침략, 공격, 침해

ⓝ the action of a state in violating by force the rights of another state, particularly its territorial rights

ⓢⓨⓝ attack, invasion, offense

ⓔⓖ The army is prepared to stop any foreign **aggression**.

ⓐ aggressive 공격적인, 침략적인

0283 ■■■

surge
[sə́:rdʒ]

파도처럼 밀려오다, 쇄도하다, 밀어닥치다

ⓥ to rise and fall, toss about, or move along on the waves

ⓢⓨⓝ rush, sweep, pour, throng

ⓔⓖ The sea **surged** against the shore.

ⓐ surgy 파도가 밀려드는, 거친 파도의, 물결이 높은

0284 ■□□

belch
[béltʃ]

트림하다, 분출하다

ⓥ to expel gas noisily from the stomach through the mouth

ⓢⓨⓝ eruct, burp

ⓔⓖ Volcanoes **belch** carbon dioxide and steam into the air even while not erupting magma.

ⓝ belching 트림

0285 ■■□

contemplate
[kántəmplèit]

심사숙고하다, 곰곰 생각하다, 묵상하다

ⓥ to look at or view with continued attention; observe or study thoughtfully

ⓢⓨⓝ consider, cogitate, meditate

ⓔⓖ The company is **contemplating** a huge expansion eastward.

ⓝ contemplation 명상, 묵상

0286 ■■□

stout
[stout]

뚱뚱한, 용감한

ⓐ bulky in figure; bold, brave, or dauntless

ⓢⓨⓝ fat, plump, bulk; fearless, gallant, courageous

ⓔⓖ He is described as being a short, **stout** man, and was believed to have been very religious.

ⓐ stout-hearted 용감한, 대담한

0287 ■■■

beguile
[bigáil]

현혹하다, 속이다, 기만하다
ⓥ to influence by trickery, flattery, etc.
ⓢⓨⓝ cheat, mislead, delude
ⓔ.ⓖ. She is a slick salesman who **beguiles** unwary customers.
ⓝ beguilement 기만, 속임

0288 ■■□

sustain
[səstéin]

떠받치다, 지탱하다
ⓥ to support, hold, or bear up from below; bear the weight of, as a structure
ⓢⓨⓝ support, hold, maintain
ⓔ.ⓖ. New York's commercial life has been **sustained** by a steady stream of foreign business.
ⓐ sustainable 지탱할 수 있는, 유지할 수 있는

DAY
05

0289 ■■□

exploit
[iksplóit]

개척하다, 개발하다, 착취하다
ⓥ to utilize, esp. for profit; turn to practical account
ⓢⓨⓝ use, utilize, abuse
ⓔ.ⓖ. The rocks are colorful, with a brilliance that may be **exploited** by shining.
ⓐ exploitative 자원 개발의, 착취적인

0290 ■□□

ritual
[rítʃuəl]

종교적 의식, 의례
ⓝ an established or prescribed procedure for a religious or other rite
ⓢⓨⓝ ceremony, cult, rite
ⓔ.ⓖ. In China, those **rituals** begin as young as the age of three.
ⓐ ritualistic 의식의, 의식주의의

0291 ■■■

prodigal
[prádigəl]

낭비하는
ⓐ wastefully or recklessly extravagant
ⓢⓨⓝ lavish, extravagant
ⓔ.ⓖ. People should not be **prodigal** in their expenditure.
ⓝ prodigality 낭비, 방탕

0292 ■■□

belittle
[bilítl]

과소평가하다, 얕보다

ⓥ to represent or speak of as contemptibly small or unimportant

ⓢⓨⓝ minimize, denigrate, derogate

ⓔ.ⓖ. Don't **belittle** other people's success.

0293 ■□□

complexity
[kəmpléksəti]

복잡성, 복잡한 것

ⓝ the state or quality of being complex

ⓢⓨⓝ intricacy, complication

ⓔ.ⓖ. This mission takes the level of **complexity** up a notch.

ⓐ complex 복잡한, 얽히고설킨

0294 ■□□

rigid
[rídʒid]

딱딱한, 단단한, 뻣뻣한

ⓐ stiff or unyielding; not pliant or flexible

ⓢⓨⓝ hard, stiff, fixed, inflexible

ⓔ.ⓖ. There's a very **rigid** social hierarchy in their society.

ⓝ rigidity 단단함, 강직, 경직

0295 ■□□

segment
[ségmənt]

구획, 단편, 조각

ⓝ one of the parts into which something naturally separates or is divided

ⓢⓨⓝ piece, part, fragment, division, portion, section

ⓔ.ⓖ. They're already having a huge impact on entire **segments** of the economy.

ⓐ segmental 부분의, 구분의, 부분으로 갈라진

0296 ■□□

molecule
[máləkjùːl]

(화학, 물리) 분자

ⓝ the smallest physical unit of an element or compound, consisting of one or more like atoms in an element and two or more different atoms in a compound

ⓢⓨⓝ fragment, particle

ⓔ.ⓖ. A **molecule** of water consists of two atoms of hydrogen and one atom of oxygen.

ⓐ molecular 분자의, 분자로 된

0297 ■□□

transact
[trænsǽkt]

집행하다, 처리하다, 취급하다
ⓥ to carry on or conduct (business, negotiations, activities)
ⓢⓨⓝ handle, treat, execute, manage
ⓔ.ⓖ. He **transacts** business with a large number of stores.
ⓝ transaction 처리, 취급, 처치

0298 ■□□

creed
[kríːd]

교의, 사도신경, 신념, 주의
ⓝ any system, doctrine, or formula of religious belief, as of a denomination
ⓢⓨⓝ tenet, doctrine, dogma
ⓔ.ⓖ. Our democratic faith is more than the **creed** of our country.

0299 ■■□

speculation
[spèkjuléiʃən]

사색, 심사숙고, 성찰, 투기
ⓝ the contemplation or consideration of some subject
ⓢⓨⓝ contemplation, consideration, gamble
ⓔ.ⓖ. You need some time to engage in **speculation** on humanity's ultimate destiny.
ⓥ speculate 사색하다, 깊이 생각하다, 투기하다

0300 ■■□

enhance
[inhǽns]

높이다, 강화하다
ⓥ to raise to a higher degree
ⓢⓨⓝ intensify, magnify
ⓔ.ⓖ. We should envision a program that will **enhance** the students, the faculty, and both universities.
ⓝ enhancement 상승, 증대, 강화

DAY
05

Day

06

microbe	⬝⬝⬝	☐☐☐	**astronomical**	⬝⬝⬝	☐☐☐
drug-resistant	⬝⬝⬝	☐☐☐	**ditch**	⬝⬝⬝	☐☐☐
supercharge	⬝⬝⬝	☐☐☐	**diffuse**	⬝⬝⬝	☐☐☐
plump	⬝⬝⬝	☐☐☐	**distress**	⬝⬝⬝	☐☐☐
curb	⬝⬝⬝	☐☐☐	**ample**	⬝⬝⬝	☐☐☐
cut	⬝⬝⬝	☐☐☐	**distinct**	⬝⬝⬝	☐☐☐
sore	⬝⬝⬝	☐☐☐	**adjoin**	⬝⬝⬝	☐☐☐
specify	⬝⬝⬝	☐☐☐	**chaos**	⬝⬝⬝	☐☐☐
tremble	⬝⬝⬝	☐☐☐	**elicit**	⬝⬝⬝	☐☐☐
amid	⬝⬝⬝	☐☐☐	**deplore**	⬝⬝⬝	☐☐☐
patent	⬝⬝⬝	☐☐☐	**imperialize**	⬝⬝⬝	☐☐☐
truce	⬝⬝⬝	☐☐☐	**acquaint**	⬝⬝⬝	☐☐☐
conceive	⬝⬝⬝	☐☐☐	**eliminate**	⬝⬝⬝	☐☐☐
exempt	⬝⬝⬝	☐☐☐	**animate**	⬝⬝⬝	☐☐☐
fester	⬝⬝⬝	☐☐☐	**dose**	⬝⬝⬝	☐☐☐
technically	⬝⬝⬝	☐☐☐	**embrace**	⬝⬝⬝	☐☐☐
forge	⬝⬝⬝	☐☐☐	**impose**	⬝⬝⬝	☐☐☐
frugal	⬝⬝⬝	☐☐☐	**encroach**	⬝⬝⬝	☐☐☐
gay	⬝⬝⬝	☐☐☐	**lucrative**	⬝⬝⬝	☐☐☐
generic	⬝⬝⬝	☐☐☐	**legitimate**	⬝⬝⬝	☐☐☐
grunt	⬝⬝⬝	☐☐☐	**endow**	⬝⬝⬝	☐☐☐
tumble	⬝⬝⬝	☐☐☐	**behold**	⬝⬝⬝	☐☐☐
vanity	⬝⬝⬝	☐☐☐	**engross**	⬝⬝⬝	☐☐☐
manipulate	⬝⬝⬝	☐☐☐	**solitary**	⬝⬝⬝	☐☐☐
tyrant	⬝⬝⬝	☐☐☐	**epithet**	⬝⬝⬝	☐☐☐
dwindle	⬝⬝⬝	☐☐☐	**high-profile**	⬝⬝⬝	☐☐☐
transmit	⬝⬝⬝	☐☐☐	**unwitting**	⬝⬝⬝	☐☐☐
monopoly	⬝⬝⬝	☐☐☐	**devote**	⬝⬝⬝	☐☐☐
antipathy	⬝⬝⬝	☐☐☐	**punctual**	⬝⬝⬝	☐☐☐
ventilate	⬝⬝⬝	☐☐☐	**equivalent**	⬝⬝⬝	☐☐☐

0301 ■□□

microbe
[máikroub]

세균
ⓝ a microorganism, especially a pathogenic bacterium
ⓔ.ⓖ. The **microbe** is not the cause of disease.

0302 ■□□

drug-resistant
[drʌg rizístənt]

약에 내성이 있는
ⓐ the reduction in effectiveness of a medication in treating a disease or condition
ⓢⓨⓝ drug-fast
ⓔ.ⓖ. In the United States, 1.2 percent of TB cases were multi-**drug resistant**.

0303 ■□□

supercharge
[súper·chàrge]

(엔진 등에) 과급(過給)하다, 강화시키다, (감정·긴장·에너지 등을) 지나치게 들이다
ⓥ to charge with an abundant or excessive amount, as of energy, emotion, or tension
ⓔ.ⓖ. The engine was **supercharged**, giving it a output of 420 hp.

0304 ■□□

plump
[plʌmp]

살찐
ⓐ slightly fat
ⓢⓨⓝ bulky, pudgy
ⓞⓟⓟ skinny
ⓔ.ⓖ. The baby is **plump**.

0305 ■□□

curb
[kəːrb]

(말의) 재갈, 고삐, 재갈을 물리다, 억제하다(=check)
ⓝ a swelling on the back of a horse's hock, caused by spraining a ligament

0306 ■□□

cut
[kʌt]

베인 상처
ⓝ to break the surface of something using a sharp tool, especially a knife
ⓔ.ⓖ. **cuts** and bruises on body

0307 ■□□

sore
[sɔːr]

감정이 상한, 따끔거리는, 상처(인후염)
ⓐ upset and angry
ⓢⓨⓝ cross, eggy
ⓔ.ⓖ. What's he so **sore** at us for?

0308 ■□□

specify
[spésəfài]

명시하다
ⓥ identify clearly and definitely
ⓢⓨⓝ particularize, enumerate
ⓔ.ⓖ. It did not **specify** the cause of death.

0309 ■□□

tremble
[trémbl]

떨다, 전율하다, 떨리다
ⓥ to shake involuntarily with quick, short movements, as from fear, excitement, weakness, or cold
ⓢⓨⓝ shake, quake, quiver
ⓔ.ⓖ. The very thought of the terrible accident makes me **tremble**.
ⓐ trembling 떨리는, 전율하는

0310 ■□□

amid
[əmíd]

~의 한복판에, ~에 둘러싸여
ⓟ in the middle of; surrounded by; among
ⓢⓨⓝ among, between
ⓔ.ⓖ. She appeared on the stage **amid** a thunderous handclapping of the audience.

0311 ■■□

patent
[pǽtnt]

특허, 특허권(증)
ⓝ the exclusive right granted by a government to an inventor to manufacture, use, or sell an invention for a certain number of years
ⓢⓨⓝ copyright, license
ⓔ.ⓖ. The company submitted the **patent** for the government's approval.
ⓐⓓ patently 명백히, 틀림없이

DAY
06

0312 ■■□

truce
[trúːs]

휴전, 휴지, 정전, 중단
ⓝ a suspension of hostilities for a specified period of time by mutual agreement of the warring parties
(syn) cease-fire, armistice, cessation, halt, letup, pause
(e.g.) They made a **truce** to avoid further bloodshed.

0313 ■■□

conceive
[kənsíːv]

상상하다, 생각하다, (생각, 의견, 원한 등을) 품다, 임신하다
ⓥ to form (a notion, opinion, purpose, etc.)
(syn) imagine, think, devise, be pregnant
(e.g.) He **conceived** the project while he was on weekend.
ⓝ conception 개념, 생각

0314 ■■□

exempt
[ɪgzempt]

면제하다(받다); 면제되는
ⓥ To exempt a person or thing from a particular rule, duty, or obligation means to state officially that they are not bound or affected by it.
(syn) immune, free, excepted
(e.g.) Men in college were **exempt** from military service.
ⓝ exemption
ⓐ exemptible

0315 ■■■

fester
[festə(r)]

곪다, 심해지다
ⓥ If you say that a situation, problem, or feeling is festering, you disapprove of the fact that it is being allowed to grow more unpleasant or full of anger, because it is not being properly recognized or dealt with.
(e.g.) If you don't treat this properly, it's going to **fester**.

0316 ■□□

technically
[téch·ni·cal·ly]

엄밀히 말하면, 기술적으로, 전문적으로
ⓐⓓ in a way that is peculiar to a certain specialized field of study or activity
(e.g.) **Technically** speaking I am not a mechanic.

0317 ■■■

forge
[fɔ:rdʒ]

대장간, 연마하다, 구축하다, 꾸며내다, 위조하다

ⓥ If one person or institution forges an agreement or relationship with another, they create it with a lot of hard work, hoping that it will be strong or lasting.

ⓢⓨⓝ form, build, counterfeit

ⓔ.ⓖ. Strategic alliances are being **forged** with major European companies.

ⓝ forgeability

0318 ■■□

frugal
[fru:gl]

절약하는

ⓐ People who are frugal or who live frugal lives do not eat much or spend much money on themselves.

ⓢⓨⓝ economical, saving, thrifty

ⓔ.ⓖ. All the people in my family are **frugal** with their money.

ⓝ frugalness, frugality

0319 ■■□

gay
[geɪ]

(구식) 명랑한, 화려한

ⓐ showing or characterized by cheerfulness and lighthearted excitement; merry

ⓢⓨⓝ merry, cheerful, fancy

ⓔ.ⓖ. The garden was **gay** with red geraniums.

0320 ■■■

generic
[dʒəǀnerɪk]

포괄적인, 통칭의, 총칭의

ⓐ You use generic to describe something that refers or relates to a whole class of similar things.

ⓢⓨⓝ collective, general, common

ⓔ.ⓖ. 'Vine fruit' is the **generic** term for currants and raisins.

ⓐⓓ generically

0321 ■■■

grunt
[grʌnt]

불평하다

ⓥ If you grunt, you make a low sound, especially because you are annoyed or not interested in something.

ⓔ.ⓖ. He pulled harder on the rope, **grunting** with the effort.

ⓐⓓ gruntingly

ⓝ grunter 불평가

DAY
06

0322 ■■□

tumble
[tʌ́mbl]

넘어지다, 떨어지다
ⓥ to fall helplessly down, end over end, as by losing one's footing, support, or equilibrium; plunge headlong
ⓢⓨⓝ fall, collapse
ⓔ.ⓖ. All the passengers were **tumbled** out of the car.
ⓝ tumbler 넘어지는 사람, 곡예사

0323 ■□□

vanity
[vǽnəti]

허영심, 자만심
ⓝ excessive pride in one's appearance, qualities, abilities, achievements, etc.; character or quality of being vain
ⓢⓨⓝ conceit, pomposity, pride
ⓔ.ⓖ. Failure to be elected was a great blow to his **vanity**.
ⓐ vain 자만심이 강한, 뽐내는

0324 ■■□

manipulate
[mənípjulèit]

교묘하게 다루다, 조종하다
ⓥ to manage or influence skillfully, esp. in an unfair manner
ⓢⓨⓝ finagle, scheme
ⓔ.ⓖ. They **manipulated** the account to conceal his theft.
ⓝ manipulation 교묘한 처리, 조종, 조작

0325 ■□□

tyrant
[táiərənt]

폭군, 전제군주, 압제자
ⓝ a sovereign or other ruler who uses power oppressively or unjustly
ⓢⓨⓝ autocrat, despot, dictator, oppressor, authoritarian
ⓔ.ⓖ. People were squeezed out under the sway of a **tyrant**.
ⓐ tyrannical 전제군주적인, 압제적인, 무도한

0326 ■■■

dwindle
[dwíndl]

점차 감소하다, 점점 작아지다
ⓥ to become smaller and smaller; waste away
ⓢⓨⓝ decrease, shrink
ⓔ.ⓖ. His vast fortune has **dwindled** away.
ⓐ dwindling 점점 줄어드는

0327 ■□□

transmit
[trænsmít]

부치다, 보내다, 전달하다

ⓥ to send or forward, as to a recipient or destination
ⓢⓨⓝ dispatch, convey, send
ⓔ.ⓖ. The Olympic game was **transmitted** all over the world by satellite.
ⓝ transmission 전달, 전송

0328 ■■□

monopoly
[mənápəli]

독점, 전매

ⓝ exclusive control of a commodity or service in a particular market, or a control that makes possible the manipulation of prices
ⓔ.ⓖ. The state-run press has strongly criticized the **monopoly** for poor service, costly installation fees and expensive calling rates.
ⓥ monopolize 독점하다, 독차지하다

0329 ■□□

antipathy
[æntípəθi]

반감, 상극, 혐오하는 것

ⓝ a natural, basic, or habitual repugnance; aversion
ⓔ.ⓖ. Snakes were her greatest **antipathy**.
ⓝ sympathy 동정심, 이해

0330 ■□□

ventilate
[véntəlèit]

공기를 통하다, 환기하다

ⓥ to provide (a room, mine, etc.) with fresh air in place of air that has been used or contaminate
ⓢⓨⓝ freshen, aerate
ⓔ.ⓖ. Most machine shops today are relatively clean, well lit, and adequately **ventilated**.
ⓝ ventilation 통풍, 환기

0331 ■■■

astronomical
[æstrənámikəl]

천문학적인, 어마어마한

ⓐ extremely large, exceedingly great
ⓢⓨⓝ enormous, vast, considerable
ⓔ.ⓖ. It takes an **astronomical** amount of money to build a car factory.
ⓝ astronomy 천문학

DAY
06

0332 ■□□

ditch
[dítʃ]

수도, 도랑, 배수구

ⓝ a long, narrow excavation made in the ground by digging, as for draining or irrigating land

ⓢⓨⓝ trench, canal, channel

ⓔ.ⓖ. The man has lost his cowboy hat in a **ditch**.

ⓝ ditcher 도랑을 파는 사람(기계)

0333 ■■□

diffuse
[difjúːz]

분산(확산)시키다, 흐트러뜨리다, (빛, 열, 냄새 등을) 발산하다

ⓥ to pour out and spread, as a fluid

ⓢⓨⓝ circulate, distribute, disseminate, irradiate

ⓞⓟⓟ concentrate

ⓔ.ⓖ. The lampshade **diffused** the harsh light of the bulb.

ⓝ diffusion 발산, 보급, 유포

ⓐ diffusible

ⓐⓓ diffusely

0334 ■■□

distress
[distrés]

고통, 괴로움, 곤경

ⓝ great pain, anxiety, or sorrow; acute physical or mental suffering

ⓢⓨⓝ affliction, trouble, hardship, adversity

ⓔ.ⓖ. She was obviously in deep emotional **distress**.

ⓐ distressful 고민이 많은, 고통스러운

0335 ■■□

ample
[ǽmpl]

충분한

ⓐ fully sufficient or more than adequate for the purpose or needs

ⓢⓨⓝ plentiful, enough

ⓔ.ⓖ. You will have **ample** opportunity to ask questions after the talk.

ⓥ amplify 증대하다, 확대하다

0336 ■■□

distinct
[distíŋkt]

별개의, 전혀 다른, 독특한

ⓐ distinguished as not being the same; not identical

ⓢⓨⓝ different, discernible, discrete, separate

ⓔ.ⓖ. Rats and mice are **distinct** animals.

ⓥ distinction 구별, 식별, 차이

0337 ■■■

adjoin
[ədʒɔ́in]

인접하다, 이웃해 있다
ⓥ to be close to or in contact with
syn border, edge
e.g. England **adjoins** with Scotland.
ⓐ adjoining 서로 접한, 옆의, 부근의

0338 ■□□

chaos
[kéiɑs]

혼란, 무질서, 혼돈
ⓝ a state of utter confusion or disorder
syn confusion, derangement
e.g. If people who don't know about politics take part in it, it may lead to political **chaos**.
ⓐ chaotic 혼돈된, 무질서한

0339 ■■□

elicit
[ilísit]

도출하다, 이끌어내다, 유도하다
ⓥ to draw or bring out or forth
syn deduce, derive, educe, evoke
e.g. Her performance **elicited** wild applause.

0340 ■■■

deplore
[diplɔ́ːr]

비탄(한탄)하다, 비난(비판)하다
ⓥ to regret deeply or strongly; lament
syn lament, bewail, grieve, moan
e.g. We cannot but **deplore** the present state of morality.
ⓐ deplorable 한탄스러운, 비통한, 슬픈

0341 ■■□

imperialize
[impíəriəlàiz]

식민화하다, 제국주의로 다스리다
ⓥ to invest with imperial authority, character, or style; to bring to the form of an empire
e.g. England **imperialized** much of the world in the last century.
ⓝ imperialist 제국주의자
ⓝ imperialism 제국주의

DAY
06

0342 ■■■

acquaint
[əkwéint]

익히 알게 하다, 정통하게 하다

ⓥ to make more or less familiar, aware, or conversant

ⓢⓨⓝ familiarize

ⓔ.ⓖ. Julia is such a out-going person so she is **acquainted** with all classes.

ⓝ acquaintance 아는 사람(사이), 알고 있음

0343 ■■■

eliminate
[ilímənèit]

제거하다, 배제하다

ⓥ to remove or get rid of, esp. as being in some way undesirable

ⓢⓨⓝ abolish, annihilate, eradicate, erase, delete

ⓔ.ⓖ. They framed a plan to **eliminate** unnecessary bureaucracy.

ⓝ elimination 제거, 배제, 삭제

0344 ■■■

animate
[ǽnəmèit]

생명을 불어넣다, 살리다

ⓥ to give life to; make alive

ⓢⓨⓝ inspire, invigorate, enliven

ⓔ.ⓖ. God **animated** the dust, and then made human with it.

ⓝ animation 생기, 활발, 활기

0345 ■□□

dose
[dóus]

(약의) 복용량, 투여량

ⓝ a quantity of medicine prescribed to be taken at one time

ⓢⓨⓝ dosage, prescription

ⓔ.ⓖ. That was the right **dose** of the right medicine and a global crisis was avoided.

ⓝ dosage 복용량, 투약량

0346 ■□□

embrace
[imbréis]

포옹하다, 껴안다, 받아들이다

ⓥ to take or clasp in the arms; press to the bosom

ⓢⓨⓝ hug, accept

ⓔ.ⓖ. He **embraced** his daughter before leaving.

ⓝ embracement 포옹

0347 ■■■

impose
[impóuz]

부과하다, 강요하다

ⓥ to put or set by or as if by authority
ⓢⓨⓝ command, compel
ⓔ.ⓖ. Many companies have **imposed** a pay freeze.
ⓝ imposition (의무, 짐, 세금 등을) 지움, 부과

0348 ■■□

encroach
[inkróutʃ]

잠식하다, 침략하다, 침입하다

ⓥ to trespass upon the property, domain, or rights of another, esp. stealthily or by gradual advances
ⓢⓨⓝ intrude, invade
ⓔ.ⓖ. A dictatorship of the majority is **encroaching** on the rights of the individual.
ⓝ encroachment 잠식, 침략, 침해

0349 ■■■

lucrative
[lúːkrətiv]

유리한, 돈이 벌리는

ⓐ profitable; moneymaking
ⓢⓨⓝ advantageous, profitable, moneymaking, remunerative
ⓔ.ⓖ. Many wheat farmers say that next year they will plant more **lucrative** crops.
ⓝ lucre 돈(특히 부당하게 얻은)

0350 ■■□

legitimate
[lidʒítəmət]

합법적인, 적합한, 타당한

ⓐ according to law; in accordance with established rules, principles, or standards
ⓢⓨⓝ lawful, legal, rightful
ⓔ.ⓖ. We will not abandon that claim to our **legitimate** right.
ⓝ legitimacy 합법성, 적법성

0351 ■■■

endow
[indáu]

재산을 증여하다, 기부하다, 기증하다

ⓥ to provide with a permanent fund or source of income
ⓢⓨⓝ bestow, contribute, fund
ⓔ.ⓖ. Nature has **endowed** her with wit and intelligence.
ⓝ endowment 증여, 기부, 기증

0352 ■■□

behold
[bihóuld]

보다, 주시하다
ⓥ to observe; look at; see
ⓢⓨⓝ notice, gaze, view
ⓔ.ⓖ. She said her heart leaped up when she **beheld** a rainbow in the sky.
ⓝ beholder 구경꾼

0353 ■■□

engross
[ingróus]

(주의, 시간을) 집중시키다, 열중시키다
ⓥ to occupy completely, as the mind or attention
ⓢⓨⓝ absorb, occupy
ⓔ.ⓖ. Their discussion **engrossed** his attention.
ⓝ engrossment 전념, 몰두

0354 ■□□

solitary
[sálətèri]

혼자의, 단독의, 외로운
ⓐ alone; without companions; unattended
ⓢⓨⓝ lonely, individual
ⓔ.ⓖ. One reason why I like the beach is its **solitary** atmosphere.
ⓝ solitude 고독, 외로움

0355 ■■□

epithet
[épəθèt]

형용어구, 별명, 칭호, 통칭
ⓝ any word or phrase applied to a person or thing to describe an actual or attributed quality
ⓢⓨⓝ nickname
ⓔ.ⓖ. "Richard the Lion-Hearted" is an **epithet** of Richard I.
ⓐ epithetic 형용하는, 형용사의

0356 ■■■

high-profile
[hái próufail]

세간의 이목을 끄는
ⓐ attracted a lot of attention or publicity
ⓔ.ⓖ. A spate of **high-profile** mergers and acquisitions in recent weeks has made 2005 the fastest start for MA activity since 2000.
ⓐ low-profile 주목을 거의 못 받는

0357 ■□□

unwitting
[ʌ̀nwítiŋ]

자신도 모르는, 부지중의

ⓐ not knowing or unaware
(syn) oblivious, unconscious, ignorant
(e.g.) Most security breaches come from users' **unwitting** interaction with password thieves.
(ad) unwittingly 자신도 모르게, 부지불식간에

0358 ■■□

devote
[divóut]

바치다, 쏟다

ⓥ to give up or appropriate to or concentrate on a particular pursuit, occupation, purpose, cause, etc.
(syn) dedicate, sacrifice
(e.g.) He **devoted** a sum of money to the relief of the poor.
ⓝ devotion 헌신, 전념

0359 ■■□

punctual
[pʌ́ŋktʃuəl]

시간을 잘 지키는, ~에 늦지 않는

ⓐ strictly observant of an appointed or regular time; not late
(syn) prompt, timely, constant
(e.g.) Danny is very diligent, **punctual**, and also sociable, and all colleagues prefer working with him.
ⓝ punctuality 시간엄수, 정확함, 꼼꼼함

DAY
06

0360 ■■■

equivalent
[ikwívələnt]

동등한, 같은 뜻의, 상응하는

ⓐ equal in value, measure, force, effect, significance, etc.
(syn) comparable, same, similar
(e.g.) His silence is **equivalent** to an admission of guilt.
ⓝ equivalence 같음, 등가

Day

07

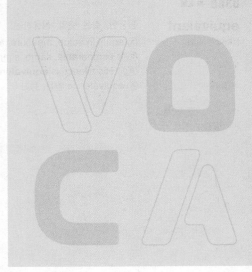

acclaim	☐☐☐		fatigue	☐☐☐
myopia	☐☐☐		congress	☐☐☐
eloquently	☐☐☐		feasible	☐☐☐
breeze	☐☐☐		deed	☐☐☐
gravitate	☐☐☐		feudal	☐☐☐
methodically	☐☐☐		deprive	☐☐☐
abort	☐☐☐		deceive	☐☐☐
back	☐☐☐		flout	☐☐☐
commodity	☐☐☐		aesthetic	☐☐☐
bait	☐☐☐		utter	☐☐☐
complementary	☐☐☐		arouse	☐☐☐
esteem	☐☐☐		dim	☐☐☐
bombard	☐☐☐		forebear	☐☐☐
clarity	☐☐☐		mammal	☐☐☐
lament	☐☐☐		abandon	☐☐☐
lay out	☐☐☐		fraud	☐☐☐
loathsome	☐☐☐		rational	☐☐☐
mandate	☐☐☐		prestige	☐☐☐
mock	☐☐☐		simplify	☐☐☐
mutiny	☐☐☐		furnish	☐☐☐
opt	☐☐☐		plural	☐☐☐
outright	☐☐☐		hallow	☐☐☐
evoke	☐☐☐		haughty	☐☐☐
excerpt	☐☐☐		copycat	☐☐☐
caution	☐☐☐		satire	☐☐☐
fossil	☐☐☐		approximate	☐☐☐
collapse	☐☐☐		simultaneous	☐☐☐
exert	☐☐☐		heritage	☐☐☐
detect	☐☐☐		accompany	☐☐☐
hypothesis	☐☐☐		cryptic	☐☐☐

0361 ■□□

acclaim
[əkléim]

갈채, 환호
ⓝ loud or enthusiastic approval or praise; acclamation
ⓢⓨⓝ kudos
ⓔ.ⓖ. The book was published to critical **acclaim**.

0362 ■□□

myopia
[máiəpi]

근시안
ⓝ lack of imagination, foresight, or intellectual insight
ⓔ.ⓖ. **Myopia**: This is the concentration on short-term issues to the exclusion of longer term considerations.

0363 ■□□

eloquently
[éləkwəntli]

유창하게
ⓐⓓ in a fluent or persuasive manner
ⓔ.ⓖ. He spoke **eloquently** on behalf of his constituents and expressed their anger at the closure in Ebbw Vale.
ⓐ eloquent 웅변을 잘하는, 유창한

0364 ■□□

breeze
[briːz]

식은 죽 먹기, 미풍
ⓝ an easy task
ⓢⓨⓝ duck soup, doss, snack
ⓔ.ⓖ. The horse won in a **breeze**.

0365 ■□□

gravitate
[grǽvətèit]

~에 끌리다
ⓥ to have a natural tendency or be strongly attracted
ⓢⓨⓝ veer
ⓔ.ⓖ. They **gravitate** towards camaraderie and then a deeper intimacy.

0366 ■□□

methodically
[məθɒdɪkliv]

체계적으로
ⓐⓓ in an orderly or systematic manner
ⓔ.ⓖ. Rescue troops search **methodically**, still hoping for survivors.

0367 ■□□

abort
[əbɔ́ːrt]

낙태시키다, 중단시키다
ⓥ to bring forth a fetus from the uterus before the fetus is viable
ⓢⓨⓝ miscarry, terminate
ⓔ.ⓖ. Does that mean you have to **abort** the child?

0368 ■■□

back
[bæk]

지지하다
ⓥ to support, as with authority, influence, help, or money
ⓢⓨⓝ support, subsidize
ⓞⓟⓟ oppose
ⓔ.ⓖ. The prime minister was **backed** a majority in parliament.

0369 ■□□

commodity
[kəmádəti]

상품, 일용품, 필수품
ⓝ an article of trade or commerce, esp. a product as distinguished from a service
ⓢⓨⓝ goods, product, stock, item
ⓔ.ⓖ. Oil is the second most valuable and essential **commodity** in the world.
ⓥ commodify 상품화하다

0370 ■□□

bait
[béit]

미끼, 먹이, 유혹하는 것
ⓝ food, or some substitute, used as a lure in fishing, trapping, etc.
ⓢⓨⓝ enticement, inducement
ⓔ.ⓖ. We caught many fish with the **bait** of an earthworm.

0371 ■■■

complementary
[kàmpləméntəri]

보완적인, 서로 보완하는
ⓐ forming a complement; completing
ⓢⓨⓝ complemental, correlative
ⓔ.ⓖ. People consuming vegetable-based diets need **complementary** proteins.
ⓝ complement 보완하는 것, 보충물

DAY
07

0372 ■■□

esteem
[istíːm]

존경하다, 존중하다, 중하게 여기다
ⓥ to regard highly or favorably; regard with respect or admiration
ⓢⓨⓝ respect, cherish
ⓔ.ⓖ. I **esteem** him for his honesty.
ⓥ disesteem 얕보다, 경시하다

0373 ■■□

bombard
[bɑmbáːrd]

포격하다, 폭격하다
ⓥ to attack or batter with artillery fire
ⓢⓨⓝ assault
ⓔ.ⓖ. The troops were **bombarded** and all soldiers fell in battle.
ⓝ bomb 폭탄

0374 ■□□

clarity
[klǽrəti]

맑음, 청명, 명백함, 명료함
ⓝ clearness or lucidity as to perception or understanding; freedom from indistinctness or ambiguity
ⓢⓨⓝ cleanliness, clearness, certainty
ⓔ.ⓖ. When tested against leading high resolution monitors, our company had the best resolution and **clarity**.
ⓐ clear 밝은, 맑은, 투명한

0375 ■■■

lament
[ləment]

애통하다, 애도
ⓥ If you lament something, you express your sadness, regret, or disappointment about it.
ⓢⓨⓝ complaint, moan, wailing
ⓔ.ⓖ. In the poem he **laments** the destruction of the countryside.
ⓝ lamentation

0376 ■■■

lay out
[lei aut]

펼치다, 투자하다, 계획하다
ⓥ to arrange or spread out; to spend (money) lavishly; to plan or contrive
ⓢⓨⓝ extend at length, reprimand, arrange

0377 ■■□

loathsome
[|loʊðsəm]

혐오스러운

ⓐ If you describe someone or something as loathsome, you are indicating how much you dislike them or how much they disgust you.

ⓔ.ᵍ. It is very **loathsome** behavior that Jake burps playfully everywhere he goes.

ⓝ loathsomeness   ⓐᵈ loathsomely

0378 ■■■

mandate
[|mændeɪt]

권한, 명령; 권한을 위임하다, 명령하다

ⓝ If a government or other elected body has a mandate to carry out a particular policy or task, they have the authority to carry it out as a result of winning an election or vote.

ⓢʸⁿ command, order, commission

ⓔ.ᵍ. The election victory gave the party a clear **mandate** to continue its programme of reform.

ⓝ mandator   ⓐ mandatory

0379 ■■□

mock
[mɑ:k]

놀리다

ⓥ If someone mocks you, they show or pretend that they think you are foolish or inferior.

ⓢʸⁿ laugh at, tease, ridicule

ⓔ.ᵍ. He's always **mocking** my French accent.

ⓝ mockery

0380 ■■■

mutiny
[mju:təni]

반란

ⓝ A mutiny is a refusal by people, usually soldiers or sailors, to continue obeying a person in authority.

ⓔ.ᵍ. Discontent among the ship's crew finally led to the outbreak of **mutiny**.

ⓐ mutinous

0381 ■■□

opt
[ɑ:pt]

택하다

ⓥ If you opt for something, or opt to do something, you choose it or decide to do it in preference to anything else.

ⓢʸⁿ choose, decide, prefer

ⓔ.ᵍ. After graduating she **opted** for a career in music.

DAY
07

0382 ■■□

outright
[|aʊtraɪt]

전면적인, 명백한
ⓐ You use outright to describe behaviour and actions that are open and direct, rather than indirect.
ⓢⓨⓝ absolute, complete, total
ⓔ.ⓖ. No one party is expected to gain an **outright** majority.
ⓐⓓ outrightly

0383 ■■■

evoke
[ivóuk]

일깨우다, 환기시키다
ⓥ to call up or produce (memories, feelings, etc.)
ⓢⓨⓝ arouse, awaken
ⓔ.ⓖ. Her letter in the newspaper **evoked** a storm of protest.

0384 ■□□

excerpt
[éksə:rpt]

발췌록, 발췌, 인용구
ⓝ a passage or quotation taken or selected from a book, document, film, or the like
ⓢⓨⓝ citation, reference, extract
ⓔ.ⓖ. In 1994, the ABC newsmagazine Prime Time Live ran **excerpts** of a Dutch documentary on euthanasia.
ⓝ excerption 발췌, 발췌록

0385 ■□□

caution
[kɔ́:ʃən]

조심, 신중, 경계
ⓝ alertness and prudence in a hazardous situation
ⓢⓨⓝ care, wariness
ⓔ.ⓖ. Let me give you a word of **caution** before you use this machine.
ⓐ cautious 조심성 있는, 신중한

0386 ■□□

fossil
[fásəl]

화석
ⓝ any remains, impression, or trace of a living thing of a former geologic age, as a skeleton, footprint, etc.
ⓢⓨⓝ relic, specimen
ⓔ.ⓖ. We know about these fantastic creatures from the **fossils** they left behind.
ⓥ fossilize 화석으로 만들다(되다)

0387 ■■□

collapse
[kəlǽps]

무너지다, 좌절되다

ⓥ to fall or cave in; crumble suddenly

ⓢⓨⓝ fail, fall, break down

ⓔⓖ The reporter announced that the building **collapsed** and buried the many workers.

0388 ■■■

exert
[igzə́ːrt]

(힘, 능력 등을) 쓰다, 행사하다, 노력하다

ⓥ to put forth or into use, as power; exercise, as ability or influence; put into vigorous action

ⓢⓨⓝ exercise, strive

ⓔⓖ His thought **exerted** a favorable influence upon the philosophers.

ⓝ exertion 노력, 진력, 분발

0389 ■■□

detect
[ditékt]

발견하다, 간파하다

ⓥ to discover or catch (a person) in the performance of some act

ⓢⓨⓝ descry, discern

ⓔⓖ I **detect** something sour in this sauce, did you add some vinegar?

ⓝ detection 간파, 탐지

0390 ■□□

hypothesis
[haipáθəsis]

가설, 가정

ⓝ a proposition, or set of propositions, set forth as an explanation for the occurrence of some specified group of phenomena

ⓢⓨⓝ premise, supposition, assumption

ⓔⓖ The results of the experiment enabled us to reject Dr. Kim's initial **hypothesis**.

ⓥ hypothesize 가설을 세우다(제기하다)

0391 ■■□

fatigue
[fətíːg]

피로, 피곤, 노동

ⓝ weariness from bodily or mental exertion

ⓢⓨⓝ exhaustion, weariness

ⓔⓖ We were half dead with **fatigue** after moving some boxes.

ⓐ fatigued 지친, 피로한

DAY
07

0392 ■□□

congress
[káŋgris]

국회, 연방, 의회

ⓝ the national legislative body of the U.S., consisting of the Senate, or upper house, and the House of Representatives, or lower house, as a continuous institution

ⓢⓨⓝ council, legislature, assembly

ⓔ.ⓖ. Finally the **Congress** will pass the bill.

ⓐ congressional 의회의, 회의의, 집회의

0393 ■■■

feasible
[fíːzəbl]

실행할 수 있는, 가능한

ⓐ capable of being done, effected, or accomplished

ⓢⓨⓝ possible, practicable

ⓔ.ⓖ. It will take quite some time before this product becomes more **feasible** to buy.

ⓐ infeasible 실현 불가능한

0394 ■□□

deed
[díːd]

행위, 업적, 공적

ⓝ something that is done, performed, or accomplished; an act

ⓢⓨⓝ action, accomplishment, achievement

ⓔ.ⓖ. The king's **deeds** have passed out of history.

ⓝ misdeed 비행, 악행

0395 ■□□

feudal
[fjúːdl]

영지의, 봉건의

ⓐ of, pertaining to, or like the feudal system, or its political, military, social, and economic structure

ⓔ.ⓖ. They tried to break down the **feudal** social system.

ⓝ feudalism 봉건제도

0396 ■■□

deprive
[dipráiv]

빼앗다, 박탈하다, 파면하다

ⓥ to remove or withhold something from the enjoyment or possession of (a person or persons)

ⓢⓨⓝ bereave, rob, dispossess

ⓔ.ⓖ. The court ruling **deprived** us of any share in the heritance.

ⓝ deprivation 박탈, 파면

0397 ■■□

deceive
[disíːv]

속이다, 기만하다, 현혹시키다

ⓥ to mislead by a false appearance or statement
ⓢⓨⓝ cheat, delude
ⓔ.ⓖ. The swindler **deceived** her with sweet words and sold the house.
ⓝ deceit 사기, 기만, 책략

0398 ■■■

flout
[fláut]

모욕하다, 업신여기다

ⓥ to treat with disdain, scorn, or contempt
ⓢⓨⓝ scoff at, mock, disregard, insult, scorn
ⓔ.ⓖ. He advised us not to **flout** the rules.
ⓐⓓ floutingly 경멸(조롱)하며

0399 ■■□

aesthetic
[esθétik]

미의, 심미적인, 미적 감각이 있는

ⓐ pertaining to a sense of the beautiful or to the science of aesthetics
ⓢⓨⓝ artistic, artful, cosmetic
ⓔ.ⓖ. I'm sure of his **aesthetic** choices.
ⓝ aestheticism 유미주의, 예술지상주의

0400 ■■□

utter
[ʌ́tər]

입 밖에 내다, 발음하다, 표명하다

ⓥ to give audible expression to; speak or pronounce
ⓢⓨⓝ say, reveal, speak, pronounce
ⓔ.ⓖ. I could not **utter** a word with a heart full of feeling.
ⓝ utterance 입 밖에 냄, 발언, 발성

0401 ■■□

arouse
[əráuz]

깨우다, 환기시키다, 자극하다

ⓥ to stir to action or strong response
ⓢⓨⓝ awake, evoke, provoke
ⓔ.ⓖ. This movie **arouses** people's attention to the calamity of war.
ⓐ aroused 흥분한

0402 ■□□

dim
[dím]

어둑한, 어스레한, 희미한
ⓐ not bright; obscure from lack of light or emitted light
ⓢⓨⓝ faint, lackluster, obscure, opaque
ⓔⓖ I think your chances of recovery from illness are **dim**.
ⓥ bedim 흐리게 하다

0403 ■■□

forebear
[fɔ́ːrbɛ̀ər]

조상, 선조
ⓝ a person from whom one is descended
ⓢⓨⓝ ancestor, forefather
ⓔⓖ Our **forebears** used fans relief from hot weather.
ⓥ bear (아이를) 낳다

0404 ■□□

mammal
[mǽməl]

포유동물
ⓝ any of various warm-blooded vertebrate animals of the class Mammalia, including humans, characterized by a covering of hair on the skin and, in the female, milk-producing mammary glands for nourishing the young
ⓔⓖ **Mammals** are animals that nurse their young with milk from their own bodies.
ⓝ mammalia 포유류

0405 ■■□

abandon
[əbǽndən]

단념하다, 포기하다, 버리다
ⓥ to leave completely and finally
ⓢⓨⓝ discard, resign
ⓔⓖ We **abandoned** the old car in the empty parking lot.
ⓝ abandonment 단념, 포기

0406 ■■□

fraud
[frɔ́ːd]

사기, 기만, 부정
ⓝ deceit, trickery, sharp practice, or breach of confidence, perpetrated for profit or to gain some unfair or dishonest advantage
ⓢⓨⓝ deceit, deception, cheat, artifice
ⓔⓖ Here are a few simple tips to protect you and your family from **fraud**.
ⓐ fraudulent 사기(행위)의, 부정의

0407 ■■□

rational
[rǽʃənl]

이성적인

ⓐ agreeable to reason
(syn) analytic, commonsensible, judicious, reasonable
(e.g.) Getting a full night's sleep will make you more **rational**.
ⓥ rationalize 합리화하다, 이론적으로 설명하다

0408 ■■□

prestige
[prestíːdʒ]

위신, 명성, 신망

ⓝ reputation or influence arising from success, achievement, rank, or other favorable attributes
(syn) fame, honor, dignity, eminence, reputation
(e.g.) The scholar's **prestige** is known through out the country.
ⓐ prestigeful 명성(신망)이 있는

0409 ■□□

simplify
[símpləfài]

간단하게 하다, 단순화하다

ⓥ to make less complex or complicated; make plainer or easier
(syn) be short(brief, plain)
(e.g.) There are many hanbok shops in Insadong selling a **simplified** version of the traditional hanbok.
ⓐ simple 간단한, 단순한

0410 ■■□

furnish
[fə́ːrniʃ]

공급하다, 제공하다, (가구 등을) 비치하다

ⓥ to provide or supply; to supply (a house, room, etc.) with necessary furniture, carpets, appliances, etc.
(syn) provide, supply
(e.g.) We have to **furnish** out the living room and then it won't look so empty.
ⓝ furnishing 가구, 비품

0411 ■□□

plural
[plúərəl]

복수의, 복수형의

ⓐ consisting of, containing, or pertaining to more than one
(syn) dual, multiple
(e.g.) The usual way to form a **plural** word is to add an —s, for example, dogs, popes, and cats.
ⓥ pluralize 복수형으로 하다, 배가하다

DAY
07

0412 ■■□

hallow
[hǽlou]

신성하게 하다, 신성한 것으로 숭배하다
ⓥ to make holy
ⓢⓨⓝ sanctify, consecrate
ⓔ.ⓖ. It is believed the Incas **hallowed** holy rivers.
ⓐ hallowed 신성한, 존경받는

0413 ■■■

haughty
[hɔ́ːti]

오만한, 건방진, 도도한, 불손한
ⓐ disdainfully proud, scornfully arrogant
ⓢⓨⓝ insolent, overbearing, snobbish, supercilious, arrogant
ⓔ.ⓖ. You should not be **haughty** with your staff.

0414 ■□□

copycat
[kápikæ̀t]

(맹목적) 모방자, (학교에서 남의 것을) 그대로 베끼는 아이
ⓝ a person or thing that copies, imitates, mimics, or follows the lead of another, as a child who says or does exactly the same as another child
ⓢⓨⓝ imitator
ⓔ.ⓖ. The films have also inspired a spree of **copycat** killing sand attacks, usually by impression able teenagers.

0415 ■■□

satire
[sǽtaiər]

풍자, 비꼼
ⓝ the use of irony, sarcasm, ridicule, or the like, in exposing, denouncing, or deriding vice, folly, etc.
ⓢⓨⓝ cynicism, mockery, parody
ⓔ.ⓖ. His movies are recognized today as classics of comic **satire**.

0416 ■■□

approximate
[əpráksəmèit]

가깝다, 비슷하다
ⓥ to come near to; approach closely to
ⓢⓨⓝ approach, come close
ⓔ.ⓖ. Her account **approximated** the truth, leaving out insignificant details.
ⓐⓓ approximately 대략, 대체로

0417 ■■□

simultaneous
[sàiməltéiniəs]

동시에 일어나는, 동시의
ⓐ existing, occurring, or operating at the same time
ⓢⓨⓝ concurrent, coincident, synchronous
ⓔ.ⓖ. The large number of **simultaneous** projects has led to work congestion.
ⓐⓓ simultaneously 동시에, 일제히

0418 ■■□

heritage
[héritiʤ]

세습, 상속, 유산, 재산
ⓝ something that comes or belongs to one by reason of birth; an inherited lot or portion
ⓢⓨⓝ inheritance, legacy
ⓔ.ⓖ. Most of my **heritage** is Irish, with some French in the family on my mother's side.
ⓥ inherit 상속하다, 물려주다

0419 ■■□

accompany
[əkʌ́mpəni]

동반하다, 따라가다
ⓥ to go along or in company with; join in action
ⓢⓨⓝ attach to, come with, go with
ⓔ.ⓖ. She went to Spain **accompanied** by her colleague.
ⓝ company 일행, 친구, 집단, 회사

DAY
07

0420 ■■□

cryptic
[kríptik]

이유를 알 수 없는, 아리송한, 신비적인
ⓐ mysterious in meaning
ⓢⓨⓝ puzzling, ambiguous, mystic, enigmatic
ⓔ.ⓖ. His **cryptic** comments confused us, so we asked his assistant for clarification
ⓐ procryptic 보호색을 가진

Day

08

protege	□□□	misconstrue	□□□
entry	□□□	derive	□□□
discrete	□□□	immune	□□□
coordinate	□□□	swarm	□□□
modular	□□□	aural	□□□
distinctive	□□□	impenetrable	□□□
deleterious	□□□	impetus	□□□
make-believe	□□□	coherent	□□□
throes	□□□	implicit	□□□
barrier	□□□	inanition	□□□
hinder	□□□	blueprint	□□□
distort	□□□	dismal	□□□
eclipse	□□□	induce	□□□
hostile	□□□	rift	□□□
implicate	□□□	tentative	□□□
ovary	□□□	hereabouts	□□□
proviso	□□□	carve	□□□
quirk	□□□	discard	□□□
resolute	□□□	anguish	□□□
restive	□□□	subordinate	□□□
rust	□□□	property	□□□
sag	□□□	anthropology	□□□
scrunch	□□□	preparatory	□□□
incubate	□□□	turnstile	□□□
instill	□□□	counterpart	□□□
hypocrite	□□□	elaborate	□□□
ghastly	□□□	ambiguity	□□□
Antarctic	□□□	wretch	□□□
ledger	□□□	assure	□□□
ignite	□□□	condemn	□□□

0421 ■■□

protege
[próutəʒèi]

제자, 후배

ⓝ a person under the patronage, protection, or care of someone interested in his or her career or welfare
syn disciple
e.g. His **protege** Medvedev won the post in March by a landslide.

0422 ■□□

entry
[éntri]

표제어, 항목, 참가, 들어감(입장)

ⓝ an item written or printed in a diary, list, ledger, or reference book
syn statement, note, memorandum
e.g. He said the **entry** was just not true.

0423 ■□□

discrete
[diskríːt]

별개의, 분리된, 불연속의

ⓐ apart or detached from others; separate; distinct
syn separate
e.g. We see counselling and consultations as two **discrete** and fairly different processes.

0424 ■□□

coordinate
[kouɔ́ːrdənèit]

조정하다, 조화시키다

ⓥ to place or class in the same order, rank, division, etc.
e.g. Continue to **coordinate** with my office.

0425 ■□□

modular
[mɑ́dʒələr]

조립식의

ⓐ employing or involving a module or modules as the basis of design or construction
e.g. Jet-powered robots will move the **modular** sections into and out of their locations.

0426 ■□□

distinctive
[distíŋktiv]

구별되는, (서로) 다른

ⓐ having a special quality, style, attractiveness, etc.
syn particular, singular
e.g. I feel this restaurant has a **distinctive** atmosphere.

0427 ■□□

deleterious 해로운
[dèlətíəriəs]
ⓐ injurious to health
ⓢⓨⓝ harmful, damaging, destructive
ⓔ.ⓖ. To my mind one of the most **deleterious** effects of the BBC is the cultural degradation that the BBC has been responsible for.

0428 ■□□

make-believe 거짓의, 가공의
['mākbə,lēv]
ⓐ imitating something real; pretend
ⓢⓨⓝ imaginary, imagined, pretended, made-up
ⓔ.ⓖ. In her **make-believe** fairy tale world everybody is so beautiful.

0429 ■■□

throes 극심한 고통
[θrooz]
ⓝ intense or violent pain and struggle, especially accompanying birth, death, or great change
ⓢⓨⓝ agony
ⓔ.ⓖ. The country is still in the **throes** of major social change.

0430 ■□□

barrier 방벽, 울타리, 요새
[bǽriər]
ⓝ anything built or serving to bar passage, as a railing, fence, or the like
ⓢⓨⓝ partition, barricade
ⓔ.ⓖ. Police erected a **barrier** to protect the performers.

0431 ■■□

hinder 방해하다, 훼방 놓다
[híndər]
ⓥ to cause delay, interruption, or difficulty in
ⓢⓨⓝ hamper, impede
ⓔ.ⓖ. The storm **hindered** our progress.
ⓝ hindrance 방해, 장애, 장애물

0432 ■■□

distort 찌푸리다, 뒤틀다
[distɔ́:rt]
ⓥ to twist awry or out of shape; make crooked or deformed
ⓢⓨⓝ deform, disfigure
ⓔ.ⓖ. Arthritis had **distorted** his hands.
ⓝ distortion 찌그러뜨림, 뒤틀림

DAY

08

0433 ■□□

eclipse
[iklíps]

(해, 달의) 식(蝕)
ⓝ the obscuration of the light of the moon by the intervention of the earth between it and the sun (lunar eclipse) or the obscuration of the light of the sun by the intervention of the moon between it and a point on the earth (solar eclipse).
ⓔ.ⓖ. During a solar **eclipse**, many people like to safely observe the sun through dark material.
ⓐ ecliptic 일식(월식)의

0434 ■■□

hostile
[hástl, -tail]

적의, 적군의, 적대적인
ⓐ of, pertaining to, or characteristic of an enemy
ⓢⓨⓝ antagonistic, inimical, malevolent, malicious, malignant
ⓔ.ⓖ. Many of the immigrants were **hostile** to each other.
ⓝ hostility 적의, 적개심, 적대 행위

0435 ■■■

implicate
[ímplikèit]

관련시키다, 연루시키다
ⓥ to show to be also involved, usually in an incriminating manner
ⓢⓨⓝ involve, tangle
ⓔ.ⓖ. More than 10 other politicians were **implicated** in the scandal.
ⓝ implication 연루, 밀접한 관계

0436 ■■■

ovary
[oʊvəri]

난소
ⓝ A woman's ovaries are the two organs in her body that produce eggs.
ⓔ.ⓖ. I know a woman who have had her **ovaries** removed.
ⓐ ovarian

0437 ■■■

proviso
[prəvaɪzoʊ]

단서, 조건
ⓝ A proviso is a condition in an agreement. You agree to do something if this condition is fulfilled.
ⓢⓨⓝ condition
ⓔ.ⓖ. Their participation is subject to a number of important **provisos**.

0438 ■■■

quirk
[kw3:rk]

별난 점, 우연

ⓝ A quirk is something unusual or interesting that happens by chance.

ⓔ·ⓖ By a strange **quirk** of fate they had booked into the same hotel.

ⓐ quirkish, quirky

0439 ■■☐

resolute
[rezəlu:t]

단호한, 확고한

ⓐ If you describe someone as resolute, you approve of them because they are very determined not to change their mind or not to give up a course of action.

ⓔ·ⓖ He became even more **resolute** in his opposition to the plan.

ⓥ resolve

ⓝ resolution

0440 ■■■

restive
[restɪv]

가만히 못 있는

ⓐ If you are restive, you are impatient, bored, or dissatisfied.

ⓢⓨⓝ restless, unsettled, nervous, edgy

ⓔ·ⓖ The audience was becoming **restive** as they waited for the performance to begin.

ⓐⓓ restively

0441 ■☐☐

rust
[rʌst]

녹

ⓝ Rust is a brown substance that forms on iron or steel, for example when it comes into contact with water.

ⓢⓨⓝ corrosion, oxidation

ⓔ·ⓖ Water had got in and **rusted** the engine.

ⓐ rusty

0442 ■■☐

sag
[sæg]

축 처지다

ⓥ When something sags, it hangs down loosely or sinks downwards in the middle.

ⓢⓨⓝ sink, bag, droop

ⓔ·ⓖ The tent began to **sag** under the weight of the rain.

DAY
08

0443 ■■■

scrunch
[skrʌntʃ]

뽀드득 소리를 내다, 구기다

ⓥ If you scrunch something, you squeeze it or bend it so that it is no longer in its natural shape and is often crushed.

ⓔⓖ He **scrunched** up the note and threw it on the fire.

0444 ■□□

incubate
[ínkjubèit]

부화하다; 숙고하다, 궁리하다

ⓥ to sit upon (eggs) for the purpose of hatching to develop or produce as if by hatching; give form to

ⓢⓨⓝ breed, nurture, produce

ⓔⓖ Chickens are usually very docile while **incubating** their eggs.

ⓝ incubation 부화, 배양, 계획

0445 ■■□

instill
[instíl]

스며들게 하다

ⓥ to infuse slowly or gradually into the mind or feelings

ⓢⓨⓝ insinuate, inject, infuse

ⓔⓖ The energetic speech he gave **instilled** us all with a sense of purpose.

ⓝ instillation 주입

0446 ■■□

hypocrite
[hípəkrit]

위선자, 겉으로 착한 척하는 사람

ⓝ a person who pretends to have virtues, moral or religious beliefs, principles, etc., that he or she does not actually possess, esp. a person whose actions belie stated beliefs

ⓢⓨⓝ dissembler, pharisee

ⓔⓖ That **hypocrite** told me yesterday that I should never smoke cigarettes.

ⓐ hypocritical 위선의, 위선자적인

0447 ■■□

ghastly
[gǽstli]

무시무시한, 유령 같은

ⓐ shockingly frightful or dreadful; resembling a ghost, esp. in being very pale

ⓢⓨⓝ horrible, ghostly

ⓔⓖ He came home from the war with **ghastly** stories.

ⓐ aghast 경악한, 겁에 질린

0448 ■□□

Antarctic
[æntá:rktik]

남극의
ⓐ at or near the south pole
ⓢⓨⓝ south-polar
ⓔ.ⓖ. The world's most abundant food source is krill which is an
   Antarctic animal.
ⓐ arctic 북극의

0449 ■■□

ledger
[lédʒər]

(은행·사업체 등에서 거래 내역을 적은) 원장, 대장부
ⓝ an account book of final entry, in which business transactions are
   recorded
ⓔ.ⓖ. He forgot to put the information in the **ledger**.

0450 ■□□

ignite
[ignáit]

불을 붙이다, 발화시키다
ⓥ to set on fire; kindle
ⓢⓨⓝ fire, kindle, light
ⓔ.ⓖ. The spark to **ignite** interest in soccer must come from the
   television networks.
ⓐ ignitable 발화성의, 점화성의

0451 ■■■

misconstrue
[mìskənstrú:]

잘못 해석하다, 오해하다
ⓥ to misunderstand the meaning of; take in a wrong sense
ⓢⓨⓝ misunderstand, misinterpret, misconceive
ⓔ.ⓖ. Don't **misconstrue** my complaint.
ⓝ misconstruction 잘못된 해석, 오해

DAY
08

0452 ■■□

derive
[diráivəbl]

끌어내다, 얻다
ⓥ to receive or obtain from a source or origin
ⓢⓨⓝ stem, obtain
ⓔ.ⓖ. She **derived** pleasure from seeing him stressed.
ⓐ derivable 끌어낼 수 있는, 추론할 수 있는

0453 ■□□

immune
[imjúːn]

면역(성)의

ⓐ protected from a disease or the like, as by inoculation
ⓔ.ⓖ. You are **immune** from the malady, as I have had it once.
ⓝ immunity 면역, 면역력

0454 ■■□

swarm
[swɔ́ːrm]

떼를 짓다, 많이 모여들다; 떼, 무리

ⓥ to fly off together in a swarm, as bees; to move about, along, forth, etc., in great numbers, as things or persons
ⓢⓨⓝ crawl, teem, flock
ⓔ.ⓖ. I saw flies were **swarming** over the trash can.
ⓝ swarmer 떼 짓는 것, 무리 중 하나

0455 ■■□

aural
[ɔ́ːrəl]

귀의, 청각의

ⓐ of or pertaining to the ear or to the sense of hearing
ⓔ.ⓖ. This animal has an **aural** apparatus more sensitive than ours, all owing it to hear far off sounds.
ⓥ auralize 마음으로 듣다, 청각화하다

0456 ■■□

impenetrable
[impénətrəbl]

꿰뚫을 수 없는, 이해할 수 없는

ⓐ not penetrable; that cannot be penetrated, pierced, entered, etc.; incapable of being understood
ⓢⓨⓝ obscure, incomprehensible
ⓔ.ⓖ. The walls of this giant fortress were completely **impenetrable**.
ⓥ penetrate 관통하다, 침입하다

0457 ■□□

impetus
[ímpətəs]

힘, 가동력, 운동력, 자극

ⓝ a moving force; impulse; stimulus
ⓢⓨⓝ momentum, incentive, motivation, impulse, stimulus
ⓔ.ⓖ. The grant for building the cultural center gave **impetus** to the city's cultural life.

0458 ■■□

coherent
[kouhíərənt]

일관성 있는, 조리 있는

ⓐ logically connected
ⓢⓨⓝ consistent
ⓔ.ⓖ. When he calm down, she was more serious and **coherent**.
ⓝ coherence 일관성, 긴밀성　　ⓥ cohere 밀착하다
ⓝ cohesion 결합(력)　　ⓐ cohesive 결합력 있는

0459 ■■□

implicit
[implísit]

함축적인, 암시적인

ⓐ implied, rather than expressly stated
ⓢⓨⓝ implied, inferred
ⓔ.ⓖ. She gave me an **implicit** permission to borrow her shirt.
ⓝ implication 암시, 함축

0460 ■■■

inanition
[inəníʃən]

영양실조, 기아

ⓝ exhaustion from lack of nourishment
ⓢⓨⓝ starvation
ⓔ.ⓖ. Every year, millions of children in Africa and Central America
die of **inanition**.

0461 ■□□

blueprint
[blúːprìnt]

청사진, 설계도, 계획

ⓝ a process of photographic printing, used chiefly in copying
architectural and mechanical drawings
ⓢⓨⓝ draft, layout
ⓔ.ⓖ. It's time for me to send these **blueprints** to the construction
crew.

DAY
08

0462 ■■□

dismal
[dízməl]

음산한, 음울한, 비참한

ⓐ causing gloom or dejection; characterized by ineptness or lack of
skill, competence, effectiveness, imagination, or interest
ⓢⓨⓝ gloomy, dreary, cheerless, melancholy
ⓔ.ⓖ. There was a **dismal** fog hanging over the town on Halloween.

0463 ■■■

induce
[indjúːs]

권유하다, 설득하다

ⓥ to lead or move by persuasion or influence, as to some action or state of mind

(syn) persuade, admonish

(e.g.) For the woman's safety, the doctors **induced** birth of the child in lieu of waiting.

ⓝ inducement 권유, 유도, 유인

0464 ■■□

rift
[ríft]

갈라진 틈, 금, 분열, 불화

ⓝ an opening made by splitting, cleaving, etc.; a break in friendly relations

(syn) breach, rupture, estrangement

(e.g.) The argument made a **rift** in their friendship.

0465 ■■■

tentative
[téntətiv]

시험적인, 임시의

ⓐ of the nature of or made or done as a trial, experiment, or attempt

(syn) provisional, temporary, experimental

(e.g.) The **tentative** agreement requires pay decreases totaling 9 percent.

ⓝ tentativeness 시험적임

0466 ■■□

hereabouts
[híərəbàuts]

이 부근에, 근처에

ⓐⓓ about this place; in this neighborhood

(syn) close to, nearby

(e.g.) I saw the car accident **hereabouts** some where.

ⓐⓓ whereabouts 어디쯤에서

0467 ■□□

carve
[káːrv]

베다, 새기다

ⓥ to cut (a solid material) so as to form something

(syn) sculpture, engrave

(e.g.) The child **carved** his name on the tree.

ⓝ carver 조각가

0468 ■■□

discard
[diskɑ́ːrd]

버리다, 처분하다
ⓥ to cast aside or dispose of; get rid of
ⓢⓨⓝ abandon, dispose of, dump
ⓔ.ⓖ. You can remove the package from the computer and **discard** it.
ⓐ discardable 포기할 수 있는, 버릴 수 있는

0469 ■■□

anguish
[ǽŋgwiʃ]

고통, 고뇌
ⓝ excruciating or acute distress, suffering, or pain
ⓢⓨⓝ affliction, agony, pain
ⓔ.ⓖ. He was in **anguish** until the doctor set his broken leg.
ⓐ anguished 번민의, 고뇌에 찬

0470 ■■□

subordinate
[səbɔ́ːrdənət]

~보다 하위의, 하급의
ⓐ placed in or belonging to a lower order or rank
ⓢⓨⓝ inferior, subject, lower
ⓔ.ⓖ. There is no doubt that education plays an essential role in **subordinate** countries.
ⓝ subordination 종속, 하위, 예속시킴

0471 ■■□

property
[prɑ́pərti]

재산, 자산, 소유물
ⓝ that which a person owns; the possession or possessions of a particular owner
ⓢⓨⓝ possession, asset
ⓔ.ⓖ. He shared his **property** with his ex-wife.
ⓐ propertied 재산이 있는

0472 ■□□

anthropology
[æ̀nθrəpɑ́lədʒi]

인류학
ⓝ the science that deals with the origins, physical and cultural development, biological characteristics, and social customs and beliefs of humankind
ⓔ.ⓖ. He was interested in **anthropology** after hearing about Ancient Egypt.
ⓝ anthropologist 인류학자

DAY
08

0473 ■■□

preparatory
[pripǽrətɔ́ːri]

준비의, 예비의
ⓐ serving or designed to prepare
(syn) preliminary, introductory
(e.g.) They made all the **preparatory** motions to begin the real dance.
ⓝ preparative 예비, 준비

0474 ■■□

turnstile
[tə́ːrnstàil]

회전식 십자문
ⓝ a structure of four horizontally revolving arms pivoted atop a post and set in a gateway or opening in a fence to allow the controlled passage of people
(e.g.) The workman is repairing the stuck **turnstile**.

0475 ■■□

counterpart
[káuntərpɑ̀ːrt]

상대, 대응 관계에 있는 사람
ⓝ a person or thing closely resembling another, esp. in function
(syn) opposite number
(e.g.) Our president is the **counterpart** of your king.

0476 ■■□

elaborate
[ilǽbərət]

공들인, 복잡한, 정교한
ⓐ worked out with great care and nicety of detail; executed with great minuteness
(syn) perfected, painstaking
(e.g.) Their investigation is considerably more **elaborate** than ours.
ⓝ elaboration 고심하여 만듦, 공들임, 정교함

0477 ■■□

ambiguity
[æ̀mbiɡjúːəti]

모호, 불명료
ⓝ doubtfulness or uncertainty of meaning or intention
(syn) obscurity, uncertainty
(e.g.) **Ambiguity** of ten functions to increase the richness and subtlety of script writing.
ⓐ ambiguous 모호한, 분명하지 않은

0478 ■■□

wretch
[rétʃ]

가련한 사람, 비참한 사람
ⓝ a deplorably unfortunate or unhappy person
ⓢⓨⓝ loser, underdog
ⓔ.ⓖ. A burglar is a **wretch** who steals the property of others.
ⓐ wretched 불쌍한, 비참한, 불행한

0479 ■■□

assure
[əʃúər]

보증하다, 책임지다
ⓥ to declare earnestly to; inform or tell positively
ⓢⓨⓝ guarantee, ensure, insure
ⓔ.ⓖ. She **assured** us that our flight would not be late.
ⓝ assurance 보증, 확신

0480 ■■□

condemn
[kəndém]

비난하다, 책망하다
ⓥ to express an unfavorable or adverse judgment on; indicate strong disapproval of
ⓢⓨⓝ censure, blame, criticize, damn
ⓔ.ⓖ. The criminal was **condemned** to life in prison.
ⓝ condemnation 비난, 규탄

DAY
08

Day

09

유희태 일반영어 ⑤
VOCA
기출 VOCA 30 days

autism	□□□	swindle	□□□
lessen	□□□	dominate	□□□
intervention	□□□	anticipate	□□□
outgrow	□□□	astray	□□□
remission	□□□	enchant	□□□
plague	□□□	stock	□□□
correct	□□□	suppress	□□□
shady	□□□	compact	□□□
business	□□□	confess	□□□
obscene	□□□	replenish	□□□
anonymous	□□□	grasp	□□□
incident	□□□	pregnant	□□□
mutter	□□□	affair	□□□
obvious	□□□	elastic	□□□
interim	□□□	uproar	□□□
shack	□□□	discriminate	□□□
shorthand	□□□	physical	□□□
sift	□□□	neolithic	□□□
simpleton	□□□	paleolithic	□□□
somber	□□□	content	□□□
specimen	□□□	rare	□□□
steadfast	□□□	scrupulous	□□□
toll	□□□	bulb	□□□
subtle	□□□	scurvy	□□□
tarry	□□□	waive	□□□
interaction	□□□	vary	□□□
assign	□□□	obscure	□□□
ornament	□□□	identify	□□□
degrade	□□□	shrew	□□□
fairy	□□□	incline	□□□

0481 ■□□

autism
[ɔ́ːtizəm]

자폐증
ⓝ a developmental disorder of variable severity that is characterized by difficulty in social interaction and communication and by restricted or repetitive patterns of thought and behavior
ⓔⓖ People with **autism** have other symptoms, too.

0482 ■□□

lessen
[lésn]

줄어들다
ⓥ to make less; reduce
ⓢⓨⓝ diminish
ⓞⓟⓟ aggrandize
ⓔⓖ It doesn't **lessen** feelings and pain, it heightens them.

0483 ■□□

intervention
[ìntərvénʃən]

개입, 중재, 해결책
ⓝ the act or fact of intervening
ⓔⓖ Government **intervention** has worsened[aggravated] the situation.

0484 ■□□

outgrow
[òut·grów]

(옷 등에 비해 사람의 몸 등이) 너무 커져 맞지 않게 되다, ~보다 더 커지다(많아지다), 나이가 들면서 ~을 그만두다(~에 흥미를 잃다)
ⓥ grow too big for (something)
ⓢⓨⓝ grow out of
ⓔⓖ About one in five children with peanut allergy **outgrow** it.

0485 ■□□

remission
[rimíʃən]

(병의) 차도, 감면
ⓝ a diminution of the seriousness or intensity of disease or pain; a temporary recovery
ⓢⓨⓝ abeyance
ⓔⓖ Ten out of twenty patients remained in **remission**.

0486 ■□□

plague
[pleig]

시달리다, 괴롭히다; 전염병, 페스트
ⓥ to trouble, annoy, or torment in any manner
ⓢⓨⓝ bedevil
ⓔⓖ I am **plagued** with about a dozen spam emails every day.

0487 ■□□

correct
[kərékt]

(계산, 관측 따위 등을) 보정(補正)하다
ⓥ remove the errors or faults from
ⓢⓨⓝ square
ⓔ.ⓖ. The Council issued a statement **correcting** some points in the press reports.
ⓝ correction

0488 ■□□

shady
[ʃéidi]

사기 치는, 그늘진
ⓐ of doubtful honesty or legality
ⓔ.ⓖ. Joseph watched a **shady**-looking bunch playing cards aboard a Mississippi steamer.

0489 ■□□

business
[bíznis]

영업(실적), 사업, 일
ⓝ the practice of making one's living by engaging in commerce
ⓢⓨⓝ performance
ⓔ.ⓖ. **Business** was booming.

0490 ■■■

obscene
[əbsíːn]

외설의, 음란한
ⓐ offensive to morality or decency
ⓢⓨⓝ indecent, depraved
ⓔ.ⓖ. **Obscene** magazines are too easily seen by children in this country.
ⓝ obscenity 외설, 음란한 행동(말)

0491 ■■□

anonymous
[ənánəməs]

작자 미상의, 익명의
ⓐ without any name acknowledged, as that of author, contributor, or the like
ⓢⓨⓝ unnamed, nameless, incognito
ⓔ.ⓖ. He sent an **anonymous** letter to the police yesterday.
ⓝ anonymity 익명, 무명

DAY
09

0492 ■□□

incident
[ínsədənt]

일어난 일, 사건
ⓝ an individual occurrence or event
ⓢⓨⓝ occurrence, event, happening
ⓔ.ⓖ. After the **incident**, he disappeared from the center stage of history.
ⓐ incidental 부수하여 일어나는, 흔히 있는

0493 ■■□

mutter
[mʌ́tər]

중얼거리다, 불평하며 말하다
ⓥ to utter words indistinctly or in a low tone, often as if talking to oneself
ⓢⓨⓝ murmur, grumble, grunt, complain
ⓔ.ⓖ. He was **muttering** something to himself in his sleep.
ⓝ muttering 투덜거림, 불평, 중얼거림

0494 ■□□

obvious
[ábviəs]

명백한, 분명한, 알기 쉬운
ⓐ easily seen, recognized, or understood; open to view or knowledge
ⓢⓨⓝ evident, apparent, clear
ⓔ.ⓖ. The error is too **obvious** to escape her notice.
ⓐⓓ obviously 명백하게, 분명히

0495 ■■□

interim
[íntərəm]

임시의
ⓐ intended to last for only a short time until sth more permanent is found
ⓔ.ⓖ. He said for those reasons the court should grant an **interim** order to give him an opportunity to prepare an objection.

0496 ■■□

shack
[ʃæk]

판잣집
ⓝ A shack is a simple hut built from tin, wood, or other materials.
ⓢⓨⓝ hut, cabin, shanty
ⓔ.ⓖ. They lived in a **shack** with a dirt floor.

0497 ■■□

shorthand
[ʃɔːrthænd]

속기, 약칭

ⓝ Shorthand is a quick way of writing and uses signs to represent words or syllables. Shorthand is used by secretaries and journalists to write down what someone is saying.

ⓔ.ⓖ. The secretary took the minutes in **shorthand**.

0498 ■■□

sift
[sɪft]

체로 치다

ⓥ If you sift a powder such as flour or sand, you put it through a sieve in order to remove large pieces or lumps.

ⓢⓨⓝ filter, strain

ⓔ.ⓖ. **Sift** the flour into a bowl.

0499 ■■□

simpleton
[sɪmpltən]

얼간이

ⓝ If you call someone a simpleton, you think they are easily deceived or not very intelligent.

ⓢⓨⓝ dunce, fool, idiot, moron

ⓔ.ⓖ. I guess that's why they call her **simpleton**.

0500 ■■□

somber
[sɑ́mbər]

어두침침한

ⓐ gloomy, depressing, or dismal

ⓢⓨⓝ dark, drab, gloomy, melancholy, grave

ⓔ.ⓖ. His face grew **somber** after he heard the news about the coup.

0501 ■■□

specimen
[spesɪmən]

견본, 샘플

ⓝ A specimen is a single plant or animal which is an example of a particular species or type and is examined by scientists.

ⓢⓨⓝ sample, example, model

ⓔ.ⓖ. Astronauts have brought back **specimens** of rock from the moon.

DAY
09

0502 ■□□

steadfast
[stédfæst]

변함없는

ⓐ If someone is steadfast in something that they are doing, they are convinced that what they are doing is right and they refuse to change it or to give up.

ⓔ.ⓖ He remained **steadfast** in his determination to bring the killers to justice.

ⓝ steadfastness, stedfastness

ⓐⓓ steadfastly, stedfastly

0503 ■□□

toll
[tóul]

사용세

ⓝ A toll is a small sum of money that you have to pay in order to use a particular bridge or road.

ⓢⓨⓝ rate, charge, fee

ⓔ.ⓖ When your computer is out of order, try our **toll** free call.

0504 ■■□

subtle
[sʌ́tl]

미묘한, 미세한, 이해하기 어려운

ⓐ fine or delicate in meaning or intent; difficult to perceive or understand

ⓢⓨⓝ detailed, fine, delicate

ⓔ.ⓖ Some **subtle** details will add depth to this painting.

ⓝ subtlety 미묘, 신비, 불가사의

0505 ■■□

tarry
[tǽri]

머무르다, 지체하다

ⓥ to remain or stay, as in a place

ⓢⓨⓝ lodge, abide, stay, remain

ⓔ.ⓖ He **tarried** in Chicago on his way to New York.

ⓝ tarrier 투숙자

0506 ■□□

interaction
[ìntərǽkʃən]

상호작용

ⓝ mutual or reciprocal action or influence

ⓢⓨⓝ communication, cooperation

ⓔ.ⓖ A smaller class allows more **interaction** between student and teacher.

ⓥ interact 상호작용하다

0507 ■■□

assign
[əsáin]

할당하다, 배당하다
ⓥ to give or allocate
(syn) allot, charge
(e.g.) He **assigned** us the best seats in the class.
ⓝ assignment 할당(된 일), 임명

0508 ■□□

ornament
[ɔ́ːrnəmənt]

꾸밈, 장식, 장식품
ⓝ an accessory, article, or detail used to beautify the appearance of something to which it is added or of which it is a part
(syn) decoration, adornment
(e.g.) A pretty girl put a ribbon in her hair as an **ornament**.
ⓐ ornamental 장식용의, 장식적인, 장식의

0509 ■■□

degrade
[digréid]

좌천시키다, 파면시키다
ⓥ to lower in dignity or estimation; bring into contempt
(syn) humble, abase, belittle
(e.g.) He felt they were **degrading** him by making him report to a supervisor.
ⓝ degradation 좌천, 파면

0510 ■□□

fairy
[féəri]

요정
ⓝ (in folklore) one of a class of supernatural beings, generally conceived as having a diminutive human form and possessing magical powers with which they intervene in human affairs.
(syn) brownie, elf, genie
(e.g.) Her slight height and cute appearance made her appear somewhat like a **fairy**.
ⓐ fairylike 요정 같은

DAY
09

0511 ■■■

swindle
[swíndl]

(돈을) 사취하다, 속이다
ⓥ to cheat (a person, business, etc.) out of money or other assets
(e.g.) Every used car salesman wants to **swindle** his customer.
ⓝ swindler 사기꾼

0512 ■■□

dominate
[dámənèit]

지배하다, 위압하다
ⓥ to rule over
ⓢⓨⓝ govern, control
ⓔ.ⓖ. They hope to **dominate** the coffee market within five years.
ⓝ dominance 우월, 권세, 지배

0513 ■■■

anticipate
[æntísəpèit]

예상(고대)하다, 예견하다
ⓥ guess or be aware of (what will happen) and take action in order
to be prepared; to realize beforehand
ⓢⓨⓝ preempt, forestall, foretaste, foresee
ⓔ.ⓖ. I **anticipate** great pleasure when I visit France.
ⓝ anticipation 예상, 예견

0514 ■■□

astray
[əstréi]

길을 잃다, 못된 길로 빠지다
ⓥ out of the right way; off the correct or known road, path, or route
ⓢⓨⓝ afield, amiss
ⓔ.ⓖ. Despite a clear map, they went **astray** and got lost.

0515 ■■□

enchant
[intʃǽnt]

요술을 걸다, 호리다, 매혹하다
ⓥ to subject to magical influence
ⓢⓨⓝ bewitch, charm
ⓔ.ⓖ. This fairytale is about witches who **enchant** handsome
princes and beautiful maidens.
ⓝ enchantment 매혹, 매력

0516 ■□□

stock
[sták]

재고품, 저장품
ⓝ a supply of goods kept on hand for sale to customers by a
merchant, distributor, manufacturer, etc.
ⓢⓨⓝ inventory, accumulation
ⓔ.ⓖ. We do not have sufficient quantities in **stock** to fill your order.
ⓝ stockpile 비축량

0517 ■■□

suppress
[səprés]

억압하다, 진압하다, 억누르다
ⓥ to put an end to the activities of (a person, body of persons, etc.)
ⓢⓨⓝ quell, quench, oppress
ⓔ.ⓖ. The riot police were sent to **suppress** the angry crowd.
ⓝ suppression 억압, 진압, 탄압

0518 ■□□

compact
[kəmpǽkt]

조밀한, 촘촘한, 밀집한
ⓐ joined or packed together; closely and firmly united
ⓢⓨⓝ dense, solid, condensed
ⓔ.ⓖ. The area was in a **compact** cluster of academies.
ⓝ compaction 꽉 채움, 밀집

0519 ■■□

confess
[kənfés]

자백하다, 고백하다
ⓥ to acknowledge or avow (a fault, crime, misdeed, weakness, etc.) by way of revelation
ⓢⓨⓝ acknowledge, avow
ⓔ.ⓖ. A detective made a man **confess** his guilt through interrogation.
ⓝ confession 자백, 고백

0520 ■■■

replenish
[ripléniʃ]

보충하다, 보급하다
ⓥ to make full or complete again, as by supplying what is lacking, used up, etc
ⓢⓨⓝ provide, replace, supplement, supply
ⓔ.ⓖ. We **replenished** the stove with wood to keep the room warm.
ⓝ replenishment 보충, 보급

0521 ■■□

grasp
[grǽsp]

붙잡다, 움켜잡다
ⓥ to seize and hold by or as if by clasping with the fingers or arms
ⓢⓨⓝ grip, take, seize, hold
ⓔ.ⓖ. She **grasped** the pole tightly as a powerful fish took her line.
ⓐ grasping 욕심 많은

DAY
09

0522 ■□□

pregnant
[prégnənt]

임신한
ⓐ having a child or other offspring developing in the body; with child or young, as a woman or female mammal
ⓢⓨⓝ enceinte, expectant, gravid
ⓔ.ⓖ. The **pregnant** women of ten want to eat strange food.
ⓝ pregnancy 임신, 임신기간

0523 ■□□

affair
[əféər]

일, 사건, 문제
ⓝ anything done or to be done; anything requiring action or effort
ⓢⓨⓝ event, business, thing, occasion
ⓔ.ⓖ. Get your **affairs** in order before we leave on vacation.

0524 ■■■

elastic
[ilǽstik]

탄력 있는, 탄성의, 신축성 있는
ⓐ capable of returning to its original length, shape, etc., after being stretched, deformed, compressed, or expanded
ⓢⓨⓝ resilient, pliant, flexible
ⓔ.ⓖ. On a lightly floured surface, knead dough until it is smooth and **elastic**, adding flour.
ⓝ elasticity 탄성, 신축성

0525 ■■□

uproar
[ʌ́prɔ̀ːr]

소란, 소동, 야단법석
ⓝ a state of violent and noisy disturbance, as of a multitude
ⓢⓨⓝ tumult, turbulence, commotion, clamor, turmoil
ⓔ.ⓖ. The whole town was in an **uproar** with the controversy.
ⓐ uproarious 떠드는, 시끄러운, 떠들썩한

0526 ■■□

discriminate
[diskrímənèit]

구별하다, 식별하다, 분리하다
ⓥ to make a distinction in favor of or against a person or thing on the basis of the group, class, or category to which the person or thing belongs rather than according to actual merit; show partiality
ⓢⓨⓝ differentiate, distinguish, segregate, separate
ⓔ.ⓖ. You should **discriminate** between friends and enemies.
ⓝ discrimination 구별, 식별

0527 ■□□

physical
[fízikəl]

육체적인
ⓐ pertaining to the body
ⓢⓨⓝ fleshly, corporal
ⓔⓖ I stay fit because my job is very **physical**.
ⓝ physics 물리학

0528 ■■□

neolithic
[nìːəlíθik]

신석기 시대의
ⓐ characteristic of the last phase of the Stone Age, marked by the domestication of animals, the development of agriculture, and the manufacture of pottery and textiles
ⓔⓖ The **Neolithic** art on pottery is very impressive.

0529 ■■□

paleolithic
[pèiliəlíθik]

구석기 시대의
ⓐ characteristic of the cultures of the late Pliocene and the Pleistocene epochs, or early phase of the Stone Age, which appeared first in Africa and are marked by the steady development of stone tools and later antler and bone artifacts, engravings on bone and stone, sculpted figures, and paintings and engravings on the walls of caves and rock-shelters: usually divided into three periods
ⓔⓖ Tim's class is studying artifacts dating from the **Paleolithic** Age.

0530 ■■□

content
[kəntént]

만족한, 안심한
ⓐ satisfied with what one is or has; not wanting more or anything else
ⓢⓨⓝ comfortable, complacent, gratified, happy, satisfied
ⓔⓖ I would be **content** to just stay in this weekend and watch movies.
ⓝ discontent 불만, 불만스러운 것

DAY
09

0531 ■□□

rare
[rέər]

드문
ⓐ coming or occurring far apart in time; unusual; uncommon
ⓢⓨⓝ occasional, scarce, sporadic
ⓔⓖ This **rare** book is worth a fortune.
ⓐⓓ rarely 좀처럼 ~ 하지 않는, 드물게

0532 ■■■

scrupulous
[skrúːpjuləs]

양심적인, 지조 있는, 성실한
ⓐ having scruples; having or showing a strict regard for what one considers right; principled
ⓔⓖ A **scrupulous** politician keeps their personal interests clear of their office.
ⓝ scrupulosity 면밀(주도)함, 꼼꼼함

0533 ■□□

bulb
[bʌlb]

전구, 공 모양의 부분
ⓝ any round, enlarged part, esp. at the end of a cylindrical object
ⓔⓖ You need to replace the light **bulb** in the hallway light.
ⓐ bulbous 둥글납작한

0534 ■□□

scurvy
[skə́ːrvi]

괴혈병
ⓝ a disease marked by swollen and bleeding gums, livid spots on the skin, prostration, etc., due to a diet lacking in vitamin C
ⓔⓖ Many sailors suffered **scurvy** due to the lack of healthy food available.
ⓐ scurvied 괴혈병에 걸린

0535 ■■■

waive
[wéiv]

포기하다, 철회하다
ⓥ to refrain from claiming or insisting on; give up
ⓢⓨⓝ renounce, surrender, forgo
ⓔⓖ We will **waive** tuition in light of your incredible test scores.
ⓝ waiver 기권, 기권증서

0536 ■■□

vary
[vέəri]

바꾸다, 변경하다
ⓥ to cause to be different from something else
ⓢⓨⓝ alter, shift
ⓔ.ⓖ. There were **varying** sizes of suitcases available.
ⓐ various 다양한
ⓝ variety 다양함

0537 ■■□

obscure
[əbskjúər]

분명치 않은, 흐릿한, 애매한
ⓐ not clear or plain
ⓢⓨⓝ vague, uncertain, ambiguous
ⓔ.ⓖ. Some of topics that you made are too **obscure** to research.
ⓝ obscurity 불분명, 모호함, 난해함

0538 ■■□

identify
[aidéntəfài]

확인하다, 증명하다, 식별하다
ⓥ to recognize or establish as being a particular person or thing; verify the identity of
ⓢⓨⓝ certify, verify, demonstrate
ⓔ.ⓖ. The name card on the baby's stroller **identified** him.
ⓝ identification 동일함, 신분증명, 신분증

0539 ■■□

shrew
[ʃrúː]

잔소리가 심한 여자, 으르렁거리는 여자
ⓝ a woman of violent temper and speech
ⓢⓨⓝ virago, termagant
ⓔ.ⓖ. She is being the **shrew** in my company.
ⓐ shrewish (여자가) 으르렁거리는, 짓궂은

0540 ■■□

incline
[inkláin]

기울이다, ~하게 만들다, ~하는 성향을 가지고 있다
ⓥ to deviate from the vertical or horizontal; to have a mental tendency, preference, etc.
ⓢⓨⓝ slant, lean, predispose
ⓔ.ⓖ. I am **inclined** to be very careful about what bank I use.
ⓝ inclination 경향, 기질, 성향

DAY
09

Day

10

variable	□□□	plow	□□□
invariably	□□□	analogous	□□□
subject	□□□	indulge	□□□
pug	□□□	ape	□□□
inanimate object	□□□	jostle	□□□
attain	□□□	maid	□□□
antidepressant	□□□	orthodox	□□□
phony	□□□	excess	□□□
nurture	□□□	convention	□□□
transcend	□□□	tug	□□□
stagger	□□□	enforce	□□□
odd	□□□	chromosome	□□□
riot	□□□	yield	□□□
fur	□□□	drift	□□□
invoke	□□□	plain	□□□
resist	□□□	exclaim	□□□
weep	□□□	scarlet	□□□
annihilate	□□□	villain	□□□
postulate	□□□	ultimate	□□□
strenuous	□□□	typography	□□□
conjunction	□□□	exhale	□□□
subdue	□□□	facet	□□□
extant	□□□	vegetation	□□□
genuine	□□□	instantaneous	□□□
lenient	□□□	likelihood	□□□
prosperous	□□□	precept	□□□
lore	□□□	civilize	□□□
criterion	□□□	twig	□□□
intuition	□□□	fare	□□□
breakdown	□□□	utensil	□□□

0541 ■■□

variable
[véəriəbəl]

변수
ⓝ a variable feature or factor
ⓔ.ⓖ. Migration was the **variable** that made this possible.
ⓥ vary

0542 ■□□

invariably
[invéəriəbli]

항상
ⓐⓓ without exception
ⓢⓨⓝ always, without fail
ⓔ.ⓖ. An emotional decision is almost **invariably** a wrong decision.
ⓐ invariable

0543 ■□□

subject
[sʌ́bdʒikt]

실험 대상자
ⓝ a person who is the focus of scientific or medical attention or
experiment
ⓢⓨⓝ guinea pig
ⓔ.ⓖ. We need female **subjects** between the ages of 18 and 40 for
the experiment.

0544 ■■■

pug
[pʌg]

들창코
ⓝ a short, broad, somewhat turned-up nose
ⓔ.ⓖ. He fix her **pug** with plastic surgery.
ⓐ puggish

0545 ■□□

**inanimate
object**
[inǽnəmit ʌ́bdʒikt]

무생물
ⓝ one that has no life
ⓢⓨⓝ inorganic
ⓔ.ⓖ. We can easily find **inanimate objects** around us.

0546 ■□□

attain
[ətéin]

얻다
ⓥ to reach, achieve, or accomplish
ⓢⓨⓝ wangle, secure, obtain, get
ⓔ.ⓖ. You've received every kind of kudos a scientist can **attain**.
ⓝ attainment

0547 ■□□

antidepressant 항우울제
[an,tīdə'presnt]
ⓝ any of a class of drugs used to alleviate depression
ⓔ.ⓖ. I personally think there should be **antidepressant** control.

0548 ■■□

phony 날조한
[fóuni]
ⓐ not real or genuine
ⓢⓨⓝ fraudulent, counterfeit, phoney
ⓔ.ⓖ. He'd phoned with some **phony** excuse she didn't believe for a minute.

0549 ■□□

nurture 양육하다, 기르다
[nə́ːrtʃər]
ⓥ to feed and protect
ⓔ.ⓖ. The Smiths **nurtured** their children in a loving environment.
ⓝ nurturance 애정 어린 돌봄, 양육

0550 ■■■

transcend 초월하다, 능가하다
[trænsénd]
ⓥ to rise above or go beyond
ⓢⓨⓝ overpass, exceed, outdo
ⓔ.ⓖ. Sports gives all men safe, common-ground small talk that can **transcend** even class and race.
ⓝ transcendence 초월, 탁월

0551 ■■□

stagger 비틀거리다, 갈지자 걸음을 걷다
[stǽgər]
ⓥ to walk, move, or stand unsteadily
ⓢⓨⓝ totter, wobble
ⓔ.ⓖ. The old man **staggered** under the heavy load of his packages.
ⓝ staggerer 비틀거리는 사람

0552 ■■□

odd 이상한, 기묘한
[ád]
ⓐ differing in nature from what is ordinary, usual, or expected
ⓢⓨⓝ strange, weird, peculiar, eccentric
ⓔ.ⓖ. I had the **odd** sensation that some one was watching me.
ⓝ oddity 이상한(괴상한) 것(사람)

DAY
10

0553 ■■□
riot
[ráiət]

폭동, 소요, 소동
ⓝ a noisy, violent public disorder caused by a group or crowd of persons, as by a crowd protesting against another group, a government policy, etc., in the streets
ⓔ.ⓖ. The **riot** was a result of the president's unfair policies.
ⓐ riotous 폭동의, 폭동을 일으키는

0554 ■□□
fur
[fɚːr]

부드러운 털, 모피
ⓝ the fine, soft, thick, hairy coat of the skin of a mammal
ⓢⓨⓝ hair, sable, fluff
ⓔ.ⓖ. The little rabbit was covered with soft gray **fur**.
ⓐ furry 부드러운 털의, 모피로 덮인

0555 ■■■
invoke
[invóuk]

청하다, 빌다, 기원하다
ⓥ to call for with earnest desire; make supplication or pray for
ⓢⓨⓝ pray, appeal, beseech, entreat
ⓔ.ⓖ. We must **invoke** the powers of the state for this crisis.
ⓝ invocation 기도, 기원, 간구

0556 ■■□
resist
[rizíst]

저항하다, 적대하다
ⓥ to withstand, strive against, or oppose
ⓢⓨⓝ oppose, abstain, withstand, battle
ⓔ.ⓖ. Farmers have long bred crop strains to **resist** cold, pests, and disease.
ⓝ resistance 저항, 반항, 적대

0557 ■□□
weep
[wiːp]

울다
ⓥ If someone weeps, they cry.
ⓢⓨⓝ cry, shed tears, sob
ⓔ.ⓖ. I could have **wept** thinking about what I'd missed.
ⓐ weepy

0558 ■■■

annihilate
[ənáiəlèit]

전멸시키다; 완패시키다

ⓥ to destroy somebody/something completely; to defeat somebody/something completely

ⓔ.ⓖ. The human race has enough weapons to **annihilate** itself.

ⓝ annihilation, annihilator

ⓐ annihilatory, annihilable, annihilative

0559 ■■■

postulate
[pɑ:stʃələit]

(이론 등의 근거로 삼기 위해 무엇이 사실이라고) 상정하다; 상정(想定)

ⓥ (formal) to suggest or accept that something is true so that it can be used as the basis for a theory, etc.

ⓔ.ⓖ. They **postulated** a 500-year lifespan for a plastic container.

ⓝ postulator, postulation

0560 ■■■

strenuous
[strenjuəs]

힘이 많이 드는, 몹시 힘든, 격렬한; 불굴의, 완강한

ⓐ needing great effort and energy; showing great energy and determination

ⓔ.ⓖ. 1. a **strenuous** climb
2. The ship went down although **strenuous** efforts were made to save it.

ⓝ strenuousness, strenuosity

ⓐⓓ strenuously

0561 ■■□

conjunction
[kəndʒʌ́ŋkʃən]

결합, 연결; 접속사

ⓝ combination, joining

ⓔ.ⓖ. Without **conjunction**, use a semicolon instead of a comma.

ⓐ conjunctional

0562 ■■■

subdue
[səbⅾúː]

진압하다; (감정을) 가라앉히다(억누르다)

ⓥ to bring somebody/something under control, especially by using force

ⓢⓨⓝ overcome, defeat, master, break

ⓔ.ⓖ. Troops were called in to **subdue** the rebels.

ⓝ subdual   ⓐ subduable

ⓐⓓ subduably

DAY
10

0563 ■■■

extant
[ekstənt]

(격식) (아주 오래된 것이) 현존(잔존)하는
ⓐ (of something very old) still in existence
ⓔ.ⓖ. **extant** remains of the ancient wall

0564 ■■□

genuine
[ʤenjuɪn]

진짜의, 진품의; 진실한, 진심 어린
ⓐ real; exactly what it appears to be; not artificial; sincere and honest; that can be trusted
ⓢyn authentic, real, actual, true, valid, legitimate, veritable, bona fide, dinkum; heartfelt, sincere, honest, earnest, real, true, frank, unaffected; frank, candid, guileless
ⓔ.ⓖ. Fake designer watches are sold at a fraction of the price of the **genuine** article.
ⓝ genuineness   ⓐd genuinely

0565 ■■□

lenient
[líːniənt]

너그러운, 인자한, 관대한
ⓐ agreeably tolerant; permissive
ⓢyn charitable, merciful, indulgent
ⓔ.ⓖ. Bob tended to be **lenient** to ward his children.
ⓝ leniency 관대, 관용

0566 ■■□

prosperous
[práspərəs]

번영하는, 부유한, 성공한
ⓐ having or characterized by financial success or good fortune
ⓢyn thriving, flourishing, successful
ⓔ.ⓖ. The harvest is a very **prosperous** time for farm companies.
ⓥ prosper 번영하다, 번창하다, 성공하다

0567 ■■■

lore
[lɔ́ːr]

(전승적) 지식, 구비설화
ⓝ the body of knowledge, esp. of a traditional, anecdotal, or popular nature, on a particular subject
ⓢyn legend, myth, mythology
ⓔ.ⓖ. Ancient **lore** suggests that once there were many rivers in this area.
ⓝ folklore 민속, 전통문화

0568 ■■□

criterion
[kraitíəriən]

표준, 기준, 규범, 척도

ⓝ a standard of judgment or criticism; a rule or principle for evaluating or testing something
ⓢⓨⓝ standard, norm, rule
ⓔ.ⓖ. A person's appetite is a good **criterion** of his health.
ⓝ criteria 표준, 기준

0569 ■□□

intuition
[intjú:ətiv]

직관, 직감

ⓝ direct perception of truth, fact, etc., independent of any reasoning process; immediate apprehension
ⓢⓨⓝ discernment, perception, instinct
ⓔ.ⓖ. Initial impressions are signals given to us by **intuition**.
ⓐ intuitive 직관적인, 직감적인

0570 ■■□

breakdown
[bréikdàun]

고장, 파손

ⓝ a breaking down, wearing out, or sudden loss of ability to function efficiently, as of a machine
ⓢⓨⓝ collapse, disruption, failure
ⓔ.ⓖ. All operations ceased after the financial **breakdown**.

0571 ■□□

plow
[pláu]

갈다, 경작하다

ⓥ to turn up (soil) with a plow
ⓔ.ⓖ. The fields were **plowed** by horse sand carts.
ⓝ plowland 경작지, 논밭

0572 ■■□

analogous
[ənǽləgəs]

유사한, 비슷한

ⓐ having analogy; corresponding in some particular
ⓢⓨⓝ correspondent, similar
ⓔ.ⓖ. A brain is **analogous** of a living computer.
ⓥ analogize 유추하다, 유사하다

DAY
10

0573 ■■■

indulge
[indʌ́ldʒ]

빠지다, 탐닉하다

ⓥ to yield to an inclination or desire; allow oneself to follow one's will
ⓢⓨⓝ addict
ⓔ.ⓖ. He **indulged** in alcohol often.
ⓝ indulgence 빠짐, 탐닉

0574 ■■□

ape
[éip]

흉내 내다, 모방하다; 유인원

ⓥ to imitate; mimic
ⓢⓨⓝ imitate, mimic
ⓔ.ⓖ. People ruin themselves by trying to **ape** their betters.

0575 ■■■

jostle
[dʒásl]

밀치다, 떠밀다

ⓥ to bump, push, shove, brush against, or elbow roughly or rudely
ⓢⓨⓝ bump, push, shove
ⓔ.ⓖ. I spent an hour **jostling** in the crowds at the department store.
ⓝ jostler 소매치기

0576 ■□□

maid
[méid]

하녀, 가정부, 소녀, 처녀

ⓝ a female servant; a girl or young unmarried woman
ⓔ.ⓖ. The young **maid** cleaned the kitchen well.
ⓝ maiden 소녀, 처녀

0577 ■■□

orthodox
[ɔ́ːrθədàks]

정설의, 정통파의

ⓐ of, pertaining to, or conforming to beliefs, attitudes, or modes of
   conduct that are generally approved
ⓔ.ⓖ. The designer has pursued the **orthodox** Korean fashions.
ⓝ orthodoxy 정통적 신념, 정통성, 정설

0578 ■■□

excess
[iksés, ékses]

초과, 과다, 과잉

ⓝ the fact of exceeding something else in amount or degree
ⓢⓨⓝ overabundance, exorbitance
ⓔ.ⓖ. **Excess** in any one thing strains the heart.
ⓐ excessive 과도의, 지나친, 엄청난

0579 ■■□

convention
[kənvénʃən]

집회, 대회, 대표자 회의

ⓝ meeting or formal assembly, as of representatives or delegates, for discussion of and action on particular matters of common concern

ⓢⓨⓝ assembly, conference, congress

ⓔⓖ The medical **convention** was busy with many doctors making speeches.

ⓐ conventional 전통적인, 인습적인

0580 ■■□

tug
[tʌg]

당기다, 끌다

ⓥ to pull at with force, vigor, or effort

ⓢⓨⓝ pull, draw, tow

ⓔⓖ A sailboat was **tugged** to shore.

ⓝ tugboat 예인선

0581 ■■□

enforce
[infɔ́:rs]

억지로 시키다, 강요하다

ⓥ to put or keep in force; compel obedience

ⓢⓨⓝ compel, force, coerce

ⓔⓖ Anti-smoking laws will be strictly **enforced**.

ⓝ enforcement 강조, 강요

0582 ■□□

chromosome
[króuməsòum]

염색체

ⓝ any of several threadlike bodies, consisting of chromatin, that carry the genes in a linear order: the human species has 23 pairs, designated 1 to 22 in order of decreasing size and X and Y for the female and male sex chromosomes respectively

ⓔⓖ Scientists have discovered some clues that suggest the key to longevity may be in a few genes on a single **chromosome**.

0583 ■■□

yield
[ji:ld]

산출하다, 내다

ⓥ to give forth or produce by a natural process or in return for cultivation

ⓢⓨⓝ furnish, supply, bear

ⓔⓖ This garden **yields** enough produce to meet all our needs.

DAY
10

0584 ■□□

drift
[dríft]

표류하다, 떠돌다

ⓥ to be carried along by currents of water or air, or by the force of circumstances
ⓢⓨⓝ float, roam, stray, wander
ⓔ.ⓖ. The boat **drifted** down stream quietly.
ⓝ drifter 표류자, 표류선

0585 ■□□

plain
[pléin]

명백한, 분명한

ⓐ clear or distinct to the eye or ear
ⓢⓨⓝ evident, clear, explicit
ⓔ.ⓖ. The **plain** truth is that he has been helping me.
ⓝ plainness 명백, 솔직

0586 ■■■

exclaim
[ikskléim]

외치다, 고함치다

ⓥ to cry out or speak suddenly and vehemently, as in surprise, strong emotion, or protest
ⓢⓨⓝ cry, scream, shout
ⓔ.ⓖ. He **exclaimed** that I should not touch his things.
ⓝ exclamation 외침, 절규

0587 ■□□

scarlet
[ská:rlit]

주홍색

ⓝ a bright-red color inclining toward orange
ⓔ.ⓖ. She was so embarrassed her face turned **scarlet**.

0588 ■■□

villain
[vílən]

악인, 악역

ⓝ a cruelly malicious person who is involved in or devoted to wicked-ness or crime
ⓔ.ⓖ. He is not a hero nor a **villain**, just a normal person.
ⓐ villainous 극악무도한, 악한

0589 ■□□

ultimate
[ʌ́ltəmət]

최후의, 최종의, 궁극적인

ⓐ last; furthest or farthest; ending a process or series
ⓢⓨⓝ last, final, eventual
ⓔ.ⓖ. Sudan is still far from the **ultimate** goal of returning home the millions of people displaced by war.
ⓝ ultimatum 최후의 말, 최후통첩

0590 ■■□

typography
[taipágrəfi]

활판술, 조판
ⓝ the art or process of printing with type
ⓔ.ⓖ. The hideous **typography** made the newspaper impossible to read.
ⓐ typographic 인쇄상의, 인쇄술의

0591 ■■□

exhale
[ekshéil]

내쉬다, 발산하다, 방출하다
ⓥ to emit breath or vapor
ⓢⓨⓝ breathe out
ⓔ.ⓖ. Remember to **exhale** as you pick up something heavy.
ⓝ exhalation 숨을 내쉼, 발산, 방출

0592 ■■□

facet
[fǽsit]

한 면, 상, 국면
ⓝ a single part or aspect of something
ⓢⓨⓝ side, aspect, phase
ⓔ.ⓖ. They carefully examined every **facet** of the diamond.

0593 ■■□

vegetation
[vèdʒətéiʃən]

초목, 식물
ⓝ all the plants or plant life of a place, taken as a whole
ⓢⓨⓝ plant
ⓔ.ⓖ. **Vegetation** becomes sparse higher up the mountains.
ⓝ vegetable 채소

0594 ■■□

instantaneous
[ìnstəntéiniəs]

즉시의, 순간의, 즉시 일어나는
ⓐ occurring, done, or completed in an instant
ⓢⓨⓝ immediate, sudden, abrupt
ⓔ.ⓖ. Customers tend to make **instantaneous** decisions about a company and its products or services.
ⓝ instant 즉시, 찰나, 순간

0595 ■□□

likelihood
[láiklihùd]

가능성, 가망
ⓝ the state of being likely or probable
ⓢⓨⓝ probability
ⓔ.ⓖ. There is a strong **likelihood** of his being elected.
ⓝ unlikelihood 사실인 것 같지 않음

DAY
10

0596 ■■■

precept
[prí:sept]

교훈, 권고, 격언
ⓝ a commandment or direction given as a rule of action or conduct
ⓢⓨⓝ instruction, edification, maxim
ⓔ.ⓖ. One of the hunting clubs **precepts** was to never hunt past the government limits.
ⓐ perceptive 교훈의

0597 ■□□

civilize
[sívəlàiz]

개화하다, 문명화하다, 교화하다
ⓥ to bring out of a savage, uneducated, or rude state; make civil; elevate in social and private life
ⓢⓨⓝ enlighten, refine
ⓔ.ⓖ. The volunteers tried to **civilize** the tribe's water system.
ⓝ civilization 문명(국), 문명인

0598 ■□□

twig
[twíg]

작은 가지, 잔가지
ⓝ a slender shoot of a tree or other plant
ⓢⓨⓝ branch
ⓔ.ⓖ. Birds build their nests out of **twigs**.
ⓐ twiggy 잔가지의, 연약한

0599 ■□□

fare
[féər]

운임, 통행료, 요금
ⓝ the price of conveyance or passage in a bus, train, airplane, or other vehicle
ⓢⓨⓝ price, charge, fee
ⓔ.ⓖ. The **fare** reduction was well received by the average bus rider.

0600 ■□□

utensil
[ju:ténsəl]

기구, 용구
ⓝ any of the instruments or vessels commonly used in a kitchen, dairy, etc.
ⓢⓨⓝ tool, implement, instrument, appliance
ⓔ.ⓖ. Her favorite kitchen **utensil** was the clean white cutting board.

MEMO

Day
11

giggle	☐☐☐	disorder	☐☐☐
censor	☐☐☐	renew	☐☐☐
peripheral	☐☐☐	glitter	☐☐☐
craft	☐☐☐	strive	☐☐☐
intermittent	☐☐☐	gratify	☐☐☐
autopsy	☐☐☐	enthusiastic	☐☐☐
underlie	☐☐☐	goad	☐☐☐
grace	☐☐☐	yawn	☐☐☐
precise	☐☐☐	annoy	☐☐☐
wizard	☐☐☐	wary	☐☐☐
affix	☐☐☐	conscious	☐☐☐
treason	☐☐☐	hoist	☐☐☐
foe	☐☐☐	equitable	☐☐☐
weary	☐☐☐	ventriloquism	☐☐☐
fragrance	☐☐☐	grin	☐☐☐
vast	☐☐☐	legal	☐☐☐
synthesis	☐☐☐	idiosyncrasy	☐☐☐
sedentary	☐☐☐	split	☐☐☐
paradox	☐☐☐	enroll	☐☐☐
contour	☐☐☐	verbal	☐☐☐
revoke	☐☐☐	sculpture	☐☐☐
malleable	☐☐☐	hairdo	☐☐☐
plausible	☐☐☐	discursive	☐☐☐
allocate	☐☐☐	illuminate	☐☐☐
utterance	☐☐☐	hog	☐☐☐
immense	☐☐☐	grotesque	☐☐☐
gloom	☐☐☐	interlocutor	☐☐☐
swamp	☐☐☐	dwarf	☐☐☐
appeal	☐☐☐	impact	☐☐☐
susceptible	☐☐☐	seal	☐☐☐

0601 ■□□

giggle
[gígəl]

낄낄거리다

ⓥ laugh lightly in a nervous, affected, or silly manner
(syn) titter
(e.g.) She started to **giggle** quietly to herself.

0602 ■■□

censor
[sénsər]

검열하다, 검열하여 삭제하다; 검열관

ⓥ examine (a book, movie, etc.) officially and suppress unacceptable parts of it
(syn) blue-pencil, bowdlerize
(e.g.) Yet the world's biggest **censor** has been unable to keep a lid on what happened.
ⓐ censorial

0603 ■■□

peripheral
[pərífərəl]

주변부의; 그다지 중요치 않은(to)

ⓐ relating to or situated on the edge or periphery of something
(syn) outer, circumferential
(e.g.) We are debating a **peripheral** aspect of the Bill.
ⓐ peripherally

0604 ■□□

craft
[kræft]

(수)공예

ⓝ an art, trade, or occupation requiring special skill, especially manual skill
(e.g.) Paper **craft** can also be a good hobby.
ⓐ crafty

0605 ■■■

intermittent
[intərmítənt]

때때로 중단되는, 간헐적인

ⓐ happens occasionally rather than continuously
(syn) sporadic, patchy
(opp) steady
(e.g.) Of course there have been **intermittent** crises.

0606 ■■□

autopsy
[ɔ́ːtɑpsi]

(사체) 부검, 검시

ⓝ an examination to discover the cause of death or the extent of disease

syn post-mortem, necropsy

e.g. The **autopsy** report gave the cause of death as poisoning.

0607 ■□□

underlie
[ʌ́ndərlaɪ]

~의 기초가 되다

ⓥ If something underlies a feeling or situation, it is the cause or basis of it.

e.g. All those issues **underlie** a problem.

0608 ■□□

grace
[greis]

~을 빛내다, 장식하다

ⓥ (of a person or thing) be an attractive presence in or on

syn adorn, decorate

e.g. He went to the beautiful old Welsh dresser that **graced** this homely room.

0609 ■■□

precise
[prisáis]

정확한, 정밀한, 명확한

ⓐ definitely or strictly stated, defined, or fixed

syn exact, correct, accurate

e.g. The plants are getting water and nutrients in **precise** amounts.

ⓝ precision 정확, 정밀, 꼼꼼함

0610 ■□□

wizard
[wízərd]

마법사, 요술쟁이

ⓝ a person who practices magic

syn magician, sorcerer, juggler

e.g. The **wizard** put a spell on the princess.

ⓝ wizardry 마법, 마술

0611 ■■□

affix
[əfíks]

첨부하다, 붙이다
ⓥ to fasten, join, or attach
ⓢⓨⓝ append, attach
ⓔ.ⓖ. Unsolicited material will not be returned unless it is accompanied by an envelope with the proper postage **affixed**.
ⓝ affixation 첨부, 부가, 덧붙임

0612 ■■■

treason
[trí:zn]

반역(죄), 배신
ⓝ the offense of acting to overthrow one's government or to harm or kill its sovereign
ⓔ.ⓖ. He was condemned of **treason** after giving the enemy secrets.
ⓐ treasonable 반역의, 배신의

0613 ■■□

foe
[fóu]

적, 원수
ⓝ a person who feels enmity, hatred, or malice toward another
ⓢⓨⓝ enemy, adversary
ⓔ.ⓖ. The young had as many friends as **foes**.

0614 ■■□

weary
[wíəri]

피곤한, 지친, 기진맥진한
ⓐ physically or mentally exhausted by hard work, exertion, strain, etc.
ⓢⓨⓝ fatigued, tired, exhausted
ⓔ.ⓖ. As the second half of the game began, the players looked determined but **weary**.
ⓐ weariless 피곤을 모르는, 지칠 줄 모르는

0615 ■□□

fragrance
[fréigrəns]

향기
ⓝ the quality of being fragrant; a sweet or pleasing scent
ⓢⓨⓝ aroma, scent, redolence
ⓔ.ⓖ. Roses have a **fragrance** enjoyed by many young lovers.
ⓐ fragrant 향기로운, 향긋한

0616 ■□□

vast
[væst, vá:st]

광대한, 거대한, 광활한
ⓐ of very great area or extent
ⓢⓨⓝ huge, immense, gigantic
ⓔ.ⓖ. We feel awed when we stand at the edge of **vast** canyons.
ⓝ vastness 광활함

0617 ■■□

synthesis
[sínθəsis]

종합, 통합, 합성
ⓝ the combining of the constituent elements of separate material or abstract entities into a single or unified entity
ⓢⓨⓝ composition, combination, unification
ⓔ.ⓖ. Creating or transforming electronic sounds became easy with the **synthesis** offered by computer software.
ⓐ synthetic 종합의, 통합적인, 합성의

0618 ■■■

sedentary
[sednteri]

(일 · 활동 등이) 주로 앉아서 하는
ⓐ (of work, activities, etc.) in which you spend a lot of time sitting down
ⓔ.ⓖ. a **sedentary** job/occupation/lifestyle
ⓝ sedentariness
ⓐⓓ sedentarily

0619 ■■□

paradox
[pærədɑ:ks]

역설적인 사람(것/상황)
ⓝ a person, thing or situation that has two opposite features and therefore seems strange
ⓢⓨⓝ contradiction, puzzle, anomaly, enigma, oddity
ⓔ.ⓖ. He was a **paradox** — a loner who loved to chat to strangers.
ⓝ paradoxer, paradoxist
ⓐ paradoxical   ⓐⓓ paradoxically

0620 ■■■

contour
[|kɑ:ntʊr]

(사물의) 윤곽; 등고선(contour line)
ⓝ the outer edges of something; the outline of its shape or form; (also contour line) a line on a map that joins points that are the same height above sea level
ⓔ.ⓖ. 1. The road follows the natural **contours** of the coastline.
2. a **contour** map (= a map that includes these lines)

0621 ■■■

revoke
[rɪvóʊk]

(격식) 폐지(철회 · 취소)하다
ⓥ to officially cancel something so that it is no longer valid
(e.g.) Your licence may be **revoked** at any time.
ⓝ revoker
(ad) revokingly

0622 ■■■

malleable
[mǽliəbl]

(사람들 · 사상 등이) 영향을 잘 받는, 잘 변하는
ⓐ (specialist) (of metal, etc.) that can be hit or pressed into different
　　shapes easily without breaking or cracking
ⓝ malleableness, malleability
(ad) malleably

0623 ■■□

plausible
[plɔ́:zəbl]

(변명 · 해명 · 설명이) 타당한 것 같은, 이치에 맞는, 그럴듯한
ⓐ (of an excuse or explanation) reasonable and likely to be true
(syn) believable, possible, likely
(e.g.) Her story sounded perfectly **plausible**.
ⓝ plausibleness, plausibility
(ad) plausibly

0624 ■■■

allocate
[ǽləkeɪt]

(특정 목적을 위해 공식적으로) 할당하다
ⓥ to give something officially to somebody/something for a particular
　　purpose
(syn) assign, grant, distribute
(e.g.) 1. A large sum has been **allocated** for buying new books for
　　　　 the library.
　　　 2. They intend to **allocate** more places to mature students
　　　　 this year.
ⓝ allocator
ⓐ allocatable

0625 ■■□

utterance
[ʌ́tərəns]

발언, 말씨, 어조
ⓝ manner of speaking; power of speaking
(e.g.) His last **utterance** was free of any fear of dying.
ⓥ utter 말하다, 발화하다

0626 ■□□

immense
[iméns]

거대한, 막대한, 광대한
ⓐ vast; huge; very great
ⓢⓨⓝ gigantic, enormous, vast, huge
ⓔ.ⓖ. An **immense** building stood before our eyes.
ⓝ immensity 광대, 거대, 막대

0627 ■□□

gloom
[glúːm]

어두침침함, 암흑, 우울, 의기소침
ⓝ total or partial darkness
ⓢⓨⓝ darkness, dimness, depression, blues
ⓔ.ⓖ. He faced his parents with a deep sense of **gloom**.
ⓐ gloomy 우울한

0628 ■□□

swamp
[swámp]

늪, 수렁
ⓝ a tract of wet, spongy land, often having a growth of certain types
of trees and other vegetation, but unfit for cultivation
ⓢⓨⓝ bog, wetland, marsh
ⓔ.ⓖ. Many people got sick in the **swamp**, because of all the
mosquitoes.
ⓐ swampy 늪 같은, 습지가 있는, 질퍽한

0629 ■□□

appeal
[əpíːl]

애원하다, 간청하다, 빌다
ⓥ to ask for aid, support, mercy, sympathy, or the like
ⓢⓨⓝ request
ⓔ.ⓖ. They **appealed** to him for more support.
ⓐ appealing 애원적인, 사람의 마음에 호소하는

0630 ■■□

susceptible
[səséptəbl]

여지 있는, 받아들이는, 허락하는
ⓐ admitting or capable of some specified treatment
ⓢⓨⓝ acceptable, admittable
ⓔ.ⓖ. Those math problems are most **susceptible** to algebraic
solving.
ⓝ susceptibility 느끼기 쉬움, 민감, 감수성

0631 ■□□

disorder
[disɔ́ːrdər]

무질서, 혼란
ⓝ lack of order or regular arrangement
ⓢⓨⓝ confusion, chaos, mess
ⓔⓖ Your house is in utter **disorder**.
ⓐ disordered 혼란된, 난잡한

0632 ■□□

renew
[rinjúː]

새롭게 하다, 다시 시작하다, 갱신하다
ⓥ to begin or take up again, as an acquaintance, a conversation, etc.
ⓢⓨⓝ resume, renovate, restart
ⓔⓖ The ID card must be **renewed** every two years.
ⓝ renewal 새롭게 하기(되기), 부흥, 재생

0633 ■■□

glitter
[glítər]

반짝반짝 빛나다, 반짝이다
ⓥ to reflect light with a brilliant, sparkling luster; sparkle with reflected light
ⓢⓨⓝ shine, glint, glister
ⓔⓖ Be careful, because all that **glitters** is not gold.
ⓐ glittering 반짝이는, 빛나는

0634 ■■□

strive
[stráiv]

노력하다, 힘쓰다, 애쓰다
ⓥ to exert oneself vigorously; try hard
ⓢⓨⓝ attempt, endeavor, exert
ⓔⓖ Those companies are known for **striving** to out perform their competitors at any cost.
ⓝ strife 투쟁, 다툼

0635 ■■■

gratify
[grǽtəfài]

만족시키다, 기쁘게 하다
ⓥ to give pleasure to (a person or persons) by satisfying desires or humoring inclinations or feelings
ⓢⓨⓝ please
ⓔⓖ Her answers served to **gratify** my interest in the course.
ⓝ gratitude 감사하는 마음, 사의

0636 ■■□

enthusiastic
[inθùːziǽstik]

열광적인, 열중한
ⓐ full of or characterized by enthusiasm
ⓢⓨⓝ fervent, zealous, ardent
ⓔ.ⓖ. He seems very **enthusiastic** about his role in the film.
ⓝ enthusiasm 열광, 열중

0637 ■■□

goad
[góud]

막대기로 찌르다(몰다), 자극하다, 격려하다, 선동하다
ⓥ to prick or drive with, or as if with a stick
ⓢⓨⓝ prod, incite, provoke, inspire, trigger
ⓔ.ⓖ. He was feeling very lazy but his friends managed to **goad** him into travelling with them.

0638 ■□□

yawn
[jɔ́ːn]

하품하다
ⓥ to open the mouth somewhat involuntarily with a prolonged, deep inhalation and sighing or heavy exhalation, as from drowsiness or boredom
ⓔ.ⓖ. It is bad manners to **yawn** in a conversation.
ⓐ yawnful 하품 나게 하는, 지루하게 하는

0639 ■□□

annoy
[ənɔ́i]

괴롭히다, 짜증나게 하다
ⓥ to disturb or bother (a person) in a way that displeases, troubles, or slightly irritates
ⓢⓨⓝ aggravate, bother, bug
ⓔ.ⓖ. It **annoys** me that she never listens to us.
ⓝ annoyance 괴롭힘

0640 ■■□

wary
[wéəri]

조심성 있는, 신중한
ⓐ being on one's guard against danger
ⓢⓨⓝ watchful, alert, vigilant, guarded, prudent
ⓔ.ⓖ. Corporate sponsors are **wary** of political movements.
ⓐ unwary 조심성 없는, 경솔한

0641 ■□□

conscious
[kɑ́nʃəs]

의식(자각)하고 있는, 깨닫고 있는
ⓐ aware of one's own existence, sensations, thoughts, surroundings, etc.
ⓢⓨⓝ aware, alert, keen
ⓔ.ⓖ. We suddenly became **conscious** of a sharp increase in the temperature.
ⓝ consciousness 의식, 자각

0642 ■■□

hoist
[hɔ́ist]

끌어 올리다, 높이 달다
ⓥ to raise or lift, esp. by some mechanical appliance
ⓢⓨⓝ lift, raise, elevate
ⓔ.ⓖ. The refrigerator is **hoisted** on to a truck.
ⓝ hoistway 승강로

0643 ■■■

equitable
[ékwətəbl]

공평한, 정당한
ⓐ characterized by equity or fairness
ⓢⓨⓝ just, right, fair, reasonable
ⓔ.ⓖ. You have to hand down an **equitable** judgment to please the public.
ⓝ equity 공평, 공정, 정당

0644 ■■■

ventriloquism
[ventríləkwìzm]

복화술
ⓝ the art or practice of speaking, with little or no lip movement, in such a manner that the voice does not appear to come from the speaker but from another source, as from a wooden dummy
ⓔ.ⓖ. He was so talented with his **ventriloquism** that he could even drink water while making the dummy "speak".
ⓥ ventriloquize 복화술로 말하다

0645 ■□□

grin
[grín]

이를 드러내고 싱긋 웃다
ⓥ to smile broadly, esp. as an indication of pleasure, amusement
ⓢⓨⓝ smile
ⓔ.ⓖ. There's nothing you can do but **grin** and bear it.

0646 ■□□

legal
[líːgəl]

법률의, 법률에 관한
ⓐ permitted by law
ⓢⓨⓝ lawful, eligible, justifiable, legitimate
ⓔ.ⓖ. After several years of **legal** proceedings judgment has been awarded in favor of the plaintiff.
ⓐ illegal 불법의, 위법의

0647 ■■■

idiosyncrasy
[idiəsíŋkrəsi]

(개인의) 특징, 특성, 개성
ⓝ a characteristic, habit, mannerism, or the like, that is peculiar to an individual
ⓢⓨⓝ peculiarity, personality
ⓔ.ⓖ. The secret to her success is detailing the little **idiosyncrasies** about the character.
ⓐ idiosyncratic (개인에게) 특유한, 기이한

0648 ■■□

split
[splít]

쪼개다, 나누다, 분리시키다
ⓥ to divide or separate from end to end or into layers
ⓢⓨⓝ divide, separate, part, cleave
ⓔ.ⓖ. Let's **split** the cost between us.
ⓝ split-up 분리, 분열, 분해

0649 ■□□

enroll
[inróul]

등록하다, 입학(입회)시키다
ⓥ to write the name of (a person) in a roll or register; place upon a list
ⓢⓨⓝ register, enlist
ⓔ.ⓖ. Fall is the time to **enroll** the new students.
ⓝ enrollment 등록, 입학

0650 ■■□

verbal
[vɔ́ːrbəl]

말의, 말에 관한, 구두의
ⓐ of or pertaining to words
ⓢⓨⓝ oral, spoken, unwritten
ⓔ.ⓖ. His ex-wife accused him of **verbal** abuse and other cruelties.
ⓥ verbalize 말로 나타내다, 언어화하다

0651 ■□□

sculpture
[skʌ́lptʃər]

조각, 조각술

ⓝ the art of carving, modeling, welding, or otherwise producing figurative or abstract works of art in three dimensions, as in relief, intaglio, or in the round

ⓔⓖ His **sculptures** are famous for their perspective.

ⓐ sculptural 조각의, 조각술의

0652 ■□□

hairdo
[héərdùː]

머리 손질, 머리 모양, 헤어스타일

ⓝ the style in which a person's hair is cut, arranged, and worn; coiffure

ⓔⓖ I'd like to change my **hairdo**.

ⓐ hairy 털이 많은, 털투성이의

0653 ■■■

discursive
[diskə́ːrsiv]

광범위한, 산만한, 종잡을 수 없는

ⓐ passing aimlessly from one subject to another

ⓢⓨⓝ digressive, rambling

ⓔⓖ The lecture notes were not in order, so soon the lesson became **discursive** and hard to follow.

ⓝ discursiveness 산만함, 두서없음

0654 ■■□

illuminate
[ilúːmənèit]

조명하다, 비추다

ⓥ to supply or brighten with light; light up

ⓢⓨⓝ illumine, lighten, enlighten, brighten

ⓔⓖ The lanterns **illuminated** the path so we were able to find our way home in the dark.

ⓝ illumination 조명, 조도

0655 ■□□

hog
[hɔ́ːg, hág]

돼지, 탐욕스럽거나 야비한 사람, 이기적인 사람

ⓝ selfish, gluttonous, or filthy person

ⓔⓖ He eats like a **hog**, shoveling food into his mouth.

ⓐ hoggish 돼지 같은, 탐욕스러운, 이기적인

0656 ■□□

grotesque
[groutésk]

괴상한, 괴기한
ⓐ odd or unnatural in shape, appearance, or character
ⓢⓨⓝ ugly, absurd, bizarre
ⓔ.ⓖ. The cake looked **grotesque** after it burned in the oven.
ⓝ grotesquerie 그로테스크한 것(성격, 언동)

0657 ■■■

interlocutor
[ìntərlákjutər]

대담자, 질문자
ⓝ a person who takes part in a conversation or dialogue
ⓢⓨⓝ speaker
ⓔ.ⓖ. If there is only two **interlocutors**, it is important for both to look at each other in eyes.
ⓐ interlocutory 대화체의, 문답체의

0658 ■□□

dwarf
[dwɔ́:rf]

난쟁이
ⓝ a person of abnormally small stature owing to a pathological condition
ⓢⓨⓝ pygmy
ⓔ.ⓖ. Many **dwarves** achieve success, showing their size doesn't interrupt their lives.
ⓐ dwarfish 난쟁이 같은, 유난히 작은

0659 ■■□

impact
[ímpækt]

충돌, 격돌
ⓝ the striking of one thing against another; forceful contact
ⓢⓨⓝ collision, clash
ⓔ.ⓖ. The **impact** of the collision tossed the motorcycle over the fence.
ⓐ impacted 충돌된, 충격 받은

0660 ■■□

seal
[síːl]

날인하다, 합의를 보다
ⓥ to affix a seal to in authorization, testimony, etc.; to assure, confirm, or bind with or as if with a seal
ⓢⓨⓝ assure, confirm, settle
ⓔ.ⓖ. They **sealed** the bargain with a hand shake.
ⓐ sealed 봉인을 한

Day

12

script	□□□	correspond	□□□
print	□□□	apt	□□□
engrave	□□□	censure	□□□
lithography	□□□	stubborn	□□□
incision	□□□	moral	□□□
gnarled	□□□	alert	□□□
din	□□□	scope	□□□
intent	□□□	exceed	□□□
tenet	□□□	connotation	□□□
unintelligible	□□□	jag	□□□
reconfigure	□□□	ennoble	□□□
epigram	□□□	rainfall	□□□
innumerable	□□□	lisp	□□□
extend	□□□	illegitimate	□□□
gruel	□□□	semantic	□□□
statement	□□□	dismiss	□□□
dispute	□□□	mediate	□□□
associate	□□□	lexical	□□□
intervene	□□□	eventual	□□□
singular	□□□	microscopic	□□□
conspicuous	□□□	span	□□□
supplant	□□□	extraordinary	□□□
emanate	□□□	dignity	□□□
entail	□□□	maturity	□□□
ravage	□□□	chronic	□□□
elucidate	□□□	immerse	□□□
commission	□□□	midst	□□□
manifestation	□□□	ophthalmology	□□□
elevate	□□□	inject	□□□
reluctant	□□□	comprise	□□□

0661 ■□□

script
[skript]

손으로 쓴 글, 대본, 유언장 초안; 원본, 정본
ⓝ the letters or characters used in writing by hand
ⓔ.ⓖ. This **script** is nearly flawless in structure and story.

0662 ■□□

print
[print]

판화, 인쇄물
ⓝ a picture or design printed from a block or plate or copied from a painting by photography
ⓢⓨⓝ replica, duplicate
ⓔ.ⓖ. This **print** reproduces well.

0663 ■■□

engrave
[engréiv]

조각하다, 명심하다
ⓥ cut or carve (a text or design) on the surface of a hard object
ⓢⓨⓝ carve, etch
ⓔ.ⓖ. My name is **engraved** on the back of the watch.

0664 ■■□

lithography
[liθágrəfi]

석판인쇄
ⓝ a method of printing in which a piece of stone or metal is specially treated so that ink sticks to some parts of it and not to others.
ⓔ.ⓖ. **Lithography** was invented in 1796.

0665 ■■■

incision
[insíʒən]

(특히 외과 수술 중의) 절개
ⓝ sharp cut made in something, for example by a surgeon who is operating on a patient
ⓔ.ⓖ. We were just about to start the "y" **incision**.

0666 ■■□

gnarled
[närld]

울퉁불퉁하고 비틀린
ⓐ knobbly, rough, and twisted, especially with age
ⓢⓨⓝ lumpy, bumpy
ⓔ.ⓖ. He must be awfully old, for his face is **gnarled** and twisted like the bark of a tree.

0667 ■■□

din
[din]

소음

ⓝ very loud and unpleasant noise
ⓔ.ⓖ. There was such a **din** that I didn't hear the phone.

0668 ■□□

intent
[intént]

의도

ⓝ intention or purpose
ⓢⓨⓝ object
ⓔ.ⓖ. The **intent** is to ease a lot of regulations on election campaigning.
ⓐⓓ intently

0669 ■□□

tenet
[ténət]

교리, 주의, 원리

ⓝ a principle or belief, especially one of the main principles of a religion or philosophy
ⓢⓨⓝ principle, creed, doctrine
ⓔ.ⓖ. Nonviolence was the fundamental **tenet** of Gandhi's philosophy.

0670 ■□□

unintelligible
[ʌnɪntelɪdʒɪbəl]

이해하기 어려운; 난해한

ⓐ impossible to understand
ⓢⓨⓝ incomprehensible, incoherent, inarticulate
ⓔ.ⓖ. I did my best to join in, but the conversation was largely **unintelligible**.

0671 ■□□

reconfigure
[riːkənfíɡjər]

변경하다

ⓥ to change the shape or formation of
ⓔ.ⓖ. Disable it before installation, then **reconfigure** it after installation if it is required.

0672 ■■■

epigram
[épəɡræm]

경구, 풍자시

ⓝ any witty, ingenious, or pointed saying tersely expressed
ⓢⓨⓝ aphorism
ⓔ.ⓖ. Oscar Wilde had a genius for **epigram**.
ⓐ epigrammatic 경구적인, 풍자시의

0673 ■■□

innumerable
[injúːmərəbl]

셀 수 없이 많은, 무수한

ⓐ very numerous
ⓢⓨⓝ countless, immeasurable, inestimable
ⓔ.ⓖ. Drugs have been the cause of **innumerable** deaths, especially in teenagers.
ⓐ numerable 셀 수 있는, 계산할 수 있는

0674 ■■□

extend
[iksténd]

연장하다, 늘이다

ⓥ to stretch out in various or all directions; spread out in area
ⓢⓨⓝ expand, outstretch
ⓔ.ⓖ. She will **extend** her hotel stay because she's enjoying it there.
ⓝ extension 확장   ⓐ extensive 넓은, 광대한

0675 ■■□

gruel
[grúːəl]

오트밀 죽

ⓝ a light, usually thin, cooked cereal made by boiling meal, esp. oatmeal, in water or milk
ⓔ.ⓖ. She is feeding a thin rice **gruel** to her sick husband.

0676 ■□□

statement
[stéitmənt]

말함, 진술문

ⓝ a single sentence or assertion
ⓢⓨⓝ instruction, affirmation
ⓔ.ⓖ. Can you explain your last **statement** more?
ⓥ state 진술하다, 성명하다, 말하다

0677 ■■□

dispute
[dispjúːt]

논쟁하다, 논의하다

ⓥ to engage in argument
ⓢⓨⓝ discuss, debate
ⓔ.ⓖ. They **disputed** with him about world peace.
ⓝ disputation 논쟁, 토론

0678 ■■□

associate
[əsóuʃièit]

연상하다, 연관 짓다

ⓥ to connect or bring into relation, as thought, feeling, memory, etc.
ⓢⓨⓝ tie in, relate, link, colligate, connect
ⓔ.ⓖ. Don't **associate** me with that incident.
ⓝ association 연상

0679 ■■□

intervene
[ìntərvíːn]

사이에 들다, 끼다, 개재하다
ⓥ to come between disputing people, groups, etc.
ⓢⓨⓝ intercede, mediate, arbitrate
ⓔ.ⓖ. The United Nations is aggressively **intervening** in foreign conflicts.
ⓝ intervention 사이에 듦, 개재, 조정, 중재

0680 ■□□

singular
[síŋgjulər]

남다른, 특이한, 비범한, 둘도 없는
ⓐ extraordinary; remarkable; exceptional
ⓢⓨⓝ extraordinary, remarkable, exceptional
ⓔ.ⓖ. He was a **singular** man, you could find no other like him in the whole of Europe.
ⓝ singularity 특이, 희한

0681 ■■■

conspicuous
[kənspíkjuəs]

눈에 잘 띄는, 튀는; 뚜렷한
ⓐ easy to see or notice; likely to attract attention
ⓢⓨⓝ obvious, clear, patent
ⓔ.ⓖ. Mary's red hair always made her **conspicuous** at school.
ⓝ conspicuousness, conspicuity
ⓐⓓ conspicuously

0682 ■■■

supplant
[səplǽnt]

(격식) (특히 낡거나 구식이 된 것을) 대신(대체)하다
ⓥ (formal) to take the place of somebody/something (especially somebody/something older or less modern)
ⓔ.ⓖ. Their work has been largely **supplanted** by the use of a computer program that fulfils the same function.
ⓝ supplanter, supplantation

0683 ■■■

emanate
[émənèit]

(격식) (어떤 느낌·특질 등을) 발하다(내뿜다)
ⓥ (formal) to produce or show something
ⓔ.ⓖ. He **emanates** power and confidence.
ⓝ emanator
ⓐ emanative, emanatory

0684 ■■■

entail
[ɪnteɪl]

수반하다
ⓥ to involve something that cannot be avoided
ⓢⓨⓝ involve, require, produce
ⓔ.ⓖ. The job **entails** a lot of hard work.
ⓝ entailment, entailer

0685 ■■■

ravage
[rævɪdʒ]

(주로 수동태로) 황폐(피폐)하게 만들다, 유린(파괴)하다
ⓥ (usually passive) ravage something to damage something badly
ⓢⓨⓝ destroy, ruin, devastate
ⓔ.ⓖ. a recession that has **ravaged** the textile industry
ⓝ ravagement, ravager

0686 ■■■

elucidate
[ilu:sɪdeɪt]

(격식) (더 자세히) 설명하다
ⓥ to make something clearer by explaining it more fully
ⓢⓨⓝ explain, illustrate, interpret
ⓔ.ⓖ. 1. He **elucidated** a point of grammar.
　　　2. I should be grateful if the Minister would **elucidate** that.
ⓝ elucidation, elucidator
ⓐ elucidative, elucidatory

0687 ■■□

commission
[kəmɪʃn]

ⓝ (보통 정부의 위임을 받은) 위원회(위원단); 수수료, 주문위탁
ⓥ 의뢰(주문)하다, 임관하다
ⓝ an official group of people who have been given responsibility to control something, or to find out about something, usually for the government; an amount of money that is paid to somebody for selling goods and which increases with the amount of goods that are sold
ⓥ give an order for or authorize the production of (something such as a building, piece of equipment, or work of art)
ⓢⓨⓝ ⓝ endeavor ⓥ bespeak
ⓔ.ⓖ. 1. The government has set up a **commission** of inquiry into the disturbances at the prison.
　　　2. In this job you work on **commission** (= are paid according to the amount you sell).
ⓥ commit
ⓐ commissional, commissionary

0688 ■■■

manifestation (어떤 것이 존재하거나 일어나고 있음을 보여주는) 징후(표명)
[mǽnɪfesteɪʃn]
　　　ⓝ an event, action or thing that is a sign that something exists or is
　　　happening; the act of appearing as a sign that something exists or is
　　　happening
　　　ⓢⓨⓝ sign, symptom, indication
　　　ⓔ.ⓖ. The riots are a clear **manifestation** of the people's discontent.
　　　ⓥ manifest
　　　ⓐ manifestative, manifestational

0689 ■■□

elevate 올리다, 들어올리다, 높이다
[élǝvèit]
　　　ⓥ to move or raise to a higher place or position; lift up
　　　ⓢⓨⓝ raise, uplift, uprear, heighten
　　　ⓔ.ⓖ. It took a special hydraulic lift to **elevate** the gigantic granite
　　　blocks into place.
　　　ⓝ elevation 높이, 고도, 해발

0690 ■■□

reluctant 마음 내키지 않는, 마지못해 하는
[rilʎktǝnt]
　　　ⓐ unwilling to do it and hesitate before doing it, or do it slowly and
　　　without enthusiasm
　　　ⓢⓨⓝ averse, disinclined, unwilling
　　　ⓔ.ⓖ. She was **reluctant** to admit the truth.
　　　ⓝ reluctance 싫음, 마지못해 함, 꺼림

0691 ■■□

correspond 일치하다, 부합하다, 조화하다
[kɔ́:rǝspánd]
　　　ⓥ to be in agreement or conformity
　　　ⓢⓨⓝ fit, harmonize, conform
　　　ⓔ.ⓖ. Your actions do not **correspond** with your words.
　　　ⓝ correspondence 일치, 조화, 상응

0692 ■■□

apt 적절한, 적당한, 경향이 있는
[ǽpt]
　　　ⓐ inclined; disposed; prone
　　　ⓢⓨⓝ proper, befitting
　　　ⓔ.ⓖ. Ambition is **apt** to carry a person to destruction.
　　　ⓝ aptitude 경향, 습성, 기질

0693 ■■□

censure
[sénʃər]

비난, 책망, 견책

ⓝ strong or vehement expression of disapproval

ⓢⓨⓝ condemnation, criticism, denunciation

ⓔⓖ The newspapers were unanimous in their **censure** of the tax proposal.

ⓝ censurer 비난하는 사람

0694 ■□□

stubborn
[stʌ́bərn]

완고한, 고집 센

ⓐ unreasonably obstinate; obstinately unmoving

ⓢⓨⓝ obstinate, dogged, persistent, incompliant

ⓔⓖ He was **stubborn** in all things, and never surrendered.

ⓝ stubbornness 완고, 완강

0695 ■□□

moral
[mɔ́:rəl]

도덕상의, 윤리의

ⓐ concerned with the principles or rules of right conduct or the distinction between right and wrong

ⓢⓨⓝ ethical, righteous, virtuous

ⓔⓖ The primary object goal is to cultivate your **moral** character.

ⓝ morale 사기, 의욕, 도덕, 도의

0696 ■■□

alert
[ələ́:rt]

민감한, 민첩한, 빈틈없는

ⓐ fully aware and attentive

ⓢⓨⓝ keen, wide-awake

ⓔⓖ He was very **alert** in answering.

ⓝ alertness 민첩함, 민감함

0697 ■□□

scope
[skóup]

범위, 영역, 시야

ⓝ extent or range of view, outlook, application, operation, effectiveness, etc.

ⓢⓨⓝ domain, range

ⓔⓖ Such subjects are not within the **scope** of this text.

ⓝ telescope 망원경

DAY
12

0698 ■■□

exceed
[iksíːd]

넘다, 능가하다
(v) to go beyond in quantity, degree, rate, etc.
(syn) surpass, excel, outdo
(e.g.) The task **exceeds** his ability.
(a) exceeding 엄청난, 대단한, 굉장한

0699 ■■■

connotation
[kànətéiʃən]

내포, 함축(된 의미)
(n) the associated or secondary meaning of a word or expression in
addition to its explicit or primary meaning
(syn) implication, nuance
(e.g.) A possible **connotation** of 'home' is 'a place of warmth, comfort,
and affection.'
(n) denotation 명시적 의미

0700 ■□□

jag
[dʒǽg]

뾰족한 끝
(n) a sharp projection on an edge or surface
(e.g.) My sweater caught on a **jag** where the door had broke.
(a) jagged 뾰족한, 들쭉날쭉한

0701 ■■□

ennoble
[inóubl]

고상하게 하다, 기품 있게 하다
(v) to elevate in degree, excellence, or respect
(syn) dignify, exalt
(e.g.) What truly **ennobled** him was his dedication to helping others.
(n) ennoblement 고상, 기품

0702 ■□□

rainfall
[réinfɔːl]

강우, 강우량, 강수량
(n) a fall or shower of rain
(e.g.) This year was much **rainfall**, so the crops should grow well.

0703 ■■□

lisp
[lísp]

혀 짧은 발음
(n) a speech defect consisting in pronouncing s and z like or nearly
like the th-sounds of thin and this, respectively
(e.g.) It is difficult to understand her because of the **lisp**.
(a) lisping 혀가 잘 돌지 않는

0704 ■■□

illegitimate
[ìlidʒítəmət]

위법의, 불법의
ⓐ not legitimate; not sanctioned by law or custom
ⓢⓨⓝ illicit, lawless, illegal
ⓔ.ⓖ. He is an **illegitimate** child, no one knows who the father is.
ⓐ legitimate 합법의, 법적인

0705 ■■■

semantic
[simǽntik]

의미의, 의미론의
ⓐ arising from the different meanings of words or other symbols
ⓔ.ⓖ. The **semantic** history of the word "black" is very political in American discussions.
ⓝ semantics 의미론

0706 ■■□

dismiss
[dismís]

해산시키다, 해고시키다
ⓥ to direct (an assembly of persons) to disperse or go
ⓢⓨⓝ disperse, scatter, discharge
ⓔ.ⓖ. The company can **dismiss** an employee in the case of misconduct.
ⓝ dismissal 해산, 해고

0707 ■■□

mediate
[mí:dièit]

조정하다, 중재하다
ⓥ to settle (disputes, strikes, etc.) as an intermediary between parties
ⓢⓨⓝ reconcile, arbitrate, conciliate, intercede
ⓔ.ⓖ. We must first **mediate** between the husband and wife before the divorce.
ⓝ mediation 조정, 중재

0708 ■■□

lexical
[léksikəl]

어휘의, 사전의
ⓐ of or pertaining to the words or vocabulary of a language, esp. as distinguished from its grammatical and syntactical aspects
ⓔ.ⓖ. Ambiguity can have both a **lexical** and a structural basis, as with phrases like 'He saw her duck'.

0709 ■□□

eventual
[ivéntʃuəl]

최후의, 결과로서 일어나는

ⓐ happening at some indefinite future time or after a series of occurrences
ⓢⓨⓝ ultimate, consequent, final
ⓔ.ⓖ. His mistakes led to his **eventual** firing.
ⓝ eventuality 예측 못할 사건, 궁극, 결말

0710 ■□□

microscopic
[màikrəskápik]

현미경으로만 볼 수 있는, 매우 작은

ⓐ so small as to be invisible or indistinct without the use of the microscope
ⓢⓨⓝ infinitesimal
ⓔ.ⓖ. The doctor studied a **microscopic** organism with a special camera.
ⓝ microscope 현미경

0711 ■□□

span
[spǽn]

거리, 폭, 기간

ⓝ a distance, amount, piece, etc., of this length or of some small extent
ⓢⓨⓝ length, term, duration
ⓔ.ⓖ. The life **span** of the average butterfly is less than one week.

0712 ■□□

extraordinary
[ikstrɔ́ːrdənèri]

비범한, 보통이 아닌

ⓐ beyond what is usual, ordinary, regular, or established
ⓢⓨⓝ exceptional, peculiar, uncommon
ⓔ.ⓖ. While he was average in other respects, his cooking was known to be **extraordinary**.
ⓐ ordinary 평상의, 보통의

0713 ■■□

dignity
[dígnəti]

존엄, 위엄, 품위

ⓝ bearing, conduct, or speech indicative of self-respect or appreciation of the formality or gravity of an occasion or situation
ⓢⓨⓝ honor, grace, prestige, ennoblement
ⓔ.ⓖ. While they can take your job and your money, they can't take your **dignity**.
ⓥ dignify 위엄 있게 하다, 존귀하게 하다

0714 ■■□

maturity
[mətʃúərəti]

성숙기, 완성기

ⓝ the state of being mature
ⓢⓨⓝ ripeness
ⓔ.ⓖ. The fish will reach **maturity** in a few days.
ⓐ mature 익은, 성숙한, 잘 발육한

0715 ■■□

chronic
[kránik]

만성적인, 오래 계속하는

ⓐ constant, inveterate
ⓢⓨⓝ continual, habitual
ⓔ.ⓖ. His disease was **chronic** and allowed no relief.
ⓝ chronicle 연대기, 기록

0716 ■■□

immerse
[imə́ːrs]

담그다, 가라앉히다, 적시다

ⓥ to plunge into or place under a liquid
ⓢⓨⓝ dip, sink
ⓔ.ⓖ. I was **immersed** in the new video game for 6 hours.
ⓝ immersion 잠금, 담금, 투입

0717 ■□□

midst
[mídst]

중앙, 한복판, 한가운데

ⓝ the position of anything surrounded by other things or parts, or occurring in the middle of a period of time, course of action, etc.
ⓢⓨⓝ center
ⓔ.ⓖ. It's not easy to find time to prepare for examination in the **midst** of your busy schedule.
ⓐ middle 한가운데의, 중앙의

0718 ■■■

ophthalmology 안과학
[àfθəlmáləʤi]
ⓝ the branch of medical science dealing with the anatomy, functions, and diseases of the eye
ⓔ.ⓖ. Laser surgery is the most exciting advancement in **ophthalmology**.
ⓝ ophthalmologist 안과 의사

DAY
12

0719 ■■□

inject 주사하다, 주입하다
[indʒékt]
ⓥ to force (a fluid) into a passage, cavity, or tissue
ⓢⓨⓝ inoculate
ⓔ.ⓖ. Farmers routinely **inject** the animals with antibiotics.
ⓝ injection 주사, 주입

0720 ■■□

comprise 포함하다, 의미하다, 구성되다
[kəmpráiz]
ⓥ to include or contain
ⓢⓨⓝ include, contain
ⓔ.ⓖ. This team is **comprised** of seven members, including one leader.
ⓝ comprisal 포함, 함유

Day
13

definite	☐☐☐	lousy	☐☐☐
superficial	☐☐☐	mandatory	☐☐☐
infer	☐☐☐	momentum	☐☐☐
abhorrent	☐☐☐	nasty	☐☐☐
unlearn	☐☐☐	persist	☐☐☐
presupposition	☐☐☐	nostalgic	☐☐☐
course	☐☐☐	oblong	☐☐☐
irresponsible	☐☐☐	disparage	☐☐☐
color	☐☐☐	oppression	☐☐☐
impertinent	☐☐☐	disregard	☐☐☐
mobilize	☐☐☐	phase	☐☐☐
victim	☐☐☐	divine	☐☐☐
shrink	☐☐☐	proportion	☐☐☐
outlet	☐☐☐	flake	☐☐☐
reverse	☐☐☐	miscreant	☐☐☐
topsoil	☐☐☐	flammable	☐☐☐
portrait	☐☐☐	enrich	☐☐☐
antonym	☐☐☐	glance	☐☐☐
rape	☐☐☐	pope	☐☐☐
quote	☐☐☐	impart	☐☐☐
perplex	☐☐☐	grind	☐☐☐
subsidiary	☐☐☐	lash	☐☐☐
repudiate	☐☐☐	idiot	☐☐☐
subterfuge	☐☐☐	dissociate	☐☐☐
setback	☐☐☐	subsequent	☐☐☐
terminology	☐☐☐	combustible	☐☐☐
alleged	☐☐☐	nocturnal	☐☐☐
prohibitive	☐☐☐	innate	☐☐☐
impermeable	☐☐☐	explode	☐☐☐
invoice	☐☐☐	prolong	☐☐☐

0721 ■□□

definite
[défənit]

분명한, 한정된, 명확한

ⓐ clearly defined or determined; not vague or general
(syn) fixed, precise, exact
(e.g.) He proposed to her but she hesitated to give a **definite** answer.
ⓐ indefinite 일정치 않은, 명확하지 않은, 애매한

0722 ■□□

superficial
[sùːpərfíʃəl]

표면상의, 외견의, 피상적인

ⓐ being at, on, or near the surface
(syn) external, outward, cursory
(e.g.) His apology sounded meaningless and **superficial**.
ⓝ superficiality 천박, 피상

0723 ■■□

infer
[infə́ːr]

추론하다

ⓥ to derive by reasoning
(syn) deduce
(e.g.) I could **infer** from his tone that he was sad.
ⓝ inference 추론

0724 ■■□

abhorrent
[æbhɔ́ːrənt]

몹시 싫은, 지겨운

ⓐ inspiring disgust and loathing; repugnant
(syn) loathsome
(e.g.) Racism is **abhorrent** to a civilized society.
(ad) abhorrently

0725 ■■□

unlearn
[ˌən'lərn]

(배운 것을 고의적으로) 잊다

ⓥ to forget or lose knowledge of
(e.g.) You must **unlearn** everything you know and believe.

0726 ■□□

presupposition 예상, 상정, 추정
[ˌpriːsʌpəˈzɪʃn]

ⓝ something that is assumed in advance or taken for granted
(syn) assumption, presumption
(e.g.) That has been the **presupposition** of our dialogue until now.

0727 ■■□

course
[kɔːrs]

(빠르게) 흐르다
ⓥ move without obstruction
(syn) pour, surge
(e.g.) Tears were **coursing** down her cheeks.

0728 ■□□

irresponsible
[ìrispánsəbəl]

무책임한
ⓐ said, done, or characterized by a lack of a sense of responsibility
(syn) rash
(opp) sensible
(e.g.) I also realised how **irresponsible** I had been in the past.
(ad) irresponsibly

0729 ■□□

color
[kʌ́lər]

채색하다, 물들다
ⓥ to give or apply color
(syn) brush
(e.g.) He **colored** her hair with a selection of blonde and brown shades.

0730 ■■□

impertinent
[impə́ːrtənənt]

무례한, 버릇없는
ⓐ not showing proper respect; rude
(opp) polite
(e.g.) Talking back to older people is **impertinent**.
(ad) impertinently

0731 ■□□

mobilize
[móubəlàiz]

동원하다(되다), 결집하다
ⓥ (of a country or its government) prepare and organize (troops) for active service
(syn) rally, deploy
(e.g.) To respond to these demands and pressures, people will **mobilize** physical and emotional resources.

0732 ■□□

victim
[víktim]

희생자, 피해자

ⓝ a person who suffers from a destructive or injurious action or agency

ⓢⓨⓝ sacrifice, casualty

ⓔ.ⓖ. These **victims** make do with instant noodles and bread instead of rice.

ⓥ victimize 희생시키다

0733 ■■□

shrink
[ʃríŋk]

줄어들다, 오그라들다

ⓥ to contract or lessen in size, as from exposure to conditions of temperature or moisture

ⓢⓨⓝ dwindle, diminish, decrease

ⓔ.ⓖ. This fabric will not **shrink** if washed in lukewarm water.

ⓐ shrinkable 줄어들기 쉬운, 수축하는

0734 ■□□

outlet
[áutlèt]

출구, 방출구

ⓝ an opening or passage by which anything is let out

ⓢⓨⓝ vent, exit

ⓔ.ⓖ. I think music is an **outlet** for my daily stress.

0735 ■■□

reverse
[rivə́ːrs]

거꾸로 하다, 반대로 하다, 뒤집다

ⓥ to turn in an opposite position

ⓢⓨⓝ transpose, interchange

ⓔ.ⓖ. The printer accidentally **reversed** two chapters of the book.

ⓝ reversal 반전, 역전, 되돌아옴

0736 ■■□

topsoil
[tápsɔ̀il]

표토

ⓝ the fertile, upper part of the soil

ⓔ.ⓖ. In this part of the valley, the **topsoil** is rich with nutrients that allow fruit to grow.

0737 ■□□

portrait
[pɔ́ːrtrit]

초상화, 인물사진

ⓝ a likeness of a person, esp. of the face, as a painting, drawing, or photograph
ⓢⓨⓝ drawing, painting, depiction
ⓔ.ⓖ. She hung a **portrait** of her grandparents in the living room.
ⓥ portray 그리다, 표현하다, 초상을 그리다

0738 ■□□

antonym
[ǽntənim]

반의어

ⓝ a word opposite in meaning to another
ⓢⓨⓝ opposite
ⓔ.ⓖ. For the scientist, "theory" is not in any way an **antonym** of "fact."
ⓝ synonym 동의어

0739 ■□□

rape
[réip]

강간하다

ⓥ to force to have sexual intercourse
ⓢⓨⓝ ravish, assault, outrage
ⓔ.ⓖ. Then he pinned her arms behind her and **raped** her.

0740 ■■□

quote
[kwóut]

인용하다, 예를 들다

ⓥ to repeat (a passage, phrase, etc.) from a book, speech, or the like, as by way of authority, illustration, etc.
ⓢⓨⓝ cite, refer, adduce
ⓔ.ⓖ. The professor **quoted** it from the text book.
ⓝ quotation 인용(문, 구, 어)

0741 ■■□

perplex
[pərpléks]

난처하게 하다, 당황하게 하다

ⓥ to cause to be puzzled or bewildered over what is not understood or certain; confuse mentally
ⓢⓨⓝ bewilder, embarrass
ⓔ.ⓖ. Her strange response **perplexed** the jury.
ⓐ perplexed 난처한, 당황한

DAY
13

0742 ■■□

subsidiary
[səbsɪdieri]

부수적인, 자회사의
ⓐ connected with something but less important than it
ⓢⓨⓝ secondary, lesser, subordinate
ⓔ.ⓖ. **subsidiary** information
ⓝ subsidiariness
ⓐⓓ subsidiarily

0743 ■■■

repudiate
[rɪpjuːdieɪt]

거부하다, 물리치다, (공식적으로) 부인하다
ⓥ to refuse to accept something
ⓔ.ⓖ. Socialism had been **repudiated** at the polls.
ⓝ subsidiariness
ⓐⓓ subsidiarily

0744 ■■■

subterfuge
[sʌbtərfjuːdʒ]

속임수
ⓝ a secret, usually dishonest, way of behaving
ⓔ.ⓖ. Journalists often use **subterfuge** to obtain material for stories.

0745 ■■■

setback
[setbæk]

차질
ⓝ a difficulty or problem that delays or prevents something, or makes a situation worse
ⓢⓨⓝ hold-up, check, defeat
ⓔ.ⓖ. The team suffered a major **setback** when their best player was injured.

0746 ■■□

terminology
[tɜːrmənɑːlədʒi]

(집합적인) 전문 용어, (어떤 개념을 나타내는) 용어들
ⓝ the set of technical words or expressions used in a particular subject
ⓔ.ⓖ. Scientists are constantly developing new **terminologies**.
ⓝ terminologist
ⓐ terminological
ⓐⓓ terminologically

0747 ■■■

alleged
[əlédʒd]

(증거 없이) 주장된, ~이라고들 말하는
ⓐ stated as a fact but without any proof
(e.g.) the **alleged** attacker/victim/killer (= that somebody says is one)

0748 ■■□

prohibitive
[prəhíbətɪv]

(가격·비용이) 엄두도 못 낼 정도로 높은(비싼); (법으로) 금지하는
ⓐ (of a price or a cost) so high that it prevents people from buying something or doing something; preventing people from doing something by law
(e.g.) 1. **prohibitive** costs
　　　 2. **prohibitive** legislation
ⓝ prohibitiveness
ⓐ prohibitively

0749 ■■■

impermeable
[ɪmpɜ́ːrmiəbl]

(액체·기체를) 통과시키지 않는, 불침투성의
ⓐ not allowing a liquid or gas to pass through
(e.g.) The insulating material should be **impermeable** to water vapour.
ⓝ impermeability, impermeableness
ⓐ impermeably

0750 ■■□

invoice
[ínvɔis]

송장
ⓝ an itemized bill for goods sold or services provided, containing individual prices, the total charge, and the terms
(syn) reckoning, bill, check
(e.g.) **Invoices** will help us track every major purchase and sale.

0751 ■□□

lousy
[láuzi]

이가 들끓는, 비열한, 혐오스러운, 형편없는
ⓐ infested with lice; mean or contemptible, wretchedly bad
(syn) disgusting, loathsome, contemptible
(e.g.) The boy had to leave the **lousy** scene.

DAY
13

0752 ■■□

mandatory
[mǽndətɔ̀:ri]

명령의, 강제의, 의무의
ⓐ authoritatively ordered
(syn) obligatory, compulsory, imperative, requisite
(e.g.) It is **mandatory** that all students take two years of math.
ⓝ ⓥ mandate 명령, 지시; 명령(요구)하다

0753 ■■□

momentum
[mouméntəm]

운동량, 추진력
ⓝ force or speed of movement; impetus, as of a physical object or course of events
(syn) impetus, force, power
(e.g.) The car gained **momentum** as it rolled down hill.

0754 ■□□

nasty
[nǽsti]

더러운, 불쾌한, 외설적인
ⓐ physically filthy; disgustingly unclean
(syn) dirty, foul, loathsome, sickening, repulsive, repellent
(e.g.) He has a **nasty** habit of exposing another's private affairs.

0755 ■■□

persist
[pərsíst]

주장하다, 우기다
ⓥ to continue steadfastly or firmly in some state, purpose, course of action, or the like, esp. in spite of opposition, remonstrance, etc.
(syn) assert, insist
(e.g.) He **persisted** in denying all knowledge of the incident to the very last.
ⓝ persistence 끈기, 고집, 버팀

0756 ■□□

nostalgic
[nɑstǽldʒə]

고향(옛날)을 그리는
ⓐ feeling happy and also slightly sad when you think about things that happened in the past
(e.g.) I was **nostalgic** for my home while living overseas.
ⓝ nostalgia 옛날을 그리워함, 향수

0757 ■■■

oblong
[ábló:ŋ]

직사각형의, 타원형의

ⓐ elongated, usually from the square or circular form
ⓔ.ⓖ. It's more convenient to use the **oblong** tables for the meeting.

0758 ■■■

disparage
[dispǽridʒ]

얕보다, 깔보다

ⓥ to speak of or treat slightingly
ⓢⓨⓝ depreciate, belittle, decry
ⓔ.ⓖ. Do not **disparage** my family.
ⓝ disparagement 경멸, 얕봄, 비난

0759 ■■■

oppression
[əpréʃən]

압박, 압제, 억압, 탄압

ⓝ the exercise of authority or power in a burdensome, cruel, or
unjust manner
ⓢⓨⓝ suppression, coercion, pressure
ⓔ.ⓖ. The people rose up against **oppression**.
ⓥ oppress 압박하다, 억압하다

0760 ■■□

disregard
[disrigá:rd]

무시하다, 경시하다, 소홀히 하다

ⓥ to pay no attention to; leave out of consideration
ⓢⓨⓝ ignore, neglect
ⓔ.ⓖ. She **disregarded** the warning signs and kept driving.
ⓐ disregardful 무시한, 경시한, 무관심한

0761 ■■□

phase
[féiz]

양상, 현상, 면, 상

ⓝ any of the major appearances or aspects in which a thing of
varying modes or conditions manifests itself to the eye or mind
ⓢⓨⓝ form, shape, facet, aspect
ⓔ.ⓖ. The government is in an intense **phase** of taxation
ⓐ phasic 국면의, 형세의

0762 ■■□

divine
[diváin]

신의, 신성의, 신이 내린
ⓐ of or pertaining to a god, esp. the Supreme Being; addressed, appropriated, or devoted to God or a god
ⓢⓨⓝ religious, sacred, godlike, holy
ⓔ.ⓖ. It's **divine** punishment for the crime you committed.
ⓝ divinity 신, 신격, 신성한 사람

0763 ■□□

proportion
[prəpóːrʃən]

비율, 정도, 크기
ⓝ comparative relation between things or magnitudes as to size, quantity, number, etc.
ⓢⓨⓝ ratio
ⓔ.ⓖ. The **proportion** of men to women in the college has changed dramatically over the years.
ⓐ proportional 비례하는, 비례의

0764 ■□□

flake
[fléik]

얇은 조각, 파편, 박편
ⓝ a small, flat, thin piece, esp. one that has been or become detached from a larger piece or mass
ⓔ.ⓖ. Some **flakes** of old paint have fallen off the wall onto the floor.

0765 ■■■

miscreant
[mískriənt]

사악한, 이단의
ⓐ depraved, villainous, or base
ⓢⓨⓝ vicious, malicious, evil
ⓔ.ⓖ. The country is under the control of a **miscreant** king.

0766 ■■□

flammable
[flǽməbl]

가연성의, 타기 쉬운
ⓐ easily set on fire
ⓢⓨⓝ combustible, inflammable
ⓔ.ⓖ. Keep matches and other **flammable** materials out of reach of children.
ⓝ flame 불꽃, 화염

0767 ■□□

enrich
[inrítʃ]

부유하게 하다, 부자가 되게 하다

ⓥ to supply with riches, wealth, abundant or valuable possessions, etc.

ⓔ.ⓖ. Our culture has been **enriched** by many other countries.

ⓝ enrichment 풍부하게 함, 농축, 강화

0768 ■■□

glance
[glǽns]

힐끗 보다, 잠깐 보다; 힐끗 봄, 얼핏 봄

ⓥ to look quickly or briefly

ⓢⓨⓝ peek, peep

ⓔ.ⓖ. He stole a **glance** at the person's ID card.

0769 ■□□

pope
[póup]

(로마) 교황

ⓝ the bishop of Rome and head of the Roman Catholic Church on earth

ⓔ.ⓖ. The **pope** has returned to Rome after his pilgrimage to Kazakhstan and Armenia.

0770 ■■□

impart
[impá:rt]

나누어 주다

ⓥ to grant a share of

ⓢⓨⓝ bestow, give

ⓔ.ⓖ. To **impart** a sense of the importance of the meeting he begins by showing a cartoon.

0771 ■□□

grind
[gráind]

갈다, 찧다, 잘게 부수다, 가루로 만들다

ⓥ to wear, smooth, or sharpen by abrasion or friction

ⓢⓨⓝ whet, grate

ⓔ.ⓖ. He **grinds** the salt brick into powder.

ⓝ grinder 분쇄기

0772 ■■□

lash
[læʃ]

채찍으로 때리다, 후려치다
ⓥ to strike or beat, as with a whip or something similarly slender and flexible
ⓢⓨⓝ whip, flog, thrash
ⓔ.ⓖ. The thief was sentenced to ten **lashes** of a whip for his crime.

0773 ■□□

idiot
[ídiət]

얼간이, 바보
ⓝ an utterly foolish or senseless person
ⓔ.ⓖ. I pretended I liked him but I said to myself that he was an **idiot**.
ⓐ idiotic 바보스러운, 백치의

0774 ■■□

dissociate
[disóuʃièit]

떼어놓다, 분리하다
ⓥ to sever the association of (oneself)
ⓢⓨⓝ separate, disengage
ⓔ.ⓖ. He tried to **dissociate** himself from his past behaviors.
ⓝ dissociation 분리, 분열, 해리

0775 ■■□

subsequent
[sʌ́bsikwənt]

다음의, 그 후의, 버금가는
ⓐ occurring or coming later or after
ⓢⓨⓝ next
ⓔ.ⓖ. **Subsequent** events proved him to be a hero.
ⓐⓓ subsequently 그 후에, 다음에, 이어서

0776 ■■□

combustible
[kəmbʌ́stəbl]

타기 쉬운, 가연성의
ⓐ capable of catching fire and burning
ⓢⓨⓝ inflammable, flammable
ⓔ.ⓖ. Gasoline vapor is highly **combustible**.
ⓝ combustibility 연소성, 가연성

0777 ■□□

nocturnal
[nɑktə́:rnl]

밤의, 야간의

ⓐ of or pertaining to the night
syn nighttime
opp diurnal 낮의, 주간의
e.g. In legends, vampires and werewolves are both exclusively **nocturnal**.

0778 ■■□

innate
[inéit]

타고난, 천부의

ⓐ existing in one from birth
syn inborn, native
opp acquired 후천적인
e.g. She has a strong **innate** sense of direction.

0779 ■□□

explode
[iksplóud]

폭발하다, 파열하다

ⓥ to expand with force and noise because of rapid chemical change or decomposition, as gunpowder or nitroglycerine
syn burst, erupt
e.g. If a gasoline tank is left in the sun it can **explode**.
ⓝ explosion 폭발, 파열

0780 ■■□

prolong
[prəlɔ́:ŋ]

늘이다, 길게 하다, 연장하다

ⓥ to lengthen out in time; extend the duration of; cause to continue longer
syn extend, elongate, prolongate
e.g. Toasting bread began as a method of **prolonging** the life of the food.
ⓝ prolongation 연장, 연기

Day

14

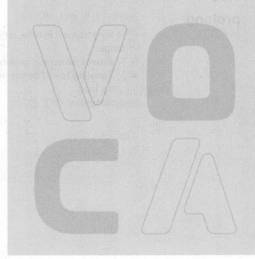

downward	☐☐☐	scheme	☐☐☐
wound	☐☐☐	unsurpassed	☐☐☐
remark	☐☐☐	disrespect	☐☐☐
vessel	☐☐☐	novelty	☐☐☐
carbohydrate	☐☐☐	pathway	☐☐☐
glucose	☐☐☐	eternal	☐☐☐
secrete	☐☐☐	misinterpret	☐☐☐
alternatively	☐☐☐	pavement	☐☐☐
maleficent	☐☐☐	incalculable	☐☐☐
ladle	☐☐☐	temporary	☐☐☐
uncanny	☐☐☐	displace	☐☐☐
incentive	☐☐☐	witchcraft	☐☐☐
snob	☐☐☐	embody	☐☐☐
primitive	☐☐☐	indifferent	☐☐☐
feast	☐☐☐	incorporate	☐☐☐
veil	☐☐☐	voracious	☐☐☐
illiberal	☐☐☐	condolence	☐☐☐
paradoxical	☐☐☐	absolute	☐☐☐
fruitful	☐☐☐	adroit	☐☐☐
inhale	☐☐☐	pernicious	☐☐☐
personnel	☐☐☐	phoneme	☐☐☐
leap	☐☐☐	rattle	☐☐☐
forestall	☐☐☐	digestion	☐☐☐
ensuing	☐☐☐	daydream	☐☐☐
rupture	☐☐☐	amiss	☐☐☐
fastidious	☐☐☐	fury	☐☐☐
succulent	☐☐☐	fragment	☐☐☐
foul	☐☐☐	skeleton	☐☐☐
compelling	☐☐☐	throng	☐☐☐
merge	☐☐☐	bang	☐☐☐

0781 ■□□

downward
[dáunwərd]

아래쪽으로, 아래로 향하는, 하향의

(ad) from a higher to a lower place or condition
(opp) upward 위로 향하는
(e.g.) As the creek flows **downward**, it widens.

0782 ■□□

wound
[wúːnd]

부상, 상처

(n) an injury, usually involving division of tissue or rupture of the integument or mucous membrane, due to external violence or some mechanical agency rather than disease
(syn) injury
(e.g.) The soldier's **wounds** were healed up after a few months.
(a) wounded 부상한, 다친

0783 ■□□

remark
[rimáːrk]

진술하다, 말하다

(v) to say casually, as in making a comment
(syn) tell
(e.g.) Someone **remarked** that tomorrow would be a rainy day.
(a) remarkable 주목할 만한, 두드러진

0784 ■□□

vessel
[vésəl]

배

(n) ship or large boat
(syn) watercraft
(e.g.) The **vessel** was tossed about in the waves for nine days.

0785 ■□□

carbohydrate
[ˌkärbəˈhīˌdrāt]

탄수화물

(n) substances, found in certain kinds of food, that provide you with energy
(e.g.) High-protein, Low-**carbohydrate** diets work!

0786 ■□□

glucose
[glúːkous]

포도당

(n) a type of sugar that gives you energy
(e.g.) **Glucose** can exist in two ring forms, Alpha and Beta.

0787 ■■□

secrete
[sikrí:t]

분비하다
ⓥ If part of a plant, animal, or human secretes a liquid, it produces it.
ⓢⓨⓝ discharge
ⓔ.ⓖ. Kissing **secretes** endorphins, which relieves pain.
ⓝ secretor

0788 ■□□

alternatively
[ôl'tərnədivlē]

그 대신에, 그렇지 않으면
ⓐⓓ as another option or possibility
ⓢⓨⓝ or
ⓔ.ⓖ. **Alternatively**, the child may have a mental impairment.

0789 ■■□

maleficent
[məléfəsənt]

유해한, 나쁜
ⓐ causing or capable of producing evil or mischief; harmful or baleful
ⓞⓟⓟ beneficent
ⓔ.ⓖ. It sounded to me like the name of some **maleficent** and sinful being.

0790 ■■□

ladle
[léidl]

국자; 국자로 뜨다
ⓝ a long-handled utensil with a cup-shaped bowl for dipping or conveying liquids
ⓢⓨⓝ scoop
ⓔ.ⓖ. It was used as a kitchen **ladle**.
ⓝ ladleful

0791 ■■□

uncanny
[ˌən'kanē]

이상한, 묘한
ⓐ beyond the ordinary or normal; extraordinary
ⓢⓨⓝ eerie, abnormal
ⓞⓟⓟ unremarkable
ⓔ.ⓖ. She was blessed with an **uncanny** connoisseur's eye for art collecting.
ⓝ uncanniness

0792 ■□□

incentive
[inséntiv]

자극, 격려, 동기

ⓝ something that incites or tends to incite to action or greater effort, as a reward offered for increased productivity

ⓢⓨⓝ motivation, encouragement, stimulation

ⓔ.ⓖ. They offered corporations **incentives** for environmental friendly planning.

ⓥ incentivize 장려하다

0793 ■■□

snob
[snáb]

신사인 체하는 속물(俗物), 지위·재산 등을 숭배하는 사람, 윗사람에게 아첨하고 아랫사람에게 거만부리는 사람

ⓝ a person who imitates, cultivates, or slavishly admires social superiors and is condescending or overbearing to others

ⓢⓨⓝ vulgarian, babbitt, Philistine, worldling

ⓔ.ⓖ. He is a **snob** who rates himself above all others.

ⓐ snobbish 속물의, 신사인 체하는

0794 ■□□

primitive
[prímətiv]

원시의, 초기의, 옛날의

ⓐ being the first or earliest of the kind or in existence, esp. in an early age of the world

ⓢⓨⓝ ancient, primary

ⓔ.ⓖ. Some **primitive** men used stones for all their tool needs.

ⓝ primitivism 원시주의

0795 ■■□

feast
[fíːst]

축하연, 잔치, 연회

ⓝ a sumptuous entertainment or meal for many guests

ⓢⓨⓝ banquet

ⓔ.ⓖ. The wedding was followed by a big **feast**.

0796 ■■□

veil
[véil]

베일로 가리다, 감추다, 숨기다

ⓥ to don or wear a veil

ⓢⓨⓝ screen, hide, conceal

ⓔ.ⓖ. In certain Islamic countries women must **veil**.

ⓐ veiled 베일로 가린, 감춘, 숨긴

0797 ■■■

illiberal
[ilíbərəl]

옹졸한, 인색한, 구두쇠의
ⓐ lacking tolerance, breadth of view, or sympathy
ⓢⓨⓝ narrow-minded, hidebound, bigoted
ⓔ.ⓖ. College students are less **illiberal** than those that never attend college.
ⓐ liberal 자유주의의, 관대한

0798 ■□□

paradoxical
[pæ̀rədáksikəl]

역설의, 자기 모순의
ⓐ a statement or proposition that seems self-contradictory or absurd but in reality expresses a possible truth
ⓔ.ⓖ. Comedians, **paradoxical** as it may seem, may more prone to depression.
ⓝ paradox 역설

0799 ■□□

fruitful
[frú:tfəl]

열매가 많이 맺는, 다산의, 열매가 좋은
ⓐ producing good results
ⓢⓨⓝ beneficial, profitable, prolific
ⓔ.ⓖ. Live a **fruitful** life as you could die at any time.
ⓐ unfruitful 헛된, 공연한, 열매를 맺지 않는

0800 ■■□

inhale
[inhéil]

들이쉬다, 호흡하다
ⓥ to breathe in; draw in by breathing
ⓔ.ⓖ. When you **inhale**, raise your arms over your head.
ⓝ inhalation 흡입

0801 ■□□

personnel
[pə̀:rsənél]

(총) 인원, (전) 직원, (전) 사원
ⓝ a body of persons employed in an organization or place of work
ⓔ.ⓖ. Personal favors must not be allowed in **personnel** relations.

0802 ■■□

leap
[lí:p]

껑충 뛰다, 뛰어오르다
ⓥ to spring through the air from one point or position to another
ⓢⓨⓝ jump, bound
ⓔ.ⓖ. The hunters **leapt** their horses over all the obstacles.

0803 ■■■

forestall
[fɔːrstɔːl]

미연에 방지하다

ⓥ to prevent something from happening or somebody from doing something by doing something first

ⓔⓖ Try to anticipate what your child will do and **forestall** problems.

ⓝ forestaller, forestallment, forestalment

0804 ■■■

ensuing
[insúːiŋ]

다음의, 뒤이은, 뒤이어 일어나는, 결과로서 따르는

ⓐ that happens after or as a result of another event

ⓔⓖ He had become separated from his parents in the **ensuing** panic.

0805 ■■■

rupture
[rʌptʃə(r)]

(수도관 등의) 파열, 단절; (관계의) 결렬

ⓝ a situation when something breaks or bursts

ⓢⓨⓝ break, tear, split

ⓔⓖ 1. the **rupture** of a blood vessel
2. **ruptures** of oil and water pipelines

ⓐ rupturable

0806 ■■■

fastidious
[fæstɪdiəs]

세심한, 꼼꼼한; (때로 못마땅함) 깔끔을 떠는, 까다로운

ⓐ being careful that every detail of something is correct

ⓔⓖ 1. Everything was planned in **fastidious** detail.
2. She wasn't very **fastidious** about personal hygiene.

ⓝ fastidiousness

ⓐⓓ fastidiously

0807 ■■■

succulent
[sʌkjələnt]

(과일·채소·고기가) 즙이 많은, (식물이) 다육성의

ⓐ (approving) (of fruit, vegetables and meat) containing a lot of juice and tasting good

ⓢⓨⓝ juicy

ⓔⓖ a **succulent** pear/steak

ⓝ succulence, succulency

ⓐⓓ succulently

0808 ■■□

foul
[faʊl]

더러운, 악취 나는; 천박한; 더럽히다, 더럽게 하다

ⓐ dirty and smelling bad
(syn) dirty, unpleasant, stinking
(e.g.) 1.**Foul** drinking water was blamed for the epidemic.
　　　2. She's in a **foul** mood.
　　　3. **foul** language
ⓝ foulness
(ad) foully

0809 ■■□

compelling
[kəmpelɪŋ]

(너무나 흥미로워서) 주목하지 않을 수 없는(눈을 뗄 수 없는); 설득력 있는, 강력한

ⓐ that makes you pay attention to it because it is so interesting and exciting; so strong that you must do something about it; that makes you think it is true
(syn) convincing, telling, powerful
(e.g.) 1. Her latest book makes **compelling** reading.
　　　2. a **compelling** need/desire
　　　3. There is no **compelling** reason to believe him.
(ad) compellingly

0810 ■■□

merge
[mɜːrdʒ]

합병(병합)하다, 합치다. 어우러지다(융합되다)

ⓥ to combine or make two or more things combine to form a single thing
(syn) combine, blend, fuse
(e.g.) 1. The banks are set to **merge** next year.
　　　2. The hills **merged** into the dark sky behind them.
ⓝ mergence

0811 ■□□

scheme
[skíːm]

계획, 설계

ⓝ a plan, design, or program of action to be followed
(syn) project, plan, strategy
(e.g.) Their **scheme** to skip class ended up getting them in trouble.
ⓝ schemer 계획자, 음모가

0812 ■■■

unsurpassed
[ʌ̀nsərpǽst]

비길 데 없는, 탁월한, 이길 사람이 없는

ⓐ not capable of being improved on
ⓢⓨⓝ unexcelled, unrivaled, unbeatable
ⓔ.ⓖ. I think she is a woman of **unsurpassed** beauty.
ⓥ surpass ~보다 낫다, 능가하다

0813 ■■□

disrespect
[dìsrispékt]

실례하다, 경시하다

ⓥ to regard or treat without respect; regard or treat with contempt
　 or rudeness
ⓢⓨⓝ belittle, ignore, neglect
ⓔ.ⓖ. We tend to **disrespect** competitors.
ⓐ disrespectful 무례한, 실례되는

0814 ■■□

novelty
[návəlti]

진기함, 신기함, 참신함

ⓝ state or quality of being novel, new, or unique
ⓢⓨⓝ newness
ⓔ.ⓖ. The **novelty** of her writing impressed me.
ⓐ novel 새로운, 신기한, 참신한

0815 ■□□

pathway
[pǽθwèi]

좁은 길

ⓝ a path which you can walk along or a route which you can take
ⓢⓨⓝ path, course, route, way
ⓔ.ⓖ. The **pathway** goes all the way to the top of the mountain.
ⓝ path 작은 길, 오솔길

0816 ■■□

eternal
[itə́:rnl]

영원한, 영구의, 불변의

ⓐ without beginning or end; lasting forever; always existing
ⓢⓨⓝ endless, everlasting, timeless, perpetual, immutable
ⓔ.ⓖ. This child is an **eternal** reminder of my departed wife.
ⓝ eternity 영원, 영구, 불멸

0817 ■■□

misinterpret
[mìsintə́:rprit]

오해하다, 오역하다

ⓥ to interpret, explain, or understand incorrectly

(syn) misconstrue, misunderstand

(e.g.) Many translators have **misinterpreted** this poem.

ⓥ interpret 설명하다, 해석하다

0818 ■□□

pavement
[péivmənt]

포장도로

ⓝ a paved road, highway, etc.

(e.g.) The **pavement** outside was slippery with the ice.

ⓥ pave 길을 포장하다

DAY
14

0819 ■■□

incalculable
[inkǽlkjuləbl]

헤아릴 수 없는, 무수한

ⓐ very numerous or great

(syn) countless, immeasurable

(e.g.) The effects of the recession on the factory is **incalculable**.

ⓐ calculable 셀 수 있는

0820 ■■□

temporary
[témpərèri]

임시적인, 잠시의, 순간의

ⓐ lasting, existing, serving, or effective for a time only; not permanent

(syn) momentary, instantaneous

(e.g.) The staff wasn't friendly to **temporary** workers.

0821 ■■□

displace
[displéis]

바꾸어 놓다, 옮겨놓다

ⓥ to move or put out of the usual or proper place

(syn) dislocate

(e.g.) When the flood waters rose, many people were **displaced** from their homes.

ⓝ displacement 바꾸어 놓기, 치환

0822 ■□□

witchcraft
[wítʃkræft]

마법, 요술

ⓝ the art or practices of a witch

(syn) sorcery, magic

(e.g.) It was thought the horoscopes were **witchcraft** in those days.

0823 ■■□

embody
[imbádi]

구체화하다, 구체적으로 표현하다, 구현하다

ⓥ to give a concrete form to; express, personify, or exemplify in concrete form

ⓢⓨⓝ concretize, actualize

ⓔⓖ For 20th century Americans, it was the skyscraper that best **embodied** the power and progress that defined their era.

ⓝ embodiment 구체화, 구현

0824 ■□□

indifferent
[indífərənt]

무관심한, 냉담한

ⓐ without interest or concern; not caring

ⓢⓨⓝ apathetic

ⓔⓖ The main reason I don't like him is his **indifferent** attitude toward the suffering of others.

ⓝ indifference 무관심함, 냉담함

0825 ■■□

incorporate
[inkɔ́ːrpərèit]

통합하다, 합병하다, 법인화하다

ⓥ to bring together (separate parts) into a single or unified whole

ⓢⓨⓝ assimilate, combine, unite

ⓔⓖ They **incorporated** their companies into one larger organization.

ⓝ incorporation 합병, 법인단체

0826 ■■□

voracious
[vɔːréiʃəs]

게걸스럽게 먹는, 식욕이 왕성한

ⓐ craving or consuming large quantities of food

ⓢⓨⓝ edacious, piggish, devouring

ⓔⓖ He has a **voracious** appetite for fruits and vegetables.

ⓝ voracity 폭식, 대식

0827 ■■■

condolence
[kəndóuləns]

애도, 조의

ⓝ expression of sympathy with a person who is suffering sorrow, misfortune, or grief

ⓢⓨⓝ consolation, solace, compassion

ⓔⓖ Please accept my sincere **condolences**.

ⓥ condole 문상하다, 조위하다, 위안하다

0828 ■□□

absolute
[ǽbsəlùːt]

절대적인, 완전한
ⓐ free from imperfection
(syn) direct, implicit, unquestioning, infinite, complete, perfect
(e.g.) I can trust him because he is a man of **absolute** sincerity.
(ad) absolutely 절대적으로, 완전히

0829 ■■□

adroit
[ədrɔ́it]

교묘한, 손재주가 있는
ⓐ expert or nimble in the use of the hands or body
(syn) dexterous, deft, artful
(e.g.) He was proud of her **adroit** control of the piano keys.
ⓐ maladroit 서투른, 솜씨없는

0830 ■■■

pernicious
[pərníʃəs]

유해한, 파괴적인, 치명적인
ⓐ causing insidious harm or ruin
(syn) fatal, ruinous, injurious, hurtful
(e.g.) Most doctors agree that drinking is a **pernicious** habit.

0831 ■■□

phoneme
[fóuniːm]

음소, 음운
ⓝ the smallest unit of sound which is significant in a language
(e.g.) These **phonemes** are particularly hard for the Korean to pronounce.
ⓐ phonemic 음소의

0832 ■■□

rattle
[rǽtl]

덜걱덜걱 소리 나다
ⓥ to give out or cause a rapid succession of short, sharp sounds, as in consequence of agitation and repeated concussions
(e.g.) The windows **rattled** in their frames from the wind.

0833 ■□□

digestion
[didʒéstʃən]

소화(작용), 소화력
ⓝ the process in the alimentary canal by which food is broken up physically, as by the action of the teeth, and chemically, as by the action of enzymes, and converted into a substance suitable for absorption and assimilation into the body
(syn) ingestion, assimilation
(e.g.) They are also high in fibre, which is vital for good **digestion** and helps to reduce bloating.
ⓥ digest 소화하다, 소화를 돕다

DAY 14

0834 ■□□

daydream
[déidri:m]

백일몽, 공상
ⓝ a reverie indulged in while awake
ⓢⓨⓝ reverie, woolgathering
ⓔ.ⓖ. It was nothing but a **daydream**.
ⓝ daydreamer 공상가, 몽상가

0835 ■■□

amiss
[əmís]

잘못되어, 빗나가, 부적당하게
ⓐⓓ out of the right or proper course, order, or condition
ⓢⓨⓝ improperly, wrongly, astray
ⓔ.ⓖ. Please remind us if there is anything **amiss** with our application.

0836 ■■□

fury
[fjúəri]

격노, 분노
ⓝ unrestrained or violent anger, rage, passion, or the like
ⓢⓨⓝ rage, wrath, anger
ⓢⓨⓝ The gods unleashed their **fury** on the offending mortal.
ⓐ furious 격노한, 분노한

0837 ■□□

fragment
[frǽgmənt]

부서진 조각, 파편
ⓝ a part broken off or detached
ⓢⓨⓝ particle, molecule, crumb
ⓔ.ⓖ. A plane was crushed to **fragments** when it struck the mountain.
ⓐ fragmentary 파편의, 단편으로 이루어진

0838 ■□□

skeleton
[skélətn]

골격, 해골
ⓝ the bones of a human or an animal considered as a whole, together forming the framework of the body
ⓔ.ⓖ. In the desert, a body will be turned into a **skeleton** in two days.

0839 ■■□

throng
[θrɔ́ːŋ]

군중, 다수, 떼
ⓝ a multitude of people crowded or assembled together
ⓢⓨⓝ crowd, mass, mob
ⓔⓖ The **throng** of people hung about in the town square.

0840 ■□□

bang
[bǽŋ]

세게 치다, 쾅 하고 닫다, 쿵 소리 나다
ⓥ to strike or beat resoundingly
ⓢⓨⓝ slam, hit
ⓔⓖ He **banged** his fist on the table angrily.

DAY
14

Day

15

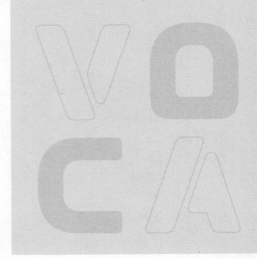

era	□□□	compensate	□□□
monologue	□□□	reprimand	□□□
rampant	□□□	implacable	□□□
observation	□□□	quell	□□□
flatten	□□□	decode	□□□
topple	□□□	replete	□□□
projectile	□□□	deserve	□□□
bound	□□□	fretful	□□□
barbed	□□□	colony	□□□
ripple	□□□	diameter	□□□
munch	□□□	bigot	□□□
striving	□□□	fertile	□□□
nursery	□□□	harrow	□□□
apathetic	□□□	assume	□□□
becket	□□□	bundle	□□□
indigent	□□□	chamber	□□□
obituary	□□□	indirect	□□□
carefree	□□□	magnitude	□□□
revert	□□□	executive	□□□
implore	□□□	psychiatrist	□□□
codify	□□□	keen	□□□
encounter	□□□	forthwith	□□□
adapt	□□□	banquet	□□□
inordinate	□□□	realm	□□□
eerie	□□□	corporation	□□□
tenuous	□□□	perverse	□□□
viable	□□□	address	□□□
attribute	□□□	drudgery	□□□
stipulate	□□□	intrepid	□□□
culprit	□□□	ominous	□□□

0841 ■■□

era
[íərə]

연대, 시대, 시기
ⓝ a period of time marked by distinctive character, events, etc.
ⓢⓨⓝ period, epoch
ⓔ.ⓖ. The use of steam for power marked the beginning of an **era**.

0842 ■□□

monologue
[mánəlɔ́ːg]

독백, 독백극
ⓝ a form of dramatic entertainment, comedic solo, or the like by a single speaker
ⓢⓨⓝ soliloquy
ⓔ.ⓖ. Participants are asked to introduce their project with a five-minute **monologue**.
ⓥ monologize 독백하다, 혼잣말하다

0843 ■■□

rampant
[rǽmpənt]

사나운, 광포한, 과격한
ⓐ violent in action or spirit
ⓢⓨⓝ raging, furious, aggressive
ⓔ.ⓖ. He grew up in a city where drug use was **rampant**.

0844 ■□□

observation
[àbzərvéiʃən]

소견, 관찰
ⓝ a remark, statement, or comment based on something one has seen, heard, or noticed
ⓢⓨⓝ pronouncement
ⓔ.ⓖ. He made a telling **observation** about Hugh.
ⓐ observant
ⓐⓓ observationally

0845 ■□□

flatten
[flǽtn]

납작하게 하다, 깨부수다
ⓥ to make flat
ⓢⓨⓝ trample, squash
ⓞⓟⓟ roughen
ⓔ.ⓖ. Place on ungreased cookie sheet, **flatten** slightly.

0846 ■■□

topple
[tápəl]

넘어지다(넘어뜨리다), 타도하다
ⓥ cause to become unsteady and fall
ⓢⓨⓝ supplant, dethrone
ⓔ.ⓖ. They now want to **topple** the Mugabe government.

0847 ■□□

projectile
[prədʒéktil]

발사체, 발사식 무기; 추진하는
ⓝ an object that is fired from a gun or other weapon
ⓔ.ⓖ. Toy guns are defined by European Standard as "**projectile** toys with stored energy" of 0.08 Joules.

0848 ■□□

bound
[baund]

껑충껑충 뛰다; 경계를 이루다
ⓥ walk or run with leaping strides
ⓢⓨⓝ capriole
ⓔ.ⓖ. The house was **bounded** on the left by a wood.

0849 ■■□

barbed
[bärbd]

가시가 돋친, 철사를 두른
ⓐ having barbs
ⓢⓨⓝ spiked
ⓔ.ⓖ. a **barbed** wire fence

0850 ■■□

ripple
[rípəl]

잔물결; 파문을 이루다
ⓝ a small wave or undulation, as on water
ⓔ.ⓖ. We think there's already been a **ripple**.
ⓐ rippleless

0851 ■■□

munch
[mʌntʃ]

우적우적 먹다
ⓥ to chew with steady or vigorous working of the jaws, often audibly
ⓢⓨⓝ champ, triturate
ⓔ.ⓖ. Rabbits **munch** carrots.

DAY
15

0852 ■□□

striving
[ˈstraɪvɪŋ]

분투
ⓝ great and tenacious efforts to do something
syn endeavor, aspire
e.g. That is a prize worth striving for, and I do not believe our
striving thus far has been in vain.

0853 ■□□

nursery
[nə́ːrsəri]

육아실, 탁아소
ⓝ a room or place set apart for young children
e.g. She had to leave her son in the care of a **nursery**.
ⓥ nurse 간호하다, 돌보다

0854 ■■□

apathetic
[æ̀pəθétpth]

무관심한, 냉담한
ⓐ showing no interest or enthusiasm
syn uninterested, unconcerned
e.g. In recent years, the student body has been recognized as one
of the most politically **apathetic** in the nation.

0855 ■■□

becket
[békit]

다림줄, 밧줄
ⓝ a short length of rope for securing spars, coils of rope, etc.
syn rope
e.g. This **becket** is old and worn-out but the sailors still may use it.

0856 ■■■

indigent
[índidʒənt]

궁핍한, 빈곤한, 결함이 있는
ⓐ lacking food, clothing, and other necessities of life because of
poverty
syn needy, poor, impoverished
e.g. This charity organization is notable for administering relief to
the **indigent**.

0857 ■■□

obituary
[oubítʃuèri]

사망기사, 사망자 약력
ⓝ a notice of the death of a person, often with a biographical
sketch, as in a newspaper
e.g. He was such a depressing person, he'd always read the
obituaries first.

0858 ■□□

carefree
[kɛ́ərfrìː]

근심 없는, 태평한, 무책임한
ⓐ without anxiety or worry
ⓢⓨⓝ unworried, indifferent
ⓔ.ⓖ. We lead a **carefree** life with no one else to worry about except ourselves.
ⓝ care 근심, 걱정거리, 불만

0859 ■■□

revert
[rivə́ːrt]

되돌아가다, 복귀하다
ⓥ to return to a former habit, practice, belief, condition, etc.
ⓢⓨⓝ return, retrace
ⓔ.ⓖ. They **reverted** to the ways of their ancestors.
ⓝ reversion 역전, 전환

0860 ■■■

implore
[implɔ́ːr]

간청하다, 애원하다
ⓥ to beg urgently or piteously, as for aid or mercy
ⓢⓨⓝ beseech, entreat, beg, plead, appeal
ⓔ.ⓖ. She **implored** the court to spare her son's life.
ⓝ imploration 탄원, 애원

DAY
15

0861 ■■□

codify
[kádəfài]

성문화하다, 체계적으로 분류하다
ⓥ to reduce (laws, rules, etc.) to a code
ⓔ.ⓖ. To protect human rights, the UN **codified** its values to make an universal standard.

0862 ■■□

encounter
[inkáuntər]

(우연히) 마주치다, 만나다
ⓥ to come upon or meet with, esp. unexpectedly
ⓢⓨⓝ meet with, be faced by[with], come across[upon], chance upon
ⓔ.ⓖ. I **encountered** an old teacher on the street.

0863 ■■□

adapt
[ədǽpt]

적응하다
ⓥ to make suitable to requirements or conditions
ⓢⓨⓝ adjust, conform
ⓔ.ⓖ. It's important to **adapt** to change if one wants to succeed.
ⓝ adaptation 적응

0864 ■■■

inordinate
[ɪnɔːrdɪnət]

(격식) 과도한, 지나친

ⓐ far more than is usual or expected

(e.g.) They spent an **inordinate** amount of time and money on the production.

ⓝ inordinateness, inordinacy　　ⓐⓓ inordinately

0865 ■■■

eerie
[ɪri]

괴상한, 으스스한

ⓐ strange, mysterious and frightening

(syn) uncanny, strange, frightening

(e.g.) I found the silence underwater really **eerie**.

ⓝ eeriness　　　　　　　　ⓐⓓ eerily

0866 ■■■

tenuous
[tenjuəs]

미약한, 보잘것없는; 극도로 허약한(가는) (그래서 쉽게 부러지는)

ⓐ so weak or uncertain that it hardly exists; extremely thin and easily broken

(e.g.) a **tenuous** hold on life

ⓝ tenuousness, tenuity　　ⓐⓓ tenuously

0867 ■■□

viable
[vaɪəbl]

실행 가능한, 성공할 수 있는; 독자 생존 가능한

ⓐ that can be done; that will be successful; (biology) capable of developing and surviving independently

(syn) workable, practical, feasible

(e.g.) 1. a **viable** option/proposition

　　　 2. **viable** organisms

ⓐⓓ viably

0868 ■■□

attribute
[ætrɪbjuːt]

(~을 …의) 결과로(덕분으로) 보다(to); 특성, 특질

ⓥ to say or believe that something is the result of a particular thing; to say or believe that somebody is responsible for doing something, especially for saying, writing or painting something

ⓝ something attributed as belonging to a person, thing, group, etc.; a quality, character, characteristic, or property

(syn) ⓥ ascribe, credit, refer　　ⓝ quality, mark

(e.g.) 1. She **attributes** her success **to** hard work and a little luck.

　　　 2. Rubber has the **attribute** stretching easily.

0869 ■■■

stipulate
[stípjulèit]

규정하다, 명기하다, 명문화하다
ⓥ to make an express demand or arrangement as a condition of agreement
(syn) specify, prescribe, ordain
(e.g.) The rental agreement **stipulates** that the deposit is non-refundable.
ⓝ stipulation 계약, 규정

0870 ■■□

culprit
[kʌ́lprit]

범죄자, 범인
ⓝ a person or other agent guilty of or responsible for an offense or fault
(syn) offender, criminal
(e.g.) The detectives searched the streets for the **culprit**.

0871 ■■■

compensate
[kámpənsèit]

보상하다, 배상하다
ⓥ to recompense for something
(syn) recompense, countervail, offset
(e.g.) He gave me one million dollars to **compensate** for my hospital bills.
ⓝ compensation 보상, 배상

0872 ■■■

reprimand
[réprəmænd]

견책하다, 징계하다
ⓥ to reprove or rebuke severely, esp. in a formal way
(syn) rebuke, scold, blame
(e.g.) He was **reprimanded** for leaving his post.

0873 ■■■

implacable
[implǽkəbl]

달래기 어려운, 인정사정없는, 무자비한
ⓐ not to be appeased, mollified, or pacified
(syn) inexorable, intransigent, unrelenting
(e.g.) They have been **implacable** customers ever since we first got their account.
ⓝ implacability 앙심 깊음, 무자비함

DAY
15

0874 ■■□

quell
[kwél]

진압하다, 정복하다, 억누르다
ⓥ to suppress, put an end to, extinguish
syn conquer, overpower, overcome, quash
e.g. The troops **quelled** the riot quickly.

0875 ■□□

decode
[di:kóud]

번역하다, 해독하다
ⓥ to translate (data or a message) from a code into the original language or form
syn translate, decipher
e.g. Once the enemy army **decoded** our cipher, we changed to another.

0876 ■■□

replete
[riplí:t]

충만한, 충분히 공급된
ⓐ abundantly supplied or provided
syn filled, abundant
e.g. The history of America is **replete** with the names of men and women who are remembered by posterity, for good or evil.
ⓝ repletion 충만, 충실, 과다

0877 ■■□

deserve
[dizə́:rv]

~할(받을) 만하다, 가치가 있다
ⓥ to merit, be qualified for, or have a claim to (reward, assistance, punishment, etc.) because of actions, qualities, or situation
syn warrant, worth
e.g. He **deserves** the highest praise for his service.
ⓝ deserver 적격자

0878 ■□□

fretful
[frétfəl]

화를 잘 내는, 안달하는, 성마른
ⓐ disposed or quick to fret
syn irritable, peevish
e.g. Children are usually **fretful** about starting school.
ⓥ fret 속 타게 하다, 안달하게 하다

0879 ■■□

colony
[káləni]

식민지, 식민

ⓝ a group of people who leave their native country to form in a new land a settlement subject to, or connected with, the parent nation

ⓔ.ⓖ. The **colony** was Dutch people who came to America for religious freedom.

ⓥ colonize 식민지로서 개척하다

0880 ■□□

diameter
[daiǽmətər]

지름, 직경

ⓝ a straight line passing through the center of a circle or sphere and meeting the circumference or surface at each end

ⓢⓨⓝ breadth, caliber

ⓔ.ⓖ. Each stalk of the pine tree was about 10 cm in **diameter**.

ⓐ diametral 직경의

DAY
15

0881 ■■□

bigot
[bígət]

고집쟁이

ⓝ a person who is utterly intolerant of any differing creed, belief, or opinion

ⓔ.ⓖ. The countryside here is full of racist **bigots** who will fight as soon as argue.

ⓐ bigoted 고집불통의

0882 ■■□

fertile
[fɔ́ːrtl]

기름진, 비옥한

ⓐ bearing, producing, or capable of producing vegetation, crops, etc., abundantly

ⓢⓨⓝ prolific, rich, productive, fruitful

ⓔ.ⓖ. Southern India is comprised of a hot and **fertile** region surrounding a dry inland plateau.

ⓥ fertilize 기름지게 하다, 비옥하게 하다

0883 ■■□

harrow
[hǽrou]

괴롭히다, 고민하게 하다

ⓥ to disturb keenly or painfully; distress the mind or feelings

ⓢⓨⓝ disturb, distress

ⓔ.ⓖ. He was **harrowed** with depression.

ⓐ harrowed 고민하는, 난처해하는

0884 ■■□

assume
[əsúːm]

가정하다
ⓥ to take for granted or without proof
ⓢⓨⓝ presume, suppose, postulate, posit
ⓔ.ⓖ. I'm going to **assume** that you will pay me back.
ⓝ assumption 가정

0885 ■□□

bundle
[bʌ́ndl]

다발, 꾸러미
ⓝ several objects or a quantity of material gathered or bound together
ⓢⓨⓝ bunch, sheaf
ⓔ.ⓖ. The boxes were tied up in **bundles** of five.

0886 ■□□

chamber
[tʃéimbər]

방, 침실
ⓝ a room, usually private, in a house or apartment, esp. a bedroom
ⓢⓨⓝ room
ⓔ.ⓖ. The designer enlarged his house to five **chambers** for office space.

0887 ■□□

indirect
[ìndərékt]

똑바르지 않은, 우회하는, 간접적인
ⓐ not in a direct course or path; deviating from a straight line
ⓢⓨⓝ mediate, secondhand, roundabout, circuitous
ⓔ.ⓖ. His reaction to the situation was **indirect**.
ⓐ direct 똑바른, 직접의

0888 ■■□

magnitude
[mǽgnətjùːd]

거대함, 중요성
ⓝ size; extent; dimensions; greatness of size, amount or importance
ⓢⓨⓝ grandeur, greatness
ⓔ.ⓖ. Never before has a drought of this **magnitude** occurred.
ⓐ magnificent 장려한, 웅장한, 장대한

0889 ■■□

executive
[igzékjutiv]

임원, 경영진

ⓝ a person or group of persons having administrative or supervisory authority in an organization

ⓢⓨⓝ director, manager, administrator

ⓔ.ⓖ. He is a responsible business **executive** and handles his credit transactions with us in a competent manner.

0890 ■□□

psychiatrist
[sikáiətrist]

정신과 의사

ⓝ a physician who practices psychiatry

ⓔ.ⓖ. He is required to meet with the company **psychiatrist** once a year.

ⓐ psychic 영혼의, 정신의

0891 ■■□

keen
[kíːn]

날카로운, 예리한

ⓐ finely sharpened, as an edge; so shaped as to cut or pierce substances readily

ⓢⓨⓝ sharp, piercing

ⓔ.ⓖ. Dogs have a **keen** sense of smell.

0892 ■■□

forthwith
[fɔ́ːrθwíð]

곧, 즉시

ⓐⓓ immediately; at once; without delay

ⓢⓨⓝ instantly, immediately, at once

ⓔ.ⓖ. Any official accused of treason should be suspended **forthwith**.

0893 ■□□

banquet
[bǽŋkwit]

연회, 향연, 축연

ⓝ a ceremonious public dinner, esp. one honoring a person, benefiting a charity, etc.

ⓢⓨⓝ feast, party

ⓔ.ⓖ. Her mother was busy preparing for a wedding **banquet**.

0894 ■■□

realm
[rélm]

왕국, 국토, 영토
ⓝ a royal domain; a community or territory over which a sovereign rules
ⓢⓨⓝ kingdom, province, region
ⓔⓖ Spiritual heroes usually have their spiritual **realms**.

0895 ■□□

corporation
[kɔ́ːrpəréiʃən]

법인, 기업, 주식회사
ⓝ an association of individuals, created by law or under authority of law, having a continuous existence independent of the existences of its members, and powers and liabilities distinct from those of its members
ⓔⓖ I heard the public **corporation** was supposed to be transferred to the private sector in the near future.
ⓐ corporate 법인(조직)의

0896 ■■□

perverse
[pərvə́ːrs]

괴팍한, 심술궂은, 외고집의
ⓐ wayward or cantankerous; persistent or obstinate in what is wrong
ⓢⓨⓝ miscreant, villainous, tenacious
ⓔⓖ How did he ever grow up to be such a **perverse** child?
ⓝ perversion 타락, 악화

0897 ■■□

address
[ədrés]

연설, 주소; 말을 걸다, (to) ~에게 전하다, 역점을 두어 다루다
ⓝ a speech or written statement, usually formal, directed to a particular group of persons
ⓢⓨⓝ speech, oration; confront, deal with
ⓔⓖ The President's **address** on the state of the economy was impressive to me.

0898 ■■■

drudgery
[drʌ́dʒəri]

고된 일, 고역
ⓝ menial, distasteful, dull, or hard work
ⓢⓨⓝ slavery
ⓔⓖ Years of **drudgery** had made her look old beyond her age.
ⓥ drudge 고역을 치르다

0899 ■■□

intrepid
[intrépid]

용맹한, 대담한
ⓐ resolutely fearless
ⓢⓨⓝ fearless, dauntless, brave, courageous, bold
ⓔ.ⓖ. Other **intrepid** entrepreneurs are finding radical new ways to sell their products.
ⓝ intrepidity 대담, 용맹, 겁없음

0900 ■■□

ominous
[ámənəs]

불길한, 나쁜 징조의
ⓐ portending evil or harm
ⓢⓨⓝ inauspicious, sinister, foreboding
ⓔ.ⓖ. **Ominous** clouds have begun to gather over village city.
ⓝ omen 징조, 조짐

DAY
15

Day

16

유희태 일반영어 ⑤
VOCA
기출 VOCA 30 days

amicable	☐☐☐	infinite	☐☐☐
deem	☐☐☐	atmosphere	☐☐☐
cathedral	☐☐☐	committee	☐☐☐
nuzzle	☐☐☐	paucity	☐☐☐
blossom	☐☐☐	coast	☐☐☐
mane	☐☐☐	reveal	☐☐☐
flat	☐☐☐	exacerbate	☐☐☐
distraction	☐☐☐	edge	☐☐☐
impudent	☐☐☐	renaissance	☐☐☐
protest	☐☐☐	adopt	☐☐☐
quack	☐☐☐	impunity	☐☐☐
trump	☐☐☐	astute	☐☐☐
neutral	☐☐☐	negligible	☐☐☐
consubstantial	☐☐☐	pragmatic	☐☐☐
fictitious	☐☐☐	turbulent	☐☐☐
metaphysics	☐☐☐	afflict	☐☐☐
tinge	☐☐☐	errand	☐☐☐
adequate	☐☐☐	reticent	☐☐☐
ponder	☐☐☐	furrow	☐☐☐
competent	☐☐☐	invade	☐☐☐
barley	☐☐☐	enthrall	☐☐☐
stratified	☐☐☐	advantageous	☐☐☐
proponent	☐☐☐	draft	☐☐☐
adjacent	☐☐☐	lyrical	☐☐☐
surmise	☐☐☐	hedge	☐☐☐
hitherto	☐☐☐	depressed	☐☐☐
strew	☐☐☐	expose	☐☐☐
encapsulate	☐☐☐	ineffectual	☐☐☐
gratitude	☐☐☐	disdain	☐☐☐
tangible	☐☐☐	scoff	☐☐☐

0901 ■■□
amicable
[æmikəbl]

우호적인, 평화적인
ⓐ characterized by or showing goodwill
syn friendly, peaceable
e.g. Korea should maintain **amicable** relations with foreign countries.
ⓝ amicability 우호, 친화, 친선

0902 ■■□
deem
[díːm]

~으로 생각하다, 간주하다
ⓥ to hold as an opinion
syn consider, judge, think, regard
e.g. She **deemed** it savvy to refuse his propose.

0903 ■□□
cathedral
[kəθíːdrəl]

대성당, 대교회
ⓝ the principal church of a diocese, containing the bishop's throne
e.g. Medieval Europeans had their great **cathedrals**.
ⓐ catholic 가톨릭교회의, 천주교의

0904 ■■□
nuzzle
[nʌzəl]

코(입)를 비비다
ⓥ to thrust the nose, muzzle, etc.
syn embrace, snuggle
e.g. train pigs to **nuzzle** truffles from the ground

0905 ■□□
blossom
[blɑ́səm]

꽃
ⓝ the flowers that appear on a tree before the fruit
syn bloom, floret
e.g. The cherry trees are in **blossom**.
ⓐ blossomy

0906 ■■□
mane
[mein]

갈기
ⓝ on a horse or lion is the long thick hair that grows from its neck
e.g. But ligers have no **mane**.

0907 ■□□

flat
[flæt]

평평한, 저조한
ⓐ horizontally level
ⓢⓨⓝ level, featureless
ⓞⓟⓟ vertical, bumpy
ⓔ.ⓖ. People used to think the earth was **flat**.
ⓝ flatness
ⓥ flatten
ⓐⓓ flatly

0908 ■□□

distraction
[dəˈstrakSH(ə)n]

(기분전환) 오락 활동, 주의집중을 방해하는 것
ⓝ an activity which is intended to entertain and amuse you
ⓢⓨⓝ pastime, entertainment
ⓔ.ⓖ. I'm usually so tired when I get home that I feel I need the **distraction**.
ⓥ distract

0909 ■□□

impudent
[ímpjədənt]

거만한
ⓐ of, relating to, or characterized by impertinence or effrontery
ⓢⓨⓝ insolent, bold as brass, arrogant
ⓔ.ⓖ. Some of them were **impudent** and insulting.
ⓝ impudence

0910 ■□□

protest
[prətést]

항변하다, 반발하다
ⓥ to make a protest or remonstrance against; object to
ⓢⓨⓝ make a fuss, oppose
ⓞⓟⓟ acquiesce
ⓔ.ⓖ. She wouldn't let him pay, and he didn't **protest**.

0911 ■■□

quack
[kwæk]

돌팔이 의사, 사기꾼
ⓝ a fraudulent or ignorant pretender to medical skill
ⓢⓨⓝ mountebank, fraud
ⓔ.ⓖ. This **quack** didn't fill your cavities.
ⓐ quackish

DAY
16

0912 ■□□

trump
[trʌmp]

~을 이기다, ~보다 우선하다
ⓥ beat (someone or something) by saying or doing something better
ⓢⓨⓝ beat, outperform
ⓔ.ⓖ. I think my people **trump** your people.
ⓐ trumpless

0913 ■□□

neutral
[njúːtrəl]

중립의, 중립국의
ⓐ not taking part or giving assistance in a dispute or war between others
ⓢⓨⓝ impartial, unbiased, unprejudiced
ⓔ.ⓖ. He has been taken a **neutral** position in the fight.
ⓝ neutralist 중립주의자

0914 ■■□

consubstantial
[kànsəbstǽnʃəl]

동질의, 동체의
ⓐ of one and the same substance, essence, or nature
ⓢⓨⓝ homogeneous, coessential, cognate
ⓔ.ⓖ. Love is **consubstantial** with anger, both springing from passion.
ⓐ substantial 실체의, 실재하는

0915 ■□□

fictitious
[fiktíʃəs]

가상의, 가공의, 거짓의
ⓐ created, taken, or assumed for the sake of concealment; not genuine
ⓢⓨⓝ imaginary, false, factitious
ⓔ.ⓖ. We loved the story, even though it was totally **fictitious**.
ⓝ fiction 소설, 허구

0916 ■□□

metaphysics
[mètəfíziks]

형이상학
ⓝ the branch of philosophy that treats of first principles, includes ontology and cosmology, and is intimately connected with epistemology
ⓔ.ⓖ. The questions of substantial world are to be answered by science, and those of **metaphysics** by holy men.

0917 ■□□

tinge
[tíndʒ]

색조를 띠게 하다, 엷게 물들이다

ⓥ to impart a trace or slight degree of some color to
ⓢⓨⓝ tint
ⓔ.ⓖ. The eastern sky was **tinged** with crimson at sunset.

0918 ■■■

adequate
[ǽdikwət]

충분한, 알맞은

ⓐ as much or as good as necessary for some requirement or
purpose; fully sufficient, suitable, or fit
ⓢⓨⓝ satisfactory, competent, sufficient, enough
ⓔ.ⓖ. This car is **adequate** for our needs.
ⓝ adequacy 적절, 타당성

0919 ■■□

ponder
[pándər]

숙고하다, 곰곰이 생각하다

ⓥ to consider something deeply and thoroughly
ⓢⓨⓝ consider, cogitate, meditate
ⓔ.ⓖ. You must **ponder** on our options for the coming semester.
ⓐ ponderable 생각할 가치가 있는

DAY
16

0920 ■■□

competent
[kámpətənt]

유능한, 능력(자격)이 있는

ⓐ having suitable or sufficient skill, knowledge, experience, etc.,
for some purpose; properly qualified
ⓢⓨⓝ able, capable, adequate, apt
ⓔ.ⓖ. He is perfectly **competent** in his decision-making.
ⓝ competence 능력, 적성

0921 ■□□

barley
[báːrli]

보리

ⓝ a widely distributed cereal plant belonging to the genus Hordeum,
of the grass family, having awned flowers that grow in tightly
bunched spikes, with three small additional spikes at each node
ⓔ.ⓖ. For thousands of years, **barley** has been used to make beer.

0922 ■■■

stratified
[strǽtəfài]

(의학) 중층-, 뭇겹-, 층상-

ⓐ A stratified society is one that is divided into different classes or social layers.

e.g. a highly **stratified**, unequal and class-divided society

0923 ■■□

proponent
[prəpóunənt]

지지자

ⓝ (formal) a person who supports an idea or course of action

syn supporter

e.g. **Proponents** argue the dam will prevent flooding.

0924 ■■□

adjacent
[ədʒéɪsnt]

인접한

ⓐ next to or near something

syn adjoining, neighbouring, nearby

e.g. The planes landed on **adjacent** runways.

ⓝ adjacency　　　　ad adjacently

0925 ■■□

surmise
[sɜːrmáɪz]

추측하다, 추정하다

ⓥ to guess or suppose something using the evidence you have, without definitely knowing

syn suspect, theory, imagine

e.g. From the looks on their faces, I **surmised** that they had had an argument.

ⓝ surmiser　　　　ⓐ surmisable

0926 ■■□

hitherto
[hɪðərtuː]

지금까지; 그때까지

ad until now

syn previously, so far, until now

e.g. a **hitherto** unknown species of moth

0927 ■■■

strew
[stru:]

흩다, 흩뿌리다

ⓥ to cover a surface with things
ⓢⓨⓝ scatter, spread
ⓔ.ⓖ. Clothes were **strewn** across the floor.
ⓝ strewer

0928 ■■■

encapsulate
[ɪnkǽpsjuleɪt]

요약하다, 압축하다

ⓥ to express the most important parts of something in a few words, a small space or a single object
ⓔ.ⓖ. The poem **encapsulates** many of the central themes of her writing.
ⓝ encapsulation

0929 ■■□

gratitude
[grǽtətjùːd]

감사(하는 마음), 사의

ⓝ the quality or feeling of being grateful or thankful
ⓢⓨⓝ thankfulness, gratefulness
ⓔ.ⓖ. He expressed his **gratitude** to everyone on the staff.
ⓥ gratify 만족시키다, 고마워하게 하다

0930 ■■□

tangible
[tǽndʒəbl]

만져서 알 수 있는, 실체적인

ⓐ capable of being touched; discernible by the touch
ⓢⓨⓝ substantial, touchable, concrete
ⓔ.ⓖ. There is no **tangible** form of love, it's all abstract and invisible.
ⓐ intangible 손으로 만질 수 없는

0931 ■■□

infinite
[ínfənət]

무한한, 끝없는

ⓐ unlimited or unmeasurable in extent of space or duration of time
ⓢⓨⓝ boundless, limitless
ⓔ.ⓖ. The Internet has opened up **infinite** possibilities.
ⓝ infinity 무한대

DAY
16

0932 ■□□

atmosphere
[ǽtməsfiər]

대기, 공기
ⓝ the gaseous envelope surrounding the earth
ⓢⓨⓝ air
ⓔⓖ I feel better because of the refreshing mountain **atmosphere**.
ⓐ atmospheric 대기중의, 공기의

0933 ■□□

committee
[kəmíti]

위원, 위원회
ⓝ a person or group of persons elected or appointed to perform some service or function, as to investigate, report on, or act upon a particular matter
ⓢⓨⓝ board, council
ⓔⓖ The **committee** will pronounce on the matter in dispute.

0934 ■■□

paucity
[pɔ́:səti]

소수, 소량, 결핍
ⓝ smallness of quantity
ⓢⓨⓝ deficiency, defect, inadequacy, scarcity, scantiness
ⓔⓖ The ultimate problem is the **paucity** of good women sprinters.

0935 ■■□

coast
[kóust]

미끄러져 나아가다, 손쉽게 얻다; 연안, 해안
ⓥ glide smoothly, obtain easily
ⓝ the land next to the sea
ⓢⓨⓝ drift, glide; seashore
ⓔⓖ She **coasted** through college; no one really saw her struggling.
ⓐ coastal 근해의, 연안의

0936 ■□□

reveal
[riví:l]

드러내다, 폭로하다
ⓥ to make known something concealed or secret
ⓢⓨⓝ disclose, divulge, unveil, expose
ⓔⓖ He refused to **reveal** his source of the information.
ⓝ revealment 폭로, 탄로

0937 ■■■

exacerbate
[igzǽsərbèit]

악화시키다, 격분시키다

ⓥ to increase the severity, bitterness, or violence of (disease, ill feeling, etc.)

ⓢⓨⓝ aggravate, provoke, worsen

ⓔ.ⓖ. This attack will **exacerbate** the already tense relations between the two countries.

ⓝ exacerbation 격화, 악화, 분노

0938 ■□□

edge
[édʒ]

가장자리, 끝, 언저리

ⓝ a line or border at which a surface terminates

ⓢⓨⓝ rim, brink, verge, margin

ⓔ.ⓖ. Grass grew along the **edges** of the road.

0939 ■□□

renaissance
[rènəsáːns]

르네상스

ⓝ the activity, spirit, or time of the great revival of art, literature, and learning in Europe beginning in the 14th century and extending to the 17th century, marking the transition from the medieval to the modern world

ⓔ.ⓖ. The application of mathematics to art, particularly in paintings, was one of the primary characteristics of **Renaissance** art.

0940 ■■□

adopt
[ədápt]

채용하다, 채택하다

ⓥ to choose or take as one's own; make one's own by selection or assent

ⓢⓨⓝ choose, select

ⓔ.ⓖ. The CEO expressed his readiness to **adopt** our proposal.

ⓝ adoption 채택, 채용

0941 ■■■

impunity
[impjúːnəti]

형벌을 받지 않음, 무사

ⓝ exemption from punishment

ⓔ.ⓖ. He was able to conduct his business with total **impunity** to local police.

ⓥ punish 벌하다, 응징하다

0942 ■■□

astute
[əstjúːt]

기민한, 눈치 빠른

ⓐ of keen penetration or discernment

ⓢⓨⓝ sagacious, foxy, clever, smart, ingenious, shrewd

ⓔ.ⓖ. It was very **astute** of him to catch your mistake.

0943 ■■□

negligible
[néglidʒəbl]

무시해도 좋은, 하찮은

ⓐ so small, trifling, or unimportant that it may safely be neglected or disregard

ⓢⓨⓝ inconsiderable, trifling, petty

ⓔ.ⓖ. Transit expenses are **negligible**.

ⓥ neglect 무시하다, 등한시하다

0944 ■□□

pragmatic
[prægmǽtik]

실용적인, 실용주의의

ⓐ of or pertaining to a practical point of view or practical considerations

ⓢⓨⓝ practical

ⓔ.ⓖ. A **pragmatic** approach to the crime problem is necessary, there has been too much irrational action.

ⓝ pragmatism 실용주의

0945 ■■□

turbulent
[tɔ́ːrbjulənt]

휘몰아치는, 사나운, 거친

ⓐ being in a state of agitation or tumult

ⓢⓨⓝ disturbed, tumultuous, blustery, violent

ⓔ.ⓖ. The sea was too **turbulent** for us to be able to sail safely.

ⓝ turbulence 휘몰아침, 사나움

0946 ■■□

afflict
[əflíkt]

괴롭히다

ⓥ to distress with mental or bodily pain; trouble greatly or grievously

ⓢⓨⓝ distress, torment, torture, bother

ⓔ.ⓖ. He was **afflicted** with debts and loneliness.

ⓝ affliction 고통, 괴로움

0947 ■□□

errand
[érənd]

심부름

ⓝ a short and quick trip to accomplish a specific purpose, as to buy something, deliver a package, or convey a message, often for someone else

ⓔ.ⓖ. The little boy went on **errands** for his mother.

0948 ■■□

reticent
[rétəsənt]

과묵한, 말을 삼가는

ⓐ disposed to be silent or not to speak freely

ⓢⓨⓝ reserved, taciturn

ⓔ.ⓖ. Men are **reticent** about their emotions.

ⓝ reticence 과묵, 말수 적음

0949 ■■□

furrow
[fə́:rou]

고랑, 도랑, 주름살

ⓝ a narrow groove made in the ground, esp. by a plow; a narrow groovelike or trenchlike depression in any surface

ⓢⓨⓝ trench

ⓔ.ⓖ. Old age plowed **furrows** in her face.

ⓐ furrowy 이랑진, 주름살이 진

0950 ■□□

invade
[invéid]

침략하다, 침입하다

ⓥ to enter forcefully as an enemy; go into with hostile intent

ⓢⓨⓝ assail, raid, encroach

ⓔ.ⓖ. During its 10,000-year history, Korea has been **invaded** over 900 times.

ⓝ invasion 침입, 침략

0951 ■■■

enthrall
[inθrɔ́:l, en-]

마음을 사로잡다

ⓥ to captivate or charm

ⓢⓨⓝ entrance, captivate, charm

ⓔ.ⓖ. I've been **enthralled** with your photographs for years.

ⓐ enthralling 마음을 사로잡는, 아주 재미있는

DAY
16

0952 ■□□

advantageous
[ædvəntéidʒəs]

유리한, 이로운, 편리한

ⓐ providing an advantage; furnishing convenience or opportunity
ⓢⓨⓝ favorable, profitable, useful, beneficial
ⓔ.ⓖ. It would be **advantageous** to you to keep silent.
ⓝ advantage 이점, 유리한 점

0953 ■□□

draft
[dræft]

밑그림, 초안, 설계, 도면

ⓝ a drawing, sketch, or design; a first or preliminary form of any
writing, subject to revision, copying, etc.
ⓢⓨⓝ drawing, sketch, design, outline
ⓔ.ⓖ. Here is the first **draft** of the timeline for the Cobblewell
company proposal.

0954 ■■□

lyrical
[lírikəl]

서정시 같은, 감상적인

ⓐ expressing deep personal emotion or observations
ⓢⓨⓝ emotional
ⓔ.ⓖ. His speech was more **lyrical** than professional, and brought
tears to the eyes of his listeners.
ⓐ lyric 서정적인, 서정시의, 음악적인

0955 ■■□

hedge
[hédʒ]

울타리

ⓝ a row of bushes or small trees planted close together, esp. when
forming a fence or boundary
ⓢⓨⓝ fence
ⓔ.ⓖ. The **hedge** is tangled with roses.

0956 ■■□

depressed
[diprést]

의기소침한, 낙담한

ⓐ sad and gloomy; dejected; downcast
ⓢⓨⓝ sad, gloomy, dejected, downcast
ⓔ.ⓖ. Most people get **depressed** when it rains for too long.
ⓝ depression 의기소침, 우울

0957 ■■□

expose
[ikspóuz]

드러내다, 노출시키다, 폭로하다
ⓥ to uncover something so that it can be seen
ⓢⓨⓝ disclose, reveal
ⓔⓖ It was the first time I was **exposed** to punk music.
ⓝ exposure 드러남, 탄로

0958 ■■□

ineffectual
[ìniféktʃuəl]

효과 없는, 쓸데없는, 무익한
ⓐ not effectual; without satisfactory or decisive effect
ⓢⓨⓝ useless, worthless, helpless, impotent
ⓔⓖ As the project manager, he seemed to be wishy-washy and **ineffectual**.
ⓐ effectual 효과적인, 유효한

0959 ■■□

disdain
[disdéin]

경멸하다, 멸시하다
ⓥ to look upon or treat with contempt
ⓢⓨⓝ despise, scorn, condemn
ⓔⓖ Do not **disdain** him because he is younger than you.
ⓐ disdainful 경멸적인

DAY
16

0960 ■□□

scoff
[skɔ́ːf]

비웃다, 조롱하다
ⓥ to speak derisively
ⓢⓨⓝ mock, jeer
ⓔⓖ Their efforts toward a peaceful settlement are not to be **scoffed** at.

Day
17

moderate	☐☐☐		**deafen**	☐☐☐	
curse	☐☐☐		**felon**	☐☐☐	
inadequate	☐☐☐		**modify**	☐☐☐	
nostrum	☐☐☐		**increment**	☐☐☐	
traipse	☐☐☐		**intimidate**	☐☐☐	
homicide	☐☐☐		**misbehave**	☐☐☐	
highlight	☐☐☐		**analyze**	☐☐☐	
mount	☐☐☐		**artifact**	☐☐☐	
thrash	☐☐☐		**latent**	☐☐☐	
canoodle	☐☐☐		**dubious**	☐☐☐	
poke	☐☐☐		**sinister**	☐☐☐	
aisle	☐☐☐		**bare**	☐☐☐	
malnutrition	☐☐☐		**mercurial**	☐☐☐	
consonant	☐☐☐		**inherent**	☐☐☐	
secure	☐☐☐		**equate**	☐☐☐	
rudimentary	☐☐☐		**harass**	☐☐☐	
analogy	☐☐☐		**uncertainty**	☐☐☐	
commercial	☐☐☐		**formal**	☐☐☐	
deride	☐☐☐		**awe**	☐☐☐	
unwieldy	☐☐☐		**throughout**	☐☐☐	
exude	☐☐☐		**bloom**	☐☐☐	
interplay	☐☐☐		**coagulate**	☐☐☐	
rudiments	☐☐☐		**reusable**	☐☐☐	
constrain	☐☐☐		**solace**	☐☐☐	
spur	☐☐☐		**cater**	☐☐☐	
feat	☐☐☐		**reprehensible**	☐☐☐	
demise	☐☐☐		**philanthropy**	☐☐☐	
furtive	☐☐☐		**meddle**	☐☐☐	
devious	☐☐☐		**ubiquitous**	☐☐☐	
provoke	☐☐☐		**bracket**	☐☐☐	

0961 ■■□

moderate
[mádərət]

알맞은, 적당한
ⓐ kept or keeping within reasonable or proper limits; not extreme,
   excessive, or intense
ⓢⓨⓝ reasonable, temperate, adequate
ⓔ.ⓖ. **Moderate** exercise plays an important role in the management
   of heart disease.
ⓝ moderation 알맞음, 중용

0962 ■□□

curse
[kə́ːrs]

저주, 악담, 독설
ⓝ the expression of a wish that misfortune, evil, doom, etc., befall a
   person, group, etc.
ⓢⓨⓝ blasphemy, cuss, denunciation
ⓔ.ⓖ. He never opens his lips without giving a **curse** or swear.

0963 ■□□

inadequate
[inǽdikwət]

부적당한, 불충분한
ⓐ not adequate or sufficient
ⓢⓨⓝ deficient, incompetent, scarce
ⓔ.ⓖ. The production is wholly **inadequate** to meet the demand.
ⓝ inadequacy 부적당, 불충분

0964 ■■□

nostrum
[nástrəm]

(성공할 가능성이 없어 보이는) 처방(대책), 엉터리 약
ⓝ a medicine sold with false or exaggerated claims and with no
   demonstrable value
ⓔ.ⓖ. We are in a world where the old **nostrums** simply no longer
   apply.

0965 ■■□

traipse
[treips]

터벅터벅 걷다
ⓥ to walk or go aimlessly or idly or without finding or reaching one's
   goal
ⓢⓨⓝ slouch, trudge
ⓔ.ⓖ. We're **traipsing** along like natural men.

0966 ■□□

homicide
[hámǝsàid]

살인
ⓝ the killing of one human being by another
ⓢⓨⓝ assassination, killing, murder

0967 ■□□

highlight
['hī,līt]

강조하다
ⓥ to emphasize or make prominent
ⓢⓨⓝ spotlight, underline, emphasize
ⓞⓟⓟ play down
ⓔ.ⓖ. Students **highlight** important parts of their textbooks.

0968 ■□□

mount
[maunt]

올라가다
ⓥ to go up; climb; ascend
ⓢⓨⓝ ascend
ⓞⓟⓟ descend
ⓔ.ⓖ. He **mounted** the steps to the front door.
ⓐ mountable

0969 ■■□

thrash
[θræʃ]

허우적거리다(몸부림치다); 때리다
ⓥ move with brute determination or violent movements
ⓔ.ⓖ. The music industry continues to **thrash** about in its death throes.

0970 ■■□

canoodle
[kǝnúːdl]

애무하다
ⓥ kiss and cuddle amorously
ⓔ.ⓖ. So after a night in separate beds, the pair spent the day **canoodling**.

0971 ■□□

poke
[pouk]

(손가락으로) 찌르다
ⓥ to prod or push, especially with something narrow or pointed, as a finger, elbow, stick, etc.
ⓢⓨⓝ jab, jolt
ⓔ.ⓖ. Don't **poke** her eye out with that stick!
ⓐ poky 비좁은

DAY
17

0972 ■□□

aisle
[áil]

복도, 통로

ⓝ a walkway between or along sections of seats in a theater or classroom

(syn) passage, pathway

(e.g.) Passengers are not permitted to smoke in the sections designated as non-smoking areas, in the **aisle** or in the washrooms.

0973 ■□□

malnutrition
[mæ̀lnjuːtríʃən]

영양부족, 영양실조

ⓝ lack of proper nutrition; inadequate or unbalanced nutrition

(e.g.) **Malnutrition** was one of the main reasons that he lost weight.

ⓝ nutrition 영양, 영양물

0974 ■□□

consonant
[kánsənənt]

자음

ⓝ a speech sound produced by occluding with or without releasing (p, b; t, d; k, g), diverting (m, n, ng), or obstructing (f, v; s, z, etc.) the flow of air from the lungs

(e.g.) Hangeul is made up of 10 vowels and 14 **consonants**, unlike English.

ⓐ consonantal 자음의

0975 ■□□

secure
[sikjúər]

안전하게 하다, 지키다

ⓥ to free from danger or harm; make safe

(syn) protect, shelter, guard

(e.g.) Sandbags **secured** the town against the flood.

ⓝ security 안전, 무사, 안보

0976 ■■□

rudimentary
[rùːdəméntəri]

기본의, 기초의

ⓐ pertaining to rudiments or first principles

(syn) elementary, primary, basic

(e.g.) She lacks even a **rudimentary** knowledge of computers.

0977 ■■□

analogy
[ənǽlədʒi]

유사, 비슷함, 유추

ⓝ a similarity between like features of two things, on which a comparison may be based

syn similarity, metaphor

e.g. Some doctors give patients very helpful **analogy** such as the heart as a pump.

ⓐ analogous 유사한, 같은

0978 ■□□

commercial
[kəmə́:rʃəl]

상업상의, 교역의, 영리적인

ⓐ of, pertaining to, or characteristic of commerce

syn mercenary, marketable

e.g. The news came down like a thunderclap on the **commercial** world.

ⓝ commerce 상업, 통상, 교역

0979 ■■□

deride
[diráid]

비웃다, 조롱하다

ⓥ to laugh at in scorn or contempt

syn mock, ridicule, scoff, jeer

e.g. They have insulted us and **derided** our family.

ⓝ derision 비웃음, 조롱

DAY

17

0980 ■■■

unwieldy
[ʌnwíːldi]

다루기 불편한

ⓐ difficult to move or control because of its size, shape or weight

e.g. The first mechanical clocks were large and rather **unwieldy**.

ⓝ unwieldiness   ad unwieldily

0981 ■■■

exude
[ɪgzúːd]

(특정한 느낌이) 물씬 풍기다

ⓥ to come out gradually in drops, as sweat, through pores or small openings

syn emanate

e.g. She **exuded** confidence.

0982 ■■■

interplay
[ɪntərpleɪ]

상호작용
ⓝ the way in which two or more things or people affect each other
ⓔⓖ the **interplay** between politics and the environment

0983 ■■■

rudiments
[ruːdɪmənts]

기본
ⓝ the most basic or essential facts of a particular subject, skill, etc.
ⓢⓨⓝ foundation, basis, groundwork
ⓔⓖ You'll only have time to learn the **rudiments** of windsurfing in
a week.

0984 ■■■

constrain
[kənstreɪn]

~하게 만들다
ⓥ force somebody to do something or behave in a particular way
ⓢⓨⓝ restrict, confine, curb
ⓔⓖ The company said that it was **constrained** to raise prices.
ⓝ constraint

0985 ■■□

spur
[spɜː(r)]

자극제, 원동력
ⓝ a fact or an event that makes you want to do something better or
more quickly
ⓢⓨⓝ stimulus, incentive, impetus
ⓔⓖ His speech was a powerful **spur** to action.
ⓝ spurrer

0986 ■■□

feat
[fiːt]

위업, 재주, 묘기
ⓝ an action or a piece of work that needs skill, strength or courage
ⓢⓨⓝ accomplishment, act, performance
ⓔⓖ The tunnel is a brilliant **feat** of engineering.
ⓐⓓ featly

0987 ■■□

demise
[dɪmaɪz]

종말, 죽음
ⓝ the end or failure of an institution, an idea, a company, etc.
ⓢⓨⓝ termination, finish
ⓔⓖ his sudden **demise**
ⓐ demisable

0988 ■■□

furtive
[fə́ːrtiv]

몰래 하는, 은밀한

ⓐ taken, done, used, etc., surreptitiously or by stealth
ⓢⓨⓝ stealthy, secret, covert, confidential
ⓔ.ⓖ. Toni cast a **furtive** glance over his shoulder.

0989 ■■□

devious
[díːviəs]

멀리 돌아가는, 구불구불한

ⓐ departing from the most direct way
ⓢⓨⓝ circuitous, indirect, remote
ⓔ.ⓖ. He seemed honest, but his intentions were **devious**.

0990 ■■□

provoke
[prəvóuk]

불러일으키다, 자극하다, 유발하다

ⓥ to stir up, arouse, or call forth (feelings, desires, or activity)
ⓢⓨⓝ arouse, incite, stimulate, spur
ⓔ.ⓖ. The mishap **provoked** a hearty laugh.
ⓐ provocative 자극하는, 불러일으키는

0991 ■□□

deafen
[défən]

귀머거리로 만들다

ⓥ to make deaf
ⓔ.ⓖ. The explosion **deafened** him for life.
ⓐ deafened 청각을 잃은

0992 ■■□

felon
[félən]

악한, 잔인한

ⓐ wicked, malicious, treacherous
ⓢⓨⓝ cruel, wicked, malicious, treacherous
ⓔ.ⓖ. Her play was a **felon** comedy about life in the 80s.
ⓝ felony 중죄

0993 ■□□

modify
[mádəfài]

변경하다, 수정하다

ⓥ to change somewhat the form or qualities of; alter partially
ⓢⓨⓝ change, amend, alter, revise
ⓔ.ⓖ. The landlady has **modified** the terms of lease.
ⓝ modification 수정, 변경

DAY
17

0994 ■■□

increment
[ínkrəmənt, íŋ-]

인상, 증가
ⓝ something added or gained; the act or process of increasing
ⓢⓨⓝ addition, increase, growth
ⓔⓖ Local newspapers and cable television stations have followed every **increment**.
ⓐ incremental 인상의, 증가의

0995 ■■□

intimidate
[intímədèit]

겁주다, 협박하다
ⓥ to force into or deter from some action by inducing fear
ⓢⓨⓝ threaten, menace, bulldoze
ⓔⓖ They carry handcuffs and guns to **intimidate** us.
ⓝ intimidation 협박, 위협

0996 ■□□

misbehave
[mìsbihéiv]

못된 짓을 하다, 품행이 좋지 않다
ⓥ to behave badly or improperly
ⓢⓨⓝ deviate
ⓔⓖ On occasion, it is necessary for students to be disciplined when they **misbehave**.
ⓝ misbehavior 버릇없음, 품행이 나쁨

0997 ■□□

analyze
[ǽnəlàiz]

분석하다, 분해하다
ⓥ to separate (a material or abstract entity) into constituent parts or elements: to examine critically, so as to bring out the essential elements or give the essence of
ⓢⓨⓝ assay, examine, inspect, investigate
ⓔⓖ Handwriting is much more difficult to **analyze** than machine-printed characters.
ⓝ analysis 분석, 분해

0998 ■□□

artifact
[ά:rtəfæ̀kt]

인공물, 가공물
ⓝ any object made by human beings
ⓔⓖ All four **artifacts** sold for prices far higher than their estimated value.
ⓐ artificial 인조의, 인공적인

0999 ■■□

latent
[léitnt]

잠재적인, 숨어 있는, 보이지 않는
ⓐ present but not visible, apparent, or actualized; existing as potential
ⓢⓨⓝ dormant, inactive, hidden, invisible
ⓔ.ⓖ. It will be helpful for you to develop your **latent** ability to detect vibrations.
ⓝ latency 잠복, 잠재, 숨어 있음

1000 ■■□

dubious
[djúːbiəs]

수상쩍은, 의심스러운
ⓐ marked by or occasioning doubt
ⓢⓨⓝ doubtful, dubitable
ⓔ.ⓖ. This report is of **dubious** authenticity.
ⓝ dubiety 의혹, 의심스러움

1001 ■■□

sinister
[sínəstər]

불길한, 사악한, 재수 없는
ⓐ threatening or portending evil, harm, or trouble
ⓢⓨⓝ ominous, inauspicious, menacing
ⓔ.ⓖ. 1. Ash clouds may look like normal weather clouds, but they are far more **sinister**.
2. In one of the folklores, they regale the moon as being **sinister**.
ⓐ sinistral 왼쪽의, 왼손잡이의

1002 ■□□

bare
[béər]

노출된, 드러난
ⓐ without covering or clothing
ⓢⓨⓝ naked, nude
ⓔ.ⓖ. She covered her **bare** shoulders with a shawl.

1003 ■■□

mercurial
[mərkjúəriəl]

변덕스러운
ⓐ changeable; volatile; fickle; flighty; erratic
ⓢⓨⓝ inconstant, indecisive
ⓔ.ⓖ. I am quite a **mercurial** person.
ⓝ mercuriality 변덕

1004 ■■□

inherent
[inhíərənt]

고유의, 본래부터의, 타고난

ⓐ existing in someone or something as a permanent and inseparable element, quality, or attribute
ⓢⓨⓝ congenital, connatural, innate, intrinsic
ⓔ.ⓖ. Logistical problems are **inherent** in the distribution of perishable goods in tropical countries.
ⓥ inhere 타고나다, 부여되어 있다

1005 ■■□

equate
[ikwéit]

같다고 간주하다, 견주다, 비교하다

ⓥ to assess the values or the similarities between two or more thing
ⓢⓨⓝ compare, equal, liken
ⓔ.ⓖ. Can we **equate** churchgoing with religion?
ⓝ equation 방정식, 평형상태

1006 ■■□

harass
[hərǽs]

괴롭히다, 귀찮게 굴다

ⓥ to disturb persistently; torment, as with troubles or cares; bother continually
ⓢⓨⓝ pester, persecute, bother
ⓔ.ⓖ. They **harassed** a state minister with repeated accusations.
ⓝ harassment 괴롭힘, 애먹음

1007 ■■□

uncertainty
[ʌnsə́:rtnti]

불확신성, 반신반의

ⓝ the state of being uncertain
ⓢⓨⓝ doubt, hesitancy, dubiety
ⓔ.ⓖ. Rarely have there been so many **uncertainties** ahead in the global economy.
ⓐ uncertain 불확실한, 미정의, 모호한

1008 ■□□

formal
[fɔ́:rməl]

형식적인, 표면적인

ⓐ being in accordance with the usual requirements, customs, etc.
ⓢⓨⓝ punctilious
ⓔ.ⓖ. The **formal** process of marriage paperwork is very serious.
ⓥ formulate 명확히 말하다, 공식화하다

1009 ■□□

awe
[ɔ́ː]

두려움, 경외
ⓝ an overwhelming feeling of wonder or admiration
ⓢⓨⓝ wonderment, amazement
ⓔ.ⓖ. We were in **awe** of the works of Bach.
ⓐ awesome 무시무시한, 굉장히 멋진

1010 ■□□

throughout
[θruːáut]

~의 도처에, ~의 구석구석까지
ⓟ in or to every part of; everywhere in
ⓢⓨⓝ around, everywhere, overall
ⓔ.ⓖ. The new technology of printing was disseminated **throughout** Asia.

1011 ■□□

bloom
[blúːm]

꽃, 개화(기)
ⓝ the flower of a plant; state of having the buds opened
ⓢⓨⓝ flower, blossom
ⓔ.ⓖ. The garden is a riot of colors with a variety of roses in full **bloom**.
ⓝ bloomer 꽃이 피는 식물

DAY 17

1012 ■■■

coagulate
[kouǽgjulèit]

응고시키다, 굳히다
ⓥ to change from a fluid into a thickened mass
ⓢⓨⓝ solidify, curdle, congeal
ⓔ.ⓖ. Let the soup stand two hours until it **coagulates**.
ⓝ coagulation 응고

1013 ■□□

reusable
[rìːjúːzəbl]

재사용할 수 있는
ⓐ capable of being used again
ⓔ.ⓖ. She separated **reusable** things from the garbage.
ⓥ reuse 재사용하다

1014 ■□□

solace
[sáləs]

위안, 위로

ⓝ comfort in sorrow, misfortune, or trouble; alleviation of distress or discomfort

ⓢⓨⓝ comfort, consolation

ⓔ.ⓖ. His sole **solace** in his loneliness and ill health was the company of novels.

1015 ■■□

cater
[kéitər]

음식을 준비하다, 공급하다

ⓥ to provide food, service, etc., as for a party or wedding

ⓢⓨⓝ provide, supply

ⓔ.ⓖ. The restaurant **caters** for individuals as well as groups with a good service.

ⓝ catering 요식 조달업, 출장 연회업

1016 ■■□

reprehensible
[rèprihénsəbl]

비난할 만한, 괘씸한

ⓐ deserving of reproof, rebuke, or censure

ⓢⓨⓝ blameworthy, condemnable

ⓔ.ⓖ. It is perfectly **reprehensible** to keep me waiting for an answer like this.

1017 ■□□

philanthropy
[filǽnθrəpi]

박애(주의), 자선

ⓝ altruistic concern for human welfare and advancement, usually manifested by donations of money, property, or work to needy persons

ⓢⓨⓝ altruism, charity, benefaction

ⓔ.ⓖ. They devoted their later years to **philanthropy**.

ⓝ philanthropist 박애주의자, 자선가

1018 ■■□

meddle
[médl]

간섭하다, 참견하다, 관여하다

ⓥ to involve oneself in a matter without right or invitation; interfere officiously and unwontedly

ⓢⓨⓝ interfere, hinder, impede

ⓔ.ⓖ. He **meddles** with every thing I do.

ⓐ meddlesome 참견하는

1019 ■■□

ubiquitous
[juːbíkwətəs]

어디에나 있는, 편재하는

ⓐ existing or being everywhere, esp. at the same time
ⓢⓨⓝ omnipresent, universal
ⓔ.ⓖ. In the 1970s robotic workers became **ubiquitous** throughout production.

1020 ■□□

bracket
[brǽkit]

까치발; (벽 등에 내단 선반[전등]의) 받침대, 브래킷

ⓝ a support, as of metal or wood, projecting from a wall or the like to hold or bear the weight of a shelf, part of a cornice
ⓔ.ⓖ. He is screwing a **bracket** to a wall to hold a nice shelf.

DAY
17

Day

18

defraud	☐☐☐	assay	☐☐☐
mundane	☐☐☐	solicit	☐☐☐
choke	☐☐☐	barn	☐☐☐
shriveled	☐☐☐	fabric	☐☐☐
patronize	☐☐☐	obsolescent	☐☐☐
famish	☐☐☐	assonance	☐☐☐
premises	☐☐☐	insult	☐☐☐
larceny	☐☐☐	terminate	☐☐☐
qualm	☐☐☐	attentive	☐☐☐
civil court	☐☐☐	laudable	☐☐☐
swerve	☐☐☐	belonging	☐☐☐
head start	☐☐☐	malignant	☐☐☐
vigilant	☐☐☐	incipient	☐☐☐
annual	☐☐☐	flint	☐☐☐
prairie	☐☐☐	mislead	☐☐☐
commonplace	☐☐☐	assassinate	☐☐☐
frenzy	☐☐☐	writhe	☐☐☐
swift	☐☐☐	concur	☐☐☐
cessation	☐☐☐	admonish	☐☐☐
inexorable	☐☐☐	miscellaneous	☐☐☐
duplicity	☐☐☐	appreciate	☐☐☐
profuse	☐☐☐	childbearing	☐☐☐
as well as	☐☐☐	disbelief	☐☐☐
constituent	☐☐☐	loathe	☐☐☐
insolent	☐☐☐	bypass	☐☐☐
shoddy	☐☐☐	despair	☐☐☐
whereby	☐☐☐	requite	☐☐☐
appoint	☐☐☐	akin	☐☐☐
enormous	☐☐☐	expand	☐☐☐
vague	☐☐☐	aptitude	☐☐☐

1021 ■■□

defraud
[difrɔ́ːd]

속여서 빼앗다, 횡령하다
- ⓥ to deprive of a right, money, or property by fraud
- (syn) deprive
- (e.g.) Dishonest employees **defrauded** the government of millions of dollars.
- ⓝ defraudation 사취, 횡령

1022 ■■□

mundane
[mʌndéin]

이승의, 현세의, 세속적인
- ⓐ of or pertaining to this world or earth as contrasted with heaven
- (syn) worldly, earthly, secular
- (e.g.) China's rising tide of nationalism has spread far beyond the **mundane** bounds of political fighting.
- ⓝ mundanity 현세, 속세

1023 ■□□

choke
[tʃóuk]

숨 막히게 하다, 질식시키다
- ⓥ to stop the breath of by squeezing or obstructing the windpipe
- (syn) strangle, stifle
- (e.g.) The reporter announced that he **choked** to death on a chicken bone.
- ⓐ choked 메인, 막힌, 숨 막히는

1024 ■■□

shriveled
[ʃrívəld]

쪼그라든, 주름살 진
- ⓐ wrinkled and contracted, especially due to loss of moisture or old age
- (e.g.) Too bad she's really a **shriveled** old, devil-worshipping witch.

1025 ■■□

patronize
[péitrənàiz]

(윗사람 행세를 하며) 가르치려 들다, 깔보는 듯한 태도로 대하다
- ⓥ treat in a way that is apparently kind or helpful but that betrays a feeling of superiority
- (syn) imperious
- (opp) humble
- (e.g.) And, honestly, I wasn't trying to **patronize** you.
- ⓝ patron

1026 ■□□

famish
[fǽmiʃ]

굶다
ⓥ to suffer or cause to suffer extreme hunger
ⓔ.ⓖ. This group was followed by a pack of **famished** wolves.

1027 ■□□

premises
[ˈpreməsəz]

부지(토지건물), 가게
ⓝ a tract of land including its buildings
ⓢⓨⓝ site
ⓔ.ⓖ. You are hereby ordered to vacate the **premises** immediately.

1028 ■■□

larceny
[lɑ́ːrsəni]

절도, 도둑질
ⓝ the crime of stealing
ⓢⓨⓝ theft, pilfering
ⓔ.ⓖ. **Larceny** is prohibited strictly by criminal laws.
ⓐ larcenous

1029 ■■□

qualm
[kwɑːm]

꺼림칙함
ⓝ an uneasy feeling or pang of conscience as to conduct; compunction
ⓢⓨⓝ misgiving, trepidation
ⓞⓟⓟ confidence
ⓔ.ⓖ. I have **qualms** about buying that house.
ⓐ qualmish
ⓝ qualmishness

1030 ■□□

civil court
[ˈsivil kôrt]

민사법정
ⓝ a court of law in which civil cases are tried and determined
ⓔ.ⓖ. The Court of Session is the superior **civil court** in Scotland.

1031 ■□□

swerve
[swəːrv]

방향을 바꾸다, 벗어나다
ⓥ change or cause to change direction abruptly
ⓢⓨⓝ veer, deviate
ⓔ.ⓖ. It wasn't quite my very own sig alert, but a few cars did have to **swerve** around me.
ⓐ swerveless

DAY
18

1032 ■□□

head start
[hed stɑːrt]

(남보다 일찍 시작해서 갖게 되는) 유리함

ⓝ an advantage given or acquired in any competition, endeavor, etc., as allowing one or more competitors in a race to start before the others

ⓔⓖ In this respect, British business comes to India with a **head start** on other countries.

1033 ■■□

vigilant
[vídʒələnt]

자지 않고 지키는, 경계하는, 방심하지 않는

ⓐ keenly watchful to detect danger; ever awake and alert

ⓢⓨⓝ wary, watchful, alert

ⓔⓖ Being ever-**vigilant** is the cost of liberty.

ⓝ vigil 철야, 밤샘, 불침번

1034 ■□□

annual
[ǽnjuəl]

1년의, 해마다의

ⓐ of, for, or pertaining to a year

ⓢⓨⓝ yearly

ⓔⓖ The **annual** rainfall is heavier than further north.

ⓝ anniversary 기념일

1035 ■□□

prairie
[préəri]

대초원

ⓝ an extensive, level or slightly undulating, mostly treeless tract of land in the Mississippi valley, characterized by a highly fertile soil and originally covered with coarse grasses, and merging into drier plateaus in the west

ⓢⓨⓝ meadow, pasture, plain

ⓔⓖ **Prairies** stretched out as far as the eyes could see.

1036 ■□□

commonplace
[kámənplèis]

평범한, 흔한, 보통의

ⓐ ordinary; undistinguished or uninteresting; without individuality

ⓢⓨⓝ ordinary, banal

ⓔⓖ Prostitution is **commonplace** in China as economic reforms widen the gap between the rich and poor.

1037 ■■□

frenzy
[frénzi]

격분, 격앙, 광포

ⓝ extreme mental agitation; wild excitement or derangement
ⓢⓨⓝ furor, distemper, ferment
ⓔ.ⓖ. The news drove him into a **frenzy**.
ⓐ frenzied 열광적인, 광포한, 격노한

1038 ■□□

swift
[swift]

빠른, 신속한

ⓐ quick or prompt to act or respond
ⓢⓨⓝ rapid, speedy, quick, prompt
ⓔ.ⓖ. Many issues remain in dispute and prospects for a **swift** resolution remain thin.
ⓝ swiftness 신속, 빠름

1039 ■■□

cessation
[seséiʃən]

정지, 휴지, 단절, 중단

ⓝ a temporary or complete stopping
ⓢⓨⓝ closure, completion, conclusion, consummation
ⓔ.ⓖ. **Cessation** of breathing in one's sleep is a problem that can cause weariness in the daytime from constantly waking up.
ⓥ cease 중단하다, 그만두다, 끝나다

1040 ■■■

inexorable
[inéksərəbl]

냉혹한, 무정한

ⓐ feeling or showing no pity
ⓢⓨⓝ severe, relentless, unrelenting, implacable, merciless, cruel, pitiless
ⓔ.ⓖ. It was the **inexorable** and timeless force of death.
ⓝ inexorability 무정, 냉혹

1041 ■■□

duplicity
[djuːplísəti]

일구이언, 표리부동

ⓝ deceitfulness in speech or conduct; speaking or acting in two different ways concerning the same matter with intent to deceive
ⓢⓨⓝ double-dealing, deceitfulness
ⓔ.ⓖ. They suspected him of **duplicity**.
ⓐ duplicitous 식언의, 불성실한

DAY
18

1042 ■■■

profuse
[prəfjuːs]

많은, 다량의
ⓐ produced in large amounts
ⓢⓨⓝ large, huge
ⓔ.ⓖ. **profuse** apologies
ⓝ profuseness, profusion   ⓐⓓ profusely

1043 ■■□

as well as

게다가
ⓐⓓ in addition to somebody/something; too
ⓢⓨⓝ equally, similarly, identically
ⓔ.ⓖ. They sell books **as well as** newspapers.

1044 ■■■

constituent
[kənstɪtuənt]

주민; 구성성분
ⓝ a person who lives, and can vote in a constituency; one of the parts of something that combine to form the whole
ⓢⓨⓝ voter, elector, component
ⓔ.ⓖ. 1. She has the full support of her **constituents**.
          2. Tar is a harmful **constituent** of tobacco smoke.
ⓥ constitute ⓝ constitution, constituency ⓐⓓ constituently

1045 ■■■

insolent
[ɪnsələnt]

버릇없는, 무례한
ⓐ extremely rude and showing a lack of respect
ⓢⓨⓝ rude, offensive, hurting
ⓔ.ⓖ. an **insolent** smile
ⓝ insolentness, insolence   ⓐⓓ insolently

1046 ■■■

shoddy
[ʃɑːdi]

조잡한, 부정직한
ⓐ made or done badly and with not enough care
ⓢⓨⓝ cosmetic, superficial, shallow
ⓔ.ⓖ. **shoddy** workmanship
ⓝ shoddiness   ⓐⓓ shoddily

1047 ■■□

whereby
[wéərbaɪ]

~하는

(ad) because of which
(e.g.) They have introduced a new system **whereby** all employees must undergo regular training.

1048 ■■□

appoint
[əpóint]

임명하다, 지명하다, 약속하다

(v) to name or assign to a position, an office, or the like
(syn) designate, name, nominate
(e.g.) We wondered if he'll **appoint** her as their new marketing manager.
(n) appointment 임명, 약속

1049 ■□□

enormous
[inɔ́:rməs]

거대한, 막대한, 엄청난

(a) greatly exceeding the common size, extent, etc.
(syn) huge, immense, gigantic
(e.g.) Archaeologists have unearthed an **enormous** ancient city built by an unknown people.
(n) enormity 거대함, 터무니없음

1050 ■□□

vague
[véig]

막연한, 모호한, 애매한

(a) not clearly or explicitly stated or expressed; not clear or distinct to the sight or any other sense
(syn) dim, faint, obscure, uncertain
(e.g.) Her **vague** fears were turning into a reality.

DAY
18

1051 ■■■

assay
[æséi]

분석하다, 검사하다

(v) to examine or analyze
(syn) test, examine, analyze
(e.g.) The investors carefully **assayed** the company's offer.

1052 ■■□

solicit

[səlísit]

간청하다, 청구하다

ⓥ to seek for (something) by entreaty, earnest or respectful request, formal application, etc.

ⓢⓨⓝ entreat, supplicate, beg, implore, beseech, request

ⓔ.ⓖ. He **solicited** aid from the church.

ⓝ solicitude 근심, 걱정, 염려

1053 ■□□

barn

[bá:rn]

헛간, 저장고, 창고

ⓝ a building for storing hay, grain, etc., and often for housing livestock

ⓢⓨⓝ storehouse, corral

ⓔ.ⓖ. My grandfather brought a shovel from the **barn**.

1054 ■□□

fabric

[fǽbrik]

직물, 천

ⓝ a cloth made by weaving, knitting, or felting fibers

ⓢⓨⓝ contexture, textile

ⓔ.ⓖ. Natural **fabrics** feel much nicer to the touch.

ⓥ fabricate 만들다, 제작하다, 가공하다

1055 ■■■

obsolescent

[àbsəlésnt]

쇠퇴해 가는, 구식의

ⓐ becoming obsolete; passing out of use, as a word

ⓢⓨⓝ out-of-date

ⓔ.ⓖ. The laws are not **obsolescent**; they are very much alive.

ⓝ obsolescence 쇠퇴, 노후, 구식화

1056 ■■■

assonance

[ǽsənəns]

음의 유사, 유음

ⓝ rhyme in which the same vowel sounds are used with different consonants in the stressed syllables of the rhyming words

ⓔ.ⓖ. "Don't mess with the best" carries **assonance** between the two -ess sounds.

1057 ■□□

insult
[insʌ́lt]

모욕하다, 욕보이다

ⓥ to treat or speak to insolently or with contemptuous rudeness
ⓢⓨⓝ affront, offend, outrage
ⓔ.ⓖ. He **insulted** me by calling me a fool.
ⓐ insulting 모욕적인, 무례한

1058 ■■□

terminate
[tə́ːrmənèit]

끝내다, 종결시키다

ⓥ to bring to an end; put an end to
ⓢⓨⓝ complete, finish, end
ⓔ.ⓖ. This project will be **terminated** due to lack of funding.
ⓐ terminative 종결시키는, 종국의

1059 ■□□

attentive
[əténtiv]

주의 깊은, 경청하는, 세심한

ⓐ characterized by or giving attention
ⓢⓨⓝ heedful, regardful, considerate
ⓔ.ⓖ. You must be more **attentive** to your work.
ⓝ attention 주의, 주목

1060 ■■□

laudable
[lɔ́ːdəbl]

칭찬할 만한, 훌륭한, 기특한

ⓐ deserving praise
ⓢⓨⓝ praiseworthy, commendable
ⓔ.ⓖ. Reorganizing the office was a **laudable** idea.
ⓐ illaudable 칭찬할 가치가 없는

1061 ■■□

belonging
[bilɔ́ːŋiŋ]

부속물, 소유물, 소지품

ⓝ a personal item that one owns
ⓢⓨⓝ possessions, property
ⓔ.ⓖ. Gather your personal **belongings** and leave the theater immediately, please.
ⓥ belong ~에 속하다, ~의 소유물이다

DAY
18

1062 ■■□

malignant
[məlígnənt]

악의(적의)가 있는, 해로운
ⓐ disposed to cause harm, suffering, or distress deliberately; feeling or showing ill will or hatred
ⓢⓨⓝ malicious, vicious, wicked
ⓔ.ⓖ. The pathology report stated my lump was **malignant**.
ⓝ malignancy 악의, 적의, 악성

1063 ■■■

incipient
[insípiənt]

시작의, 초기의, 발단의
ⓐ beginning to exist or appear; in an initial stage
ⓢⓨⓝ initiative, basic, introductory
ⓔ.ⓖ. The **incipient** jealousy of the phone call would end after her boyfriend's explanation.
ⓝ incipiency 최초, 발단, 초기

1064 ■■□

flint
[flínt]

부싯돌, 아주 단단한 물건
ⓝ a hard stone, a form of silica resembling chalcedony but more opaque, less pure, and less lustrous
ⓢⓨⓝ hard, solid, firm
ⓔ.ⓖ. Hitting **flint** against rock, the camper made a fire.
ⓐ flinty 부싯돌 같은, 아주 단단한

1065 ■■□

mislead
[mislí·d]

오도하다, 잘못 인도하다
ⓥ to lead or guide wrongly; lead astray
ⓢⓨⓝ beguile, deceive
ⓢⓨⓝ He was **misled** by his friends into a life of drinking.
ⓐ misleading 오도하는, 오해시키는, 현혹시키는

1066 ■■□

assassinate
[əsǽsənèit]

암살하다
ⓥ to kill suddenly or secretively, esp. a politically prominent person; murder premeditatedly and treacherously
ⓢⓨⓝ kill, slay
ⓔ.ⓖ. They wove a plot to **assassinate** the CEO.
ⓥ assassination 암살

1067 ■■□

writhe
[ráið]

몸부림치다, 몸부림치며 괴로워하다
ⓥ to twist the body about, or squirm, as in pain, violent effort, etc.
ⓢⓨⓝ struggle, wriggle, flounce
ⓔ.ⓖ. He **writhed** with the agony of needing to itch.

1068 ■■□

concur
[kənkə́:r]

일치하다, 동의하다
ⓥ to accord in opinion
ⓢⓨⓝ agree, accord
ⓔ.ⓖ. I think we can **concur** that this deal won't benefit the city.
ⓝ concurrence 일치, 동의

1069 ■■■

admonish
[ædmániʃ]

훈계하다, 타이르다, 충고하다
ⓥ to caution or counsel against something
ⓢⓨⓝ reprove, advise, warn
ⓔ.ⓖ. The teacher **admonished** the students to keep their voices to a low murmur.
ⓝ admonition 훈계, 경고, 충고

1070 ■■□

miscellaneous
[mìsəléiniəs]

잡다한, 갖가지의
ⓐ consisting of members or elements of different kinds; of mixed character
ⓢⓨⓝ various, diverse, sundry
ⓔ.ⓖ. There were **miscellaneous** groups protesting the government's new treaty.
ⓝ miscellany 잡다한 것

DAY
18

1071 ■■□

appreciate
[əprí:ʃièit]

진가를 인정하다, 높이 평가하다
ⓥ to value or regard highly; place a high estimate on
ⓢⓨⓝ apprize, apprise, revalue
ⓔ.ⓖ. We failed to **appreciate** their efforts and generosity.
ⓝ appreciation 진가, 식별, 감지

1072 ■■□

childbearing
[tʃáɪldberɪŋ]

출산, 분만; 출산의, 출산 가능한

ⓝ the act of producing or bringing forth children
syn childbirth, delivery
e.g. **Childbearing** teens are more common in Europe than in the United States.
ⓥ bear 아이를 낳다, 출산하다

1073 ■□□

disbelief
[disbilíːf]

불신, 의혹, 불신앙

ⓝ the inability or refusal to believe or to accept something as true
syn dubiety, incredulity, mistrust
e.g. They stared at me with total **disbelief**.
ⓝ belief 신뢰, 믿음, 확신

1074 ■■□

loathe
[louð]

몹시 싫어하다, 질색하다

ⓥ to feel disgust or intense aversion for
syn abhor, hate
e.g. I **loathe** people who spread malicious rumors.
ⓐ loathful 싫은

1075 ■□□

bypass
[báɪpɑːs]

우회로

ⓝ a road enabling motorists to avoid a city or other heavy traffic points or to drive around an obstruction
e.g. You had better use the **bypass** rather than drive through the middle of town.

1076 ■□□

despair
[dispéər]

절망, 자포자기

ⓝ loss of hope; hopelessness
syn depression, discouragement
e.g. Many people feel **despair** due to the economic crisis.
ⓐ desperate 막가는, 자포자기의

1077 ■■□

requite
[rikwáit]

보답하다, 반응을 보이다

ⓥ to make repayment or return for (service, benefits, etc.)
ⓢⓨⓝ repay, reward, recompense, compensate, remunerate, reimburse
ⓔ.ⓖ. You can't force a person to **requite** your love.
ⓝ requital 보답, 보상

1078 ■■□

akin
[əkín]

동족의, 유사한, 비슷한

ⓐ of kin; related by blood (usually used predicatively); allied by nature; having the same properties
ⓢⓨⓝ cognate, similar, analogous
ⓔ.ⓖ. Listening to his life story is **akin** to reading a good adventure novel.
ⓝ kin 친척, 친족, 일가

1079 ■□□

expand
[ikspǽnd]

넓히다, 확장하다

ⓥ to increase in extent, size, volume, scope, etc.
ⓢⓨⓝ enlarge, extend, magnify
ⓔ.ⓖ. We've increased the volume of merchandise we handle, so I'd like to **expand** the store.
ⓝ expansion 확장, 발전

1080 ■■□

aptitude
[ǽptətjùːd]

소질, 재능, 능력

ⓝ innate or acquired capacity for something
ⓢⓨⓝ talent, capability, ability
ⓔ.ⓖ. She has a special **aptitude** for mathematics and science.

DAY
18

Day

19

stampede	□□□	expunge	□□□
construe	□□□	recant	□□□
precocious	□□□	extort	□□□
fitness	□□□	nominal	□□□
choosy	□□□	lethal	□□□
posit	□□□	importune	□□□
inexplicable	□□□	sporadic	□□□
hillside	□□□	fidget	□□□
rank	□□□	attic	□□□
tuft	□□□	temerity	□□□
tufted	□□□	repulse	□□□
turf	□□□	precipitate	□□□
bleed	□□□	canny	□□□
venom	□□□	guile	□□□
voluble	□□□	boisterous	□□□
invalid	□□□	awful	□□□
respite	□□□	biblical	□□□
companion	□□□	ailment	□□□
succumb	□□□	begrudge	□□□
bloated	□□□	cache	□□□
grovel	□□□	domicile	□□□
sophisticated	□□□	galore	□□□
antagonize	□□□	havoc	□□□
subsistence	□□□	incontrovertible	□□□
equivocal	□□□	inundate	□□□
preclude	□□□	obsess	□□□
deviation	□□□	pertinent	□□□
hairline	□□□	raze	□□□
virulent	□□□	remunerate	□□□
inquire	□□□	valor	□□□

1081 ■■■

stampede
[stæmpíːd]

달아나게 하다, 쇄도하게 하다

ⓥ to scatter or flee in a stampede

ⓢⓨⓝ throng, rush

ⓔ.ⓖ. The shoppers **stampede** into the supermarket after it re-opened.

1082 ■■□

construe
[kənstrúː]

해석하다, 번역하다

ⓥ to give the meaning or intention of

ⓢⓨⓝ explain, interpret

ⓔ.ⓖ. His speech was **construed** as an attack on the government.

ⓥ misconstrue 잘못 해석하다, 오해하다

1083 ■■□

precocious
[prikóuʃəs]

조숙한, 숙성한

ⓐ unusually advanced or mature in development, esp. mental development

ⓢⓨⓝ premature, early

ⓔ.ⓖ. She is **precocious** for her age, making her own lunch like that.

ⓝ precocity 조숙

1084 ■□□

fitness
[fít·ness]

적합함

ⓝ the quality of being suitable to fulfill a particular role or task

ⓢⓨⓝ suitability, proficiency

ⓔ.ⓖ. Doubts have been expressed about his **fitness** for office.

1085 ■□□

choosy
[tʃúːzi]

까탈스러운

ⓐ hard to please, particular; fastidious, especially in making a selection

ⓢⓨⓝ fussy, overfastidious

ⓔ.ⓖ. You ain't very **choosy** about your company.

1086 ■□□

posit
[pázit]

상정하다, 사실로 받아들이다

ⓥ assume as a fact; put forward as a basis of argument

ⓢⓨⓝ postulate, hypothesize

ⓔ.ⓖ. I do not **posit** that God exists.

1087 ■□□

inexplicable
[inéksplikəbəl]

불가해한
ⓐ unable to be explained or accounted for
ⓢⓨⓝ unaccountable, unfathomable, incomprehensible
ⓞⓟⓟ explicable, understandable
ⓔ.ⓖ. The rationale for this is quite **inexplicable**.
ⓝ inexplicability
ⓐⓓ inexplicably

1088 ■□□

hillside
[híll·side]

산비탈(허리)
ⓝ the side or slope of a hill
ⓔ.ⓖ. They constructed a wooden platform on a **hillside** lot.

1089 ■□□

rank
[ræŋk]

무성한, 울창한
ⓐ growing too thickly and coarsely
ⓢⓨⓝ abundant, lush
ⓞⓟⓟ sparse
ⓔ.ⓖ. clumps of **rank** grass

1090 ■□□

tuft
[tʌft]

다발
ⓝ a bunch or cluster of small, usually soft and flexible parts, as feathers or hairs, attached or fixed closely together at the base and loose at the upper ends
ⓔ.ⓖ. His whiskers and the soft **tuft** on his chin were white.

1091 ■□□

tufted
[tʌftid]

올이 촘촘한
ⓐ having or growing in a tuft or tufts
ⓔ.ⓖ. a **tufted** duck

1092 ■□□

turf
[təːrf]

잔디
ⓝ grass and the surface layer of earth held together by its roots
ⓢⓨⓝ lawn, sward
ⓔ.ⓖ. Artificial **turf** is used since dome stadiums are indoor structures.

DAY
19

1093 ■□□

bleed
[bliːd]

피 흘리다, 출혈하다
ⓥ to lose blood from the vascular system
ⓢⓨⓝ hemorrhage
ⓔ.ⓖ. I got the fright of my life when my child ran in with his head **bleeding**.
ⓝ blood 피

1094 ■■□

venom
[vénəm]

악의, 원한, 앙심; 독(독액)
ⓝ something resembling or suggesting poison in its effect
ⓢⓨⓝ spite, malice
ⓔ.ⓖ. The **venom** of this snake is strong enough to kill an elephant.
ⓐ venomous 악의에 찬, 원한을 품은

1095 ■■□

voluble
[váluəbl]

말이 유창한, 입담 좋은
ⓐ characterized by a ready and continuous flow of words
ⓢⓨⓝ glib, talkative, fluent
ⓔ.ⓖ. She was **voluble** with anxiety.
ⓝ volubility 유창, 다변

1096 ■■□

invalid
[ínvəlid]

실효성이 없는, 무효의
ⓐ not valid; without force or foundation; void or without legal force, as a contract
ⓢⓨⓝ void, null, unavailable, inoperative
ⓔ.ⓖ. The treaty became **invalid** because it had not been ratified.
ⓐ valid 정당한, 타당한, 유효한

1097 ■■□

respite
[réspit]

일시적 중지, 휴지, 휴식
ⓝ a delay or cessation for a time, esp. of anything distressing or trying; an interval of relief
ⓢⓨⓝ lull, intermission, cessation, recess
ⓔ.ⓖ. We walked for hours with no **respite**.

1098 ■□□

companion
[kəmpǽnjən]

동료, 친구

ⓝ a person who is frequently in the company of, associates with, or accompanies another

ⓢⓨⓝ companion, buddy, comrade, associate

ⓔⓖ She always warns her children against associating with bad **companions**.

ⓐ companionable 동무로 사귈 만한, 상대하여 재미있는

1099 ■■■

succumb
[səkʌm]

굴복하다, 압도당하다

ⓥ to give way to superior force

ⓢⓨⓝ yield, surrender, capitulate

ⓔⓖ During the recession the government had **succumbed** to pressure for tax expansion.

1100 ■■□

bloated
[blóutid]

부푼, 부은, 살찐

ⓐ puffed up, overlarge, excessively fat

ⓢⓨⓝ swollen, turgid, obese

ⓔⓖ We were **bloated** from overeating last night.

ⓥ bloat 부풀게 하다, 팽창시키다

1101 ■■□

grovel
[grá:vl]

비굴하게 굴다, 굽실거리다, 굴복하다

ⓥ to humble oneself or act in an abject manner, as in great fear or utter servility

ⓢⓨⓝ truckle, flatter, kneel

ⓔⓖ The new employee **groveled** at the feet of his boss.

ⓝ groveler

ⓐ groveling 비굴한, 천한, 슬슬 기는

1102 ■■□

sophisticated
[səfístıkeıtıd]

세련된, 정교한

ⓐ having a lot of experience of the world and knowing about fashion, culture and other things that people think are socially important

ⓢⓨⓝ complex, complicated, advanced

ⓔⓖ the **sophisticated** pleasures of city life

ⓐⓓ sophisticatedly

DAY
19

1103 ■■□

antagonize
[æntǽgənaɪz]

적대감을 불러일으키다
ⓥ antagonize somebody to do something to make somebody angry with you
ⓢⓨⓝ counteract
ⓔ.ⓖ. Not wishing to **antagonize** her further, he said no more.
ⓝ antagonization, antagonisation
ⓐ antagonizable, antagonisable

1104 ■■■

subsistence
[səbsɪstəns]

최저 생활
ⓝ the state of having just enough money or food to stay alive
ⓢⓨⓝ living, livelihood, maintenance
ⓔ.ⓖ. to live below (the) **subsistence** level

1105 ■■■

equivocal
[ɪkwɪvəkl]

모호한
ⓐ not having one clear or definite meaning or intention
ⓢⓨⓝ unclear, vague, dubious
ⓔ.ⓖ. She gave an **equivocal** answer, typical of a politician.
ⓝ equivocalness, equivocality
ⓐⓓ equivocally

1106 ■■■

preclude
[prɪkluːd]

못 하게 하다
ⓥ to prevent something from happening or somebody from doing something
ⓢⓨⓝ ban, reject, exclude
ⓔ.ⓖ. Lack of time **precludes** any further discussion.
ⓝ preclusion
ⓐ precludable, preclusive
ⓐⓓ preclusively

1107 ■■□

deviation
[diːviéɪʃən]

일탈
ⓝ the act of moving away from what is normal or acceptable; a difference from what is expected or acceptable
ⓔ.ⓖ. a **deviation** from the plan
ⓝ deviationism, deviationist

1108 ■■□

hairline
[hérlaɪn]

가느다란 선
ⓝ a very thin crack or line
ⓔ.ⓖ. a **hairline** crack

1109 ■□□

virulent
[vírjulənt]

유독한, 맹독의, 유해한
ⓐ actively poisonous; intensely noxious
ⓢⓨⓝ toxic, deadly, fatal
ⓔ.ⓖ. Plagues are the result of particularly **virulent** and contagious diseases.
ⓝ virulence 독성, 악의

1110 ■■■

inquire
[inkwáiər]

묻다, 알아보다
ⓥ to seek information by questioning
ⓢⓨⓝ ask, question
ⓔ.ⓖ. The two leaders **inquired** about Iran's nuclear program.
ⓝ inquiry 질문, 문의, 조회

1111 ■□□

expunge
[ɪkspʌndʒ]

지우다, 삭제하다
ⓥ to strike or blot out
ⓢⓨⓝ erase, obliterate
ⓔ.ⓖ. The mistake was something he had tried to **expunge** from his work records.

1112 ■■□

recant
[rikǽnt]

취소하다, 철회하다
ⓥ to withdraw or disavow (a statement, opinion, etc.), esp. formally
ⓢⓨⓝ retract, withdraw, revoke, cancel
ⓔ.ⓖ. He had refused after torture to **recant** his confession.
ⓝ recantation 취소

1113 ■■□

extort
[ikstɔ́ːrt]

강탈하다, 강요하다
ⓥ to wrest or wring (money, information, etc.) from a person by violence, intimidation, or abuse of authority; obtain by force, torture, and threat
ⓢⓨⓝ extract, despoil, plunder, wrest, wring
ⓔ.ⓖ. He **extorted** a large sum of money from the company.
ⓝ extortion 강요, 강탈

DAY
19

1114 ■□□

nominal
[nάmənl]

이름만의, 명목상의

ⓐ being such in name only
ⓢⓨⓝ putative, so-called
ⓔ.ⓖ. As he was still not legally allowed to run a company, his brother became its **nominal** head.
ⓥ nominalize 명사화하다

1115 ■■□

lethal
[líːθəl]

죽음의, 치사의, 치명적인

ⓐ of, pertaining to, or causing death
ⓢⓨⓝ deadly, fatal
ⓔ.ⓖ. The cobra's poison is **lethal**.
ⓝ lethality 치명적임

1116 ■■■

importune
[impɔːrtjúːn]

성가시게 부탁하다, 조르다

ⓥ to press or beset with solicitations; demand with urgency or persistence
ⓢⓨⓝ pester, solicit
ⓔ.ⓖ. He began to **importune** her with offers of help.
ⓝ importunity 끈질긴 요구

1117 ■■□

sporadic
[spərǽdik]

때때로 일어나는, 우발적인

ⓐ (of similar things or occurrences) appearing or happening at irregular intervals in time
ⓢⓨⓝ occasional, periodic
ⓔ.ⓖ. There still seems to be **sporadic** gun fighting in the streets of Iraq.

1118 ■■□

fidget
[fídʒit]

안절부절못하다, 안달하다

ⓥ to move about restlessly, nervously, or impatiently
ⓔ.ⓖ. Her nervousness made her **fidget** about in her chair.
ⓐ fidgety 안절부절못하는, 조바심 내는

1119 ■□□

attic
[ǽtik]

다락방

ⓝ the part of a building, esp. of a house, directly under a roof

ⓔ.ⓖ. Later while cleaning the **attic**, I found many things I had completely forgotten.

1120 ■■□

temerity
[təmérəti]

무모한 행위, 만용

ⓝ reckless boldness

ⓢⓨⓝ rashness, audacity, effrontery

ⓔ.ⓖ. He is a difficult student who has the **temerity** to challenge his teacher's command.

ⓐ temerarious 무모한, 무분별한

1121 ■■□

repulse
[ripʌ́ls]

격퇴하다, 물리치다

ⓥ to drive back; to keep away

ⓢⓨⓝ repel

ⓔ.ⓖ. They employed a stratagem to **repulse** the invading army.

ⓝ repulsion 격퇴

1122 ■■□

precipitate
[prisípitèit]

촉진시키다, 마구 재촉하다

ⓥ to hasten the occurrence of; bring about prematurely, hastily, or suddenly

ⓢⓨⓝ hasten, accelerate

ⓔ.ⓖ. An insult now would **precipitate** the outbreak of war.

ⓝ precipitation 촉진, 다급, 눈이나 비와 같은 강수

1123 ■■■

canny
[kǽni]

신중한, 조심성 많은

ⓐ cautious in one's actions

ⓢⓨⓝ careful, prudent

ⓔ.ⓖ. He had a **canny** disposition, which made him a great father.

DAY
19

1124 ■■□

guile
[gail]

교활, 엉큼함
ⓝ insidious cunning in attaining a goal; crafty or artful deception
ⓢⓨⓝ duplicity, trickery, fraud, craft
ⓔ.ⓖ. It took all of his **guile** to get the job.
ⓐ guileful 교활한, 음험한

1125 ■■□

boisterous
[bɔ́istərəs]

시끄러운, 요란한, 거친, 사나운, 난폭한
ⓐ rough and noisy; noisily jolly or rowdy; clamorous; unrestrained
ⓢⓨⓝ uproarious, obstreperous, impetuous
ⓔ.ⓖ. The children were having a **boisterous** game of catch on the playground.

1126 ■□□

awful
[ɔ́ːfəl]

지독한, 심한, 무서운, 무시무시한
ⓐ extremely bad, inspiring fear
ⓢⓨⓝ unpleasant, ugly, dreadful, terrible
ⓔ.ⓖ. It's **awful** the way they made her leave the house.
ⓝ awfulness 두려움, 장엄, 지독함

1127 ■□□

biblical
[bíblikəl]

성경의, 성경에 있는
ⓐ of or in the Bible
ⓔ.ⓖ. This kind of revenge was almost **biblical** in its seriousness.
ⓝ bible 성경

1128 ■■■

ailment
[éilmənt]

병, 불쾌, 불안
ⓝ a physical disorder or illness, esp. of a minor or chronic nature
ⓢⓨⓝ malady, disease, illness, sickness
ⓔ.ⓖ. Diabetes is a lifestyle **ailment**, though genetics is a significant factor.

1129 ■■■

begrudge
[bigrʌ́dʒ]

시기하다, 시샘하다
ⓥ to envy or resent the pleasure or good fortune of (someone)
ⓢⓨⓝ envy
ⓔ.ⓖ. Don't **begrudge** my new job, you will have your own soon.

1130 ■■□

cache
[kæʃ]

은닉처, 저장소

ⓝ a hiding place, esp. one in the ground, for ammunition, food, treasures, etc.

ⓢⓨⓝ hideout, reservoir

ⓔ.ⓖ. They found a **cache** of weapons in the criminal's home.

1131 ■□□

domicile
[dάməsàil]

처소, 집, 주소

ⓝ a place of residence; abode; house or home

ⓢⓨⓝ residence, dwelling, habitation

ⓔ.ⓖ. Any change of **domicile** should be followed by notifying authorities.

1132 ■■□

galore
[gəlɔ́ːr]

많은, 풍부한

ⓐ in abundance; in plentiful amounts

ⓢⓨⓝ abounding, plentiful

ⓔ.ⓖ. You'll be able to find cakes **galore**.

1133 ■■□

havoc
[hǽvək]

파괴, 황폐, 대혼란

ⓝ great destruction or devastation; ruinous damage

ⓢⓨⓝ devastation, destruction, ruination

ⓔ.ⓖ. The tornado brought **havoc** to the small town.

1134 ■■□

incontrovertible
[inkὰntrəvə́ːrtəbl]

논쟁의 여지가 없는, 부정할 수 없는

ⓐ not controvertible; not open to question or dispute

ⓢⓨⓝ indisputable, incontestable, undeniable, unquestionable

ⓔ.ⓖ. We have **incontrovertible** proof of what happened.

ⓥ controvert 논의하다, 논쟁하다

1135 ■■□

inundate
[ínəndèit]

범람시키다, 물에 잠기게 하다

ⓥ to flood; cover or overspread with water

ⓢⓨⓝ overflow, whelm

ⓔ.ⓖ. The creek overflowed its banks and **inundated** the fields.

ⓝ inundation 범람, 침수

DAY
19

1136 ■■□

obsess
[əbsés]

사로잡히다, 괴롭히다

ⓥ to dominate or preoccupy the thoughts, feelings, or desires of (a person); beset, trouble, or haunt persistently or abnormally

ⓢⓨⓝ torment, afflict

ⓔ.ⓖ. She was so **obsessed** with video games that it made her lose her job.

ⓝ obsession 강박관념, 망상, 집념

1137 ■■□

pertinent
[pə́ːrtənənt]

적절한, 타당한

ⓐ pertaining or relating directly and significantly to the matter at hand

ⓢⓨⓝ appropriate, fitting, fit, suitable, applicable

ⓔ.ⓖ. She had asked some **pertinent** questions for the manager.

ⓐ impertinent 적절치 않은, 관계없는

1138 ■■□

raze
[réiz]

파괴하다, 무너뜨리다

ⓥ to tear down; level to the ground

ⓢⓨⓝ demolish, destroy

ⓔ.ⓖ. The Vikings often would **raze** cities, leaving nothing standing.

1139 ■■■

remunerate
[rimjúːnərèit]

보수를 주다, 보상하다

ⓥ to pay or reward for work, trouble, etc.

ⓢⓨⓝ reward, recompense

ⓔ.ⓖ. You will be **remunerated** for your effort.

ⓝ remuneration 보수, 보상

1140 ■■□

valor
[vǽlər]

용기, 용맹

ⓝ boldness or determination in facing great danger, esp. in battle

ⓢⓨⓝ courage, bravery, boldness

ⓔ.ⓖ. His **valor** is known throughout the land.

ⓐ valorous 씩씩한, 용감한

MEMO

Day
20

유희태 일반영어 ⑤
VOCA
기출VOCA 30days

bloodstream	☐☐☐	blemish	☐☐☐
burial	☐☐☐	propitious	☐☐☐
incisive	☐☐☐	integral	☐☐☐
lap	☐☐☐	sinecure	☐☐☐
gong	☐☐☐	fraught	☐☐☐
amnesia	☐☐☐	abdicate	☐☐☐
muffle	☐☐☐	corroborate	☐☐☐
entreat	☐☐☐	bourgeois	☐☐☐
baton	☐☐☐	epilog	☐☐☐
outweigh	☐☐☐	frontier	☐☐☐
ping	☐☐☐	metaphor	☐☐☐
curious	☐☐☐	skeptic	☐☐☐
relegate	☐☐☐	interject	☐☐☐
fortuitous	☐☐☐	frenzied	☐☐☐
culpable	☐☐☐	breach	☐☐☐
characteristic	☐☐☐	permeate	☐☐☐
cognitive	☐☐☐	recoil	☐☐☐
conduct	☐☐☐	malady	☐☐☐
conservation	☐☐☐	antithesis	☐☐☐
precedence	☐☐☐	slaughter	☐☐☐
luminous	☐☐☐	squeak	☐☐☐
refinement	☐☐☐	stammer	☐☐☐
cumbersome	☐☐☐	bumptious	☐☐☐
rapport	☐☐☐	nomadic	☐☐☐
dainty	☐☐☐	incoherent	☐☐☐
attest	☐☐☐	flounder	☐☐☐
continent	☐☐☐	virtuosity	☐☐☐
cyclical	☐☐☐	subterranean	☐☐☐
detach	☐☐☐	ostentatious	☐☐☐
succinct	☐☐☐	tribe	☐☐☐

1141 ■□□

bloodstream
[blʌ́dstriːm]

피의 흐름, 혈류
ⓝ the blood flowing through a circulatory system
ⓔⓖ They help transport nutrients between cells and keep calcium moving along through the **bloodstream** to where it's needed.

1142 ■■□

burial
[bériəl]

매장, 토장
ⓝ the act or ceremony of burying
ⓢⓨⓝ interment
ⓔⓖ Most **burials** take place in the night, to keep from disturbing people.
ⓥ bury 묻다, 매장하다

1143 ■■□

incisive
[insáisiv]

예리한, 재빠른, 기민한
ⓐ remarkably clear and direct
ⓢⓨⓝ sharp, keen, acute, shrewd
ⓔⓖ He is a shrewd strategist with an **incisive** mind.

1144 ■□□

lap
[læp]

무릎
ⓝ the flat area between the waist and knees of a seated person
ⓢⓨⓝ knee
ⓔⓖ When you sit down, place the napkin in your **lap**.

1145 ■■■

gong
[gɔːŋ]

징, (영구)훈장
ⓝ a metal disk with a turned rim, giving a resonant note when struck
ⓔⓖ Oh wait, I think I hear a **gong**.
ⓐ gonglike

1146 ■■■

amnesia
[æmníːʒə]

기억상실
ⓝ complete or partial loss of memory
ⓔⓖ It is very rare for **amnesia** patients to have a complete blackout.
ⓐ amnesic

1147 ■□□

muffle
[mʌ́fəl]

소리를 죽이다
ⓥ to deaden (sound) by wrappings or other means
ⓢⓨⓝ dampen, mute
ⓔ.ⓖ. **Muffled** rock music from the house next door.

1148 ■□□

entreat
[ɛntríːt]

간청(애원)하다
ⓥ to ask (a person) earnestly
ⓢⓨⓝ beseech, implore
ⓔ.ⓖ. I shall **entreat** his pardon for not having done it earlier.
ⓝ entreaty
ⓐⓓ entreatingly

1149 ■□□

baton
[bǽtən]

지휘봉, (릴레이에서 주자들이 주고받는) 배턴
ⓝ a staff symbolizing office or authority, especially one carried by a field marshal
ⓔ.ⓖ. The guard is changing, the **baton** passing on.

1150 ■□□

outweigh
[òut·wéigh]

~보다 더 중요하다
ⓥ to exceed in value, importance, influence, etc.
ⓢⓨⓝ supersede
ⓔ.ⓖ. It is true that the positive effects of unification would **outweigh** any cost.

1151 ■■□

ping
[piŋ]

이메일(문자)을 보내다
ⓥ to make contact with (someone) by sending a brief electronic message, as a text message
ⓔ.ⓖ. I'll **ping** it to you later.

1152 ■□□

curious
[kjúəriəs]

기이한, 호기심을 일으키는
ⓐ eager to know or learn something
ⓢⓨⓝ bizarre, queer, eerie
ⓔ.ⓖ. There was a **curious** mixture of people in the audience.

DAY
20

1153 ■■■

relegate
[réləgèit]

좌천시키다, 격하시키다

ⓥ to send or consign to an inferior position, place, or condition
ⓢⓨⓝ consign, demote, deport
ⓔ.ⓖ. She was **relegated** to a less important post.
ⓝ relegation 좌천

1154 ■■□

fortuitous
[fɔːrtjúːɪtəs]

뜻밖의, 우연한

ⓐ happening or produced by chance
ⓢⓨⓝ accidental, incidental
ⓔ.ⓖ. Their success is the result of a **fortuitous** combination of luck and outside support.
ⓝ fortuity 우연성, 우연

1155 ■■□

culpable
[kʌ́lpəbl]

비난할 만한, 괘씸한

ⓐ deserving blame or censure
ⓢⓨⓝ blameworthy, censurable, reprehensible, blamable
ⓔ.ⓖ. I hold him **culpable** because he is the only adult.
ⓝ culpability 유죄

1156 ■■■

characteristic
[kæriktərístik]

특징적인, 독특한, 특질 있는

ⓐ pertaining to, constituting, or indicating the character or peculiar quality of a person or thing
ⓢⓨⓝ typical, distinctive
ⓔ.ⓖ. Red and gold are the **characteristic** colors of fall.
ⓥ characterize 특징을 기술하다, 성격을 묘사하다

1157 ■■□

cognitive
[kɑ́gnitiv]

인식의, 인식력이 있는

ⓐ of or pertaining to the mental processes of perception, memory, judgment, and reasoning, as contrasted with emotional and volitional processes
ⓔ.ⓖ. The accident has significantly impaired her **cognitive** function.
ⓝ cognition 인식, 인지

1158 ■■□

conduct
[kándʌkt]

행위, 행동

ⓝ personal behavior; way of acting; bearing or deportment
ⓢⓨⓝ act, deed, behavior
ⓔ.ⓖ. His **conduct** is always in line with our club's standards.

1159 ■■□

conservation
[kànsərvéiʃən]

보존, 유지, 보호

ⓝ the act of conserving; prevention of injury, decay, waste, or loss
ⓢⓨⓝ preservation, protection, keeping
ⓔ.ⓖ. **Conservation** is the key to helping the environment.
ⓥ conserve 보존하다, 보호하다

1160 ■■□

precedence
[présədəns, prisí:-]

우선(함)(over)

ⓝ the condition of being more important than somebody else and therefore coming or being dealt with first
ⓔ.ⓖ. She had to learn that her wishes did not take **precedence** over other people's needs.

1161 ■■□

luminous
[lú:mɪnəs]

야광의

ⓐ shining in the dark
ⓔ.ⓖ. **luminous** paint
ⓝ luminousness, luminosity
ⓐⓓ luminously

1162 ■■□

refinement
[rɪfaɪnmənt]

개선

ⓝ a small change to something that improves it
ⓔ.ⓖ. This particular model has a further **refinement**.
ⓥ refine

1163 ■■■

cumbersome
[kʌmbərsəm]

크고 무거운, 다루기 힘든

ⓐ large and heavy; difficult to carry
ⓔ.ⓖ. **cumbersome** machinery
ⓝ cumbersomeness, cumbrousness
ⓐⓓ cumbersomely, cumbrously

DAY
20

1164 ■■□

rapport
[ræpɔː(r)]

(친밀한) 관계

ⓝ a friendly relationship in which people understand each other very well

e.g. She understood the importance of establishing a close **rapport** with clients.

1165 ■■□

dainty
[deɪnti]

앙증맞은

ⓐ small and delicate in a way that people find attractive

e.g. **dainty** feet

ⓝ daintiness

ⓐd daintily

1166 ■■■

attest
[ətest]

증명하다

ⓥ to show or prove that something is true

e.g. Contemporary accounts **attest** to his courage and determination.

ⓝ attestant, attestation

ⓐ attestable

1167 ■□□

continent
[kɑ́ntənənt]

대륙, 육지

ⓝ one of the main landmasses of the globe, usually reckoned as seven in number (Europe, Asia, Africa, North America, South America, Australia, and Antarctica)

syn mainland

e.g. India used to be its own **continent**, away from mainland Asia.

ⓐ continental 대륙의, 대륙성의

1168 ■■□

cyclical
[síklɪkəl]

순환의, 주기적인

ⓐ revolving or recurring in cycles; characterized by recurrence in cycles

e.g. These financial ups and downs are **cyclical**.

ⓝ cycle 순환, 주기

1169 ■□□

detach
[ditǽʧ]

떼다, 떼어내다, 분리하다
ⓥ to unfasten and separate
ⓢⓨⓝ remove, disengage, disunite
ⓔ.ⓖ. We designed the flashlight to **detach** from the bicycle.
ⓝ detachment 분리, 이탈

1170 ■■□

succinct
[səksíŋkt]

간단명료한, 간결한
ⓐ expressed in few words
ⓢⓨⓝ concise, terse
ⓔ.ⓖ. The writing is perceptive, **succinct** and mercilessly realistic.

1171 ■■□

blemish
[blémiʃ]

손상하다, 흠내다, 해치다
ⓥ to destroy or diminish the perfection of
ⓢⓨⓝ harm, impair, tarnish
ⓔ.ⓖ. The book is **blemished** by long, ineffective descriptions.

1172 ■■■

propitious
[prəpíʃəs]

호의를 가진, 자비로운, 길조의
ⓐ presenting favorable conditions
ⓢⓨⓝ favorable
ⓔ.ⓖ. The weather is **propitious** for fishing today.
ⓐ unpropitious 불길한, 불운한

1173 ■■□

integral
[íntigrəl]

구성요소로서의, 절대 필요한, 없어서는 안 될
ⓐ of, pertaining to, or belonging as a part of the whole; constituent or component; necessary to the completeness of the whole
ⓢⓨⓝ essential, indispensable, requisite
ⓔ.ⓖ. Internet marketing has become **integral** with sales.
ⓝ integrality 완전(성), 절대필요성

1174 ■■■

sinecure
[sáinikjùər]

한직(한가한 직종)
ⓝ an office or position requiring little or no work, esp. one yielding profitable returns
ⓔ.ⓖ. They found him an exalted **sinecure** as a ambassador.

DAY
20

1175 ■■■

fraught
[frɔːt]

~으로 충만한
ⓐ filled or laden (with)
⟨syn⟩ filled
⟨e.g.⟩ The first attempts were **fraught** with struggles.
ⓥ be fraught with ~으로 충만한

1176 ■■■

abdicate
[ǽbdəkèit]

물러나다, 퇴위하다
ⓥ to renounce or relinquish a throne, right, power, claim, responsibility, or the like, esp. in a formal manner
⟨syn⟩ resign, quit
⟨e.g.⟩ The aging founder of the firm decided to **abdicate**.
ⓝ abdication 퇴위, 사직, 포기

1177 ■■■

corroborate
[kərábərèit]

확실하게 하다, 확증하다
ⓥ to make more certain
⟨syn⟩ confirm, verify, authenticate
⟨e.g.⟩ He **corroborated** my version of the story.
ⓝ corroboration 확증, 보강증거

1178 ■■□

bourgeois
[búərʒwaː]

중산계급의, 속물의, 물질만능적인
ⓐ belonging to, characteristic of, or consisting of the middle class; conventional, dominated or characterized by materialistic pursuits or concerns
⟨syn⟩ materialistic
⟨e.g.⟩ The **bourgeois** understand nothing about the working class.
ⓝ bourgeoisie 부르주아 계급, 중산계급

1179 ■□□

epilog
[epiloːk]

에필로그
ⓝ a speech, usually in verse, delivered by one of the actors after the conclusion of a play
⟨e.g.⟩ In the **epilog**, we find out the main character was really a hero.
ⓝ prolog 프롤로그

1180 ■□□

frontier
[frʌntíər]

국경, 변경
ⓝ the part of a country that borders another country
(syn) boundary, border
(e.g.) At the **frontier**, many soldier are trained to stand guard.

1181 ■■□

metaphor
[métəfɔ̀:r]

은유
ⓝ a figure of speech in which a term or phrase is applied to something to which it is not literally applicable in order to suggest a resemblance
(e.g.) Commonly, a red rose is a **metaphor** for love.
ⓐ metaphoric 은유의, 은유적인

1182 ■■□

skeptic
[sképtik]

의심 많은 사람, 회의론자
ⓝ a person who questions the validity or authenticity of something purporting to be factual
(syn) disbeliever, pessimist
(e.g.) Some **skeptics** don't believe the war was about human rights.
ⓐ skeptical 의심 많은, 회의적인

1183 ■■□

interject
[ìntərdʒékt]

불쑥 끼워넣다, 사이에 끼우다
ⓥ to insert between other things
(syn) interpose
(e.g.) He listened thoughtfully, **interjecting** only when he need clarification.
ⓝ interjection 감탄사

1184 ■■□

frenzied
[frénzid]

열광적인, 광포한
ⓐ wildly excited or enthusiastic
(syn) frenetic, feverish, furious
(e.g.) His baseball swing was **frenzied**, no accuracy but great power.
ⓝ frenzy 격분, 격앙

DAY
20

1185 ■■□

breach
[bríːtʃ]

위반, 불이행

ⓝ the act or a result of breaking; an infraction or violation, as of a law, trust, faith, or promise

ⓢⓨⓝ infraction, contravention, infringement

ⓔ.ⓖ. The prosecution alleges that the company is in **breach** of the contract.

1186 ■■■

permeate
[páːrmièit]

배어들다, 스며들다

ⓥ to pass into or through every part of

ⓢⓨⓝ pervade, infiltrate

ⓔ.ⓖ. The smell of flowers **permeated** the garden.

ⓝ permeation 침투, 삼투

1187 ■■□

recoil
[rikóil]

후퇴하다, 뒷걸음치다

ⓥ to draw back; start or shrink back, as in alarm, horror, or disgust

ⓢⓨⓝ blench, flinch

ⓔ.ⓖ. The boy **recoiled** at the sight of the vegetables.

1188 ■■□

malady
[mǽlədi]

(만성)병, 병폐

ⓝ any disorder or disease of the body; any undesirable or disordered condition

ⓢⓨⓝ ailment, disease

ⓔ.ⓖ. For this **malady**, we must use natural medicine.

1189 ■■□

antithesis
[æntíθəsis]

대조, 정반대

ⓝ opposition; contrast

ⓢⓨⓝ opposite, contraposition

ⓔ.ⓖ. These two words form are the **antithesis** of one another.

ⓐ antithetic 대조되는, 정반대의

1190 ■■□

slaughter
[slɔ́:tər]

도살하다, 살육하다

ⓥ to kill or butcher (animals), esp. for food; to kill in a brutal or violent manner
ⓢⓨⓝ butcher, massacre, slay
ⓔ.ⓖ. Both countries **slaughtered** thousands of snakes.
ⓐ slaughterous 살육을 좋아하는, 살생하는

1191 ■■□

squeak
[skwíːk]

찍찍 소리내다, 끽끽거리다

ⓥ to utter or emit a short, sharp, shrill sound
ⓢⓨⓝ creak
ⓔ.ⓖ. My boots **squeaked** a little as I walked across the wet floor.

1192 ■■□

stammer
[stǽmər]

말을 더듬다

ⓥ to speak with involuntary breaks and pauses, or with spasmodic repetitions of syllables or sounds
ⓢⓨⓝ stutter, falter
ⓔ.ⓖ. She **stammers** when she feels awkward.
ⓝ stammerer 말더듬이

1193 ■■■

bumptious
[bʌ́mpʃəs]

오만한, 거만한

ⓐ offensively self-assertive
ⓢⓨⓝ arrogant, conceited
ⓔ.ⓖ. He is a **bumptious** and young upstart, much to the annoyance of his peers.

1194 ■■□

nomadic
[noumǽdik]

유목의, 방랑의

ⓐ of, pertaining to, or characteristic of nomads
ⓢⓨⓝ migrant, vagrant
ⓔ.ⓖ. The Gypsies were **nomadic** in Europe, moving constantly from city to city.
ⓝ nomad 유목민, 방랑자

DAY
20

1195 ■■□

incoherent
[ìnkouhíərənt]

모순된, 일관되지 않은
ⓐ without logical or meaningful connection
ⓢⓨⓝ incongruous, inconsistent
ⓔ.ⓖ. You are tired, and your explanations are becoming totally **incoherent**.
ⓝ incoherence 논리가 맞지 않음, 모순

1196 ■■□

flounder
[fláundər]

발버둥치다, 허우적거리다
ⓥ to struggle with stumbling or plunging movements
ⓢⓨⓝ squirm, wriggle, writhe, struggle
ⓔ.ⓖ. The fish **floundered** on the shore, trying to get back into the water.

1197 ■■□

virtuosity
[və́ːrtʃuásəti]

탁월한 기량, 명인 연기
ⓝ the character, ability, or skill of a virtuoso
ⓔ.ⓖ. At that time, his **virtuosity** on the piano had no parallel in the blues.
ⓝ virtuoso 거장, 명인, 대가

1198 ■■□

subterranean
[sʌ̀btəréiniən]

지하의, 숨은, 비밀의
ⓐ existing, situated, or operating below the surface of the earth
ⓢⓨⓝ underground, hidden, secret, covert
ⓔ.ⓖ. The **subterranean** work machines were necessary to finish the subway.

1199 ■■■

ostentatious
[àstentéiʃəs, -tən-]

드러내는, 과시하는
ⓐ characterized by or given to pretentious or conspicuous show in an attempt to impress others
ⓢⓨⓝ pretentious, boastful
ⓔ.ⓖ. They made an **ostentatious** display of our country's military strength.
ⓝ ostentation 겉치레, 허식

1200 ■□□

tribe
[tráib]

부족, 종족

ⓝ a group of people of the same race, language, and customs, especially in a developing country

ⓢⓨⓝ race, people, family, clan, lineage

ⓔ.ⓖ. Many **tribes** became extinct when they came into contact with Western diseases.

ⓐ tribal 종족의, 부족의

Day

21

timorous	□□□	bulwark	□□□
inhibit	□□□	vivid	□□□
gregarious	□□□	divergent	□□□
fleeting	□□□	abrogate	□□□
flank	□□□	saturate	□□□
press conference	□□□	poignant	□□□
respond	□□□	repress	□□□
coalition	□□□	asperity	□□□
reach	□□□	beleaguer	□□□
expound	□□□	persevere	□□□
referendum	□□□	glutton	□□□
brusque	□□□	indigenous	□□□
jeopardize	□□□	lurid	□□□
imminent	□□□	covenant	□□□
flamboyant	□□□	overt	□□□
bristle	□□□	vain	□□□
albeit	□□□	rash	□□□
premise	□□□	grumble	□□□
scurry	□□□	consummate	□□□
rule of thumb	□□□	fallacious	□□□
menace	□□□	babble	□□□
envision	□□□	manifold	□□□
eccentric	□□□	assiduous	□□□
conductive	□□□	impeccable	□□□
commend	□□□	desist	□□□
wholly	□□□	brawl	□□□
abreast	□□□	hoax	□□□
levity	□□□	beholden	□□□
spew	□□□	conjecture	□□□
interlope	□□□	gullible	□□□

1201 ■■□

timorous
[tímərəs]

겁 많은, 두려움 많은

ⓐ full of fear
syn fearful, timid
e.g. The new staff was **timorous** when dealing with customers.

1202 ■■□

inhibit
[inhíbit]

억제하다, 제지하다

ⓥ to restrain, hinder, arrest, or check (an action, impulse, etc.)
syn prohibit, forbid, restrain, hinder
e.g. Washing one's hands regularly can help **inhibit** the spread of disease.
ⓝ inhibition 금지, 억제

1203 ■■□

gregarious
[grigέəriəs]

사교적인, 떼 지어 사는, 군거성의

ⓐ fond of the company of others; living in flocks or herds, as animals
syn sociable, companionable, affable
e.g. He is such a **gregarious** and outgoing dinner guest.

1204 ■■□

fleeting
[fléet·ing]

순식간의, 찰나적인

ⓐ passing swiftly
syn transient, momentary
e.g. Their time together will be **fleeting**.
ⓝ fleetingness
ad fleetingly

1205 ■■□

flank
[flæŋk]

옆구리; ~의 호위를 받다

ⓝ the side of an animal or a person between the ribs and hip
syn haunch, side
e.g. He'll try and escape through the left **flank**.

1206 ■□□

press conference
[préss cònference]

기자회견
ⓝ an interview given to journalists by a prominent person in order to make an announcement or answer questions
(e.g.) He was primed with the latest news for the **press conference**.

1207 ■□□

respond
[rispónd]

~에 반응하다(to)
ⓥ to make a return by some action as if in answer
(syn) riposte
(e.g.) You did not **respond** to his name.

1208 ■□□

coalition
[kòuəlíʃən]

연합
ⓝ a combination or alliance, especially a temporary one between persons, factions, states, etc.
(syn) alliance, partnership, affiliation
(e.g.) The New York Immigration **Coalition** protects the rights and interests of immigrant communities.
ⓝ coalitionist
ⓐ coalitional

1209 ■■□

reach
[riːtʃ]

(가까운) 거리(범위), 강변
ⓝ the distance to which someone can stretch out their hand
(syn) range
(e.g.) The glasses was tantalizingly out of **reach**.
ⓝ reachability
ⓐ reachable

1210 ■□□

expound
[ikspáund]

(자세히) 설명하다
ⓥ explain systematically and in detail
(syn) set forth, advance
(e.g.) Feel free to **expound** on your vague and unfounded comment.

1211 ■□□

referendum
[rèfəréndəm]

국민투표

ⓝ a general vote by the electorate on a single political question which has been referred to them for a direct decision
ⓢⓨⓝ public vote, poll, ballot
ⓔ.ⓖ. A confirmatory **referendum** was rejected.

1212 ■■□

brusque
[brʌ́sk]

퉁명스러운, 무뚝뚝한

ⓐ abrupt in manner
ⓢⓨⓝ blunt, rough, impolite
ⓔ.ⓖ. A **brusque** complaint greeted his unexpected return.
ⓝ brusquerie 무뚝뚝함, 매정함

1213 ■■□

jeopardize
[dʒépərdàiz]

위험에 빠뜨리다, 위태롭게 하다

ⓥ to put in jeopardy
ⓢⓨⓝ endanger, imperil
ⓔ.ⓖ. He **jeopardized** his life every time he went diving in the river.
ⓝ jeopardy 위험

1214 ■■□

imminent
[ímənənt]

절박한, 촉박한

ⓐ likely to occur at any moment
ⓢⓨⓝ impending
ⓔ.ⓖ. Since he worked hard, his raise was **imminent**.
ⓝ imminence 절박, 촉박

1215 ■■□

flamboyant
[flæmbɔ́iənt]

현란한, 눈부신, 이채를 띤

ⓐ strikingly bold or brilliant; conspicuously dashing and colorful
ⓢⓨⓝ showy, brilliant, ornate
ⓔ.ⓖ. His **flamboyant** style is unfit for this respectable law firm.
ⓝ flamboyance 화려함, 현란함

1216 ■■□

bristle
[brísl]

곤두서다, 성내다, 초조해하다

ⓥ to stand or rise stiffly, like bristles; to become rigid with anger or irritation

ⓢⓨⓝ rage

ⓔ.ⓖ. The man **bristled** angrily when I asked him to move.

ⓐ bristled 센 털이 있는, 곤두선

1217 ■■□

albeit
[ɔːlbíːit]

~임에도 불구하고

ⓐ conj; although; even if

ⓢⓨⓝ although, even if

ⓔ.ⓖ. They noted that East Timor has moderated its behavior over the years, **albeit** very slowly.

1218 ■■□

premise
[prémis]

전제

ⓝ a proposition supporting or helping to support a conclusion

ⓢⓨⓝ thesis, presupposition, assumption

ⓔ.ⓖ. The proof was wrong because of a faulty **premise**.

1219 ■■□

scurry
[skə́ːri]

허둥지둥 달리다, 잰 걸음으로 서두르다

ⓥ to go or move quickly or in haste

ⓢⓨⓝ scamper, sprint, hasten, hurry

ⓔ.ⓖ. When the lights went on residents went **scurrying** for cover.

1220 ■■□

rule of thumb
['rul əv 'θʌm]

경험법칙

ⓔ.ⓖ. You can use a **rule of thumb** for choosing a weight.

1221 ■■□

menace
[menəs]

위협적인 존재; (어조·분위기 등으로 느껴지는) 위협

ⓝ person or thing that is likely to cause serious harm

ⓢⓨⓝ nuisance, plague, pest

ⓔ.ⓖ. A new initiative aimed at beating the **menace** of illegal drugs.

ⓝ menacer ⓐ menacing ⓐⓓ menacingly

1222 ■■□

envision
[ɪnvɪʒn]

(특히 앞으로 바라는 일을) 마음속에 그리다(상상하다)
ⓥ to envisage it
ⓢⓨⓝ imagine, visualize, picture
ⓔⓖ In the future we **envision** a federation of companies.

1223 ■■□

eccentric
[ɪksentrɪk]

괴짜인, 별난, 기이한
ⓐ to behave in a strange way, and have habits or opinions that are different from those of most people
ⓢⓨⓝ odd, strange, peculiar
ⓔⓖ He is an **eccentric** character who likes wearing a beret and dark glasses.
ⓝ eccentricity   ⓐⓓ eccentrically

1224 ■■□

conductive
[kəndʌktɪv]

(열 · 전기 등을) 전도하는, 전도성의
ⓐ A conductive substance is able to conduct things such as heat and electricity.
ⓔⓖ Salt water is much more **conductive** than fresh water is.
ⓐⓓ conductively

1225 ■■□

commend
[kəmend]

(특히 공개적으로) 칭찬하다, 추천하다, 권하다
ⓥ to praise them formally
ⓢⓨⓝ praise, acclaim, applaud
ⓔⓖ She was **commended** on her handling of the situation.
ⓝ commender, commendation, commendableness
ⓐ commendatory, commendable
ⓐⓓ commendably

1226 ■□□

wholly
[hóulli]

전적으로, 완전히
ⓐⓓ entirely, totally, altogether, quite
ⓢⓨⓝ completely, thoroughly
ⓔⓖ My attention is **wholly** consumed with finals.
ⓐ whole 전체의, 모든, 완전한

1227 ■■□

abreast
[əbrést]

나란히, ~와 병행하여
(ad) side by side; beside each other in a line
(syn) side by side, beside, in a row, abeam
(e.g.) The children walked two **abreast** down the street.

1228 ■■□

levity
[lévəti]

경거망동, 경솔, 변덕
(n) lightness of mind, character, or behavior; lack of appropriate seriousness or earnestness
(syn) rashness, hastiness
(e.g.) We tried to add **levity** to the meeting with some jokes.

1229 ■■□

spew
[spjúː]

토하다
(v) to discharge the contents of the stomach through the mouth
(syn) vomit, throw up
(e.g.) After the boat ride, I had to **spew**.

1230 ■■■

interlope
[intərlóup]

허가 없이 영업하다, 참견하다
(v) to intrude into some region or field of trade without a proper license; to thrust oneself into the affairs of others
(syn) trespass, poach, encroach, meddle
(e.g.) He said the United Nations would **interlope** in Middle Eastern affairs too much.
(n) interloper 남의 일에 참견하고 나서는 사람

1231 ■■□

bulwark
[búlwərk]

성채, 보루
(n) a wall of earth or other material built for defense
(syn) rampart, fortress
(e.g.) Outside the city was a **bulwark** which had no importance any more.

1232 ■□□

vivid
[vívid]

선명한, 밝은, 발랄한, 생기 있는
ⓐ strikingly bright or intense, as color, light, etc.; full of life
ⓢⓨⓝ brilliant, bright, lively, animated
ⓔ.ⓖ. The poet gives a **vivid** description of the lady.
ⓐⓓ vividly 생생하게, 선명하게

1233 ■■□

divergent
[divə́:rdʒənt, dai-]

분기하는, 갈라지는; (관습 등에서) 일탈한; (의견 등이) 다른
ⓐ different from each other
ⓞⓟⓟ convergent
ⓔ.ⓖ. There are two people who have **divergent** views on this question.

1234 ■■■

abrogate
[ǽbrəgèit]

폐기하다
ⓥ to abolish by formal or official means; annul by an authoritative act
ⓢⓨⓝ repeal, revoke, rescind, nullify, void, invalidate
ⓔ.ⓖ. The treaty was **abrogated** by declaration of the king.
ⓝ abrogation 폐기

1235 ■■■

saturate
[sǽtʃərèit]

흠뻑 적시다, 담그다
ⓥ to soak, impregnate, or imbue thoroughly or completely
ⓢⓨⓝ soak, impregnate, imbue
ⓔ.ⓖ. The carpet was **saturated** from the leaky pipe.
ⓐ saturated 스며든, 흠뻑 젖은

1236 ■■■

poignant
[pɔ́injənt]

마음 아픈, 통렬한
ⓐ keenly distressing to the feelings
ⓢⓨⓝ bitter, agonizing
ⓔ.ⓖ. The museum guard made **poignant** remarks to a group of tourists.
ⓝ poignancy 날카로움, 신랄함

1237 ■■□

repress
[riprés]

억제하다, 억누르다

ⓥ to keep under control, check, or suppress (desires, feelings, actions, tears, etc.)

syn suppress

e.g. **Repressing** tears is no more helpful to our body than keeping laughter back is.

ⓝ repression 억제, 제지

1238 ■■■

asperity
[əspérəti]

거침, 무뚝뚝함, 거친 말

ⓝ harshness or sharpness of tone, temper, or manner

syn severity, acrimony, sharpness

e.g. The student's honest mistake did not warrant such **asperity**.

ⓐ aspirate 거친, 까칠한

1239 ■■□

beleaguer
[bilíːgər]

포위하다, 에워싸다

ⓥ to surround or beset, as with troubles

syn surround, beset

e.g. Further cutbacks will only **beleaguer** the economy.

1240 ■■□

persevere
[pə̀ːrsəvíər]

인내하다, 견뎌내다

ⓥ to persist in anything undertaken; maintain a purpose in spite of difficulty, obstacles, or discouragement; continue steadfastly

syn endure, persist

e.g. Faith helped them **preserve** through the troubling times.

ⓝ perseverance 인내, 끈기

1241 ■■□

glutton
[glʌ́tn]

대식가, 폭식가

ⓝ a person who eats and drinks excessively or voraciously

syn hog, gourmand

e.g. He is such a **glutton** during all the holiday meals.

ⓐ gluttonous 많이 먹는, 탐욕스러운

1242 ■■□

indigenous
[indídʒənəs]

토착의, 지역 고유의

ⓐ originating in and characteristic of a particular region or country
ⓢⓨⓝ native, connatural, innate
ⓔ.ⓖ. Ginseng is **indigenous** to the soil of Gaeseong.
ⓝ indigene 본토박이, 토착민

1243 ■■□

lurid
[lúərid]

소름 끼치는, 무서운, 끔찍한

ⓐ gruesome, horrible, revolting
ⓢⓨⓝ gruesome, horrible, revolting
ⓔ.ⓖ. The scandal cast a **lurid** light on the person.

1244 ■■□

covenant
[kʌ́vənənt]

계약

ⓝ a promise to sb, or a legal agreement, especially one to pay a
regular amount of money to sb/sth
ⓢⓨⓝ contract
ⓔ.ⓖ. Let's not forget, the **covenant** between God and His people,
was about the coming Messiah and the kingdom of God.

1245 ■■□

overt
[ouvə́ːrt]

명백한, 공공연한

ⓐ open to view or knowledge; not concealed or secret
ⓢⓨⓝ plain, manifest, apparent, public
ⓔ.ⓖ. So far, there haven't been any **overt** mistakes.

1246 ■□□

vain
[véin]

헛된, 헛수고의

ⓐ ineffectual or unsuccessful
ⓢⓨⓝ fruitless, useless, unavailing
ⓔ.ⓖ. All of his suggestions were in **vain**, nothing changed.
ⓝ vanity 허무함, 덧없음

1247 ■■□

rash
[rǽʃ]

무분별한, 경솔한

ⓐ acting or tending to act too hastily or without due consideration
ⓢⓨⓝ impetuous, reckless, venturous, incautious, precipitate, indiscreet,
foolhardy
ⓔ.ⓖ. It was **rash** of you to buy the house without talking to your wife.

1248 ■■□

grumble
[grʌ́mbl]

투덜거리다, 불평하다

ⓥ to murmur or mutter in discontent; complain sullenly

ⓢⓨⓝ grunt, complain

ⓔ.ⓖ. He **grumbled** at his father for not buying him a video game.

1249 ■■□

consummate
[kʌ́nsəmèit]

완성하다, 완료하다

ⓥ to bring to a state of perfection; to complete (an arrangement, agreement, or the like) by a pledge or the signing of a contract

ⓢⓨⓝ fulfill, complete, perfect, finish, accomplish, achieve

ⓔ.ⓖ. The company **consummated** its agreement with the sale of the property.

ⓝ consummation 완성, 완료, 성취

1250 ■■□

fallacious
[fəléiʃəs]

그릇된, 허위의

ⓐ containing a fallacy; logically unsound

ⓢⓨⓝ illogical, false

ⓔ.ⓖ. The story he gave the police was **fallacious**.

1251 ■■□

babble
[bǽbl]

불명료한 소리를 내다, 쓸데없는 말을 하다

ⓥ to utter sounds or words imperfectly, indistinctly, or without meaning

ⓔ.ⓖ. The child **babbled** on excitedly about his new toy.

ⓝ babbler 수다쟁이

1252 ■■□

manifold
[mǽnəfòuld]

가지각색의, 여러 가지의, 잡다한

ⓐ of many kinds; numerous and varied

ⓢⓨⓝ various, multitudinous

ⓔ.ⓖ. They don't understand **manifold** cultural differences within a community.

1253 ■■■

assiduous
[əsídʒuəs]

끊임없는, 계속하는, 근면한
ⓐ constant in application or effort; working diligently at a task
(syn) continuous, persistent, diligent
(e.g.) He was always **assiduous** in taking notes, because his memory was weak.
ⓝ assiduity 부지런함, 근면

1254 ■■■

impeccable
[impékəbl]

결점 없는, 죄 없는
ⓐ having no flaws
(syn) flawless, irreproachable, faultless
(e.g.) His record was **impeccable**, which impressed the board.
ⓐ impeccant 죄 없는, 결백한

1255 ■■□

desist
[dizíst]

그만두다, 단념하다
ⓥ to cease, as from some action or proceeding
(syn) stop, cease
(e.g.) The government has asked that you **desist** selling alcohol.

1256 ■■■

brawl
[brɔ́ːl]

말다툼하다, 싸움하다
ⓝ to quarrel angrily and noisily
(syn) wrangle, squabble, fight
(e.g.) The two baseball teams **brawled** after the run was scored.
ⓐ brawling 시끄러운, 떠들썩한

1257 ■■■

hoax
[hóuks]

골탕 먹임, 짓궂은 장난
ⓝ something intended to deceive or defraud
(syn) deception, fraud, fake, imposture, humbug
(e.g.) It was learned later that the UFO was a **hoax** perpetrated by children.

1258 ■■■

beholden
[bihóuldən]

은혜를 입은, 신세 진
ⓐ obligated; indebted
(syn) obligated, indebted, owing
(e.g.) He was **beholden** to no one.

1259 ■■□

conjecture
[kəndʒéktʃər]

추측하다, 어림짐작하다

ⓥ to conclude or suppose from grounds or evidence insufficient to ensure reliability

ⓢⓨⓝ surmise, suppose, presume

ⓔ.ⓖ. We **conjectured** that the next train would be less crowded.

ⓐ conjecturable 추측할 수 있는

1260 ■■□

gullible
[gʌ́ləbl]

잘 속는

ⓐ easily deceived or cheated

ⓢⓨⓝ credulous

ⓔ.ⓖ. This replica was sold to a **gullible** tourist as a valuable original.

ⓝ gullibility 잘 속음

Day

22

coerce	☐☐☐		mendacious	☐☐☐	
spontaneous	☐☐☐		pecuniary	☐☐☐	
apathy	☐☐☐		backslide	☐☐☐	
revile	☐☐☐		sumptuous	☐☐☐	
lookout	☐☐☐		underwrite	☐☐☐	
monotheism	☐☐☐		rife	☐☐☐	
buttress	☐☐☐		nebulous	☐☐☐	
recuperate	☐☐☐		bogus	☐☐☐	
rusty	☐☐☐		repose	☐☐☐	
reputed	☐☐☐		omnivorous	☐☐☐	
aspire	☐☐☐		disparate	☐☐☐	
myriad	☐☐☐		edifice	☐☐☐	
declaim	☐☐☐		sultry	☐☐☐	
burgeon	☐☐☐		badger	☐☐☐	
urbane	☐☐☐		frown	☐☐☐	
utilitarian	☐☐☐		opulence	☐☐☐	
expedite	☐☐☐		lush	☐☐☐	
decimate	☐☐☐		supplicate	☐☐☐	
tantalizing	☐☐☐		decadence	☐☐☐	
sediment	☐☐☐		penance	☐☐☐	
deflect	☐☐☐		juxtapose	☐☐☐	
withstand	☐☐☐		browse	☐☐☐	
coinage	☐☐☐		plight	☐☐☐	
crave	☐☐☐		cope	☐☐☐	
barometer	☐☐☐		incompatible	☐☐☐	
tortuous	☐☐☐		blare	☐☐☐	
conjugal	☐☐☐		brink	☐☐☐	
coup	☐☐☐		fabricate	☐☐☐	
amnesty	☐☐☐		demur	☐☐☐	
exonerate	☐☐☐		escalate	☐☐☐	

1261 ■■□

coerce
[kouɔ́ːrs]

강제하다, 강요하다
ⓥ to compel by force, intimidation, or authority, esp. without regard for individual desire or volition
ⓢⓨⓝ compel, force
ⓔ.ⓖ. They **coerced** him into selling his house.

1262 ■■□

spontaneous
[spɑntéiniəs]

자발적인, 임의의, 자연적인
ⓐ coming or resulting from a natural impulse or tendency; without effort or premeditation
ⓢⓨⓝ natural, unconstrained
ⓔ.ⓖ. Something **spontaneous** and surprising will impress her more than a big plan.

1263 ■□□

apathy
[ǽpəθi]

무관심
ⓝ absence or suppression of passion, emotion, or excitement
ⓢⓨⓝ indifference, torpor, unconcern
ⓞⓟⓟ enthusiasm
ⓔ.ⓖ. The ignorance and **apathy** of the people is the problem.

1264 ■■□

revile
[riváil]

매도하다
ⓥ to speak abusively
ⓢⓨⓝ condemn, censure
ⓔ.ⓖ. But I do **revile** his decision.
ⓝ revilement

1265 ■■□

lookout
[lúkàut]

경계(guard), 감시(watch)
ⓝ a watch kept, as for something that may happen
ⓔ.ⓖ. The thieves had their **lookout** at the corner.

1266 ■■□

monotheism
[mɑ́nəθiːìzm]

일신교
ⓝ the doctrine or belief that there is only one God
ⓞⓟⓟ polytheism
ⓔ.ⓖ. Polytheism is the belief in more than one God, and **monotheism** is the belief in one God.

1267 ■■□

buttress
[bʌ́tris]

지지대; 지탱해주다, 힘을 실어주다
ⓝ a projecting support of stone or brick built against a wall
ⓢⓨⓝ prop, abutment
ⓔ.ⓖ. The final structural element of Gothic architecture is the flying **buttress**.

1268 ■■□

recuperate
[rikjú:pərèit]

회복하다, 만회하다
ⓥ regain health or strength
ⓢⓨⓝ recover, convalesce
ⓔ.ⓖ. The doctor thought you needed some more time to **recuperate**.
ⓝ recuperation
ⓐ recuperative

1269 ■□□

rusty
[rʌ́sti]

녹슨, 예전 같지 않은
ⓐ covered with or affected by rust
ⓢⓨⓝ oxidized, tarnished
ⓔ.ⓖ. **Rusty** iron is of little use to anyone.
ⓝ rust

1270 ■□□

reputed
[ripjú:tid]

~라고 평판이 나(알려져) 있는
ⓐ widely known and well thought of
ⓢⓨⓝ respected
ⓞⓟⓟ obscure
ⓔ.ⓖ. It is **reputed** to be of value in kidney-diseases.

1271 ■■□

aspire
[əspáiər]

열망하다, 포부를 가지다
ⓥ to long, aim, or seek ambitiously; be eagerly desirous, esp. for something great or of high value
ⓢⓨⓝ long, yearn, desire
ⓔ.ⓖ. Few people who **aspire** to fame ever achieve it.
ⓝ aspiration 포부, 대망, 열망

1272 ■■□

myriad
[míriəd]

매우 많은 것, 무수
ⓝ a very great or indefinitely great number of persons or things
ⓔ.ⓖ. A **myriad** of stars were twinkled in the night sky.

1273 ■■□

declaim
[dikléim]

낭독하다, 열변을 토하다
ⓥ to speak aloud in an oratorical manner; make a formal speech
ⓢⓨⓝ declare, proclaim
ⓔ.ⓖ. The senator **declaimed** from the steps of the capitol building.

1274 ■■□

burgeon
[bə́ːrdʒən]

갑자기 출현(발전)하다
ⓥ to grow or develop quickly
ⓢⓨⓝ flourish, develop, grow, advance
ⓔ.ⓖ. His **burgeoning** skill with the rifle made him famous.
ⓐ burgeoning 급증하는, 급성장하는

1275 ■□□

urbane
[əːrbéin]

도시의, 세련된
ⓐ having the polish and suavity regarded as characteristic of sophisticated social life in major cities; reflecting elegance, sophistication
ⓢⓨⓝ refined, cultured
ⓔ.ⓖ. She describes him as **urbane** and of great wisdom.

1276 ■■□

utilitarian
[juːtɪlɪtériən]

(격식) 실용적인; (철학) 공리주의의
ⓐ based on the idea that the morally correct course of action is the one that produces benefit for the greatest number of people.
ⓔ.ⓖ. True education cannot be purely **utilitarian**.

1277 ■■□

expedite
[ekspədaɪt]

더 신속히 처리하다
ⓥ to cause it to be done more quickly
ⓔ.ⓖ. We tried to help you **expedite** your plans.
ⓝ expediter

1278 ■■■

decimate
[desɪmeɪt]

(주로 수동태로) (특정 지역의 동식물이나 사람들을) 대량으로 죽이다; 심하게 훼손하다(약화시키다)
ⓥ To decimate something such as a group of people or animals means to destroy a very large number of them.
ⓔ.ⓖ. The rabbit population was **decimated** by the disease.
ⓝ decimation, decimator

1279 ■■■

tantalizing
[tǽntəlàiziŋ]

애타게 하는, 감질나게 하는

ⓐ having or exhibiting something that provokes or arouses expectation, interest, or desire, especially that which remains unobtainable or beyond one's reach

(e.g.) The **tantalizing** aroma of fresh coffee wafted towards them.

1280 ■■□

sediment
[sedɪmənt]

침전물, (지리) 퇴적물

ⓝ Solid material that settles at the bottom of a liquid, especially earth and pieces of rock that have been carried along and then left somewhere by water, ice, or wind

(syn) dregs, grounds, residue

(e.g.) Many organisms that die in the sea are soon buried by **sediment**.

ⓐ sedimentous

1281 ■■■

deflect
[dɪflekt]

(특히 무엇에 맞고 난 뒤) 방향을 바꾸다, (관심 · 비판 등을) 피하다(모면하다)

ⓥ to act in a way that prevents it from being directed towards you or affecting you

(syn) turn aside, bend

(e.g.) He raised his arm to try to **deflect** the blow.

ⓝ deflector

ⓐ deflectable

1282 ■■■

withstand
[wɪðstǽnd]

견뎌(이겨)내다

ⓥ If something or someone withstands a force or action, they survive it or do not give in to it.

(syn) resist, suffer, bear

(e.g.) They had **withstood** siege, hunger and deprivation

ⓝ withstander

1283 ■■■

coinage
[kɔɪnɪdʒ]

주화, 화폐 제도(통화), 새로 만들어진 말(구), 신조어

ⓝ the coins which are used in a country

(e.g.) Roman **coinage**

ⓥ coin

1284 ■■□

crave
[kréiv]

열망하다, 갈망하다
ⓥ to long for; want greatly; desire eagerly
ⓢⓨⓝ yearn for, hunger for
ⓔ.ⓖ. Teenagers may claim they want privacy, but they also **crave** connections with people around them.

1285 ■□□

barometer
[bərámətər]

기압계, (일반적인 의미의) 측정기준
ⓝ any instrument that measures atmospheric pressure
ⓔ.ⓖ. A **barometer** was on display at the weather station.
ⓐ barometric 기압(계)의

1286 ■□□

tortuous
[tɔ́ːrtʃuəs]

구불구불한, 꼬인, 비틀린
ⓐ full of twists, turns, or bends; not direct or straightforward, as in procedure or speech
ⓢⓨⓝ twisting, winding, crooked, intricate, circuitous
ⓔ.ⓖ. These long work days are **tortuous.**
ⓥ torture 비틀다, 곡해하다

1287 ■■□

conjugal
[kándʒugəl]

부부의, 혼인의
ⓐ of, pertaining to, or characteristic of marriage
ⓢⓨⓝ matrimonial, nuptial, connubial
ⓔ.ⓖ. The prisoners were allowed quiet **conjugal** visits in a quiet room.
ⓝ conjugality 혼인, 부부관계(생활)

1288 ■■□

coup
[kúː]

일격, 대히트, 대성공
ⓝ a highly successful, unexpected stroke, act, or move
ⓢⓨⓝ accomplishment, triumph
ⓔ.ⓖ. The military has made a **coup** attempting to overthrow the government.

DAY
22

1289 ■□□

amnesty
[ǽmnəsti]

대사, 특사

ⓝ a general pardon for offenses, esp. political offenses, against a government, often granted before any trial or conviction
ⓢⓨⓝ absolution, remission, pardon
ⓔ.ⓖ. He was granted **amnesty** and allowed to stay free.

1290 ■■■

exonerate
[igzánərèit]

무고함을 밝히다, 무죄가 되게 하다

ⓥ to clear, as of an accusation; free from guilt or blame
ⓢⓨⓝ exculpate
ⓔ.ⓖ. He was **exonerated** of all charges after the confessor appeared.
ⓝ exoneration 면죄, 면제

1291 ■■□

mendacious
[mendéiʃəs]

거짓의, 거짓말하는

ⓐ telling lies, esp. habitually
ⓢⓨⓝ untruthful, dishonest, lying
ⓔ.ⓖ. Most advertising is perceived to be **mendacious**.
ⓝ mendacity 허위, 거짓말

1292 ■■□

pecuniary
[pikjúːnièri]

금전(상)의, 벌금(형)의

ⓐ of or pertaining to money; consisting of or given or exacted in money or monetary payments
ⓢⓨⓝ financial, monetary
ⓔ.ⓖ. We are in a state of **pecuniary** woe.

1293 ■■□

backslide
[bǽkslàid]

(악습으로) 되돌아가다, 타락하다

ⓥ to relapse into bad habits, sinful behavior, or undesirable activities
ⓢⓨⓝ relapse
ⓔ.ⓖ. After three months of dieting, she would **backslide** into bad study habits.

1294 ■■■

sumptuous
[sΛmptʃuəs]

값비싼, 고가의, 호화스러운
ⓐ entailing great expense, as from choice materials, fine work, etc.
ⓢⓎⓝ costly, luxurious, lavish, splendid
ⓔ.ⓖ. The King asked for a **sumptuous** banquet.

1295 ■■□

underwrite
[Λndərráit]

서명 승낙하다, 기명 승인하다
ⓥ to sign one's name, as to a document; to show agreement with or to support by or as if by signing one's name to, as a statement or decision
ⓔ.ⓖ. This bill was **underwritten** by both companies involved.

1296 ■■□

rife
[ráif]

유행하는, 유포되어 있는
ⓐ of common or frequent occurrence; in widespread existence, activity, or use
ⓢⓎⓝ prevalent, widespread, epidemic
ⓔ.ⓖ. Cheating is **rife** in this teacher's classroom.

1297 ■■□

nebulous
[nébjuləs]

흐린, 불투명한
ⓐ hazy, vague, indistinct, or confused
ⓢⓎⓝ vague, obscure, ambiguous
ⓔ.ⓖ. We only had a **nebulous** vision of what we would have to do in the class.
ⓝ nebulosity 모호함

1298 ■■□

bogus
[bóugəs]

가짜의, 사이비의
ⓐ not genuine
ⓢⓎⓝ counterfeit, spurious, sham, fraudulent, pseudo, fake, phony
ⓔ.ⓖ. It turned out that his degree was **bogus**, and he had never gone to university.

1299 ■■□

repose
[ripóuz]

휴식
ⓝ the state of reposing or being at rest
ⓢⓎⓝ rest, sleep, relaxation
ⓔ.ⓖ. He had a blank expression while in **repose**.
ⓐ reposeful 평온한, 조용한

DAY
22

1300 ■■□

omnivorous
[ɑmnívərəs]

잡식성의
@ eating all kinds of foods indiscriminately
(syn) edacious, voracious
(e.g.) Human are **omnivorous**, eating fruits, meats, cheeses, and almost anything else.
(n) omnivore 탐식가, 잡식동물

1301 ■■□

disparate
[díspərət]

다른, 공통점이 없는
@ distinct in kind; essentially different
(syn) dissimilar, unlike, distinct, different
(e.g.) The two companies had **disparate** sets of ideas about the future of the merger.

1302 ■■□

edifice
[édəfis]

건물, 대건축물
(n) a building, esp. one of large size or imposing appearance
(syn) building
(e.g.) The Empire State Building was a magnificent **edifice** symbolizing man's achievement.

1303 ■■□

sultry
[sʌ́ltri]

무더운, 후텁지근한
(syn) oppressively hot and close or moist
(syn) sweltering, muggy
(e.g.) The southern US states are **sultry** and steamy in the summertime.

1304 ■■□

badger
[bǽdʒər]

집적대다, 조르다, 괴롭히다; 오소리
(v) to harass or urge persistently
(syn) pester, nag, harass
(e.g.) The lawyer was trying to **badger** the witness into a confession.

1305 ■□□

frown
[fráun]

눈살을 찌푸리다, 난색을 표하다
(v) to contract the brow, as in displeasure or deep thought
(syn) scowl
(e.g.) We could see her **frown** after receiving the gift, and knew she wasn't content.
@ frowning 찌푸린 얼굴의, 불쾌한

1306 ■■■

opulence
[ápjuləns]

부유, 풍부
ⓝ wealth, riches, or affluence
ⓢⓨⓝ abundance, wealth, riches, affluence
ⓔⓖ The ruling classes lived in **opulence** while others died of starvation.
ⓐ opulent 부유한, 풍부한

1307 ■■□

lush
[lʌʃ]

청청한, 싱싱한, 우거진
ⓐ (of vegetation, plants, grasses, etc.) luxuriant
ⓢⓨⓝ succulent
ⓔⓖ The **lush** forest is the best place to grow flowers.

1308 ■■■

supplicate
[sʌ́pləkèit]

간청하다, 기원하다
ⓥ to pray humbly; make humble and earnest entreaty or petition
ⓢⓨⓝ implore, solicit, beseech
ⓔⓖ Each day, the priest **supplicates** and honors God.
ⓝ supplication 간청, 탄원, 기원

1309 ■■□

decadence
[dékədəns]

타락, 퇴폐
ⓝ the act or process of falling into an inferior condition or state
ⓢⓨⓝ deterioration, degeneration, retrogression, decline
ⓔⓖ Some historians hold that the fall of Rome can be attributed to **decadence**.
ⓐ decadent 퇴폐적인, 퇴폐기의

1310 ■■□

penance
[pénəns]

참회, 후회, 고해성사
ⓝ a punishment undergone in token of penitence for sin
ⓢⓨⓝ confession, remorse
ⓔⓖ The common **penance** is the monotonous repetition of prayer.

1311 ■■□

juxtapose
[dʒʌ́kstəpòuz]

병렬하다, 병치하다
ⓥ to place close together or side by side, esp. for comparison or contrast
ⓔⓖ The technique the playwright uses most often is to **juxtapose** things for dramatic effect.

1312 ■□□

browse
[bráuz]

띄엄띄엄 읽다, 훑어보다
ⓥ to look through or glance at casually
ⓢⓨⓝ glance, scan, skim
ⓔⓖ He's **browsing** my books for something to read.
ⓝ browser 띄엄띄엄 읽는 사람, 컴퓨터 브라우저

1313 ■■■

plight
[plait]

곤경, 궁지
ⓝ a condition, state, or situation, esp. an unfavorable or unfortunate one
ⓢⓨⓝ difficulty, predicament
ⓔⓖ His **plight** is desperate since losing his job.

1314 ■■□

cope
[kóup]

대처하다, 처리하다
ⓥ to struggle or deal, esp. on fairly even terms or with some degree of success
ⓢⓨⓝ confront, wrestle, strive
ⓔⓖ I have been **coping** with the loss of my pencil.

1315 ■■□

incompatible
[inkəmpǽtəbl]

성미가 맞지 않는, 양립할 수 없는, 조화되지 않는
ⓐ not compatible; unable to exist together in harmony
ⓢⓨⓝ discordant, inconsistent
ⓔⓖ This program is **incompatible** with my computer, I need another one.
ⓝ incompatibility 양립할 수 없음, 불일치, 불화합성

1316 ■■■

blare
[bléər]

울려퍼지다, 크게 울리다
ⓥ to emit a loud, raucous sound
ⓢⓨⓝ resound
ⓔⓖ The elephants **blared** their call.

1317 ■□□

brink
[bríŋk]

가장자리, 직전
ⓝ the edge or margin of a steep place or of land bordering water; a crucial or critical point, esp. of a situation or state beyond which success or catastrophe occurs
ⓢⓨⓝ rim, verge
ⓔⓖ The those countries were on the **brink** of fighting.

1318 ■■□

fabricate
[fǽbrikèit]

만들다, 제작하다, 가공하다, (가짜로) 만들어내다

ⓥ to make by art or skill and labor, to concoct in order to deceive

ⓢⓨⓝ construct, manufacture

ⓔ.ⓖ. The story was **fabricated**, none of it actually happened.

ⓝ fabrication 제조, 구성, 사기

1319 ■■■

demur
[dimə́ːr]

난색을 표하다, 이의를 제기하다, 반대하다

ⓥ to make objection, esp. on the grounds of scruples; take exception

ⓢⓨⓝ object

ⓔ.ⓖ. They wanted to make him the CEO, but he **demurred**.

ⓝ demurral 이의, 항변

1320 ■■□

escalate
[éskəlèit]

단계적으로 확대되다, 차츰 오르다

ⓥ to increase in intensity, magnitude, etc.

ⓢⓨⓝ advance, mount, increase

ⓔ.ⓖ. The arguing **escalated** into fighting.

ⓝ escalation (단계적) 확대, 증가

MEMO

Day

23

cumulative	☐☐☐	compensatory	☐☐☐
recondite	☐☐☐	fetish	☐☐☐
halo	☐☐☐	taboo	☐☐☐
depository	☐☐☐	imprudent	☐☐☐
mausoleum	☐☐☐	imperative	☐☐☐
glade	☐☐☐	taint	☐☐☐
irresponsive	☐☐☐	contemptuous	☐☐☐
peerage	☐☐☐	absurd	☐☐☐
compassion	☐☐☐	puny	☐☐☐
resounding	☐☐☐	debris	☐☐☐
free-range	☐☐☐	disperse	☐☐☐
learning rate	☐☐☐	obliterate	☐☐☐
delude	☐☐☐	congenial	☐☐☐
mortal	☐☐☐	hoard	☐☐☐
enunciate	☐☐☐	detriment	☐☐☐
baffle	☐☐☐	longevity	☐☐☐
embellish	☐☐☐	lethargic	☐☐☐
perseverance	☐☐☐	paramount	☐☐☐
intact	☐☐☐	remiss	☐☐☐
interlock	☐☐☐	aversion	☐☐☐
deplete	☐☐☐	gist	☐☐☐
prowess	☐☐☐	transient	☐☐☐
threshold	☐☐☐	ardent	☐☐☐
commence	☐☐☐	constrict	☐☐☐
fuss	☐☐☐	prodigy	☐☐☐
introspective	☐☐☐	exult	☐☐☐
balk	☐☐☐	invective	☐☐☐
burrow	☐☐☐	voluminous	☐☐☐
bigwig	☐☐☐	retrospect	☐☐☐
perpetuate	☐☐☐	pungent	☐☐☐

1321 ■■□

cumulative
[kjúːmjulətiv]

누적하는, 누적의

ⓐ increasing or growing by accumulation or successive additions

ⓢⓨⓝ additive, accumulative

ⓔ.ⓖ. It is simple pleasures, such as seeing a child smile, which have a **cumulative** effect on our moods.

ⓝ cumulus 퇴적, 누적

1322 ■■■

recondite
[rékəndàit]

심오한, 난해한

ⓐ dealing with very profound, difficult, or abstruse subject matter

ⓢⓨⓝ profound, difficult, abstruse

ⓔ.ⓖ. Her poems are **recondite** in subject-matter, showing the depth of her knowledge and thought.

1323 ■■□

halo
[héilou]

후광

ⓝ circle of light that is shown in pictures round the head of a holy figure such as a saint or angel

ⓢⓨⓝ nimbus, aureole

ⓔ.ⓖ. She even looks like a angel with a **halo**.

1324 ■□□

depository
[dipázitɔ̀ːri]

보관소

ⓝ a place where objects can be stored safely

ⓢⓨⓝ repository

ⓔ.ⓖ. The preferred solution was a deep nuclear waste **depository**.

1325 ■■□

mausoleum
[mɔ̀ːsəlíːəm]

묘(능)

ⓝ a building, especially a large and stately one, housing a tomb or tombs

ⓢⓨⓝ crypt, sepulcher

ⓔ.ⓖ. His ashes were taken to Rome and placed in Hadrian's **mausoleum**.

1326 ■■□

glade
[gleid]

작은 빈터(공터)

ⓝ grassy space without trees in a wood or forest

ⓔ.ⓖ. The path ended in a **glade**.

1327 ■□□

irresponsive
[ìrispάnsiv]

~에 반응이 없는(to)

ⓐ not responsive to someone or something

ⓔ.ⓖ. Mute, close, **irresponsive** to any glancing light, his dress is like himself.

1328 ■■□

peerage
[píəridʒ]

귀족(의 지위)

ⓝ those holding a hereditary or honorary title

ⓔ.ⓖ. The hereditary **peerage**, taken as a whole, is unrepresentative of today's Britain.

1329 ■□□

compassion
[kəmpǽʃən]

연민, 동정심

ⓝ sympathetic pity and concern for the sufferings or misfortunes of others

ⓢⓨⓝ empathy, sympathy

ⓞⓟⓟ indifference

ⓔ.ⓖ. She had **compassion** for the little dog and took it home.

1330 ■□□

resounding
[rizáundiŋ]

강력한, 울려퍼지는

ⓐ loud and clear

ⓢⓨⓝ tremendous, enormous

ⓔ.ⓖ. It landed with a **resounding** electronic thud.

1331 ■■□

free-range
[fríːreindʒ]

놓아 기른

ⓐ kept in natural conditions, with freedom of movement

ⓔ.ⓖ. Omega 6 oils are present in **free-range** poultry and eggs, wholegrain bread, cereals, corn oil and nuts.

1332 ■□□

learning rate
[lə́ːrniŋ reit]

학습률; 학습속도

ⓝ learning speed

ⓔ.ⓖ. This is very useful since slow **learning rate** would lead to the decrease in effectiveness of work.

1333 ■■□

delude
[dilúːd]

속이다, 현혹하다
ⓥ to mislead the mind or judgment of
ⓢⓨⓝ deceive, cheat, defraud, gull
ⓔⓖ He was so **deluded** he thought the company needed him.
ⓝ delusion 현혹, 기만

1334 ■□□

mortal
[mɔ́ːrtl]

죽어야 할 운명의, 필멸의
ⓐ subject to death; having a transitory life
ⓔⓖ A man is deliberately designed to be **mortal**. He grows, he
　　ages, and he dies.
ⓝ mortality 죽음을 면할 수 없는 운명(성질)

1335 ■■■

enunciate
[inʌ́nsièit]

선언하다, 발표하다
ⓥ to announce or proclaim; to state or declare definitely
ⓔⓖ It is important to **enunciate** when speaking in loud situations,
　　otherwise it is too difficult to understand.
ⓝ enunciation 선언

1336 ■■□

baffle
[bǽfl]

당황하게 하다
ⓥ to confuse, bewilder, or perplex
ⓢⓨⓝ frustrate, confound
ⓔⓖ He was **baffled** by the difficult language in the novel.
ⓝ bafflement 곤혹, 당혹

1337 ■■□

embellish
[imbéliʃ]

미화하다, 장식하다
ⓥ to beautify by or as if by ornamentation
ⓢⓨⓝ beautify, ornament, adorn
ⓔⓖ Many churches were richly **embellished**.
ⓝ embellishment 꾸밈, 장식

1338 ■■□

perseverance
[pɜ̀ːrsəvírəns]

인내(심)
ⓝ the quality of continuing with something even though it is difficult
ⓔⓖ They showed great **perseverance** in the face of difficulty.
ⓥ persevere　　　　　　　　ⓐ perseverant

1339 ■■□

intact
[ɪntækt]

(하나도 손상되지 않고) 온전한, 전혀 다치지 않은

ⓐ complete and has not been damaged or changed
ⓢⓨⓝ undamaged, whole, complete
ⓔⓖ Most of the cargo was left **intact** after the explosion.
ⓝ intactness   ⓐⓓ intactly

1340 ■■□

interlock
[ɪntərlɑ:k]

서로 맞물리다(맞물리게 하다)

ⓥ to fit together firmly
ⓔⓖ Things that **interlock** or are **interlocked** go between or through each other so that they are linked.

1341 ■■□

deplete
[dɪpli:t]

(남아 있는 것이 충분하지 않을 정도로) 대폭 감소시키다(격감시키다)

ⓥ To deplete a stock or amount of something means to reduce it.
ⓢⓨⓝ use up, reduce, drain
ⓔⓖ Food supplies were severely **depleted**.
ⓝ depletion
ⓐ depletable, depletive, depletory

1342 ■■□

prowess
[praʊəs]

(절묘한) 기량(솜씨)

ⓝ one's great skill at doing something
ⓢⓨⓝ skill, ability, talent
ⓔⓖ He's always bragging about his **prowess** as a cricketer.

1343 ■■□

threshold
[θreʃhoʊld]

문지방, 한계점

ⓝ The threshold of a building or room is the floor in the doorway, or the doorway itself.
ⓢⓨⓝ entrance, doorway, door
ⓔⓖ She stood hesitating on the **threshold**.

1344 ■■□

commence
[kəmens]

시작되다(하다)

ⓥ to begin
ⓢⓨⓝ embark on, start, open
ⓔⓖ The meeting is scheduled to **commence** at noon.
ⓝ commencer, commencement

DAY
23

1345 ■□□

fuss
[fʌs]

수선을 떨다, 야단법석을 떨다, 안절부절못하다
ⓥ to make a fuss; make much ado about trifles
ⓔ.ⓖ. You'll never finish the job if you **fuss** over nuances.
ⓐ fussy 야단법석하는, 소란스러운

1346 ■□□

introspective
[intrəspéktiv]

내성(內省)적인, 자기반성의
ⓐ considering one's own internal state or feelings
ⓔ.ⓖ. **Introspective** people put their attention on their own concerns and thoughts in place of socializing with others.
ⓥ introspect 자기 반성하다

1347 ■■□

balk
[bɔ́ːk]

방해하다, 좌절시키다
ⓥ to stop, as at an obstacle, and refuse to proceed or to do something specified
ⓢⓨⓝ retard, obstruct, impede, prevent
ⓔ.ⓖ. The coach **balked** at me when I tried to leave practice early.

1348 ■■□

burrow
[bə́ːrou]

은신처, 굴
ⓝ a hole or tunnel in the ground made by a rabbit, fox, or similar animal for habitation and refuge
ⓢⓨⓝ shelter, refuge
ⓔ.ⓖ. The bear hibernates in a shallow **burrow**.

1349 ■■□

bigwig
[bígwìg]

중요 인물, 높은 사람, 거물
ⓝ an important person, esp. an official
ⓢⓨⓝ personage, VIP, magnate
ⓔ.ⓖ. He is a **bigwig** in the oil business.

1350 ■■■

perpetuate
[pərpétʃuèit]

영존시키다, 영속시키다
ⓥ to preserve from extinction or oblivion
ⓢⓨⓝ maintain, preserve, keep going, immortalize
ⓔ.ⓖ. This stereotype is a myth **perpetuated** by the media.
ⓝ perpetuation 영구, 영속

1351 ■■□

compensatory
[kəmpénsətɔ́ːri]

보상의, 보수의

ⓐ serving to compensate, as for loss, lack, or injury
ⓢⓨⓝ compensative, remunerative
ⓔ.ⓖ. The jury awarded some money in **compensatory** damages.
ⓝ compensation 보상, 보수

1352 ■■□

fetish
[fétiʃ]

주물(呪物), 물신(物神), 미신의 대상

ⓝ an object regarded with awe as being the embodiment or habitation of a potent spirit or as having magical potency
ⓔ.ⓖ. Some primitive people made a **fetish** of rivers and creeks.
ⓝ fetishism 주물 숭배

1353 ■□□

taboo
[təbúː]

금기, 꺼림

ⓝ a prohibition or interdiction of anything; exclusion from use or practice
ⓢⓨⓝ inhibition, prohibition
ⓔ.ⓖ. Our society places a **taboo** on spitting in public.

1354 ■■□

imprudent
[imprúːdnt]

경솔한, 무모한

ⓐ not prudent; lacking discretion
ⓢⓨⓝ incautious, rash, indiscreet
ⓔ.ⓖ. It was **imprudent** to make the announcement before the contract was signed.
ⓝ imprudence 경솔, 무분별
ⓝ prudence 신중, 분별력

1355 ■■□

imperative
[impérətiv]

피할 수 없는, 필수적인, 긴급한

ⓐ absolutely necessary or required
ⓢⓨⓝ unavoidable, urgent
ⓔ.ⓖ. It is **imperative** that students dedicate passion along with reason to their studies.

1356 ■■□

taint
[téint]

더러움, 얼룩, 오점, 수치, 오명

ⓝ a trace of something bad, offensive, or harmful; a trace of dishonor or discredit

ⓢⓨⓝ defect, spot, flaw, fault, disgrace, dishonor, infamy, stigma

ⓔ.ⓖ. The scandal left a **taint** on his reputation.

ⓐ taintless 더러워지지 않은, 순결한

1357 ■■■

contemptuous
[kəntémptʃuəs]

얕잡아보는, 경멸적인, 무시하는

ⓐ showing or expressing contempt or disdain

ⓢⓨⓝ scornful, disdainful, sneering, insolent, arrogant, supercilious, haughty

ⓔ.ⓖ. He was **contemptuous** of the very rich.

ⓝ contempt 경멸, 멸시, 모욕

1358 ■■□

absurd
[æbsə́:rd]

불합리한, 부조리한

ⓐ utterly or obviously senseless, illogical, or untrue; contrary to all reason or common sense; laughably foolish or false

ⓢⓨⓝ irrational, nonsensical, illogical

ⓔ.ⓖ. The accusation was **absurd** because a child could never drive a car.

ⓝ absurdity 부조리, 불합리, 모순

1359 ■■□

puny
[pjú:ni]

아주 작은, 미약한, 보잘것없는

ⓐ of less than normal size and strength; petty or minor

ⓢⓨⓝ petty, weak, unimportant; insignificant

ⓔ.ⓖ. The child made a **puny** struggle against her teacher.

1360 ■■□

debris
[dəbrí:]

파편, 부스러기

ⓝ the remains of anything broken down or destroyed

ⓢⓨⓝ fragment, splinter, ruins, rubble

ⓔ.ⓖ. **Debris** from the plane crash washed up on shore.

DAY

23

1361 ■■□

disperse
[dispə́:rs]

흩뜨리다, 흩어지게 하다

ⓥ to drive or send off in various directions; to spread widely

ⓢⓨⓝ scatter, disseminate

ⓔ.ⓖ. As soon as the police arrived, the crowd was **dispersed** to keep things peaceful.

ⓐ dispersed 흩어진, 분산된

1362 ■■■

obliterate
[əblítərèit]

지우다, 말소하다

ⓥ to remove or destroy all traces of; do away with; destroy completely

ⓢⓨⓝ efface, remove, destroy

ⓔ.ⓖ. The explosion left the house totally **obliterated**.

ⓝ obliteration 말소, 삭제

1363 ■■□

congenial
[kəndʒí:njəl]

같은 성질의, 마음이 맞는, 알맞은

ⓐ agreeable, suitable, or pleasing in nature or character; suited or adapted in spirit, feeling, temper, etc.

ⓢⓨⓝ agreeable, suitable, compatible

ⓔ.ⓖ. We found the foreigners most **congenial**.

ⓝ congeniality 일치, 화합

1364 ■■□

hoard
[hɔ́:rd]

비장, 저장, 축적; 저장하다, 매장하다

ⓝ a supply or accumulation that is hidden or carefully guarded for preservation, future use, etc.

ⓢⓨⓝ stockpile, reserve, cache, store, stock

ⓔ.ⓖ. He discovered a **hoard** of hidden food that had been hidden by the prisoners.

1365 ■■□

detriment
[détrəmənt]

손해, 손실

ⓝ loss, damage, disadvantage, or injury

ⓢⓨⓝ loss, damage, disadvantage, injury

ⓔ.ⓖ. Children spend too much time on schoolwork, to the **detriment** of their happiness.

ⓐ detrimental 해로운, 불리한

1366 ■□□

longevity
[lɑndʒévəti]

장수, 수명

ⓝ a long individual life; great duration of individual life

ⓔ.ⓖ. This family is known for their **longevity**, many people live over 100 years.

ⓐ longevous 장수의, 수명이 긴

1367 ■□□

lethargic
[ləθɑ́ːrdʒik]

기면성의, 혼수상태의, 무기력한

ⓐ of, pertaining to, or affected with lethargy

ⓢⓨⓝ drowsy, sluggish, lazy, indolent, torpid

ⓔ.ⓖ. The medicine makes him **lethargic** and unable to get out of bed in the mornings.

ⓝ lethargy 기면, 혼수상태, 무기력감

1368 ■□□

paramount
[pǽrəmàunt]

최고의, 주요한, 탁월한

ⓐ chief in importance or impact

ⓢⓨⓝ supreme, principal, prime, first, chief, main, primary, cardinal, preeminent

ⓔ.ⓖ. The child's wellbeing is **paramount**.

ⓝ paramountcy 최고권, 우월

1369 ■■□

remiss
[rimís]

태만한, 게으른

ⓐ negligent, careless, or slow in performing one's duty, business, etc.

ⓢⓨⓝ negligent, careless, lazy

ⓔ.ⓖ. He's terribly **remiss** in his duties, leaving other people to pick up the slack.

1370 ■■□

aversion
[əvə́ːrʒən]

싫음, 반감, 혐오

ⓝ strong feeling of dislike, opposition, repugnance, or antipathy

ⓢⓨⓝ antipathy, dislike, opposition, repugnance

ⓔ.ⓖ. He also says he has no **aversion** about doing accounting work.

ⓐ aversive 혐오의

1371 ■□□

gist
[dʒist]

요점, 요지
ⓝ the main or essential part of a matter
ⓢⓨⓝ point, essence
ⓔ.ⓖ. I didn't hear every word of the lecture, but I got the **gist**.

1372 ■■□

transient
[trǽnʃənt]

덧없는, 무상한, 일시의
ⓐ not lasting, enduring, or permanent; lasting only a short time; existing briefly
ⓢⓨⓝ transitory, temporary
ⓔ.ⓖ. He had a **transient** notion to write her a letter.

1373 ■■□

ardent
[áːrdənt]

열렬한, 열심인
ⓐ having, expressive of, or characterized by intense feeling; intensely devoted, eager, or enthusiastic
ⓢⓨⓝ fervent, passionate, zealous, fervid, eager, impassioned, avid
ⓔ.ⓖ. He was an **ardent** fan of the sport for decades.
ⓝ ardency 열심, 열렬함

1374 ■■□

constrict
[kənstríkt]

압축하다, 수축하다, 억제(제한)하다
ⓥ to draw or press in; cause to contract or shrink; to slow or stop the natural course or development of
ⓢⓨⓝ compress, inhibit, restrain, restrict
ⓔ.ⓖ. The wire around his arm **constricted** his ability to reach.
ⓝ constriction 압축, 수축

1375 ■■□

prodigy
[prádədʒi]

천재, 신동
ⓝ a person, esp. a child or young person, having extraordinary talent or ability
ⓢⓨⓝ genius, virtuoso
ⓔ.ⓖ. 1. The child **prodigy** was already writing music at the age of five.
2. Einstein was a **prodigy** in the field of science.
ⓐ prodigious 기이한, 놀라운

1376 ■■■

exult
[igzʌ́lt]

크게 기뻐하다, 기뻐 날뛰다

ⓥ to show or feel a lively or triumphant joy; rejoice exceedingly; be highly elated or jubilant

ⓢⓨⓝ delight, glory, revel

ⓔ.ⓖ. They **exulted** over their overall championship of the games.

ⓝ exultation 환희, 크게 기뻐함

1377 ■■■

invective
[invéktiv]

비난, 독설, 욕설

ⓝ vehement or violent denunciation, censure, or reproach

ⓢⓨⓝ contumely, scorn, obloquy

ⓔ.ⓖ. A woman screamed a racist **invective** at the family.

1378 ■■□

voluminous
[vəlúːmənəs]

여러 권의, 부피가 큰, 대형의

ⓐ forming, filling, or writing a large volume or many volumes

ⓢⓨⓝ bulky, copious

ⓔ.ⓖ. The doctor kept **voluminous** notes on Pablo Picasso.

ⓝ volume 부피, 양, 용적, 용량

1379 ■■□

retrospect
[rétrəspèkt]

회고, 추억, 회상

ⓝ contemplation of the past; a survey of past time, events, etc.

ⓢⓨⓝ hindsight, review, re-examination

ⓔ.ⓖ. In **retrospect**, I could have used my time in college to learn more.

ⓐ retrospective 회고의

1380 ■■□

pungent
[pʌ́ndʒnet]

톡 쏘는, 찌르는, 날카로운, 신랄한

ⓐ sharply affecting the organs of taste or smell, as if by a penetrating power; caustic, biting, or sharply expressive

ⓢⓨⓝ biting, acrid, sarcastic, mordant, cutting, acrimonious, bitter

ⓔ.ⓖ. The garlic sauce had a **pungent** aroma.

ⓝ pungency 얼얼함, 매움, 신랄함

MEMO

Day

24

유희태 일반영어 ⑤
VOCA
기출VOCA 30days

adamant	☐☐☐	hideous	☐☐☐
vulnerable	☐☐☐	soothe	☐☐☐
alleviate	☐☐☐	elusive	☐☐☐
spiral	☐☐☐	rummage	☐☐☐
extraterrestrial	☐☐☐	boorish	☐☐☐
cold shoulder	☐☐☐	indolent	☐☐☐
outdo	☐☐☐	upbraid	☐☐☐
ingenious	☐☐☐	cursory	☐☐☐
ingenuous	☐☐☐	platitude	☐☐☐
freak	☐☐☐	blot	☐☐☐
illustrious	☐☐☐	lucid	☐☐☐
infallible	☐☐☐	seep	☐☐☐
panacea	☐☐☐	atypical	☐☐☐
eradicate	☐☐☐	revamp	☐☐☐
sedate	☐☐☐	brisk	☐☐☐
equanimity	☐☐☐	rend	☐☐☐
serenity	☐☐☐	heed	☐☐☐
revere	☐☐☐	gaudy	☐☐☐
judicious	☐☐☐	blunder	☐☐☐
inclement	☐☐☐	snarl	☐☐☐
lateral	☐☐☐	unearth	☐☐☐
primordial	☐☐☐	curtail	☐☐☐
apparatus	☐☐☐	malign	☐☐☐
nadir	☐☐☐	barter	☐☐☐
precarious	☐☐☐	rustic	☐☐☐
guileless	☐☐☐	jubilant	☐☐☐
balmy	☐☐☐	heckle	☐☐☐
elapse	☐☐☐	brittle	☐☐☐
stale	☐☐☐	shiftless	☐☐☐
finicky	☐☐☐	flabby	☐☐☐

1381 ■■□

adamant
[ǽdəmənt]

견고한, 단호한, 확고한

ⓐ utterly unyielding in attitude or opinion in spite of all appeals, urgings, etc.

(syn) resolute, inflexible, rigid, uncompromising

(e.g.) Sammy was **adamant** in refusing to marry Jane.

ⓐ adamantine 불굴의, 굳센

1382 ■■□

vulnerable
[vΛlnərəbl]

상처입기 쉬운, 공격받기 쉬운, 비난받기 쉬운, 취약성이 있는

ⓐ capable of or susceptible to being wounded or hurt, as by a weapon; open to moral attack, criticism, temptation, etc.

(syn) susceptible, helpless, unprotected, defenceless

(e.g.) The people from this country are most **vulnerable** to this disease.

ⓝ vulnerability 상처받기 쉬움, 약점이 있음, 취약성

1383 ■□□

alleviate
[əlíːvièit]

완화하다

ⓥ to make easier to endure

(syn) deaden, ease

(opp) aggravate

(e.g.) Double-deckers are expected to help **alleviate** the shortage of seats.

1384 ■□□

spiral
[spáiərəl]

나선형으로 움직이다, 급등(급증)하다

ⓥ move in a spiral course

(syn) swirl, gyrate

(e.g.) Vines **spiraled** upward toward the roof.

ⓝ spire (교회) 첨탑

1385 ■□□

extraterrestrial
[èxtra·terréstrial]

외계의

ⓐ outside, or originating outside, the limits of the earth

(e.g.) The search for **extraterrestrial** life has been going on for many decades.

1386 ■■□

cold shoulder 무시, 냉대
[kould ʃóuldər]

ⓝ a show of deliberate indifference or disregard
ⓢⓨⓝ snub, spurn
ⓔ.ⓖ. He was given the **cold shoulder** in the team.

1387 ■□□

outdo 능가하다
[autduː]

ⓥ to surpass in execution or performance
ⓢⓨⓝ surpass, outshine
ⓔ.ⓖ. Handel was keen to **outdo** his rivals at the Senesino-directed company.

1388 ■■□

ingenious 기발한, 독창적인
[indʒíːnjəs]

ⓐ characterized by cleverness or originality of invention or construction
ⓢⓨⓝ creative, innovative
ⓞⓟⓟ unimaginative
ⓔ.ⓖ. The plot, when it winds up and unwinds, is **ingenious**.

1389 ■■□

ingenuous 순진한, 사람을 잘 믿는
[indʒénjuːəs]

ⓐ innocent and unsuspecting
ⓢⓨⓝ naive, trusting
ⓞⓟⓟ disingenuous
ⓔ.ⓖ. She is interested in an **ingenuous** man.
ⓝ ingenuousness
ⓐⓓ ingenuously

1390 ■□□

freak 괴짜, 기이한 사람
[friːk]

ⓝ a person regarded as strange because of their unusual appearance or behavior
ⓢⓨⓝ eccentric, maverick
ⓔ.ⓖ. He looked at me as if I were some kind of **freak**.
ⓐ freaky

1391 ■□□

illustrious
[ilʌ́striəs]

걸출한, 저명한
ⓐ highly distinguished; renowned; famous
ⓢⓨⓝ eminent, acclaimed
ⓔ.ⓖ. His **illustrious** achievements will be permanently remembered.

1392 ■■□

infallible
[infǽləbl]

절대 오류가 없는, 절대 확실한
ⓐ absolutely trustworthy or sure
ⓢⓨⓝ unerring, unfailing, faultless
ⓔ.ⓖ. His record showed him to be an **infallible** driver.
ⓝ infallibility 무과실성, 절대 확신

1393 ■■□

panacea
[pæ̀nəsíːə]

만병통치약
ⓝ a remedy for all disease or ills
ⓢⓨⓝ elixir, nostrum, catholicon
ⓔ.ⓖ. There is no easy **panacea** for cancer.

1394 ■■□

eradicate
[irǽdəkèit]

뿌리 뽑다, 박멸하다
ⓥ to remove or destroy utterly
ⓢⓨⓝ obliterate, uproot, exterminate, annihilate, extirpate
ⓔ.ⓖ. The antibiotics will **eradicate** any traces of infection.
ⓝ eradication 근절, 박멸

1395 ■■□

sedate
[sidéit]

차분한, 침착한
ⓐ calm, quiet, or composed; undisturbed by passion or excitement
ⓢⓨⓝ unruffled, unperturbed
ⓔ.ⓖ. Her home was a **sedate** and comfortable place in the mountains.
ⓐ sedative 진정의, 달래는

1396 ■■■

equanimity
[iːkwəníməti]

평정, 침착, 태연
ⓝ mental or emotional stability or composure, esp. under tension or strain
ⓢⓨⓝ calmness, equilibrium, serenity
ⓔ.ⓖ. The judge made the decision that rightly ended the conflict, with total **equanimity** and peace of mind.

1397 ■■□

serenity
[sərénəti]

고요함, 청명
ⓝ the state or quality of being serene, calm, or tranquil
ⓢⓨⓝ sereneness, composure, calm, peacefulness, peace
ⓔⓖ When she slept, she appeared in a state of perfect **serenity**.
ⓐ serene 고요한, 잔잔한, 평온한

1398 ■■□

revere
[rivíər]

숭배하다, 경외하다, 존경하다
ⓥ to regard with respect tinged with awe
ⓢⓨⓝ respect, worship, venerate
ⓔⓖ The British **revered** the invention of the steam engine as proof of their great destiny.
ⓐ reverend 숭상할 만한, 거룩한
ⓝ the reverend 신부, 목사

DAY
24

1399 ■■□

judicious
[dʒuːdíʃ.əs]

분별력 있는, 사려 깊은
ⓐ having or showing reason and good judgment in making decisions
ⓔⓖ We should make **judicious** use of the resources available to us.

1400 ■■□

inclement
[ɪnklemənt]

(춥거나 비가 오는 등으로) 좋지 못한(궂은)
ⓐ Weather is unpleasantly cold or stormy.
ⓔⓖ The game was suspended due to **inclement** weather.
ⓝ inclementness, inclemency
ⓐⓓ inclemently

1401 ■■□

lateral
[lætərəl]

옆(측면)의; 옆(측면)으로의
ⓐ relating to the sides of something, or moving in a sideways direction
ⓔⓖ McKinnon estimated the **lateral** movement of the bridge to be between four and six inches.
ⓐⓓ laterally

1402 ■■□

primordial
[praɪmɔːrdiəl]

태고의, (감정 · 욕구가) 원시(원초)적인

ⓐ to belong to a very early time in the history of the world

(e.g.) Twenty million years ago, Idaho was populated by dense **primordial** forest.

ⓝ primordiality

ⓐⓓ primordially

1403 ■■■

apparatus
[æpərætəs]

기구, 장치; (주로 단수로) (특히 정당 · 정부의) 조직체(기구)

ⓝ The apparatus of an organization or system is its structure and method of operation.

(syn) organization, system, network

(e.g.) Firefighters needed breathing **apparatus** to enter the burning house.

1404 ■■□

nadir
[néidər]

밑바닥, 최하점

ⓝ the point on the celestial sphere directly beneath a given position or observer and diametrically opposite the zenith; the lowest point; point of greatest adversity or despair

(syn) bottom, floor, foot, depths

(e.g.) At this **nadir** of creativity, it seems like no one conceives an original thought or style.

1405 ■■■

precarious
[prɪkeriəs]

불안정한; 위태로운

ⓐ (of a situation) not safe or certain; dangerous

(syn) insecure, dangerous, tricky

(e.g.) He earned a **precarious** living as an artist.

ⓝ precariousness

ⓐⓓ precariously

1406 ■□□

guileless
[gáillis]

교활하지 않은, 정직한

ⓐ free from guile; sincere; honest; straightforward; frank

(syn) artless, ingenuous, naive, unsophisticated

(e.g.) The apology the child gave was genuine and **guileless**.

ⓝ guile 교활, 음흉함

1407 ■■□

balmy
[bάːmi]

향기의, 온화한
ⓐ mild and refreshing; soft; soothing; having the qualities of balm
ⓢⓨⓝ fair, gentle, temperate, clement, fragrant
ⓔⓖ The islands here are a popular tourist destination due to the **balmy** climate.
ⓝ balm 향유

1408 ■■□

elapse
[ilǽps]

(시간이) 경과하다, 지나다
ⓥ (of time) to slip or pass by
ⓔⓖ Thirty minutes **elapsed** before the dinner was served.

1409 ■□□

stale
[steɪl]

싱싱하지 못한, 김빠진
ⓐ not fresh; vapid or flat, as beverages; dry or hardened as a bread
ⓢⓨⓝ tasteless, insipid
ⓔⓖ She had left the plastic bag open and the bread went **stale**.

1410 ■■□

finicky
[fíniki]

몹시 까다로운
ⓐ excessively particular or fastidious; difficult to please
ⓢⓨⓝ exacting, demanding, meticulous; choosy, picky
ⓔⓖ Even at the finest of restaurants she was a **finicky** eater.

1411 ■■□

hideous
[hídiəs]

끔찍한, 섬뜩한
ⓐ horrible or frightful to the senses; repulsive; very ugly
ⓢⓨⓝ monstrous, dreadful, appalling
ⓔⓖ The monster he painted was absolutely **hideous**.

1412 ■□□

soothe
[súːð]

달래다, 위로하다
ⓥ to tranquilize or calm, as a person or the feelings; to mitigate, assuage, or allay, as pain, sorrow, or doubt
ⓢⓨⓝ relieve, comfort, allay, alleviate, appease, mollify
ⓔⓖ We used music to **soothe** the upset children.
ⓐ soothing 달래는, 위로하는

1413 ■■□

elusive
[ilúːsiv]

피하는, 달아나는, 정의하기 어려운

ⓐ eluding clear perception or complete mental grasp; hard to express or define

ⓔ.g. The effects of the disease are well-known, but its origin remains **elusive**.

1414 ■■□

rummage
[rʌmɪdʒ]

뒤지다, 샅샅이 찾다

ⓥ to search thoroughly or actively through (a place, receptacle, etc.), esp. by moving around, turning over, or looking through contents

ⓢⓨⓝ ransack

ⓔ.g. He **rummaged** through his house looking for extra change.

1415 ■■□

boorish
[búəriʃ]

막돼먹은, 본데없는

ⓐ of or like a boor

ⓢⓨⓝ rude, unmannered

ⓔ.g. His **boorish** attitude earned him few friends.

ⓝ boor 무례한 사람

1416 ■■■

indolent
[índələnt]

게으른, 나태한

ⓐ having or showing a disposition to avoid exertion

ⓢⓨⓝ sluggish, torpid, slothful

ⓔ.g. You are consistently **indolent**, so we have to fire you.

ⓝ indolence 게으름, 나태

1417 ■■□

upbraid
[ʌpbréid]

신랄하게 비판(비난)하다

ⓥ to find fault with or reproach severely

ⓢⓨⓝ reprove, blame, censure

ⓔ.g. The student was **upbraided** for his dirty uniform.

ⓐ upbraiding 나무라는, 비난하는

1418 ■■□

cursory
[kə́ːrsəri]

서두르는, 마구잡이의

ⓐ going rapidly over something, without noticing details

ⓢⓨⓝ hasty, quick, brief, passing, haphazard

ⓔ.g. He gave the class a **cursory** introduction.

1419 ■■□

platitude
[plǽtitjùːd]

상투어, 진부, 평범

ⓝ a flat, dull, or trite remark, esp. one uttered as if it were fresh or profound

ⓢⓨⓝ cliché, truism

ⓔ.ⓖ. His speech was full of **platitudes**, with no true spirit of its own.

ⓐ platitudinous 평범한, 하찮은

1420 ■□□

blot
[blɑːt]

얼룩, 오점, 오명

ⓝ a spot or stain; a blemish on a person's character or reputation

ⓢⓨⓝ spot, stain, stigma, disgrace, dishonor, infamy

ⓔ.ⓖ. The only **blot** on his record was the one time he was late to work.

DAY
24

1421 ■■□

lucid
[lúːsid]

명쾌한, 번쩍이는, 투명한, 명석한

ⓐ shining or bright; easily understood, completely intelligible or comprehensible

ⓢⓨⓝ clear, lucent

ⓔ.ⓖ. After a full night's sleep, her thinking was totally **lucid**.

1422 ■□□

seep
[siːp]

새다, 스며나오다

ⓥ to pass, flow, or ooze gradually through a porous substance

ⓢⓨⓝ leak, ooze

ⓔ.ⓖ. The rain **seeped** through the ceiling.

ⓐ seepy 물이 스며나오는

1423 ■□□

atypical
[eitípikəl]

전형적이 아닌, 부정형의

ⓐ not typical; not conforming to the type

ⓢⓨⓝ irregular, abnormal

ⓔ.ⓖ. This type of bird was **atypical** because it was particularly small.

ⓐ typical 전형적인, 대표적인

1424 ■■□

revamp
[rivǽmp]

개조하다, 혁신하다, 쇄신하다
ⓥ to renovate, redo, or revise
ⓢⓨⓝ renovate, redo, revise
ⓔ.ⓖ. We've decided to **revamp** the sales floor.

1425 ■□□

brisk
[brɪsk]

활발한, 기운찬
ⓐ quick and active
ⓢⓨⓝ lively, energetic, vigorous, active, dynamic
ⓔ.ⓖ. A **brisk** walk in the morning always wakes me up properly.

1426 ■■□

rend
[rend]

찢다, 잘게 부수다, 나누다
ⓥ to separate into parts with force or violence; to tear apart, split, or divide
ⓢⓨⓝ separate, split, divide
ⓔ.ⓖ. The sails of the ship were **rent** in the store.

1427 ■■□

heed
[hiːd]

주의하다, 조심하다
ⓥ to give careful attention to
ⓢⓨⓝ pay attention to, listen to, take notice of, consider, note
ⓔ.ⓖ. If you would have **heeded** my warning, you wouldn't be in this spot.
ⓐ heedful 주의 깊은, 조심하는

1428 ■■□

gaudy
[gɔ́ːdi]

화려한, 야한, 저속한
ⓐ brilliantly or excessively showy
ⓢⓨⓝ garish, meretricious
ⓔ.ⓖ. Her **gaudy** bright shirt hat attracted our attention.
ⓝ gaud 외양만 번지르르한 싼 물건

1429 ■■□

blunder
[blʌndə(r)]

큰 실수, 대실책

ⓝ a gross, stupid, or careless mistake
syn error, mistake
e.g. This little **blunder** at my job cost the company thousands of dollars.
ⓐ blundering 실수하는, 서투른, 어색한

1430 ■□□

snarl
[snɑːrl]

으르렁거리다, 호통치다

ⓥ to growl threateningly or viciously; to speak in a surly or threatening manner
syn bark, hurl, bawl
e.g. The dog **snarled** at the cat.

1431 ■□□

unearth
[ʌn3ːrθ]

발굴하다, 발견하다, 밝히다

ⓥ to dig or get out of the earth; to uncover or bring to light by search, inquiry, etc.
syn dig, excavate, discover, find
e.g. An ancient city was **unearthed** by scientists.

1432 ■■□

curtail
[kəːrtéil]

짧게 줄이다, 단축하다, 생략하다

ⓥ to cut short; cut off a part of
syn abridge, reduce, diminish, shorten
e.g. It will be necessary to **curtail** production until the new supplies come in.

1433 ■■□

malign
[məláin]

해로운, 악의 있는

ⓐ evil in effect
syn pernicious, baleful, injurious
e.g. The gloomy house had a **malign** influence upon her pleasant mood.
ⓐ malignant 악의가 있는

1434 ■■□

barter
[bάːrtər]

교환하다, 교역하다

ⓥ to exchange in trade, as one commodity for another

ⓢⓨⓝ trade, exchange

ⓔ.ⓖ. If you **barter**, you can get rid of some extra apples and get something different and nice.

1435 ■□□

rustic
[rʌstɪk]

시골의, 시골뜨기의

ⓐ pertaining to, or living in the country, as distinguished from towns or cities

ⓢⓨⓝ rural

ⓔ.ⓖ. The house was small but had a **rustic** charm.

1436 ■■□

jubilant
[dʒúːbələnt]

좋아하는, 기쁨에 넘치는

ⓐ showing great joy, satisfaction, or triumph

ⓢⓨⓝ rejoicing, exultant

ⓔ.ⓖ. The team was **jubilant** about the coming championship.

ⓝ jubilance 환희

1437 ■■□

heckle
[hékl]

야유하다, 힐문하다

ⓥ to harass (a public speaker, performer, etc.) with impertinent questions or gibes

ⓢⓨⓝ decry, ridicule, jeer, mock

ⓔ.ⓖ. The actor tried hard to ignore the **heckling**.

1438 ■■□

brittle
[brítl]

부서지기 쉬운, 깨지기 쉬운

ⓐ breaking readily with a comparatively smooth fracture, as glass; easily damaged or destroyed

ⓢⓨⓝ fragile, frail, breakable

ⓔ.ⓖ. Damage from too much sun had made the wood **brittle**.

1439 ■■□

shiftless
[ʃíftlis]

기력 없는, 주변머리 없는

ⓐ lacking in resourcefulness; lacking in incentive, ambition, or aspiration

ⓢⓨⓝ lazy, slothful, careless, indolent, sluggish

ⓔⓖ The younger children were **shiftless** and naive.

1440 ■□□

flabby
[flǽbi]

축 늘어진, 연약한, 맥이 없는

ⓐ hanging loosely or limply, as flesh or muscles

ⓢⓨⓝ loose, enervated, flaccid

ⓔⓖ After so many big holiday dinners, I'm a little more **flabby**.

DAY

24

Day

25

유희태 일반영어 ⑤
VOCA
기출VOCA 30 days

trudge	□□□	flap		□□□
blunt	□□□	bolster		□□□
prospect	□□□	hassle		□□□
implode	□□□	sully		□□□
pestilence	□□□	tread		□□□
lifelong	□□□	anomaly		□□□
pretense	□□□	slander		□□□
dot	□□□	bashful		□□□
playfulness	□□□	plunge		□□□
trigger	□□□	harangue		□□□
fetus	□□□	innocuous		□□□
doleful	□□□	surfeit		□□□
truckle	□□□	bombastic		□□□
heresy	□□□	flaunt		□□□
fervid	□□□	nimble		□□□
smuggle	□□□	trample		□□□
ramble	□□□	batch		□□□
haven	□□□	foible		□□□
blush	□□□	strident		□□□
perpetual	□□□	boost		□□□
adherent	□□□	toady		□□□
ingenuity	□□□	shudder		□□□
spell	□□□	hapless		□□□
culminate	□□□	concomitant		□□□
destitute	□□□	naughty		□□□
apex	□□□	forerunner		□□□
spurious	□□□	tingle		□□□
emit	□□□	bulge		□□□
bask	□□□	efficacy		□□□
propagate	□□□	hackneyed		□□□

1441 ■■□

trudge
[trʌdʒ]

터벅터벅 걷다
ⓥ to walk laboriously or wearily along or over
ⓢⓨⓝ tramp
ⓔ.ⓖ. The soldiers dutifully **trudged** across the swamps.

1442 ■■□

blunt
[blʌnt]

퉁명스러운, 무뚝뚝한
ⓐ abrupt in address or manner
ⓢⓨⓝ curt, abrupt
ⓔ.ⓖ. He can be **blunt**, which will upset strangers.

1443 ■□□

prospect
[práspekt]

전망
ⓝ the possibility or likelihood of some future event occurring
ⓢⓨⓝ anticipation, chances
ⓔ.ⓖ. He could not reconcile himself to the **prospect** of losing her.
ⓐ prospective 장래의, 유망한
ⓐ prospectless 가망 없는

1444 ■■□

implode
[implóud]

자체적으로(내부에서부터) 파열되다
ⓥ collapse or cause to collapse violently inwards
ⓢⓨⓝ collapse
ⓞⓟⓟ explode
ⓔ.ⓖ. The market was sure to **implode** at some time.

1445 ■□□

pestilence
[péstələns]

역병, 전염병
ⓝ a deadly or virulent epidemic disease
ⓢⓨⓝ plague
ⓔ.ⓖ. A **pestilence** is overhanging the land.
ⓐ pestilent

1446 ■□□

lifelong
[láiflɔ̀(ː)ŋ]

평생 동안의, 일생의, 필생의
ⓐ lasting or remaining in a particular state throughout a person's life
ⓔ.ⓖ. Her **lifelong** dream was to be a famous actress.

1447 ■□□

pretense
[priténs]

가식, 허위, 겉치레
ⓝ pretending or feigning
ⓢⓨⓝ dissembling
ⓔ.ⓖ. Israel of targeting Islamic countries under the **pretense** of achieving peace.
ⓥ pretend

1448 ■□□

dot
[dɑt]

점을 찍다
ⓥ mark with a small spot or spots
ⓢⓨⓝ bespeckle, stipple
ⓔ.ⓖ. Add broth and **dot** with remaining butter.
ⓐ dotty 약간 미친(모자라는) (=eccentric)
ⓐ dotal 지참금의

1449 ■■□

playfulness
[pléifəlnes]

장난기
ⓝ the quality of being light-hearted or full of fun
ⓔ.ⓖ. This clever **playfulness**, which raised a smile mid-dance, is what Doherty did best, and did briefly.

1450 ■□□

trigger
[trígər]

촉발하다, 유발하다, 방아쇠를 당기다
ⓥ cause (an event or situation) to happen or exist
ⓢⓨⓝ precipitate, activate
ⓔ.ⓖ. The current recession was **triggered** by a slump in consumer spending.

1451 ■□□

fetus
[fíːtəs]

태아
ⓝ an animal or human being in its later stages of development before it is born
ⓢⓨⓝ embryo
ⓔ.ⓖ. The mother and the **fetus** are both healthy.

DAY
25

1452 ■□□

doleful
[dóʊlf]

서글픈, 슬픈
ⓐ sad and sorrowful
ⓢⓨⓝ mournful, melancholy
ⓔ.ⓖ. After dropping his ice cream, he looked up at me with a **doleful** look.

1453 ■■□

truckle
[trʌ́kl]

굴종(맹종)하다, 굽실굽실하다
ⓥ to submit or yield obsequiously or tamely
ⓢⓨⓝ submit, yield, cringe
ⓔ.ⓖ. Don't **truckle** to younger people.

1454 ■■□

heresy
[hérəsi]

이교, 이단
ⓝ opinion or doctrine at variance with the orthodox or accepted doctrine, esp. of a church or religious system
ⓢⓨⓝ paganism, heterodoxy, heathenism
ⓔ.ⓖ. It was considered **heresy** to even say the name of their leader.
ⓐ heretical 이교의, 이단의

1455 ■□□

fervid
[fɔ́ːrvid]

타오르는 듯한, 열렬한, 열정적인
ⓐ heated or vehement in spirit, enthusiasm, etc.
ⓢⓨⓝ ardent, fervent, impassioned
ⓔ.ⓖ. He's been one of the most **fervid** supporters of the government.
ⓝ fervidity 열렬, 열심

1456 ■□□

smuggle
[smʌgl]

밀수하다, 몰래 갖고 오다
ⓥ to import or export (goods) secretly, in violation of the law, esp. without payment of legal duty
ⓢⓨⓝ bootleg
ⓔ.ⓖ. The drugs were **smuggled** in the country on ships.
ⓝ smuggler 밀수업자

1457 ■■□

ramble
[ræmbl]

(어슬렁어슬렁) 거닐다, 산책하다
ⓥ to wander around in a leisurely, aimless manner
⑤ⓨ⑩ stroll, saunter, amble, stray, straggle
ⓔ.ⓖ. They **rambled** across the desert, finding no true home.
ⓝ rambler 어슬렁거리는 사람

1458 ■■□

haven
[héivn]

항구, 정박소; 피난처, 안식처
ⓝ a harbor or port; any place of shelter and safety
⑤ⓨ⑩ harbor, refuge, asylum
ⓔ.ⓖ. The Pope declared the country a safe **haven** for the refugees.

1459 ■□□

blush
[blʌʃ]

얼굴을 붉히다, 부끄러워하다
ⓥ to redden, as from embarrassment or shame
⑤ⓨ⑩ redden, be ashamed
ⓔ.ⓖ. The flowers he gave her made her **blush**.
ⓐ blushing 얼굴이 빨개진, 부끄러움을 잘 타는

DAY
25

1460 ■■□

perpetual
[pərpétʃuəl]

끊임없이 계속되는, 빈번한
ⓐ A perpetual feeling, state, or quality is one that never ends or changes.
⑤ⓨ⑩ everlasting, permanent, endless
ⓔ.ⓖ. They lived in **perpetual** fear of being discovered.
ⓥ perpetuate ⓝ perpetuity ⓐⓓ perpetually

1461 ■■□

adherent
[ədhírənt]

(정당·사상 등의) 지지자
ⓝ someone who holds a particular belief or supports a particular person or group
ⓔ.ⓖ. This idea is gaining **adherents**.
ⓥ adhere   ⓐⓓ adherently

1462 ■■□

ingenuity
[ɪndʒənuːəti]

기발한 재주, 재간, 독창성

ⓝ Ingenuity is skill at working out how to achieve things or skill at inventing new things.

ⓢⓨⓝ creativity, innovation

ⓔ.ⓖ. 1. Inspecting the nest may require some **ingenuity**.
2. Some historic painters, so called geniuses, thrived on their own **ingenuity**.

ⓐ ingenious

1463 ■■□

spell
[spel]

일정 기간의 시간, 주문

ⓝ A spell of a particular type of weather or a particular activity is a short period of time during which this type of weather or activity occurs.

ⓢⓨⓝ span, duration, interval

ⓔ.ⓖ. a **spell** of warm weather

1464 ■■□

culminate
['kʌlmɪneɪt]

드디어(결국) ~이 되다

ⓔ.ⓖ. The Jeju Festival **culminated** in the traditional fan dance.

1465 ■■□

destitute
[|destɪtuːt]

~이 결여된

ⓔ.ⓖ. They seem **destitute** of ordinary human feelings.

1466 ■■□

apex
[eɪpeks]

꼭대기, 정점

ⓝ The apex of an organization or system is the highest and most important position in it.

ⓢⓨⓝ top, summit, peak

ⓔ.ⓖ. At 37, she'd reached the **apex** of her career.

1467 ■■■

spurious
[spjúəriəs]

가짜의, 위조의

ⓐ not genuine, authentic, or true; not from the claimed, pretended, or proper source

ⓢⓨⓝ counterfeit, bogus, mock, phony

ⓔ.ⓖ. The rumors about him were **spurious**.

1468 ■□□

emit
[imɪt]

방사하다, 내뿜다, 내다

ⓥ to send forth (liquid, light, heat, sound, particles, etc.); to give forth or release (a sound)
ⓢⓨⓝ discharge, give out, utter
ⓔ.ⓖ. The kitchen **emitted** a delicious aroma.
ⓝ emission 방사, 내뿜음, 발사

1469 ■□□

bask
[bæsk]

햇볕을 쬐다

ⓥ to lie in or be exposed to a pleasant warmth
ⓢⓨⓝ sunbathe
ⓔ.ⓖ. Lizards are cold-blooded and must **bask** in the sun to stay warm.

1470 ■■□

propagate
[prɑ́pəgèit]

번식(증식)시키다, 보급시키다

ⓥ to cause (an organism) to multiply by any process of natural reproduction from the parent stock; to spread (a report, doctrine, practice, etc.) from person to person
ⓢⓨⓝ proliferate, breed, spread, disseminate
ⓔ.ⓖ. The type of corn which grew faster was **propagated** widely in the hopes it would help with famine problems.
ⓝ propagation 번식, 증식, 보급

1471 ■□□

flap
[flæp]

펄럭이다, 휘날리다

ⓥ to swing or sway back and forth loosely, esp. with noise
ⓢⓨⓝ flitter, flutter
ⓔ.ⓖ. The flag **flapped** wildly in the stormy winds.
ⓐ flappy 느슨한, 헐렁한, 동요한

1472 ■■□

bolster
[bóulstər]

지지하다, 보강하다, 기운 내게 하다

ⓥ to support with or as with a pillow or cushion; to add to, support, or uphold
ⓢⓨⓝ strengthen, sustain, aid, reinforce, fortify
ⓔ.ⓖ. This positive letter should **bolster** your confidence.

1473 ■□□

hassle
[hǽsl]

혼란, 혼전, 싸움
ⓝ a problem brought about by pressures of time, money, incon-
venience, etc.
ⓢⓨⓝ quarrel, clash
ⓔ.ⓖ. Getting this visa in such a hurry was a **hassle**.

1474 ■■□

sully
[sʌ́li]

훼손하다, 더럽히다
ⓥ to soil, stain, or tarnish
ⓢⓨⓝ taint, blemish, contaminate
ⓔ.ⓖ. It would have **sullied** the atmosphere and made for great difficulties.

1475 ■□□

tread
[tred]

밟다, 걷다, 지나가다
ⓥ to set down the foot or feet in walking
ⓢⓨⓝ step, walk
ⓔ.ⓖ. **Tread** lightly through enemy territory.

1476 ■■□

anomaly
[ənάməli]

변칙, 예외, 이례
ⓝ a deviation from the common rule, type, arrangement, or form
ⓢⓨⓝ oddity, irregularity, exception, abnormality, inconsistency,
eccentricity
ⓔ.ⓖ. His mistake was an **anomaly** and usually his preference is
flawless.
ⓐ anomalous 변칙의, 예외의

1477 ■■□

slander
[slǽndər]

중상, 욕설
ⓝ a malicious, false, and defamatory statement or report
ⓢⓨⓝ defamation, calumny
ⓔ.ⓖ. The **slander** ruined his reputation for years.
ⓐ slanderous 중상적인, 비방적인

1478 ■■□

bashful
[bǽʃfəl]

수줍어하는, 부끄럼 타는
ⓐ uncomfortably diffident and easily embarrassed
ⓢⓨⓝ shy, timid
ⓔ.ⓖ. He is quite **bashful**, don't be surprised if he doesn't speak.

1479 ■■□

plunge
[plʌndʒ]

던져 넣다, 내던지다
ⓥ to cast or thrust forcibly or suddenly into something, as a liquid, a penetrable substance, a place, etc.
ⓢⓨⓝ immerse, submerge
ⓔ.ⓖ. The dog **plunged** into the pond chasing the stick.

1480 ■□□

harangue
[hərǽŋ]

긴 연설, 열변
ⓝ a scolding or a long or intense verbal attack
ⓢⓨⓝ tirade, declamation, address
ⓔ.ⓖ. The **haranguing** of referees is absolutely ridiculous.

1481 ■■□

innocuous
[inákjuəs]

해가 없는, 독이 없는
ⓐ not harmful or injurious
ⓢⓨⓝ harmless, hurtless
ⓔ.ⓖ. The most **innocuous** kinds of fish are usually plainly colored.

1482 ■■□

surfeit
[sə́ːrfit]

과다, 과도, 폭식, 과음
ⓝ an excessive amount; excess or overindulgence in eating or drinking
ⓢⓨⓝ intemperance, excess, surplus
ⓔ.ⓖ. There was a **surfeit** of meal choices.

1483 ■■□

bombastic
[bɑmbǽstik]

과장된, 허풍 떠는
ⓐ high-sounding; high-flown; inflated; pretentious
ⓢⓨⓝ exaggerated, ostentatious, magniloquent
ⓔ.ⓖ. The newer artists are more **bombastic** about their work.
ⓝ bombast 호언장담, 허풍

1484 ■■□

flaunt
[flɔːnt]

과시하다
ⓥ to parade or display ostentatiously
ⓢⓨⓝ vaunt, show off
ⓔ.ⓖ. He happily **flaunted** his new watch.
ⓐ flaunty 과시하는

1485 ■■□

nimble
[nímbl]

민첩한, 재빠른
ⓐ quick and light in movement; moving with ease
⒮ⓨⓝ agile, active, rapid
ⓔ.ⓖ. Someone who is **nimble** can move their fingers, hands, or legs quickly.

1486 ■■□

trample
[trǽmpl]

내리밟다, 짓밟다, 유린하다, 무시하다
ⓥ to tread or step heavily and noisily; to act in a harsh, domineering, or cruel manner, as if treading roughly
⒮ⓨⓝ stamp, tread, infringe, devastate
ⓔ.ⓖ. The football players have **trampled** on my flowers.

1487 ■□□

batch
[bætʃ]

1회분, 한 묶음
ⓝ a quantity or number coming at one time or taken together
⒮ⓨⓝ group, lot, number, bunch, gang, set, pack, flock, troop
ⓔ.ⓖ. The first **batch** of cookies tasted better than the second.

1488 ■■□

foible
[fɔ́ibl]

약점, 결점, 단점
ⓝ a minor weakness or failing of character
⒮ⓨⓝ flaw, defect, shortcoming
ⓔ.ⓖ. The only **foible** with Jeff is his bad temper.

1489 ■■□

strident
[stráidnt]

귀에 거슬리는, 소리가 불쾌한
ⓐ making or having a harsh sound; having a shrill, irritating quality or character
⒮ⓨⓝ squawky, creaking
ⓔ.ⓖ. Her once beautiful singing fell into **strident** shouts.
ⓝ stridence 삐걱거림, 귀에 거슬림

1490 ■□□

boost
[buːst]

밀어올리다, 밀어주다
ⓥ to lift or raise by pushing from behind or below; to advance or aid by speaking well of
⒮ⓨⓝ upraise, promote
ⓔ.ⓖ. If you can **boost** me up, I can see over this fence.
ⓝ booster 후원자

1491 ■■□

toady
[tóudi]

알랑거리다, 아첨하다
ⓥ to be the toady (an obsequious flatterer)
ⓢⓨⓝ flatter, truckle
ⓔ.ⓖ. For years he was **toadying** for a major company boss.
ⓝ toadyism 사대주의

1492 ■□□

shudder
[ʃʌdər]

(공포, 추위로) 떨다
ⓥ to tremble with a sudden convulsive movement, as from horror,
   fear, or cold
ⓢⓨⓝ quiver, shiver, tremble
ⓔ.ⓖ. He **shuddered** at the appearance of his rival.
ⓐ shuddering 떠는, 몸서리치는, 오싹하는

1493 ■■□

hapless
[hǽplis]

운이 나쁜, 불운한
ⓐ unlucky or unfortunate
ⓢⓨⓝ unlucky, luckless, unfortunate
ⓔ.ⓖ. The new secretary was **hapless** and unorganized.
ⓝ hap 우연, 운

1494 ■■□

concomitant
[kankámətənt]

수반하는, 동시에 일어나는
ⓐ existing or occurring with something else, often in a lesser way
ⓢⓨⓝ accompanying, concurrent, associated
ⓔ.ⓖ. There are **concomitant** detrimental side effects to the medicine.
ⓝ concomitance 수반, 부수

1495 ■□□

naughty
[nɔ́ːti]

개구쟁이의, 장난이 심한, 버릇없는
ⓐ disobedient and mischievous (used esp. in speaking to or about
   children)
ⓢⓨⓝ willful, wayward, misbehaving
ⓔ.ⓖ. That **naughty** boy keep cheating off his neighbor's paper.

DAY
25

1496 ■□□

forerunner
[fɔ́:rʌnə(r)]

선구자, 선조, 전조, 예보
ⓝ predecessor; an omen, sign, or indication of something to follow
ⓢⓨⓝ ancestor, forebear, precursor, portent
ⓔ.ⓖ. The **forerunners** of the motorcycle were bicycles.

1497 ■□□

tingle
[tíŋgl]

쑤시다, 얼얼하다, 욱신거리다
ⓥ to have a sensation of slight prickles, stings, or tremors, as from cold, a sharp blow, excitement, etc.
ⓢⓨⓝ sting
ⓔ.ⓖ. There was a **tingling** in my hands after being outside in the cold for so long.

1498 ■■□

bulge
[bʌldʒ]

부풀다, 불룩하다
ⓥ to swell or bend outward
ⓢⓨⓝ protrude
ⓔ.ⓖ. Her pocket **bulged** with an orange.

1499 ■■□

efficacy
[éfikəsi]

효능, 효험
ⓝ capacity for producing a desired result or effect
ⓢⓨⓝ effectiveness, efficiency
ⓔ.ⓖ. Scientists from the East and West disagree on the **efficacy** of the vast majority traditional medicines.
ⓐ efficacious 효과 있는, 효험 있는

1500 ■■□

hackneyed
[hǽknid]

낡은, 진부한
ⓐ made commonplace or trite
ⓢⓨⓝ stale, banal
ⓔ.ⓖ. The language of this book wears on because it is so **hackneyed**.
ⓐ unhackneyed 참신한, 독창적인

MEMO

Day

26

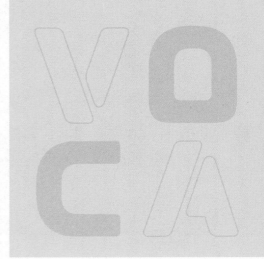

malinger	☐☐☐		scorch	☐☐☐	
ferment	☐☐☐		usurp	☐☐☐	
embryo	☐☐☐		leery	☐☐☐	
adjutant	☐☐☐		swelter	☐☐☐	
rucksack	☐☐☐		frail	☐☐☐	
peel	☐☐☐		eventuate	☐☐☐	
stack	☐☐☐		bribe	☐☐☐	
pat	☐☐☐		paltry	☐☐☐	
tuck	☐☐☐		lanky	☐☐☐	
milestone	☐☐☐		freakish	☐☐☐	
shove	☐☐☐		swap	☐☐☐	
beckon	☐☐☐		jeer	☐☐☐	
thwart	☐☐☐		parry	☐☐☐	
machination	☐☐☐		glare	☐☐☐	
foster	☐☐☐		condone	☐☐☐	
brag	☐☐☐		menial	☐☐☐	
shabby	☐☐☐		penurious	☐☐☐	
haggard	☐☐☐		bestow	☐☐☐	
attenuate	☐☐☐		jargon	☐☐☐	
loiter	☐☐☐		swagger	☐☐☐	
mutilate	☐☐☐		venerable	☐☐☐	
deject	☐☐☐		glossy	☐☐☐	
configuration	☐☐☐		extraneous	☐☐☐	
truism	☐☐☐		irksome	☐☐☐	
wield	☐☐☐		burnish	☐☐☐	
arbiter	☐☐☐		archaic	☐☐☐	
incumbent	☐☐☐		emulate	☐☐☐	
breed	☐☐☐		sullen	☐☐☐	
bulky	☐☐☐		query	☐☐☐	
lewd	☐☐☐		debilitate	☐☐☐	

1501 ■□□

malinger
[məlíŋgər]

꾀병을 부리다
ⓥ to pretend illness, esp. in order to shirk one's duty, avoid work, etc.
(e.g.) He **malingered** in order to get out of his classes.
ⓝ malingerer 꾀병쟁이

1502 ■□□

ferment
[fə́ːrment]

발효시키다
ⓥ to act upon as a ferment
(e.g.) Alcohol comes from **fermented** grains.
ⓝ fermentation 발효(작용)

1503 ■□□

embryo
[émbriòu]

배아
ⓝ an unborn animal or human being in the very early stages of development
(syn) fetus
(e.g.) Some also object over the possibility the procedure could harm the **embryo** in an unknown way.

1504 ■■■

adjutant
[ǽdʒətənt]

부관
ⓝ an officer in the army who deals with administrative work
(e.g.) I've notified the **adjutant**, change in schedule.

1505 ■■□

rucksack
[rúck·sàck]

배낭
ⓝ a type of knapsack carried by hikers, bicyclists, etc.
(e.g.) He keeps a **rucksack** packed and ready to go at all times.

1506 ■□□

peel
[piːl]

껍질을 벗기다
ⓥ remove the outer covering or skin from a fruit or vegetable
(syn) pare, trim
(e.g.) I was **peeling** potatoes in the kitchen when he called.
ⓐ peelable

1507 ■□□

stack
[stæk]

무더기, 더미

ⓝ a pile of objects, typically one that is neatly arranged

ⓢⓨⓝ heap, mound

ⓔⓖ There's another **stack** of dirty plates in the dishpan.

1508 ■■□

pat
[pæt]

톡톡 치다

ⓥ touch quickly and gently with the flat of the hand

ⓢⓨⓝ tap, dab

ⓔⓖ He **patted** his sister's hand consolingly.

1509 ■■□

tuck
[tʌk]

(끝부분을 단정하게) 밀어넣다(접다)

ⓥ push, fold, or turn so as to hide them or hold them in place

ⓢⓨⓝ insert, thrust

ⓔⓖ Your shirt is hanging out. **Tuck** it in.

1510 ■□□

milestone
[máilstòun]

이정표, 획기적 사건

ⓝ a stone set up beside a road to mark the distance in miles to a particular place

ⓔⓖ **Milestone** is set along the road.

1511 ■■□

shove
[ʃʌv]

밀다, 밀치다

ⓥ to push roughly or rudely

ⓢⓨⓝ push, jostle

ⓔⓖ He **shoved** her off her bike.

1512 ■■□

beckon
[békən]

신호하다, 손짓으로 부르다

ⓥ to signal, summon, or direct by a gesture of the head or hand

ⓢⓨⓝ signal, summon

ⓔⓖ The stranger **beckoned** us to come nearer.

DAY
26

1513 ■■□

thwart
[θwɔːrt]

훼방 놓다, 방해하다
ⓥ to oppose successfully; prevent from accomplishing a purpose
ⓢⓨⓝ hinder, obstruct
ⓔ.ⓖ. The security guard **thwarted** his attempt to steal.
ⓐⓓ thwartedly

1514 ■■□

machination
[mækənéiʃən]

음모, 책략
ⓝ the act of plotting
ⓢⓨⓝ scheme, plot, intrigue, stratagem
ⓔ.ⓖ. The **machinations** of the government are apparent here.
ⓥ machinate 꾸미다, 음모하다

1515 ■□□

foster
[fɔ́ːstər]

육성하다, 촉진하다
ⓥ to promote the growth or development of
ⓢⓨⓝ further, encourage, promote
ⓔ.ⓖ. We **foster** a warm, loving environment here.
ⓝ fosterage 양육, 육성, 촉진

1516 ■□□

brag
[bræg]

자랑하다
ⓥ to use boastful language
ⓢⓨⓝ boast
ⓔ.ⓖ. He would always **brag** egotistically about his income.
ⓝ bragger 허풍쟁이

1517 ■□□

shabby
[ʃǽbi]

초라한, 낡아빠진
ⓐ impaired by wear, use, etc; showing conspicuous signs of wear
or neglect
ⓢⓨⓝ tatty, worn, ragged, scruffy, tattered, threadbare, antiquated
ⓔ.ⓖ. His clothes were plain and **shabby**.

1518 ■□□

haggard
[hǽgərd]

여윈, 수척한, 초췌한

ⓐ having a gaunt, wasted, or exhausted appearance, as from prolonged suffering, exertion, or anxiety

ⓢⓨⓝ gaunt, worn

ⓔ.ⓖ. He always looked **haggard** after a long shift.

1519 ■■■

attenuate
[əténjuèit]

약하게 하다, 희박하게 하다

ⓥ to weaken or reduce in force, intensity, effect, quantity, or value

ⓢⓨⓝ lessen, weaken

ⓔ.ⓖ. You could never eliminate error, but preparation and training could **attenuate** it.

ⓝ attenuation 쇠약, 수척

1520 ■■■

loiter
[lɔ́itər]

빈둥거리다, 어슬렁어슬렁 걷다, 늑장부리다

ⓥ to linger aimlessly or as if aimless in or about a place

ⓢⓨⓝ dawdle, linger, tarry

ⓔ.ⓖ. The teenagers **loitered** in front of the comic book shop.

1521 ■■□

mutilate
[mju:tileit]

훼손하다

ⓥ If a person or animal is mutilated, their body is severely damaged, usually by someone who physically attacks them.

ⓢⓨⓝ damage, disable, cripple

ⓔ.ⓖ. The body had been badly **mutilated**.

ⓝ mutilator, mutilation

ⓐ mutilative

1522 ■■□

deject
[didʒékt]

낙담시키다

ⓥ to have a depressing effect on; dispirit; dishearten

ⓢⓨⓝ disappoint, discourage, depress

DAY
26

1523 ■■☐

configuration

[kənfɪɡjəreɪʃn]

배열, 배치 형태

ⓝ A configuration is an arrangement of a group of things.

ⓢⓨⓝ perimeter, profile, contour

ⓔ.ⓖ. Time of Day **configuration** saved successfully.

ⓝ configurationism

ⓐ configurational, configurative

ⓐⓓ configurationally

1524 ■■☐

truism

[truːɪzəm]

뻔한 말

ⓝ a statement that is so obviously true that it is almost not worth saying

ⓔ.ⓖ. It has become a **truism** that every woman wants to choose how she delivers her baby.

ⓐ truistic

1525 ■■☐

wield

[wiːld]

(권력·권위 등을) 행사하다, 힘을 휘두르다

ⓥ If you wield a weapon, tool, or piece of equipment, you carry and use it.

ⓢⓨⓝ exercise

ⓔ.ⓖ. She **wields** enormous power within the party.

ⓝ wielder   ⓐ wieldy

1526 ■■☐

arbiter

[ɑ́ːrbətər]

중재인, 조정자

ⓝ a person empowered to decide matters at issue

ⓢⓨⓝ judge, umpire

ⓔ.ⓖ. He was the final **arbiter** on the conditions of their divorce.

ⓥ arbitrate 중재하다, 조정하다

1527 ■■■

incumbent

[ɪnkʌ́mbənt]

현직의, 재직의

ⓐ holding an indicated position, role, office, etc., currently

ⓔ.ⓖ. The **incumbent** president has the support of the people, but his new rival really wants the position.

ⓝ incumbency 현직, 재직기간

1528 ■□□

breed
[briːd]

새끼를 낳다, 번식하다, 자라다
ⓥ to produce (offspring)
(syn) bear, hatch, engender, procreate
(e.g.) Lots of animals **breed** only at certain times of the year.
ⓝ breeding 번식, 양육

1529 ■□□

bulky
[bʌlki]

부피가 큰, 거대한, 너무 커서 다루기 힘든
ⓐ of relatively large and cumbersome bulk or size
(syn) massive, ponderous
(e.g.) His new uniform was too **bulky** to be comfortable.
ⓝ bulk 부피, 용적, 크기

1530 ■□□

lewd
[luːd]

외설적인, 음탕한, 음란한
ⓐ inclined to, characterized by, or inciting to lust or lechery;
    obscene or indecent, as language or songs
(syn) lascivious, salacious, lustful
(e.g.) After he drank, the old man often told **lewd** stories.

DAY
26

1531 ■□□

scorch
[skɔːrtʃ]

태우다, 그슬리다
ⓥ to affect the color, taste, etc., of by burning slightly
(syn) char
(e.g.) Leaving the cake in the stove too long had **scorched** it.
ⓐ scorched 탄, 그을은

1532 ■■■

usurp
[juːsə́ːrp]

빼앗다, 탈권하다
ⓥ to seize and hold (a position, office, power, etc.) by force or
    without legal right
(syn) capture, seize, wrest
(e.g.) His aim was to **usurp** the king.
ⓝ usurpation 강탈, 탈취, 권리 침해

1533 ■□□

leery
[líəri]

상스러운 눈초리의, 의심 많은
ⓐ wary; suspicious
ⓢⓨⓝ distrustful, wary, suspicious
ⓔ.ⓖ. We were all **leery** about the new digital scheduling system, but it worked fine.

1534 ■■□

swelter
[swéltər]

더위 먹다, 더위에 지치다
ⓥ to suffer from oppressive heat
ⓔ.ⓖ. The heat inside the car with closed doors was **sweltering**.
ⓐ sweltering 더위에 지친, 무더운

1535 ■□□

frail
[freɪl]

무른, 연약한
ⓐ having delicate health; not robust
ⓢⓨⓝ weak, feeble
ⓔ.ⓖ. After being sick in bed for months, he was a little **frail** and weak.
ⓝ frailty 여림, 무름, 약함

1536 ■■□

eventuate
[ivéntʃuèit]

~결과가 되다, ~으로 끝나다
ⓥ to have issue; to be the issue or outcome
ⓢⓨⓝ result, come about, end
ⓔ.ⓖ. This course of decision making will **eventuate** in a total economic shutdown.

1537 ■□□

bribe
[braɪb]

뇌물, 유혹물
ⓝ money or any other valuable consideration given or promised with a view to corrupting the behavior of a person, esp. in that person's performance as an athlete, public official, etc.
ⓔ.ⓖ. The politician was arrested for accepting **bribes**.
ⓝ bribery 뇌물수수

1538 ■■□

paltry
[pɔ́ːltri]

얼마 안 되는, 하찮은, 보잘것없는
ⓐ ridiculously or insultingly small; utterly worthless
ⓢⓨⓝ minor, inconsiderable, slight, insignificant
ⓔ.ⓖ. It was a **paltry** sum, but the symbolic giving of it was important.

1539 ■□□

lanky
[læŋki]

마르고 키 큰, 호리호리한
ⓐ ungracefully thin and rawboned
ⓢⓨⓝ gaunt, skinny
ⓔ.ⓖ. He was **lanky** and tall, like a bird.

1540 ■□□

freakish
[fríːkiʃ]

변덕스러운, 괴상한, 장난의
ⓐ markedly unusual or abnormal
ⓢⓨⓝ strange, queer, odd, unusual, grotesque
ⓔ.ⓖ. The monster costume made him look **freakish**.
ⓝ freak 이상 현상, 변칙, 기형

1541 ■□□

swap
[swɑːp]

바꾸다, 교환하다
ⓥ to exchange, barter, or trade, as one thing for another
ⓢⓨⓝ exchange, trade, switch, interchange, barter
ⓔ.ⓖ. We **swap** the lunches our mothers had given because we didn't
like them.

1542 ■■□

jeer
[dʒɪr]

조롱하다, 놀리다
ⓥ to speak or shout derisively; scoff or gibe rudely
ⓢⓨⓝ sneer, insult, mock
ⓔ.ⓖ. They **jeered** at the performer.

1543 ■■□

parry
[pǽri]

받아넘기다, 슬쩍 피하다, 회피하다
ⓥ to turn aside; evade or dodge
ⓢⓨⓝ avert, elude, prevent, obviate, preclude
ⓔ.ⓖ. The man tried to stab me with his umbrella, but I **parried** with
my own.

1544 ■■□

glare
[gler]

섬광, 눈부신 빛
ⓝ a very harsh, bright, dazzling light
ⓢⓨⓝ blaze, flash
ⓔ.ⓖ. The **glare** from the sun made me unable to see the road.
ⓐ glary 번쩍번쩍 빛나는, 눈부신

DAY
26

1545 ■■■

condone
[kəndóun]

묵과하다, 용서하다
Ⓥ to disregard or overlook (something illegal, objectionable, or the like)
ⓢⓨⓝ overlook, excuse, forgive, pardon
ⓔ.ⓖ. Our company does not **condone** the use of drugs.
ⓝ condonation 용서, 묵과

1546 ■■□

menial
[míːniəl]

시시한, 지루한, 천한
ⓐ lowly and sometimes degrading; servile or submissive
ⓢⓨⓝ boring, dull, servile, submissive
ⓔ.ⓖ. Without a college degree, the only jobs I could find were those involving **menial** tasks.

1547 ■■■

penurious
[pənjúəriəs]

인색한, 궁핍한
ⓐ extremely stingy; extremely poor
ⓢⓨⓝ miserly, destitute, indigent
ⓔ.ⓖ. He was quite often **penurious**, and saved his money tightly.

1548 ■■□

bestow
[bistóu]

주다, 수여하다
Ⓥ to present as a gift; confer
ⓢⓨⓝ give, grant, vouchsafe, award
ⓔ.ⓖ. The award was **bestowed** upon the brightest student.
ⓝ bestowal 증여, 수여

1549 ■□□

jargon
[dʒáːrgən]

은어, 전문어
ⓝ the language, esp. the vocabulary, peculiar to a particular trade, profession, or group
ⓢⓨⓝ parlance, idiom, usage
ⓔ.ⓖ. This technical **jargon** was difficult to understand.

1550 ■□□

swagger
[swǽgər]

오만한 태도로 걷다, 으스대다
Ⓥ to walk or strut with a defiant or insolent air; to boast or brag noisily
ⓢⓨⓝ strut
ⓔ.ⓖ. The boxer **swaggered** around the ring.
ⓐ swaggering 뽐내며 걷는, 으스대는

1551 ■■□

venerable
[vénərəbl]

존경할 만한, 덕망 있는

ⓐ commanding respect because of great age or impressive dignity
ⓢⓨⓝ honorable, respectable
ⓔ.ⓖ. Our captain was a famous and **venerable** man.
ⓝ veneration 존경, 숭배

1552 ■□□

glossy
[glási]

광택이 나는, 번질번질한

ⓐ having a shiny or lustrous surface
ⓢⓨⓝ shining, polished, glazed
ⓔ.ⓖ. The sidewalk was **glossy** with the thin layer of rain.
ⓝ gloss 광택, 윤

1553 ■■■

extraneous
[ikstréiniəs]

외래의, 외부에 발생한, 이질적인

ⓐ introduced or coming from without; not belonging or proper to a thing
ⓢⓨⓝ external, foreign
ⓔ.ⓖ. Any **extraneous** costs will be cut.

1554 ■■□

irksome
[ə́ːrksəm]

진저리(싫증)나는, 지루한

ⓐ annoying; irritating; exasperating
ⓢⓨⓝ tedious, tiresome
ⓔ.ⓖ. The sound of the neighbor's dogs was becoming **irksome**.
ⓥ irk 지루하게 하다, 짜증나게 하다

1555 ■■□

burnish
[bə́ːrniʃ]

닦다, 갈다, 윤나다

ⓥ to polish (a surface) by friction; to make smooth and bright
ⓢⓨⓝ polish, furbish
ⓔ.ⓖ. After we **burnished** our silverware, they all shone brightly.
ⓝ burnisher 연마기

1556 ■■□

archaic
[aːrkéiik]

고풍의, 예스러운

ⓐ marked by the characteristics of an earlier period
ⓢⓨⓝ antiquated
ⓔ.ⓖ. The house was **archaic**, it looked as if it might not have running water.

DAY
26

1557 ■■■

emulate
[émjulèit]

경쟁하다, 우열을 겨루다
ⓥ to rival with some degree of success
ⓢⓨⓝ rival, compete
ⓔ.ⓖ. Her clothing always **emulates** the runway fashions of New York.
ⓝ emulation 경쟁, 겨룸

1558 ■□□

sullen
[sʌlən]

부루퉁한, 기분이 언짢은
ⓐ persistently and silently ill-humored
ⓢⓨⓝ sulky, bad-tempered
ⓔ.ⓖ. His mood was silent and **sullen** after he lost his wallet.

1559 ■■□

query
[kwíəri]

묻다, 질문하다, 의문을 가지다
ⓥ to ask or inquire about; to question as doubtful or obscure
ⓢⓨⓝ question, inquire
ⓔ.ⓖ. He was **queried** about his involvement in the robbery.

1560 ■■□

debilitate
[dibílətèit]

쇠약(허약)하게 하다
ⓥ to make weak or feeble
ⓢⓨⓝ enfeeble, weaken, deplete, enervate, devitalize
ⓔ.ⓖ. Her cancer left her **debilitated**.
ⓝ debility 쇠약

MEMO

Day

27

bland	☐☐☐	refute	☐☐☐
gruesome	☐☐☐	blink	☐☐☐
passe	☐☐☐	staunch	☐☐☐
misshapen	☐☐☐	obese	☐☐☐
huddle	☐☐☐	sparse	☐☐☐
dead on	☐☐☐	topography	☐☐☐
underhand	☐☐☐	fatalistic	☐☐☐
master	☐☐☐	cognizant	☐☐☐
gut feeling	☐☐☐	fortress	☐☐☐
hub	☐☐☐	quotient	☐☐☐
deter	☐☐☐	homogeneous	☐☐☐
glean	☐☐☐	provincialism	☐☐☐
stoop	☐☐☐	arithmetic	☐☐☐
relent	☐☐☐	wart	☐☐☐
stint	☐☐☐	effervescent	☐☐☐
stringent	☐☐☐	astonish	☐☐☐
aberrant	☐☐☐	revelation	☐☐☐
hallmark	☐☐☐	confidential	☐☐☐
modulate	☐☐☐	dross	☐☐☐
stratify	☐☐☐	infamy	☐☐☐
offset	☐☐☐	damnation	☐☐☐
probe	☐☐☐	dilettante	☐☐☐
hoodwink	☐☐☐	dementia	☐☐☐
exodus	☐☐☐	deteriorate	☐☐☐
extrinsic	☐☐☐	ornamentation	☐☐☐
vigil	☐☐☐	protrusion	☐☐☐
stifle	☐☐☐	asymmetric	☐☐☐
bleak	☐☐☐	detract	☐☐☐
falter	☐☐☐	monolithic	☐☐☐
tenacious	☐☐☐	cling	☐☐☐

1561 ■■□

bland
[blænd]

부드러운, 온화한, 지루한

ⓐ pleasantly gentle or agreeable
ⓢⓨⓝ pleasant, affable, mild, amiable
ⓔ.ⓖ. The soup was completely **bland**.

1562 ■□□

gruesome
[grúːsəm]

섬뜩한, 소름 끼치는

ⓐ causing great horror; horribly repugnant
ⓢⓨⓝ grisly, horrific, horrible, ghastly
ⓔ.ⓖ. Driving on a freeway we come across a **gruesome** accident.
ⓝ grue 몸서리, 전율

1563 ■■□

passe
[pæséi]

유행이 지난

ⓐ no longer fashionable
ⓢⓨⓝ out of date, behind the times
ⓔ.ⓖ. I think that blouse is a bit **passe**.

1564 ■■□

misshapen
[misʃéipən]

기형의, 모양이 정상이 아닌

ⓐ not having the normal or natural shape or form
ⓢⓨⓝ deformed, malformed
ⓔ.ⓖ. Prions are nothing more than rogue or **misshapen** proteins.

1565 ■□□

huddle
[hʌ́dl]

(보통 춥거나 무서워서) 옹송그리며 모이다

ⓥ to gather or crowd together in a close mass
ⓢⓨⓝ throng, cluster
ⓔ.ⓖ. As many as 5,000 penguins will **huddle** to keep warm!

1566 ■■□

dead on
[ded ɔn]

바로 정확히

ⓐ exactly right, accurate, or pertinent
ⓔ.ⓖ. The subway was **dead on** time.

1567 ■■□

underhand
[ʌ́ndəhænd]

부정직한

ⓐ not open and aboveboard; secret and crafty or dishonorable
ⓢⓨⓝ dishonest, fraudulent
ⓔⓖ I suggest to you that what they have done today is sneaky, **underhand** and cowardly.

1568 ■□□

master
[mǽːstər]

~의 주인이 되다, 지배하다, 통달하다

ⓥ gain control of; overcome
ⓢⓨⓝ conquer, vanquish
ⓔⓖ He that is **master** of himself will soon be master of others.
ⓝ mastery 숙달, 통달
ⓝ masterdom 교사의 신분(직), 석사학위
ⓐ masterly 능수능란한

1569 ■■□

gut feeling
[gʌt fíːliŋ]

육감, 직감

ⓝ an instinctive feeling, as opposed to an opinion based on facts
ⓔⓖ The Islamic Penal code of Iran allows a judge to rule according to his **gut feeling** instead of hard evidence.

1570 ■□□

hub
[hʌb]

중심, 중추

ⓝ a center around which other things revolve or from which they radiate; a focus of activity, authority, commerce, transportation, etc.
ⓢⓨⓝ core, pivot, heart, center
ⓔⓖ Greece used to be the **hub** of the western world.

1571 ■■□

deter
[ditə́ːr]

그만두게 하다, 단념시키다

ⓥ to discourage or restrain from acting or proceeding
ⓢⓨⓝ discourage, inhibit, put off, frighten, intimidate, dissuade
ⓔⓖ The criminals were **deterred** by the new serious laws.

DAY
27

1572 ■■□

glean
[gliːn]

(이삭을) 줍다, 수집하다, 모으다
ⓥ to gather slowly and laboriously, bit by bit; to learn, discover, or find out, usually little by little or slowly
ⓢⓨⓝ gather, amass
ⓔ.ⓖ. We could **glean** from his expression that the interview had gone well.
ⓝ gleaning 이삭줍기, 수집

1573 ■□□

stoop
[stuːp]

웅크리다, 구부리다
ⓥ to bend the head and shoulders, or the body generally, forward and downward from an erect position
ⓢⓨⓝ crouch, bend
ⓔ.ⓖ. He **stooped** to tie his shoe.

1574 ■■□

relent
[rilént]

마음이 누그러지다, 가엾게 여기다
ⓥ to soften in feeling, temper, or determination; become more mild, compassionate, or forgiving
ⓢⓨⓝ pity, commiserate
ⓔ.ⓖ. I thought his intense questions would never **relent**.
ⓐ relentless 냉혹한, 가차없는

1575 ■■□

stint
[húdwɪŋk]

절약하다, 아끼다
ⓥ to be frugal; get along on a scanty allowance
ⓢⓨⓝ spare, save
ⓔ.ⓖ. They **stinted** and scrimped to save for years and years to save for a new bicycle.

1576 ■■□

stringent
[strɪndʒənt]

엄중한
ⓐ very strict and that must be obeyed
ⓢⓨⓝ strict, tough, rigorous
ⓔ.ⓖ. **stringent** air quality regulations
ⓝ stringency
ⓐⓓ stringently

1577 ■■□

aberrant

[æberənt]

도리를 벗어난, 일탈적인

ⓐ not usual or not socially acceptable
ⓔ.ⓖ. **aberrant** behaviour
ⓝ aberrance
ⓐⓓ aberrantly

1578 ■■□

hallmark

[hɔ:lmɑ:rk]

특징

ⓝ a feature or quality that is typical of somebody/something
ⓢⓨⓝ trademark, sure sign, telltale sign
ⓔ.ⓖ. The regime adopted the style which was to become its **hallmark** in the 1960s.

1579 ■■■

modulate

[mɑ:dʒəleɪt]

(크기 · 강도 등을) 조절하다

ⓥ change the quality of your voice in order to create a particular effect by making it louder, softer, lower, etc.
ⓢⓨⓝ control, regulate, adjust
ⓔ.ⓖ. He carefully **modulated** his voice.
ⓝ modulator
ⓐ modulative

1580 ■■■

stratify

[strætɪfaɪ]

층을 이루게 하다, 계층화하다

ⓥ arrange something in layers or strata
ⓔ.ⓖ. a highly **stratified** society
ⓐ stratified

1581 ■■□

offset

[|ɔ:fset;|ɑ:f-]

상쇄하다

ⓥ to use one cost, payment or situation in order to cancel or reduce the effect of another
ⓢⓨⓝ make up for, cancel out
ⓔ.ⓖ. Prices have risen in order to **offset** the increased cost of materials.

1582 ■■□

probe
[proʊb]

캐묻다, 캐다, 조사하다

ⓥ to ask questions in order to find out secret or hidden information about somebody/something

⟮syn⟯ examine, go into, investigate

⟮e.g.⟯ He didn't like the media **probing** into his past.

ⓝ prober

ⓐ probeable

1583 ■■□

hoodwink
[hʊdwɪŋk]

속이다, 농락하다

ⓥ to deceive or trick

⟮syn⟯ dupe, cheat, swindle

⟮e.g.⟯ We were **hoodwinked** into buying a new house, when really we didn't want one.

1584 ■■□

exodus
[éksədəs]

탈출, 이동

ⓝ a going out; a departure or emigration, usually of a large number of people

⟮syn⟯ migration, departure

⟮e.g.⟯ We see an **exodus** of people losing their homes that are foreclosed on.

1585 ■■□

extrinsic
[ikstrínsik]

외래의, 비본질적인, 외부로부터의

ⓐ not essential or inherent; not a basic part or quality

⟮syn⟯ extraneous, external

⟮e.g.⟯ One of the **extrinsic** services of the church is to clean the street.

ⓐ intrinsic 본질적인, 고유의

1586 ■■□

vigil
[vídʒəl]

철야, 밤샘, 불침번

ⓝ wakefulness maintained for any reason during the normal hours for sleeping

⟮syn⟯ awareness, lookout, watchfulness

⟮e.g.⟯ We held a **vigil** for the actor who recently died.

ⓐ vigilant 자지 않고 있는, 경계하고 있는

1587 ■■□

stifle
[stáifl]

억누르다, 숨을 막다, 질식시키다

ⓥ to quell, crush, or end by force; to suffer from difficulty in breathing, as in a close atmosphere
ⓢⓨⓝ suppress, repress, choke, suffocate
ⓔ.ⓖ. These people were trying to **stifle** the truth.
ⓐ stifling 숨 막힐 듯한, 답답한

1588 ■■□

bleak
[bliːk]

황량한, 처량한, 삭막한

ⓐ bare, desolate, and often windswept
ⓢⓨⓝ dreary, desolate, dismal
ⓔ.ⓖ. The job market in the recession was **bleak**.

1589 ■■□

falter
[fɔ́ːltər]

비틀거리다, 넘어지다, 주춤하다

ⓥ to move unsteadily; to hesitate or waver in action, purpose, intent, etc.
ⓢⓨⓝ stumble, hesitate, waver
ⓔ.ⓖ. You will **falter** a few times when you first try to walk.

1590 ■■■

tenacious
[tənéiʃəs]

고집하는, 끈기 있는

ⓐ holding fast; characterized by keeping a firm hold
ⓢⓨⓝ pertinacious, patient, stubborn, obstinate, pigheaded
ⓔ.ⓖ. The politician was quite **tenacious** about getting his law approved, he never would quit.
ⓝ tenacity 고집, 끈기

1591 ■■□

refute
[rifjúːt]

논박하다, 반박하다

ⓥ to prove to be false or erroneous, as an opinion or charge
ⓢⓨⓝ disprove, rebut
ⓔ.ⓖ. All of the accusations were later **refuted**.
ⓝ refutation 논박, 반박

DAY
27

1592 ■□□

blink
[blɪŋk]

눈을 깜박거리다, 깜작이다

ⓥ to open and close the eye, esp. involuntarily; wink rapidly and repeatedly

ⓢⓨⓝ nictitate, flicker, bat

ⓔ.ⓖ. Toni **blinked** in the bright sunlight.

ⓐ blinking 깜박거리는

1593 ■■□

staunch
[stɔːntʃ]

든든한, 견고한, 충실한

ⓐ firm or steadfast in principle, adherence, loyalty, etc.; characterized by firmness, steadfastness, or loyalty

ⓢⓨⓝ loyal, faithful, stalwart, firm, sound, true, trusty, steadfast

ⓔ.ⓖ. The governments rules were **staunch** concerning immigration.

1594 ■□□

obese
[oubíːsəti]

비만인, 뚱뚱한

ⓐ very fat or overweight

ⓢⓨⓝ corpulent, fat, overweight, plump, chubby, gross

ⓔ.ⓖ. I have lived with the physical and emotional pain of being struggled with being **obese** all my life.

ⓝ obesity 비만, 비대

1595 ■■□

sparse
[spáːrs]

드문, 희박한

ⓐ existing only in small amounts

ⓢⓨⓝ scant, scarce, meager

ⓔ.ⓖ. The information available on the subject is **sparse**.

1596 ■□□

topography
[təpáːgrəfi]

지형, 지형학

ⓝ the science of describing an area of land, or making maps of it

ⓢⓨⓝ geomorphology

ⓔ.ⓖ. The **topography** of this region has changed a lot because of geological folds and faults.

ⓝ topographer 지형학자

ⓐ topographical 지형학의

1597 ■■□

fatalistic
[feɪtə́lɪstɪk]

운명론적인

ⓐ believing that there is nothing you can do to prevent events from happening

ⓔ.ⓖ. Young people are almost **fatalistic** about having accidents as novice drivers.

ⓝ fatalism 운명론, 체념

1598 ■■□

cognizant
[kάgnəzənt]

인식하고 있는, 알고 있는

ⓐ If someone is cognizant of something, they know about it and understand it.

ⓔ.ⓖ. We are **cognizant** of the problem.

1599 ■□□

fortress
[fɔ́ːrtrəs]

요새

ⓝ a large strong building used for defending an important place

ⓢⓨⓝ castle, stronghold, citadel, fastness

ⓔ.ⓖ. Fear of terrorist attack has turned the conference centre into a **fortress**.

1600 ■□□

quotient
[kwóʊʃnt]

(나눗셈의) 몫

ⓝ the amount or degree of a quality, feeling etc in a person, thing, or situation

ⓔ.ⓖ. When six is divided by three, the **quotient** is two.

1601 ■■□

homogeneous
[hoʊmədʒíːniəs]

동종의, 동질의

ⓐ consisting of people or things that are all of the same type

ⓢⓨⓝ unvarying, similar, identical

ⓔ.ⓖ. Some governments want a **homogeneous** national identity.

1602 ■■■

provincialism
[prəvínʃlɪzəm]

편협성, 고루함

ⓝ provincial attitudes

ⓔ.ⓖ. Despite its obvious **provincialism**, the arts festival was a huge success.

1603 ■□□

arithmetic
[əríθmətɪk]

산수, 연산, 계산
ⓝ the science of numbers involving adding, multiplying etc
ⓢⓨⓝ mathematics, maths
ⓔ.ⓖ. I think there's something wrong with your **arithmetic**.

1604 ■□□

wart
[wɔːrt]

(피부에 생기는) 사마귀
ⓝ a small hard raised part on someone's skin
ⓔ.ⓖ. His hands are covered with **warts**.
ⓐ warty 사마귀가 잔뜩 난, 사마귀 투성이의

1605 ■■□

effervescent
[efərvésnt]

열광하는, 기운이 넘치는
ⓐ someone who is effervescent is very happy, excited, and active
ⓢⓨⓝ ecstatic, electric
ⓔ.ⓖ. I have an **effervescent** personality.
ⓝ effervescence 감격, 흥분, 활기

1606 ■□□

astonish
[əstɑ́ːnɪʃ]

깜짝 놀라게 하다
ⓥ to surprise someone very much
ⓢⓨⓝ surprise, amaze, shock, startle, astound, stun
ⓔ.ⓖ. Her reply **astonished** me.
ⓝ astonishment 깜짝 놀람

1607 ■□□

revelation
[revəléɪʃn]

폭로, 드러냄, (신의) 계시
ⓝ a surprising fact about someone or something that was previously secret and is now made known
ⓢⓨⓝ disclosure, divulgence
ⓔ.ⓖ. He resigned after **revelations** about his affair.
ⓐ revelatory 알게 하는
ⓐ revelational 천계(계시)의

1608 ■□□

confidential
[kɑ:nfidénʃl]

비밀의, 기밀의, 은밀한

ⓐ spoken or written in secret and intended to be kept secret
(syn) secret, privy, private
(e.g.) Doctors are required to keep patients' records completely **confidential**.
ⓝ confidentialness 비밀성, 기밀성
ⓝ confidentiality 비밀(을 지켜야 하는 상황), 비밀리

1609 ■□□

dross
[drɔ:s;drɑ:s]

싸구려 (물건들); 찌꺼기

ⓝ something that is of very low quality
(syn) cheapie, cheapy
(e.g.) Most of the poems were pretentious **dross**.

1610 ■■□

infamy
[ínfəmi]

악명, 오명, 악행

ⓝ the state of being evil or well known for evil things
(e.g.) Property developers earned their **infamy** in the years when the country felt like a huge building site.

1611 ■■□

damnation
[dæmnéɪʃn]

지옥살이, 파멸

ⓝ when someone is punished by being sent to hell after their death, or the state of being in hell for ever
(e.g.) If you do otherwise, you risk eternal **damnation**.
ⓝ Damnation of Faust 파우스트의 영겁(永劫)의 벌

1612 ■■□

dilettante
[dɪlətǽnti]

딜레탕트, 호사가

ⓝ someone who is not serious about what they are doing or does not study a subject thoroughly
(syn) lover, devotee, enthusiast
(e.g.) He's a professional artist, not a **dilettante**.
ⓝ dilettantism 취미로 하는 일, 아마추어 예술

DAY
27

1613 ■■□

dementia
[dɪménʃə]

치매
ⓝ an illness that affects the brain and memory, and makes you gradually lose the ability to think and behave normally
ⓔ.ⓖ. **Dementia** (defined as memory impairment accompanied by aphasia, apraxia, or agnosia) is the critical feature of Alzheimer's disease.
ⓝ senile dementia 노인성 치매

1614 ■■□

deteriorate
[dɪtíriəreɪt]

악화되다, 더 나빠지다
ⓥ to develop into a bad or worse situation
ⓢⓨⓝ worsen, degenerate, slump
ⓔ.ⓖ. The argument **deteriorated** into a fight.
ⓝ deterioration 악화, (가치의) 하락

1615 ■□□

ornamentation
[ɔ:rnəmentéɪʃn]

장식
ⓝ decoration on an object that makes it look attractive
ⓢⓨⓝ decoration, patterns, ornament
ⓔ.ⓖ. The chairs were comfortable, functional and free of **ornamentation**.
ⓐ ornamental 장식의

1616 ■■■

protrusion
[proʊtrú:ʒn]

돌출, 돌출부
ⓝ something that sticks out
ⓔ.ⓖ. A **protrusion** of rock gave us shelter from the storm.
ⓥ protrude 튀어나오다, 돌출되다

1617 ■■■

asymmetric
[èɪsəmétrɪk]

불균형의, 부조화의, 비대칭적인
ⓐ having two sides that are different in shape
ⓔ.ⓖ. Linguists are studying the **asymmetric** use of Creole by parents and children.
ⓝ asymmetry 불균형, 부조화, 비대칭

1618 ■■□

detract
[dɪtrǽkt]

(가치 · 평판 따위를) 떨어뜨리다, 줄이다
ⓥ to make something seem less good
⑤ⓨⓝ derogate, devalue, devaluate
ⓔ.ⓖ. One mistake is not going to **detract** from your achievement.
ⓝ detraction 감손, 훼손, 비난

1619 ■■□

monolithic
[mànəlíθɪk]

모놀리스의, 돌(바위) 하나로 된; 획일적인, 통제된
ⓐ made of only one stone; characterized by massiveness, total
uniformity, rigidity, invulnerability, etc.
ⓔ.ⓖ. There are two types of churches at Lalibela, rock-hewn and
monolithic.
ⓝ monolith 모놀리스, 획일화된 통제체제

1620 ■□□

cling
[klɪŋ]

꼭 달라붙다, 매달리다
ⓥ to hold someone or something tightly, especially because you do
not feel safe
⑤ⓨⓝ clutch, grip, grasp
ⓔ.ⓖ. Passengers **clung** desperately onto the lifeboats.
ⓝ clinger 애착을 못 버리는 사람, 고집하는 사람

DAY
27

Day
28

pensive	☐☐☐	paradigmatic	☐☐☐
indignant	☐☐☐	inert	☐☐☐
fan	☐☐☐	sash	☐☐☐
tinker	☐☐☐	summons	☐☐☐
laborious	☐☐☐	litany	☐☐☐
breathlessly	☐☐☐	chalice	☐☐☐
skid	☐☐☐	impinge	☐☐☐
nurturant	☐☐☐	felicity	☐☐☐
underlying	☐☐☐	queer	☐☐☐
epic	☐☐☐	untenanted	☐☐☐
shrivel	☐☐☐	ghostliness	☐☐☐
proclaim	☐☐☐	piazza	☐☐☐
locomotion	☐☐☐	chintz	☐☐☐
avail	☐☐☐	matriculate	☐☐☐
transcription	☐☐☐	fiddle	☐☐☐
emphatically	☐☐☐	decimal	☐☐☐
molecular biology	☐☐☐	wobble	☐☐☐
impede	☐☐☐	thud	☐☐☐
undermine	☐☐☐	sprint	☐☐☐
haphazard	☐☐☐	hustle	☐☐☐
legible	☐☐☐	flimsy	☐☐☐
metamorphosis	☐☐☐	eddy	☐☐☐
mutation	☐☐☐	perilous	☐☐☐
chilling	☐☐☐	inch	☐☐☐
archetype	☐☐☐	herpetology	☐☐☐
consign	☐☐☐	foliage	☐☐☐
till	☐☐☐	vertebrate	☐☐☐
equilibrium	☐☐☐	mite	☐☐☐
optimal	☐☐☐	Court of Appeal	☐☐☐
expertise	☐☐☐	err	☐☐☐

1621 ■■□

pensive
[pénsɪv]

깊은 생각에 잠긴, 수심 어린
ⓐ thinking a lot about something, especially because you are worried or sad
(syn) thoughtful
(e.g.) He looked suddenly **pensive**.

1622 ■□□

indignant
[indígnənt]

화난
ⓐ feeling or showing anger or annoyance at what is perceived as unfair treatment
(syn) aggrieved, disgruntled
(e.g.) He was **indignant** because a bus splashed water on him.
ⓝ indignity 수모, 모욕

1623 ■□□

fan
[fæn]

부채질하다
ⓥ cool by waving something to create a current of air
(syn) air, ventilate
(e.g.) She would have to wait in the truck, **fanning** herself with a piece of cardboard.
ⓐ fanlike 부채꼴의

1624 ■■□

tinker
[tíŋkər]

(떠돌이) 땜장이; 어설프게 손보다, 서투르게 만지다
ⓝ a person who travels from place to place mending metal utensils as a way of making a living
(e.g.) The **tinker** barely managed to earn his living.

1625 ■□□

laborious
[ləbɔ́ːriəs]

고된
ⓐ requiring considerable effort and time
(syn) heavy, arduous, grueling, onerous
(e.g.) That may be a bit **laborious**.
ⓝ labor 노동, 근로

1626 ■□□

breathlessly
[bréθlisli]

숨 가쁘게, 숨을 죽이고

(ad) in a way that involves gasping for breath
(e.g.) The tension mounts as the **breathlessly** awaited moment approaches: the unveiling of the 2005 Playmate of the Year.

1627 ■■□

skid
[skid]

미끄러지다

(v) to slide along without rotating, as a wheel to which a brake has been applied
(syn) slip, slide
(e.g.) The car went into a **skid** as the driver lost control, and caused the accident.
(a) skiddy

1628 ■■□

nurturant
[nɔ́ːrtʃənt]

자애로운, 양육하는

(a) relating to the fact of taking care of or nurturing, or the ability to do so, in both a physical and emotional manner
(syn) benevolent
(e.g.) Extensive verbal give-and-take is allowed, and parents are warm and **nurturant** toward the child.
(n) (v) nurture 양육; 양육하다

1629 ■□□

underlying
[ʌ̀ndəláiiŋ]

밑에 있는, 기초가 되는, 근원적인

(a) lying or situated beneath, as a substratum
(syn) fundamental
(e.g.) the **underlying** rock formation

DAY
28

1630 ■□□

epic
[épik]

큰, 엄청난, 서사시의

(a) heroic or grand in scale or character
(syn) ambitious, Herculean
(e.g.) Even the harshest music critic said the night was full of magic and the concert was a series of **epic** performances.

1631 ■■□

shrivel
[ʃrívl]

쪼글쪼글해지다; 쪼글쪼글하게 만들다
ⓥ to become or make something dry and wrinkled as a result of heat, cold or being old
e.g. The leaves on the plant had **shrivelled** up from lack of water.

1632 ■■□

proclaim
[prəkléim]

선언하다, 선포하다
ⓥ to say publicly or officially that something important is true or exists
syn announce, declare
e.g. The President **proclaimed** the republic's independence.
ⓝ proclamation 선언, 발표, 공포

1633 ■■□

locomotion
[lòukəmóuʃən]

운동, 이동
ⓝ movement or the ability to move
syn movement
e.g. A fish uses its fins for **locomotion**.
ⓐ locomotive 이동(운동)하는, 이동(운동)력이 있는

1634 ■□□

avail
[əvéil]

쓸모가 있다, 가치가 있다
ⓥ If you avail yourself of an offer or an opportunity, you accept the offer or make use of the opportuntiy.
e.g. Such arguments will not **avail**.

1635 ■■□

transcription
[trænskrípʃən]

필사, 베낀 것
ⓝ Transcription of speech or text is the process of transcribling it.
e.g. The full **transcription** of the interview is attached.

1636 ■■□

emphatically
[imfǽtik, em-]

명확하게, 뚜렷하게
ⓐⓓ If you say something emphatically, you say it in a forceful way which shows that you fell very strongly about what you are saying.
e.g. He has always **emphatically** denied the allegations.

1637 ■■□

molecular biology
[moulékjulər baiáːlədʒi/-ɔ́l-]

분자 생물학

ⓝ Molecular biology is the study of the structure and function of the complex chemicals that are found in living things.

ⓔⓖ He's giving a series of lectures on **molecular biology**.

1638 ■■□

impede
[ɪmpíːd]

지연시키다, 방해하다

ⓥ to delay or stop the progress of something

ⓢⓨⓝ interrupt, disrupt

ⓔⓖ Work on the building was **impeded** by severe weather.

ⓝ impediment

ⓐⓓ impedingly

1639 ■■□

undermine
[ʌndərmaɪn]

약화시키다

ⓥ to make something, especially somebody's confidence or authority, gradually weaker or less effective

ⓢⓨⓝ weaken, sabotage, subvert

ⓔⓖ This crisis has **undermined** his position.

ⓝ underminer

ⓐⓓ underminingly

1640 ■■□

haphazard
[hæphǽzərd]

무계획적인, 되는 대로의

ⓐ with no particular order or plan; not organized well

ⓢⓨⓝ random, inadvertent, incidental

ⓔⓖ The books had been piled on the shelves in a **haphazard** fashion.

ⓝ haphazardness

ⓐⓓ haphazardly

DAY
28

1641 ■■□

legible
[lédʒəbl]

읽을(알아볼) 수 있는, 또렷한

ⓐ clear enough to read

ⓔⓖ **legible** handwriting

ⓝ legibleness

ⓐⓓ legibly

1642 ■■■

metamorphosis
[mètəmɔ́ːrfəsis]

변형, 변신, 대변모

ⓝ When a metamorphosis occurs, a person or thing develops and changes into something completely different.

(e.g.) Even before his **metamorphosis**, there was a communication problem within the family.

1643 ■■□

mutation
[mjuːtéiʃən]

변화, 변성; 돌연변이

ⓝ the act or process of mutating; change; alteration

(e.g.) Scientists have found a genetic **mutation** that appears to be the cause of Huntington's disease.

1644 ■□□

chilling
[ʧíliŋ]

냉랭한, 냉담한

ⓐ If you describe something as chilling, you mean it is frightening.

(e.g.) He described in **chilling** detail how he attacked her during one of their frequent rows.

1645 ■■□

archetype
[áːrkitàip]

원형, 전형

ⓝ An archetype is something that is considered to be a perfect or typical example of a particular kind of person or thing, because it has all their most important characteristics.

(e.g.) He came to this country 20 years ago and is the **archetype** of the successful Asian businessman.

1646 ■■■

consign
[kənsáin]

건네주다, 교부하다

ⓥ to consign something or someone to a place where they will be forgotten about, or to an unpleasant situation or place, means to put them there

(e.g.) For decades, many of Malevich's works were **consigned** to the basements of Soviet museums.

1647 ■□□

till
[til]

돈궤, 카운터의 돈 서랍

ⓝ A till is the drawer of a cash register, in which the money is kept.

1648 ■■■

equilibrium
[iːkwəlíbriəm]

평형상태, 균형, 평정
ⓝ Equilibrium is a balance between several different influences or aspects of a situation.
ⓢⓨⓝ balance
ⓔⓖ Most natural systems are in a state of **equilibrium**.

1649 ■■□

optimal
[áptəməl/ɔ́pt-]

최선(최적)의
ⓐ The optimum or optimal level or state of something is the best level or state that it could achieve.
ⓔⓖ A cool room is **optimal** for good sleep.

1650 ■□□

expertise
[èkspərtíːz]

전문가의 의견, 전문기술
ⓝ Expertise is special skill or knowledge that is acquired by training, study, or practice.
ⓔⓖ The problem is that most local authorities lack the **expertise** to deal sensibly in this market.

1651 ■■□

paradigmatic
[pæ̀rədigmǽtik]

모범이 되는, 예증의
ⓐ You can describe something as paradigmatic if it acts as a model or example for something.
ⓔⓖ Their great academic success was paraded as **paradigmatic**.

1652 ■■□

inert
[inə́ːrt]

활발하지 못한, 둔한, 생기가 없는
ⓐ someone or something that is inert does not move at all
ⓢⓨⓝ slow, slack, quit
ⓔⓖ He covered the **inert** body with a blanket.

1653 ■■□

sash
[sæʃ]

창틀, 새시
ⓝ A sash window is a window which consists of two frames placed one above the other. The window can be opened by sliding one frame over the other.
ⓔⓖ The spacious bathroom had its own **sash** window.

DAY
28

1654 ■■□

summons
[sʌ́mənz]

소환, 호출(장)

ⓝ A summons is an official order to appear in court.

ⓔ.ⓖ. She had received a **summons** to appear in court.

1655 ■■□

litany
[lítəni]

탄원, 장황한 이야기

ⓝ If you describe what someone says as a litany of things, you mean that you have heard it many times before, and you think it is boring or insincere.

ⓔ.ⓖ. She remained in the doorway, listening to his **litany** of complaints against her client.

1656 ■■□

chalice
[tʃǽlis]

성배, 성작

ⓝ A chalice is a large gold or silver cup with a stem. Chalices are used to hold wine in the Christian service of Holy Communion.

ⓔ.ⓖ. The priest raised a golden **chalice** from the altar.

1657 ■■■

impinge
[impíndʒ]

치다, 부딪치다, 충돌하다

ⓥ Something that impinges on you affects you to some extent.

ⓔ.ⓖ. The waves **impinge** against the rocks.

1658 ■■■

felicity
[filísəti]

경사, 더없는 행복

ⓝ Felicity is great happiness and pleasure.

ⓢⓨⓝ joy, pleasure, happiness

ⓔ.ⓖ. The children brought much **felicity** into their parents' lives.

1659 ■■□

queer
[kwiər]

이상한, 기묘한, 의심스러운

ⓐ Something that is queer is strange.

ⓢⓨⓝ odd, strange, suspicious

ⓔ.ⓖ. If you ask me, there's something a bit **queer** going on.

1660 ■□□

untenanted
[ʌnténəntid]

(토지, 집이) 임대되어 있지 않은

ⓔ.ⓖ. All trickle transfer sales are of vacant **untenanted** homes.

1661 ■□□

ghostliness
[góustlinis]

유령 같음
ⓝ the quality of being ghostly
(e.g.) Their **ghostliness** forces us to be alert to our own fragile lives.

1662 ■□□

piazza
[piǽzə/-ǽtsə]

광장, 시장, 회랑, 복도 현관
ⓝ A piazza is a large open square in a town or city, especially in Italy.
(syn) verandah, porch
(e.g.) They were seated at a table outside a pub in a pleasant **piazza** close by St Paul's.

1663 ■□□

chintz
[tʃints]

사라사 무명(커튼, 의자 커버용)
ⓝ Chintz is a cotton fabric decorated with flowery patterns.
(e.g.) The bedroom walls would be papered with **chintz**.

1664 ■■□

matriculate
[mətríkjəlèit]

대학 입학을 허가하다
ⓥ In some countries, if you matriculate, you register formally as a student at a university, or you satisfy the academic requirements necessary for registration for a course.
(e.g.) Most people who **matriculate** into business schools have an average of five years of work experience.

1665 ■■□

fiddle
[fídl]

바이올린, 하찮은 일
ⓝ violin
(e.g.) In memory everything seems to happen to music. That explains the **fiddle** in the wings.

1666 ■■□

decimal
[désəməl]

십진법의, 소수의
ⓐ A decimal system involves counting in units of ten.
(e.g.) Calculate it to three **decimal** places.

DAY
28

1667 ■■□

wobble
[wάbəl/wɔ́bəl]

흔들리다, 떨리다, 흔들리게 하다

ⓥ If something or someone wobbles, they make small movements from side to side, for example because they are unsteady.

(syn) shake, waver

(e.g.) Don't **wobble** the table — I'm trying to write.

1668 ■□□

thud
[θʌd]

퍽, 털썩, 쿵

ⓝ A thud is a dull sound, such as that which a heavy object makes when it hits something soft.

(syn) bump, thud, thump, clonk

(e.g.) She tripped and fell with a sickening **thud**.

1669 ■□□

sprint
[sprint]

(단거리를) 역주하다

ⓥ The sprint is a short, fast running race.

(syn) dash

(e.g.) He set the U.S. record for the 100-meter **sprint**.

1670 ■■□

hustle
[hʌ́səl]

세게 밀다, 밀고 나아가다

ⓥ If you hustle someone, you try to make them go somewhere or do something quickly, for example by pulling or pushing them along.

(e.g.) The guards **hustled** Harry out of the car.

1671 ■■□

flimsy
[flímzi]

박약한, 얄팍한, 하찮은

ⓐ A flimsy object is weak because it is made of a weak material, or is badly made.

(e.g.) He lives in a **flimsy** little house that has no electricity.

1672 ■■□

eddy
[édi]

소용돌이, 회오리(바람)

ⓝ An eddy is a movement in water or in the air which goes round and round instead of flowing in.

(syn) whirl, swirl

(e.g.) The rocks in the river caused swirls and **eddies** in the water.

1673 ■■□

perilous
[pérələs]

위험한, 위험이 많은, 모험적인
ⓐ Something that is perilous is very dangerous.
ⓢⓨⓝ risky, dangerous, precarious
ⓔ.ⓖ. The ways to the top of the mountain are quite **perilous**.

1674 ■■□

inch
[intʃ]

조금씩 움직이다
ⓥ To inch somewhere means to move there very slowly and carefully, or to make something do this.
ⓔ.ⓖ. I **inched** the car forward.

1675 ■■□

herpetology
[hə̀ːrpətálədʒi/-tól-]

파충류학
ⓝ Herpetology is the study of reptiles and amphibians.
ⓔ.ⓖ. More and more people are becoming interested in **herpetology** every day.

1676 ■□□

foliage
[fóuliidʒ]

잎, 잎의 무성함
ⓝ The leaves of a plant are referred to as its foliage.
ⓔ.ⓖ. My love for Linton is like the **foliage** in the woods.

1677 ■■□

vertebrate
[vɔ́ːrtəbrèit, -rit]

척추동물, 척추가 있는
ⓝ A vertebrate is a creature which has a spine. Mammals, birds, reptiles, and fish are vertebrates.
ⓔ.ⓖ. The discovery was written in an issue of the Journal of **Vertebrate** Paleontology.

1678 ■□□

mite
[mait]

진드기 (무리)
ⓝ Mites are very tiny creatures that live on plants, for example, or in animals' fur.
ⓢⓨⓝ tick
ⓔ.ⓖ. The **mites** created fear among Chinese people.

DAY
28

1679 ■□□

Court of Appeal

상소 법원

ⓝ A Court of Appeal is a court which deals with appeals against legal judgments.

ⓔ.ⓖ. The **Court of Appeal** reversed the decision.

1680 ■■□

err
[əːr, εər]

잘못하다, 틀리다, 그르치다

ⓥ If you err, you make a mistake.

ⓔ.ⓖ. All men are liable to **err**.

MEMO

Day

29

antipsychotic	☐☐☐	mirth	☐☐☐
cue	☐☐☐	substantiate	☐☐☐
involve	☐☐☐	inextricable	☐☐☐
demonize	☐☐☐	inadvertent	☐☐☐
infinitesimal	☐☐☐	bleach	☐☐☐
meritorious	☐☐☐	marigold	☐☐☐
underrate	☐☐☐	apricot	☐☐☐
little game	☐☐☐	amber	☐☐☐
regardless	☐☐☐	shovelful	☐☐☐
Amendments	☐☐☐	rafter	☐☐☐
pharmacology	☐☐☐	rack	☐☐☐
milieu	☐☐☐	thistle	☐☐☐
hover	☐☐☐	attorney	☐☐☐
instigate	☐☐☐	hatchet	☐☐☐
preponderance	☐☐☐	butcher	☐☐☐
projection	☐☐☐	josh	☐☐☐
manipulation	☐☐☐	carob	☐☐☐
bemuse	☐☐☐	fissure	☐☐☐
virtuoso	☐☐☐	venomous	☐☐☐
reincarnate	☐☐☐	cowardice	☐☐☐
apotheosis	☐☐☐	deify	☐☐☐
psychopath	☐☐☐	dethrone	☐☐☐
impairment	☐☐☐	soak	☐☐☐
amygdala	☐☐☐	prosodic	☐☐☐
underpinning	☐☐☐	squirmy	☐☐☐
adversary	☐☐☐	slumber	☐☐☐
conglomerate	☐☐☐	solipsistic	☐☐☐
taproot	☐☐☐	inclination	☐☐☐
zapper	☐☐☐	subjectivity	☐☐☐
entomology	☐☐☐	discrepancy	☐☐☐

1681 ■■□

antipsychotic
[æntisaikátik, -tai-]

항정신병의; 항정신병약, 정신병 치료약

ⓐ preventing or treating psychosis

ⓔ.ⓖ. **Antipsychotic** medications are the most commonly prescribed medications to treat schizophrenia.

1682 ■□□

cue
[kjuː]

계기, 신호, 단서

ⓝ a hint or indication about how to behave in particular circumstances

ⓔ.ⓖ. My teacher joked about such attitudes and I followed her **cue**.

1683 ■□□

involve
[inválv]

~을 필요로 하다, (필연적으로) ~을 수반하다, ~을 복잡하게 하다

ⓥ If a situation or activity involves something, that thing is a necessary part or consequence of it.

ⓢⓨⓝ entail, mean, demand, require

ⓔ.ⓖ. Nicky's job **involves** spending quite a lot of time with other people.

1684 ■□□

demonize
[díːmənàiz]

악마화하다

ⓥ to turn into a demon or make demonlike

ⓔ.ⓖ. It's easy to **demonize** and vilify that which you don't personally know.

1685 ■■□

infinitesimal
[infìnitésəməl]

극소수의, 극미량의

ⓐ extremely small

ⓢⓨⓝ tiny, minuscule

ⓞⓟⓟ huge

ⓔ.ⓖ. It was a tiny, tiny, **infinitesimal** percentage of the material that we are reviewing.

ⓝ infinitesimalness 극소

1686 ■■□

meritorious
[mèritɔ́ːriəs]

가치 있는, 칭찬할 만한

ⓐ deserving praise, reward, esteem, etc.

ⓢⓨⓝ praiseworthy, admirable, exemplary

ⓔ.ⓖ. We think we have a **meritorious** case.

1687 ■□□

underrate
[ˌʌndəˈreɪt]

과소평가하다, 얕보다

Ⓥ underestimate the extent, value, or importance of someone or something
Ⓢⓨⓝ discount, undervalue, belittle
Ⓞⓟⓟ overrate
Ⓔⓖ That is not to **underrate** the importance of focusing veterinary effort on BSE.

1688 ■□□

little game
[lítl geim]

잔꾀, 술책

Ⓝ a person's secret intention or business
Ⓔⓖ so that's his **little game**!

1689 ■□□

regardless
[rigάːrdlis]

어떻든지(간에)

ⓐ without paying attention to the present situation
Ⓢⓨⓝ anyway, at any rate, at all events, whether or not
Ⓔⓖ Despite her recent surgery she has been carrying on **regardless**.
Ⓝ regardlessness 무관심

1690 ■■□

Amendments
[əˈmendmənt]

(미국 헌법의) 수정 조항

Ⓔⓖ The **Amendments** are before us for debate.

1691 ■■□

pharmacology
[fὰːrməkάlədʒi/-kɔ́l-]

약리학, 약물학

Ⓝ Pharmacology is the branch of science relating to drugs and medicines.
Ⓔⓖ In the middle ages, alchemy was widely connected to astrology and **pharmacology**.

DAY
29

1692 ■■□

milieu
[miljə́ː, -ljúː/míːljəː]

주위, 환경

Ⓝ Your milieu is the group of people or activities that you live among or are familiar with.
Ⓢⓨⓝ environment
Ⓔⓖ They stayed, safe and happy, within their own social **milieu**.

1693 ■■□

hover
[hʌvər]

(허공을) 맴돌다
ⓥ to stay in the air in one place
ⓢⓨⓝ float, fly, hang
ⓔ.ⓖ. A hawk **hovered** over the hill.
ⓝ hoverer
ⓐⓓ hoveringly

1694 ■■■

instigate
[ɪnstɪɡeɪt]

실시(착수)하게 하다
ⓥ to make something start or happen, usually something official
ⓢⓨⓝ urge, force
ⓔ.ⓖ. The government has **instigated** a programme of economic reform.
ⓝ instigation
ⓐ instigative
ⓐⓓ instigatingly

1695 ■■□

preponderance
[prɪpɑ:ndərəns]

(수적으로) 우세함, 더 많음
ⓝ If there is a preponderance of one type of people or things in a group, there are more of them than others.
ⓔ.ⓖ. There is still a **preponderance** of male managers in the profession.

1696 ■■□

projection
[prədʒekʃn]

(현 상황을 근거로 한 규모·비용·양 등의) 예상(추정); 투사, 투영, 영사
ⓝ [countable] an estimate or a statement of what figures, amounts, or events will be in the future, or what they were in the past, based on what is happening now; [uncountable, countable] the act of putting an image of something onto a surface; an image that is shown in this way
ⓢⓨⓝ forecast, estimate, reckoning
ⓔ.ⓖ. 1. Sales have exceeded our **projections**.
2. the **projection** of three-dimensional images on a computer screen
ⓥ project
ⓝ projectionist
ⓐ projective, projectional

1697 ■■■

manipulation
[mənìpjuléiʃən]

교묘히 다루기, 속임

ⓝ a manipulating or being manipulated; skillful handling or operation, artful management or control, etc.

e.g. The **manipulation** of reality is called editing.

1698 ■■□

bemuse
[bimjúːz]

멍하게 하다, 생각에 잠기게 하다

ⓥ If something bemuses you, it puzzles or confuses you.

e.g. He was rather **bemused** by children.

1699 ■□□

virtuoso
[və̀ːrtʃuóusou, -zou]

예술의 거장, 음악의 대가

ⓝ A virtuoso is someone who is extremely good at something, especially at playing a musical instrument.

syn maestro, great artist

e.g. He was gaining a reputation as a remarkable **virtuoso**.

1700 ■■■

reincarnate
[rìːinkáːrneit]

환생시키다

ⓥ If people believe that they will be reincarnated when they die, they believe that their spirit will be born again and will live in the body of another person or animal.

e.g. This man is the devil **reincarnated**.

1701 ■■■

apotheosis
[əpàθióusis/əpɔ̀θ-]

신격화, 미화, 숭배

ⓝ If something is the apotheosis of something else, it is an ideal or typical example of it.

e.g. The Oriental in Bangkok is the **apotheosis** of the grand hotel.

1702 ■■■

psychopath
[sáikoupæ̀θ]

정신병질자

ⓝ A psychopath is someone who has serious mental problems and who may act in a violent way without feeling sorry for what they have done.

syn maniac, lunatic

e.g. She was abducted by a dangerous **psychopath**.

DAY

29

1703 ■■■

impairment
[impédəmənt]

손상, 해침, 감손

ⓝ If someone has an impairment, they have a condition which prevents their eyes, ears, or brain from working properly.

ⓢⓨⓝ disability, defect

ⓔ.ⓖ. He has a visual **impairment** in the right eye.

1704 ■□□

amygdala
[əmígdələ]

편도류, 편도선

ⓝ an almond-shaped part, such as a tonsil or a lobe of the cerebellum

1705 ■■□

underpinning
[ʌ́ndərpìniŋ]

받침, 토대, 지주, 지지물

ⓝ a structure of masonry, concrete, etc, placed beneath a wall to provide support

ⓔ.ⓖ. APEC leaders stressed the critical role of **underpinning** economic recovery.

1706 ■■□

adversary
[ǽdvərsèri/-səri]

적, 상대, 대항자

ⓝ Your adversary is someone you are competing with, or arguing or fighting against.

ⓢⓨⓝ rival, competitor, antagonist

ⓔ.ⓖ. His political **adversaries** were creating a certain amount of trouble for him.

1707 ■■□

conglomerate
[kənglάmərət/-glóm-]

재벌, 거대 기업; 결합시키다, 결합하다

ⓝ A conglomerate is a large business firm consisting of several different companies.

ⓔ.ⓖ. It was up against Samsung, Korea's largest **conglomerate**.

1708 ■■□

taproot
[tǽprùːt]

주근, 곧은 뿌리, 성장의 요인

ⓝ the large single root of plants such as the dandelion, which grows vertically downwards and bears smaller lateral roots

1709 ■■□

zapper
[zǽpər]

리모콘; (해충, 잡초 등의) 마이크로파 구제장치
ⓝ Zapper is a small device that you use to control a television, video, or stereo from a distance.
ⓔ.ⓖ. In the final part, many flies die in a bug **zapper**.

1710 ■■□

entomology
[èntəmɑ́lədʒi/
-mɔ́l-]

곤충학
ⓝ Entomology is the study of insects.
ⓔ.ⓖ. He had bachelor's degrees in chemistry and biology and a master's in **entomology**.

1711 ■■□

mirth
[məːrθ]

명랑, 유쾌, 환희
ⓝ Mirth is amusement which you express by laughing.
ⓢⓨⓝ pleasure, delight, gaiety
ⓔ.ⓖ. The performance produced much **mirth** among the audience.

1712 ■■□

substantiate
[səbstǽnʃièit]

성립시키다, 실체화하다
ⓥ To substantiate a statement or a story means to supply evidence which proves that it is true.
ⓢⓨⓝ prove, demonstrate
ⓔ.ⓖ. There is little scientific evidence to **substantiate** the claims.

1713 ■■□

inextricable
[inékstrikəbəl]

풀 수 없는, 뒤엉킨, 헤어날 수 없는
ⓐ If there is an inextricable link between things, they cannot be considered separately.
ⓔ.ⓖ. This debate is about the **inextricable** links between health and education.

1714 ■■■

inadvertent
[inədvə́ːrtənt]

부주의한, 소홀한, 태만한
ⓐ An inadvertent action is one that you do without realizing what you are doing.
ⓢⓨⓝ negligent, hasty, rash
ⓔ.ⓖ. I happily accept that it was **inadvertent**.

DAY

29

1715 ■■□

bleach
[bliːʧ]

희게 하다, 표백하다
ⓥ If you bleach something, you use a chemical to make it white or pale in colour.
ⓢⓨⓝ decolorize, decolor
ⓔ.ⓖ. These products don't **bleach** the hair.

1716 ■□□

marigold
[mǽrəgòuld]

금잔화, 금송화
ⓝ A marigold is a type of yellow or orange flower.

1717 ■□□

apricot
[éiprəkàt, ǽp-/-kɒ̀t]

살구, 살구빛, 살구빛의
ⓝ An apricot is a small, soft, round fruit with yellowish-orange flesh and a stone inside.
ⓔ.ⓖ. She spread **apricot** jelly on her toast.

1718 ■□□

amber
[ǽmbər]

호박, 황갈색; 황갈색의
ⓝ Amber is a hard yellowish-brown substance used for making jewellery.
ⓔ.ⓖ. I found a lot of **amber** jewelry when I traveled in Russia.

1719 ■□□

shovelful
[ʃʌ́vəlfùl]

한 삽 가득(한 양)
ⓝ scoopful, spadeful

1720 ■■□

rafter
[rǽftər, rɑ́ːftər]

서까래; 뗏목을 만드는 사람, 타는 사람
ⓝ Rafters are the sloping pieces of wood that support a roof.

1721 ■□□

rack
[ræk]

파괴, 황폐, 고문대
ⓝ If you say that someone is on the rack, you mean that they are suffering either physically or mentally.

1722 ■□□

thistle
[θísl]

엉겅퀴

ⓝ A thistle is a wild plant which has leaves with sharp points and purple flowers.

ⓔ.ⓖ. It is funding research on milk **thistle**.

1723 ■□□

attorney
[ətɔ́ːrni]

대리인, 변호사, 검사

ⓝ In the United States, an attorney or attorney at law is a lawyer.

ⓔ.ⓖ. Did his **attorney** contact you about the trial?

1724 ■□□

hatchet
[hǽtʃit]

자귀(도끼)

ⓝ A hatchet is a small axe that you can hold in one hand.

ⓔ.ⓖ. I use a **hatchet** to chop wood for the fire.

1725 ■□□

butcher
['bʊtʃə]

고깃간 주인; 고깃간

ⓝ A butcher is a shopkeeper who cuts up and sells meat. Some butchers also kill animals for meat and make foods such as sausages and meat pies.

ⓔ.ⓖ. I found the best **butcher** of the meeting.

1726 ■■□

josh
[dʒɑʃ/dʒɔʃ]

놀리다, 조롱하다, 속이다

ⓥ to tease (someone) in a bantering way

ⓔ.ⓖ. Don't **josh** about somebody's hair style.

1727 ■□□

carob
[kǽrəb]

캐럽(쥐엄나무 비슷한 교목)

ⓝ A carob or carob tree is a Mediterranean tree that stays green all year round. It has dark brown fruit that tastes similar to chocolate.

ⓔ.ⓖ. In my experience a straight substitution of **carob** for chocolate doesn't work.

DAY
29

1728 ■■□

fissure
[fíʃər]

터진 자리, 틈, 균열

ⓝ A fissure is a deep crack in something, especially in rock or in the ground.

ⓢⓨⓝ crack

ⓔ.ⓖ. The **fissure** in the ground is so deep.

1729 ■■□

venomous
[vénəməs]

독이 있는, 독액을 분비하는; 앙심에 찬

ⓐ If you describe a person or their behaviour as venomous, you mean that they show great bitterness and anger towards someone.

ⓢⓨⓝ deadly, lethal, poisonous, toxic

ⓔ.ⓖ. She hurled **venomous** words at them.

1730 ■□□

cowardice
[káuərdis]

겁, 소심, 비겁

ⓝ Cowardice is cowardly behaviour.

ⓔ.ⓖ. He openly accused his opponents of **cowardice**.

ⓐ cowardly 겁 많은, 소심한

1731 ■■□

deify
[díːəfài]

신으로 삼다, 신성시하다

ⓥ If someone is deified, they are considered to be a god or are regarded with very great respect.

ⓔ.ⓖ. The Romans used to **deify** their emperors.

1732 ■■□

dethrone
[diθróun]

(왕을) 퇴위시키다

ⓥ remove (a monarch) from power

ⓔ.ⓖ. The palace guard **dethroned** the emperor.

1733 ■□□

soak
[souk]

(액체 속에) 담그다. 흠뻑 적시다

ⓥ make or allow (something) to become thoroughly wet by immersing it in liquid

ⓢⓨⓝ steep, wet

ⓔ.ⓖ. I usually **soak** the beans overnight.

1734 ■■■

prosodic
[prəsádik/-sɔ́d-]

작시법의, 운율법에 맞는
ⓐ of, or according to the principles of, prosody
ⓝ metrics, prosody

1735 ■■□

squirmy
[skwə́ːrm]

꿈틀거리는, 꼼지락거리는, 우물쭈물하는
ⓐ moving with a wriggling motion
ⓔ.g. You don't want to get too close to a **squirmy** cat's skin with sharp scissors!
ⓥ squirm

1736 ■□□

slumber
[slʌ́mbər]

잠; 잠을 자다
syn sleep, doze, snooze
ⓔ.g. She fell into a deep and peaceful **slumber**.

1737 ■■■

solipsistic
[sálipsìzəm, sóul-/sɔ́l-]

유아독존적인
ⓔ.g. Perhaps these people are **solipsistic** and so cannot break free of their illusion.

1738 ■■□

inclination
[ìnklənéiʃən]

(~하려는) 의향, 경향
ⓝ an attitude of mind especially one that favors one alternative over others
syn desire, longing, aspiration
ⓔ.g. He had an **inclination** to give up too easily.

1739 ■■□

subjectivity
[sʌ̀bdʒektívəti]

주관성, 주관(주의)
ⓝ judgment based on individual personal impressions and feelings and opinions rather than external facts
ⓔ.g. Taste in art is in the realm of **subjectivity**.

1740 ■■□

discrepancy
[diskrépənsi]

차이, 불일치
ⓝ a difference between conflicting facts or claims or opinions
syn disagreement, difference, variation
ⓔ.g. There was a **discrepancy** between what they ordered and the bill they received.

DAY
29

Day

30

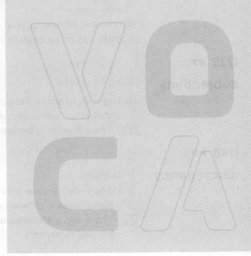

bemoan	☐☐☐	reign	☐☐☐
shortcoming	☐☐☐	throb	☐☐☐
penchant	☐☐☐	noontide	☐☐☐
deform	☐☐☐	brim	☐☐☐
diversification	☐☐☐	nevermind	☐☐☐
romp	☐☐☐	superintend	☐☐☐
endeavor	☐☐☐	providence	☐☐☐
solitude	☐☐☐	scoffingly	☐☐☐
recess	☐☐☐	scrape	☐☐☐
requisition	☐☐☐	momentarily	☐☐☐
roundabout	☐☐☐	nothingness	☐☐☐
bewildered	☐☐☐	wilt	☐☐☐
torture	☐☐☐	rite of passage	☐☐☐
desolate	☐☐☐	radical	☐☐☐
flaw	☐☐☐	ill-fitting	☐☐☐
downplay	☐☐☐	greenlight	☐☐☐
combat	☐☐☐	residual	☐☐☐
scoundrel	☐☐☐	humble	☐☐☐
constituency	☐☐☐	bureaucratic	☐☐☐
fluctuate	☐☐☐	entourage	☐☐☐
overlay	☐☐☐	decompose	☐☐☐
emblematic	☐☐☐	long-standing	☐☐☐
pedigree	☐☐☐	landfill	☐☐☐
imprison	☐☐☐		

1741 ■■□

bemoan
[bimóun]

한탄하다

ⓥ regret strongly

ⓢⓨⓝ bewail, lament, mourn, regret, rue

ⓔⓖ They sat **bemoaning** the fact that no one would give them a chance.

1742 ■□□

shortcoming
[ʃɔ́:rtkʌmiŋ]

(주로 복수로) 결점, 단점

ⓝ a fault in somebody's character, a plan, a system, etc.

ⓢⓨⓝ failing, fault, weakness

ⓔⓖ She made me aware of my own **shortcomings**.

1743 ■■■

penchant
[péntʃənt]

애호

ⓝ a special liking for something

ⓔⓖ She has a **penchant** for champagne.

1744 ■■□

deform
[difɔ́:rm]

변형시키다, 기형으로 만들다

ⓥ assume a different shape or form; alter the shape of (something) by stress

ⓔⓖ The disease had **deformed** his spine.

1745 ■■□

diversification
[divə́:rsəfikéiʃən]

다양화, 다양성, 잡다한 상태

ⓝ (especially in business) the act of developing a wider range of products, interests, skills, etc. in order to be more successful or reduce risk

ⓔⓖ the company's **diversification** into health care products

1746 ■■□

romp
[rɑmp/rɔmp]

즐겁게 뛰놀다; (경마, 경주의) 쾌주, 낙승, 오락물

ⓥ play boisterously

ⓝ an easy victory

ⓔⓖ kids are **romping** around in the snow.

1747 ■■□

endeavor
[endévər]

노력, 시도; 노력하다, 시도하다

ⓝ earnest and conscientious activity intended to do or accomplish something

ⓢⓨⓝ attempt, effort, try

ⓔ.ⓖ. No important **endeavor** that required innovation was done without risk.

1748 ■■□

solitude
[sálitjùːd/sɔ́li-]

고독

ⓝ the state or situation of being alone

ⓔ.ⓖ. He enjoyed his moments of **solitude** before the pressures of the day began.

1749 ■□□

recess
[ríːses, risés]

휴회 기간, 움푹 들어간 부분

ⓝ A recess is a break between the periods of work of an official body such as a committee, a court of law, or a government.

ⓢⓨⓝ break, interval, alcove, hollow

ⓔ.ⓖ. 1. The judge called a short **recess**.
2. We love a **recess** for books.

1750 ■■□

requisition
[rèkwəzíʃən]

요청, 신청, 요구

ⓝ the act of requiring; an authoritative request or demand, especially by a military or public authority that takes something over (usually temporarily) for military or public use

ⓔ.ⓖ. The request for **requisition** of these materials is denied.

1751 ■■□

roundabout
[raundəbaut]

로터리; 우회하는, 에두르는

ⓝ a place where two or more roads meet, forming a circle that all traffic must go around in the same direction

ⓢⓨⓝ indirect, devious, tortuous

ⓔ.ⓖ. At the **roundabout**, take the second exit.

ⓝ roundaboutness

DAY
30

1752 ■■□

bewildered
[biwíldər]

당혹한, 갈피를 못 잡은

ⓐ perplexed by many conflicting situations or statements; filled with bewilderment

ⓢⓨⓝ confused

ⓔ.ⓖ. She was **bewildered** by their questions.

1753 ■□□

torture
[tɔ́ːrtʃər]

고문

ⓝ extreme mental distress; unbearable physical pain

ⓢⓨⓝ torment, illtreatment

ⓔ.ⓖ. His confessions were made under **torture**.

1754 ■■■

desolate
[désəlit]

황량한, 적막한, 너무나 외로운; 고적하게 만들다

ⓐ providing no shelter or sustenance; crushed by grief

ⓔ.ⓖ. 1. It was a completely **desolate** area, like a desert.
2. She had been **desolated** by the death of her friend.

1755 ■□□

flaw
[flɔː]

결함, 결점

ⓝ A flaw in something such as a theory or argument is a mistake in it, which causes it to be less effective or valid.

ⓔ.ⓖ. There is always a **flaw** in the character of a tragic hero.

1756 ■□□

downplay
[,daʊnˈpleɪ]

경시하다, 대단치 않게 생각하다

ⓥ represent as less significant or important

ⓢⓨⓝ understate, minimize

ⓔ.ⓖ. The coach is **downplaying** the team's poor performance.

1757 ■□□

combat
[kʌ́mbæt, kʌ́m-]

전투, 싸움; (좋지 않은 일의 발생이나 악화를) 방지하다

ⓝ Combat is fighting that takes place in a war.

ⓥ If people in authority combat something, they try to stop it happening.

ⓢⓨⓝ fight, war, conflict

ⓔ.ⓖ. 1. The man volunteered to enter **combat** in Vietnam.
2. The body also uses apoptosis to **combat** cancer.

1758 ■■□

scoundrel
[skáundrəl]

(비열한) 악당

ⓝ a wicked or evil person; someone who does evil deliberately
ⓔ.ⓖ. Violence is the last resort of a **scoundrel**.

1759 ■■■

constituency
[kənstítʃuənsi]

(국회의원을 선출하는) 선거구; (특정 지역의) 선거구민(유권자들)

ⓝ A constituency is an area for which someone is elected as the representative in a parliament or government.
ⓔ.ⓖ. Unemployment is high in her **constituency**.

1760 ■■□

fluctuate
[flʌ́ktʃuèit]

변동(등락)을 거듭하다

ⓥ If something fluctuates, it changes a lot in an irregular way.
ⓔ.ⓖ. During the crisis, oil prices **fluctuated** between $20 and $40 a barrel.

1761 ■■□

overlay
[òverláy]

덮어씌우다, (어떤 감정 · 기운을) 더하다; 덮어씌우는(입히는) 것

ⓥ If something is overlaid with something else, it is covered by it.
ⓔ.ⓖ. 1. The place was **overlaid** with memories of his childhood.
2. wood **overlaid** with gold

1762 ■■□

emblematic
[èmbləmǽtik]

상징적인

ⓐ serving as a symbol of a particular quality or concept; symbolic
ⓢⓨⓝ symbolic
ⓔ.ⓖ. The dove is **emblematic** of peace.

1763 ■■□

pedigree
[pédəgrìː]

족보, 혈통서

ⓝ The recorded ancestry or lineage of a person or family
ⓢⓨⓝ lineage, family
ⓔ.ⓖ. She was proud of her long **pedigree**.

DAY
30

1764 ■■□

imprison
[imprízən]

투옥하다

ⓥ If someone is imprisoned, they are locked up or kept somewhere, usually in prison as a punishment for a crime or for political opposition.

ⓢⓨⓝ jail, confine

ⓔ.ⓖ. Our aim should be to catch, convict and **imprison** more terrorists.

1765 ■■□

reign
[rein]

(왕의) 통치 기간; 다스리다, 통치하다

ⓝ the period of rule of a monarch

ⓥ hold royal office; rule as monarch

ⓢⓨⓝ besupreme, predominate

ⓔ.ⓖ. I'm relieved and pleased Eriksson's futile **reign** is over.

1766 ■□□

throb
[θrɑːb]

두근거림

ⓝ a strong, regular beat or sound; a steady pulsation

ⓢⓨⓝ fluttering

ⓔ.ⓖ. the **throb** of the ship's engines

1767 ■■□

noontide
[nóon·tide]

한낮 (무렵)

ⓝ noon

ⓢⓨⓝ noontime

ⓔ.ⓖ. A wild cry suddenly cleft the **noontide** stillness.

1768 ■■□

brim
[brim]

그득 채우다

ⓥ be full to the point of overflowing

ⓢⓨⓝ be full, well over

ⓔ.ⓖ. Tears **brimmed** in her eyes.

1769 ■■■

nevermind
[névərmàind]

주의, 배려, 용무, 책임

ⓔ.ⓖ. It's no **nevermind** of yours.

1770 ■■□

superintend
[sùːpərinténd]

관리, 감독하다

ⓥ be responsible for the management or arrangement of (an activity or organization); oversee

ⓢⓨⓝ supervise

ⓔ.ⓖ. Her job is to **superintend** the production process.

1771 ■■■

providence
[právədəns/próv-]

(신의) 섭리

ⓝ God, or a force which is believed by some people to arrange the things that happen to us

ⓔ.ⓖ. I trust in divine **providence**.

1772 ■□□

scoffingly
[skɔːf, skɑf]

조롱하듯이

ⓐⓓ speaking to someone or about something in a scornfully derisive or mocking way

ⓢⓨⓝ mockingly

ⓔ.ⓖ. 'You, a scientist?', he said **scoffingly**.

1773 ■□□

scrape
[skreɪp]

긁어내다; 긁힌 상처

ⓥ remove it, especially by pulling a sharp object over the surface

ⓔ.ⓖ. I **scraped** the side of my car on the wall.

1774 ■□□

momentarily
[móuməntèri/-təri]

잠깐 동안, 금방

ⓐⓓ for a very short time

ⓢⓨⓝ for a while

ⓔ.ⓖ. She was **momentarily** frozen by the sight.

1775 ■□□

nothingness
['nʌθ.ɪŋ.nəs]

무(無), 공허; 존재하지 않음, 없음

ⓝ the fact of not existing

ⓢⓨⓝ absence

ⓔ.ⓖ. Another theme that caught my attention was "**Nothingness**."

DAY
30

1776 ■■□

wilt
[wɪlt]

시들다, 시들게 하다
ⓥ gradually bends downwards and becomes weak because it needs more water or is dying
ⓢⓨⓝ droop, wither
ⓔ.ⓖ. Do not season until ready to serve or vegetables will **wilt**.

1777 ■■■

rite of passage
[ˌraɪt əv ˈpæs.ɪdʒ]

통과의례
ⓝ a ceremony performed in some cultures at times when an individual changes his status, for example, as at puberty and marriage
ⓔ.ⓖ. Chickenpox was once considered a **rite of passage** for most children.

1778 ■■□

radical
[rǽdikəl]

근본적인, 철저한; 급진적인, 과격한
ⓐ relating to or affecting the fundamental nature of something; characterized by departure from tradition
ⓢⓨⓝ fundamental, revolutionary
ⓔ.ⓖ. 1. One is more **radical** than the other.
2. There is a **radical** difference.

1779 ■■□

ill-fitting
[ˌɪlˈfitɪŋ]

(크기·모양이) 안 맞는
ⓐ of the wrong size or shape for the person wearing it
ⓔ.ⓖ. He was wearing a helmet that was either **ill-fitting** or with the strap undone.

1780 ■□□

greenlight
[ˌgriːnˈlaɪt]

승인을 내리다
ⓥ give permission to go ahead with (a project)
ⓢⓨⓝ approve of
ⓔ.ⓖ. They refused to **greenlight** his script until he did a major rewrite.

1781 ■■□

residual
[rizídʒuəl]

(어떤 과정이 끝나고 난 뒤에) 남은, 잔여(잔류)의
ⓐ remaining after the greater part or quantity has gone
ⓢⓨⓝ remnantal
ⓔ.ⓖ. We shall leave a **residual** member of staff in Islamabad.

1782 ■□□

humble
[hʌ́mbəl]

겸손한; (예의상 자기를 낮추는 표현에서) 초라한; (신분이) 미천한

ⓐ having or showing a modest or low estimate of one's importance; (of an action or thought) offered with or affected by a modest estimate of one's importance; (of a thing) of modest pretensions or dimensions

ⓢⓨⓝ modest

ⓔ.ⓖ. 1. I felt very **humble** when meeting her.
　　2. my **humble** apologies
　　3. She came from a **humble**, unprivileged background.

1783 ■□□

bureaucratic
[bjùərəkrǽtik]

관료주의적인

ⓐ relating to a system of government in which most of the important decisions are taken by state officials rather than by elected representatives

ⓔ.ⓖ. The report revealed a great deal of **bureaucratic** inefficiency.

1784 ■■□

entourage
[à:nturá:ʒ]

(주요 인물의) 수행단

ⓝ a group of people attending or surrounding an important person

ⓢⓨⓝ retinue

ⓔ.ⓖ. The president visited China with his **entourage**.

1785 ■■□

decompose
[dì:kəmpóuz]

분해하다, 분해되다

ⓥ make or become rotten; decay or cause to decay

ⓔ.ⓖ. Over time, dead leaves **decompose** into the ground.

1786 ■□□

long-standing
['lɔŋ,stændɪŋ]

오래된

ⓐ having existed or continued for a long time

ⓢⓨⓝ long-lasting

ⓔ.ⓖ. This is a custom of **long-standing** in this district.

1787 ■□□

landfill
[lǽnd·fìl]

쓰레기 매립; 쓰레기 매립지

ⓝ a method of getting rid of very large amounts of rubbish by burying it in a large deep hole

ⓔ.ⓖ. The map shows the position of the new **landfills**.

DAY 30

Appendix
& Index

유희태 일반영어 ⑤
VOCA
기출VOCA 30days

Appendix

PHRASAL VERB

● Separable Transitive Phrasal Verbs

back up (=support)	뒷받침하다, 도와주다
bear out (=support)	지탱하다, 지원하다, 지지하다
beef up (=fortify)	보강하다, 강화하다
blow up (=inflate)	부풀리다, 날려버리다
break in (=make usable)	길들이다, 훈련시키다
break out (=unveil, make available)	달아나다, 벗어나다, 탈피하다
bring up (=broach)	꺼내다, 불러일으키다
bring off (=execute a task successfully)	해내다
brush off (=reject)	무시하다, 거절하다
call off (=abandon, cancel)	취소하다, 중지하다, 포기하다
call up (=telephone)	전화를 걸다
carry out (=execute)	수행하다, 이행하다
clean up (=make clean and tidy)	치우다, 청소하다, 정화하다
clean out (=remove all objects)	말끔히 씻어 내다, 깨끗이 치우다
clear up (=resolve)	해결하다, 설명하다
check out (=investigate)	조사하다, 확인하다
empty out (=remove something from a container)	텅 비게 하다, 몽땅 비워 내다, 텅 비다
figure out (=solve, find a solution)	이해하다, 알아내다, 계산해내다
fill in (=supply information)	정보를 주다, 자세히 알리다, 대신하다
fill out (=complete a form)	기입하다
get back (=reacquire)	되찾다
give back (=return)	돌려주다, 응수하다, 앙갚음하다
give up (=abandon)	그만두다, 포기하다, 단념하다
hand in (=submit)	제출하다, 내다, 인계하다
hand out (=distribute)	나누어주다
hand over (=give something to someone)	넘겨주다, 이양하다
hold up (=delay)	견디다, 지체되다
jot down (=write)	쓰다, 적다
keep out (=deny access)	억제하다, 억압하다
leave out (=omit)	빠뜨리다, 빼다, 배제시키다, 생략하다, 무시하다
line up (=form in a line)	줄을 서다, 줄을 이루다
lock in (=secure)	가두다, 감금하다
look over (=examine)	훑어보다, 살펴보다

look up (=find information)	찾아보다, 방문하다
make out (=discern, recognize)	알아보다, 알아듣다
make up (=fabricate)	이루다, 형성하다
open up (=unlock a door, show something hidden)	마음을 터놓다
pay back (=settle debts, get revenge)	갚다, 상환하다
pick out (=select)	고르다, 선발하다
pick up (=acquire, obtain, fetch)	듣게 되다, 알게 되다, 익히게 되다
point out (=indicate)	가리키다, 지적하다, 주목하다
put off (=postpone)	취소하다, 미루다, 연기하다
put on (=dress)	입다, 쓰다, 끼다, 걸치다
put out (=place outside, extinguish)	내다 놓다
rule out (=eliminate)	배제하다, 제외시키다
set up (=arrange, erect)	세우다, 건립하다, 준비하다
sort out (=separate, solve)	정리하다, 해결하다, 구분하다
spread out (=move apart, unfold)	몸을 뻗다, 넓은 공간을 차지하다
take on (=undertake)	착수하다, 떠맡다, 고용하다
try on (=test for size)	입어보다
try out (=test)	시험해보다
take off (=undress)	벗다, 벗기다
take on (=assume)	일을 맡다, 책임을 지다
talk over (=discuss)	~에 대해 이야기를 나누다, 논의하다
track down (=find, locate)	~을 찾아내다
turn down (=refuse)	거절하다, 거부하다
turn off (=deactivate)	신경을 끊다, 정지시키다
turn on (=activate)	작동시키다, 활성화시키다, 관심을 갖게 하다
turn over (=place with other side up)	뒤집다, 뒤집히다
use up (=exhaust supply)	다 써버리다
work out (=develop, solve)	계산하다, 이해하다
work over (=beat badly)	두들겨 패다
wrap up (=cover, finish)	마무리 짓다
zip up (=close)	지퍼로 잠그다, 지퍼로 잠기다

❷ Ergative Phrasal Verbs

(1) unpaired

break down (=stop functioning)	고장나다
break up (=disintegrate)	부서지다
catch on (=become popular)	유행하다
come apart (=disintegrate)	부서지다
come up (=arise)	오르다, 올라가다
crop up (=appear)	갑자기 나타나다
die down (=abate)	점점 잦아들다
die out (=disappear)	멸종되다
doze off (=fall asleep)	잠이 들다
drag on (=continue too long)	질질 끌다
dry up (=end [supply of money, food, water, etc.])	고갈되다
end up (=finish)	끝내다
fall behind (=lose ground)	(~에) 뒤지다
fall out (=become loose and come out)	헐거워지다
grow up (=mature, increase)	성장하다
pass away (=die)	돌아가시다
pass out (=become unconscious)	의식을 잃다, 기절하다
show up (=appear)	나타나다
sink in (=become comprehensible)	충분히 이해되다
taper off (=decrease)	(수 · 양 · 정도가) 점점 줄어들다
wind down (=decrease)	(열의 · 활동 따위가) 약화되다

(2) paired

blow up	~을 폭파하다	heat up	~을 뜨겁게 데우다
break off	~을 분리시키다	open up	~을 열다, 개방하다
break up	~을 부수다	slow down	~을 늦추다
build up	~을 창조(개발)하다	thaw out	~를 녹이다
burn down	태워 없애다	wake up	~을 깨우다
burn up	~을 다 태워버리다	warm up	~을 데우다
cheer up	~을 응원하다	wear down	~을 닳아빠지게 하다
clear up	(날씨가) 개다 (=weather)	wear out	~을 써서 낡게 하다, 닳게 하다
close down	폐쇄(폐업)하다		

❸ Prepositional Verbs

abide by	~을 준수하다[지키다]	laugh at	~을 비웃다
account for	~을 해명하다, ~의 이유가 되다	lead to	~로 이어지다, ~을 초래하다
agree on	~에 동의하다	lie about	~에 대해 거짓말하다
allow for	~을 감안하다[참작하다]	listen to	~에 귀를 기울이다
apply for	~에 지원하다	look at	~을 보다
approve of	~을 승인하다	look for	~을 바라다, ~을 찾다
ask for	~에 대해 묻다[~를 찾다]	object to	~에 반대하다
bank on	~에 의지하다; ~을 기대하다	part with	~와 헤어지다
call for (=require)	~을 필요로 하다	reason with	~을 설득하다
call on (=visit)	~을 방문하다	refer to	~와 관련이 있다, ~에 대해 언급하다
comment on	~에 주석을 달다	resort to	~에 의지하다
conform to	~을 따르다, ~에 맞추다	result in	~을 야기하다
consent to	~에 동의하다, ~을 비준하다	see about (=attend to something)	~을 처리하다
consist of	~으로 이루어지다[구성되다]	serve as	~의 역할을 하다
contribute to	~에 기여하다	smile at	~을 보고 미소짓다
decide on	~으로 결정하다	stand for (=represent)	~을 나타내다[상징하다]
depend on	~에 의존하다	stare at	~을 응시하다
differ from	~와 다르다	tamper with	~을 간섭하다
enlarge on(=expand in greater detail)	더 상세히 말하다[쓰다]	wait for	~을 기다리다
go through(=search, pass through)	~을 살펴보다[조사하다]	wait on	~의 시중을 들다
hint at	~을 암시하다[내비치다]	watch for	(~이 나타나기·발생하기를) 기다리다
hope for	~을 기대하다	worry about	~에 대해 걱정하다
insist on	~을 주장[요구]하다		

❹ Phrasal Prepositional Verbs

break in on (=interrupt)	(갑자기) ~에 침입하다, 끼어들다
bring (someone /something) in on (=enlist the help of someone/something)	도움을 요청하다
cash in on (=take advantage of)	~을 이용하다

come in for (=be due or receive criticism/praise, etc.)	(특히 좋지 않은 것을) 받다
come up with (=produce, devise)	생산하다, 제시하다, 제안하다
come down to (=amount to)	결국 ~이 되다, ~에 이르다
come down with (=contract)	병에 걸리다
cry out for (=seriously require)	절실히 필요로 하다, 간절히 바라다
cut in on (=interrupt)	~을 방해하다
do away with (=exterminate)	죽이다, 그만두다, 처분하다, 폐지하다
face up to (=acknowledge)	인정하다, 받아들이다, 직시하다
fall back on (=rely on if necessary)	기대다, 의지하다
get along with (=coexist peacefully)	~와 잘 지내다
get away with (=escape without punishment)	교묘히 모면하다, 무사히 빠져나가다
get out of (=avoid doing something, escape)	회피하다, 떠나다, 나가다
go along with (=accept, cooperate)	동의하다, 찬성하다, 동조하다
go out for (=become engaged in an activity)	얻으려고 애쓰다, ~을 하러 나가다
go through with (=carry out, execute, e.g., a plan)	탐색하다, 수행하다, 거치다
hold on to (=retain)	유지하다, 고수하다, 지키다
look down on(=hold in lesser esteem)	낮춰 보다, 얕보다, 경시하다
look forward to (=anticipate)	기대하다, 고대하다
look in on (=visit, call on)	방문하다
look up to (=admire)	우러러보다, 존경하다
measure up to (=meet a standard)	~대로 되다
own up to (=admit)	~을 인정하다
pick up on (=comprehend)	이해하다, 알아차리다
play along with (=cooperate)	협조하다, 협력하다, 동의하다, 동의하는 척하다
put up with (=tolerate)	참다, 참고 견디다
put (someone) up to (=induce someone to do something)	~을 부추기다, 설득하다
put (something) down to (=ascribe something to)	~을 ~의 탓으로 보다
play (someone) off against (=create strife between two people)	남을 누구와 반목시켜 어부지리를 얻다
run up against (=encounter)	~에 맞부딪치다, ~와 충돌하다
stand up to (=withstand pressure or scrutiny)	잘 견디다, 오래 가다
take (something) out on (=direct anger, frustration at someone)	~에게 화풀이하다, 분풀이하다

DATIVE VERBS

❶ To dative verbs that optionally take the dative movement rule

allot	hand	play	slip
assign	hand back	preach	supply
award	issue	quote	take
bring	leave	read	teach
cable	lend	rent	tell
cede	loan	sell	throw
feed	mail	send	toss
forward	offer	serve	type
give	owe	ship	wire
give back	pass	show	write
grant	pay	sing	

❷ To dative verbs that are restricted to the prepositional pattern

administer	display	propose	roll
admit	donate	push	say
announce	explain	recite	slide
confess	extend	recommend	state
contribute	float	recount	submit
convey	haul	relay	suggest
communicate	illustrate	repeat	transfer
declare	indicate	report	transport
describe	introduce	restore	
deliver	mention	return	
demonstrate	narrate	reveal	

❸ For dative verbs that optionally take the dative movement rule

bake	dig	hire	plow
boil	donate	leave	prepare
build	draw	make	print
buy	draw up	mix	quote
call	fetch	order	reserve
catch	find	pack	roast
choose	fix	paint	save
cook	fry	peel	sing
cut	get	pick out	spare
design	guarantee	play	

❹ For dative verbs that are restricted to the prepositional word order

acquire	copy	kill	select
answer	correct	look over	sew
capture	create	obtain	take down
carry	dance	plain	take over
cash	eat	recite	unload
clean up	examine	remove	whistle
collate	finish	repeat	
complete	fix	retrieve	
compose	guard	sacrifice	

중요 숙어

a factor of two
2배

a train of
일련의, 따라오는
(e.g.) His death set in motion a train of events that led to the outbreak of war.

acute effect
단기 효과(=short-term effect)

age out of
나이가 들어 ~로부터 벗어나다(=mature out of)

aid in
~을 돕다

all over the place
엉망인
(e.g.) The government is all over the place on this.

ask A for loan
A에게 대출(차용)을 부탁하다
(e.g.) He ask a bank for a loan.

at long intervals
간혹, 오랜 시간을 두고
(e.g.) Above all, let him eat regularly and not at too long intervals.

barge in
불쑥 끼어들다
(e.g.) I'm sorry to barge in like this, but I have a problem I hope you can solve.

be attributable to
~에 기인하다
(e.g.) Part of their popularity and success must be attributable to their denominational status.

be committed to
~에 헌신(전념)하다
(e.g.) Government will continue to be committed to this problem.

be dotted with
여기저기 흩어 놓다(흩어져 있다), 산재하다
e.g. Campsites used to be dotted with tents arranged in a circle.

be entitled to
~에 대한 자격이 되다; ~가 주어지다
e.g. I understand I could be entitled to more of a discount.

be meant to
~하기로 되어 있다
e.g. I guess it wasn't meant to be.

be saddled with
~을 짊어지다, 싫어하다
e.g. He's unlikely to be saddled with the public's hatred by proxy.

be subject to
~에 종속되다, ~의 대상이다
e.g. Any changes proposed would be subject to consultation.

be up to par
기대에 부응하다, 수준에 달하다
e.g. The classroom computers were not quite up to par with today's needs.

be worse off
더욱더 궁색한
e.g. The increase in taxes means that we'll be £40 a month worse off than before.

belong in
~에 속하다(알맞다)
e.g. Police officers do not belong in schools.

bluff one's way through
(곤란한 상황을) 허세를 부려 성공적으로 넘기다
e.g. How to bluff your way through the world of art - an idiot's guide by Steve Smith.

burn to
~에 사로잡혀 있다, ~에 안달 나 있다
e.g. People who burn to win fame, will be ruined some day.

by virtue of

~덕택에, ~위하여
(syn) via, by dint of
(e.g.) By virtue of the 2001 and 2005 general election results, Conservatives have remained in Opposition.

carry around

들고 다니다
(e.g.) It's compact enough to carry around in your pocket.

cash a bond

채권을 현금화하다
(e.g.) He said he cashed a bond.

catch on

유행하다(인기를 얻다), 이해하다
(e.g.) This design will surely catch on splendidly with young people.

cost a fortune

엄청나게 비싸다
(e.g.) The first is that flashy cars cost a fortune to run.

count sheep

(잠이 오지 않을 때 잠들기 위해) 머릿속으로 양을 세다
(e.g.) I was counting sheep.

deal with

~과 거래하다; 상대하다; 다루다
(e.g.) Nobody wanted to deal with that client.

deceive A into B

A를 속여 B하게 하다
(e.g.) In previous years, the regime tried to deceive the US into increasing pressures on the residents of Ashraf.

delve into

탐구(조사)하다(=probe)
(e.g.) Bomb the System is the first feature in over 20 years to delve into the world of graffiti art.

depart from

~에서 벗어나다
(e.g.) The greater the lines depart from being parallel, the greater the strength of the interaction.

desperate to
~하려고 필사적인
(e.g.) It's a friendly game but both teams will be desperate to win.

doctor-issued
의사가 발행한
(e.g.) The doctor issued an ultimatum: start stop-smoking or die.

easy call
쉬운 선택
(e.g.) I'd booked well in advance it was equivalent, and hence an easy call.

edge out
서서히 몰아내다
(e.g.) France edged out the British team by less than a second.

feel flattered
아첨당하고 있다고 느끼다
(e.g.) I feel greatly flattered by your compliment.

feel obliged (to)
~할 의무감이 들다
(e.g.) I feel obliged to introduce a new stuff.

fill (in) time
시간을 보내다
(e.g.) The operation performed, the leg in plaster, the question now is what to do to fill in the time.

fly in the face of
~에 위배되다
(e.g.) Ann made it a practice to fly in the face of standard procedures.

fold over
접다
(e.g.) Place filling across middle and fold over.

foot the bill
비용을 부담하다
(e.g.) BBC News should foot the bill and downsize if necessary.

for anything else

다른 것들에 대해서는

(e.g.) I think he could see I didn't have a lot of aptitude for anything else.

---

for that matter

그 점에 있어서

(e.g.) I am partly responsible for that matter.

---

get A out of the way

A를 제거하다, 피하다

(e.g.) Let's schedule a meeting on it for later this week and get it out of the way.

---

give away

폭로하다, 누설하다, 나누어 주다

(e.g.) I won't give away the ending—you have to go see it!

---

given (that)

~을 고려하면; ~을 고려할 때

(e.g.) Given his political connections, he thought he was untouchable.

---

given to

~하는 버릇이 있는

(e.g.) He's given to going for long walks on his own.

---

gnaw at

~를 오랫동안 괴롭히다

(e.g.) The doubts continued to gnaw at me.

---

go out of one's way

굳이(일부러) ~하다

(syn) make a special effort

(e.g.) I went out of my way to please my mom.

---

gorge on

~을 게걸스럽게 먹다(=binge on)

(e.g.) But once home I'd have dinner then gorge on bread and cheese.

---

hang out

걸려 있다

(e.g.) hang out [hoist] a flag half-mast high

---

have the stomach to

~하려고 하다; ~할 배포가 있다

hold one's breath

숨을 죽이다
(e.g.) Second, hold your breath for three seconds.

---

hold one's ground

입장을 고수하다, 공격에 견디다
(syn) stand one's ground, stick to one's guns
(e.g.) He hold tenaciously to his ground.

---

impute A to B

A를 B에게 전가하다(씌우다)
(e.g.) It is grossly unfair to impute blame to the United Nations.

---

in relation(ship) to

~와 결부해서, ~에 관해서
(e.g.) He is the sixth person to be arrested in relation to the coup plot.

---

in the first place

애(시당)초, 우선
(e.g.) This is why we're here in the first place.

---

in the service of

~에 이용되어, ~에 복무하여
(e.g.) His father was a court official in the service of the Holy Roman Emperor, and so was his grandfather.

---

in the throes

극심한 고통을 겪는
(e.g.) Despite being in the throes of school exams, Tamsin made the long trek from Liverpool.

---

just about

거의
(syn) almost, to all intents and purposes
(e.g.) The company just about broke even last year.

---

keep A at bay

A를 저지하다
(syn) hold off
(e.g.) Dogs will keep them at bay for a while.

---

keep A clear for B

B를 위해 A를 정리해두다, B가 A를 피하도록 하다
(e.g.) keep the ring clear for boxers.

---

keep one's eyes peeled on　　눈을 똑바로 뜨고 지켜보다, 계속 경계를 하고 있다
　　(e.g.) Keep your eyes peeled on the road.

keep pace with　　~와 보조를 맞추다, ~에 따라가다
　　(e.g.) Our systems have to keep pace with those changes.

kiss off　　~을 거절하다; 무시하다; 피하다
　　(e.g.) I sent them a complain but they just kissed it off.

kneel down　　무릎 꿇다
　　(e.g.) There was a moment when he knelt down and saluted.

loom large　　(걱정·위기 등이) 크게 다가오다
　　(e.g.) Issues such as immigration and asylum loom large in our consciousness.

make a case　　논거의 정당함을 입증하다, ~에 대한 의견을 진술하다
　　(e.g.) You could make a case for a rise in taxes in order to reduce public borrowing.

make a face　　얼굴을 찌푸리다
　　(e.g.) Why'd you make a face?

make a splash　　세상을 깜짝 놀라게 하다, 평판이 자자해지다
　　(e.g.) Lastly, you don't have to do anything fancy to make a splash.

make a stand　　일정한 입장을 견지하다, 저항하다
　　(e.g.) We need to make a stand on these issues.

make room for　　~에 양보하다
　　(e.g.) Would you please move along and make room for this old man?

make way for	~에 길을 열어주다, (사람이 지나가도록) 자리를 내주다
	(e.g.) The crowd parted right and left to make way for the party.
no shortage	많은
	(syn) many
	(e.g.) There is no shortage of wars in this world.
on net	요컨대(in sum)
out of place	제자리에 있지 않은, (특정한 상황에) 맞지 않는(부적절한)
	(syn) muddled, ill at ease
	(e.g.) There's not a thing out of place.
out of thin air	난데없이
phase out	단계적 철수하다, 폐지하다
	(e.g.) The UK Government had hoped for a 2010 phase out.
play a part in	일익을 담당하다
	(syn) contribute
	(e.g.) Behavior, Environment and Genetics also play a part in obesity.
plump for	~을 (신중히) 선택하다, ~에게 표를 던지다(=support)
	(e.g.) Mr King is plumping for "quantitative easing", or printing money.
propensity for	~하는 성향(버릇)
	(e.g.) Europe has a propensity for ostrich-ism.
put A on full blast	A를 가장 세게 틀다
	(e.g.) I put my stereo on full blast and enjoy music.
put forth an effort	노력하다
	(syn) make an effort
	(e.g.) You know, we all put forth a great effort.

put forward　　　　(사람들 앞에) 나서다; 나타나다; 제안하다

put out of existence　　~을 죽이다, 소멸시키다

relative to　　~에 비례해서, ~에 관하여
(syn) in proportion to
(e.g.) Singapore has the world's highest execution rate relative to its population.

resort to　　~을 일으키다, ~에 의지하다
(e.g.) They resorted to bribery to get what they wanted.

round the clock　　계속해서 쭉, 밤낮으로
(e.g.) Chanel Ten was the only station not playing round the clock 9/11 stories.

run out of　　~이 떨어지다, 다 써버리다
(syn) be used up
(e.g.) We just happened to run out of that product.

select against　　도태시키다

settle on　　~을 결정하다
(e.g.) We all settled on plan A.

shed light on　　(문제 등에 대해) 해결의 실마리를 던져 주다, 보다 분명하게 하다
(syn) cast/throw light on
(e.g.) We will shed light on the truth.

sit around　　빈둥거리다; 빈둥거리며 세월을 보내다; 둘러앉다
(e.g.) And I don't sit around all day.

skim through　　~을 대충 읽다(=read quickly)
(e.g.) It was terrible to even skim through it.

slip by　　~을 (슬쩍) 통과하다(get by unnoticed)
(e.g.) Don't let this opportunity slip by.

take A into consideration

A를 고려하다

e.g. The ranking is based on a points system that takes the chart success of each group into consideration.

---

take out a mortgage on

~을 저당 잡히다

e.g. I could take out a mortgage on my house.

---

to a degree

어느 정도; 꽤

e.g. The data are subject to a degree of statistical error.

---

to date

지금까지

e.g. We have fifteen people enrolled to date.

---

to one's surprise

놀랍게도

e.g. To my surprise, he was my brother.

---

to some extent

얼마간, 어느 정도까지, 다소

e.g. To some extent it is true.

---

track down

~을 찾아내다

syn trace, detect

e.g. I don't know where that old story came from, I've never been able to track it down.

---

tune into

~로 채널을 맞추다

e.g. Tune into 104.4 FM.

---

turn out

만들어내다, 생산하다(produce)

e.g. The factory turns out thousands of cars a week.

---

upwards of

~이상

e.g. In some Chicago districts, Kennedy got upwards of 95% of the vote with upwards of 95% turnout.

walk abroad	활보하다; 만연하다
walk away from	~로부터 걸어 나오다; 벗어나다; 이탈하다 (e.g.) Don't walk away from the right path.
weigh down	~을 짓누르다 (e.g.) It is the accumulation of all the above evidence types that weigh down the case at hand.
with a view to	~할 생각(목적)으로 (e.g.) They came to this island with a view to digging up the ruins.
with that said	그렇긴 하지만 (e.g.) With that said, however, the hatred I feel for politicians is incredible.
writing-off	탕감, 감가상각, 평가인하 (e.g.) Their banks are still writing off bad debts.

Index

유희태 일반영어 ⑤

기출 VOCA 30 days

초판 **1쇄**	2012년 2월 20일
2판 1쇄	2015년 2월 10일
3판 1쇄	2018년 3월 26일
4판 1쇄	2021년 1월 4일
2쇄	2021년 7월 30일
3쇄	2023년 1월 5일
4쇄	2024년 4월 25일

저자와의
협의하에
인지생략

저자 유희태 **발행인** 박 용 **발행처** (주)박문각출판
표지디자인 박문각 디자인팀
등록 2015. 4. 29. 제2015-000104호
주소 06654 서울시 서초구 효령로 283 서경 B/D
팩스 (02) 584-2927
전화 교재 문의 (02) 6466-7202

정 가 18,000원
ISBN 979-11-6444-566-0